Engraved by J. C. Buttre

GOV^R. JOHN HAYNES.

From a portrait in the State House at Hartford Ct.

Engraved for the New England History

Since the publication of this History, Mr. Charles F. Winthrop of New York has shown me a portrait of his ancestor, Governor Fitz John Winthrop, which is the same as the copy in the State House at Hartford, incorrectly named Governor John Haynes.

C. W. E.

THE

NEW ENGLAND HISTORY,

FROM THE

DISCOVERY OF THE CONTINENT

BY THE

NORTHMEN, A.D. 986,

TO THE

PERIOD WHEN THE COLONIES DECLARED THEIR INDEPENDENCE, A.D. 1776.

BY

CHARLES W. ELLIOTT,

MEMBER OF THE NEW YORK, OHIO AND CONNECTICUT HISTORICAL SOCIETIES.

IN TWO VOLUMES.

VOL. I.

NEW YORK:

CHARLES SCRIBNER, 377 & 379 BROADWAY;

LONDON: TRUBNER & COMPANY.

1857.

STEREOTYPED BY
THOMAS B. SMITH,
82 & 84 Beekman St. N. Y.

PRINTED BY
GEO RUSSELL & CO.,
Beekman Street.

PREFACE.

I AM aware that much has been written, and well written, about New England and her History. Valuable and minute histories of towns, counties, and colonies exist, and her general History or Chronology has been incorporated into various elaborate works; but when, some years since, I undertook to examine New England life, with a desire to trace the growth of ideas and principles, through her active struggles and unremitting labors from the beginning, I met with difficulties. It seemed to me that for the general reader the local histories were too detailed, and the general history was too chronological and disconnected: it seemed, too, that the peculiar and marked development of man there was worthy of a more simple, compact, and picturesque re-presentation than it had received, and that, if it could be so re-presented to the reader of this day, it would be a commendable work to do. This is what I have attempted.

Few will doubt that, however well History may have been written, it is desirable that it should be re-written from time to time, by those who look from an advanced position; it is, of course, only necessary to say, that I have written from the democratic stand-point of to-day, believing it to be the true one from which to see and judge the past. With no conscious wish to exalt or depress the Puritans, it has been my aim to see them fairly, and represent them truly, while I have not hesitated to praise or blame when truth seemed to demand it. The historian is not a chronologer only, without sympathy for the right, or hatred of the wrong. It seems to me that he ought to feel quickly, and appreciate justly, and to state clearly and positively; for there is great danger that what is written without feeling will be read without interest.

It is altogether possible that I may have failed to give prominence to some important event—and, of course, no writer is above criticism—but the great reading public, I trust, will pardon a slight deviation from the beaten track, in the attempt made to group those events which have a natural and necessary connection, into single chapters, so that a continuous narrative may be presented, rather than a broken record of disconnected events. At the end of the second volume will be found a chronological table, containing many facts which did not fall into place elsewhere.

Many valuable books now challenge the attention of the reader; and I can only ask, that whatever good this work may contain will sooner or later be accepted.

C. W. E.

NEW YORK, January, 1857.

CONTENTS OF VOL. I.

CHAPTER I.

THE NORTHMEN IN NEW ENGLAND.—A.D. 986.

CHAPTER II.

RISE OF THE PURITANS IN ENGLAND.

CHAPTER III.

THE PURITANS BECOME PILGRIMS.

CHAPTER IV.

THE EMBARKATION.

CHAPTER V.

THE VOYAGE.

CHAPTER VI.

THE LANDING.

CHAPTER VII.

WINTER SETTLEMENT OF PLYMOUTH.

CHAPTER VIII.

WELCOME.

CHAPTER IX.

DEATH.

CHAPTER X.

NEW COMERS.

CHAPTER XI.

LANDS, CATTLE, ETC.

CHAPTER XII.

WESTON'S COLONY.

CHAPTER XIII.

INDIAN EMBASSIES.

CHAPTER XIV.

WAR.

CHAPTER XV.

THE GOVERNMENT.

CHAPTER XVI.

THEIR CHURCH.

CHAPTER XVII.

MASSACHUSETTS BAY.

CHAPTER XVIII.

THE CHARTER TRANSFERRED TO NEW ENGLAND.

CHAPTER XIX.

SETTLEMENT OF BOSTON.

CHAPTER XX.

SETTLEMENTS AT THE TIME OF WINTHROP'S COMING.

CHAPTER XXI.

FORTIFIED TOWN.

CHAPTER XXII.

WINTHROP, DUDLEY, VANE, AND ENDICOTT.

CHAPTER XXIII.

THE GOVERNMENT.

CHAPTER XXIX.

THE PEQUOT WAR.

CHAPTER XXX.

THE DEATH OF MIANTONOMOH.

CHAPTER XXXI.

MRS. HUTCHINSON.

CHAPTER XXXII.

THE GREAT CAMBRIDGE SYNOD.

CHAPTER XXXIII.

SAMUEL GORTON.

CHAPTER XXXIV.

THE CONFEDERATION.

CHAPTER XXXV.

THE VASSAL AND CHILDE DISTURBANCE.

CHAPTER XXXVI.

PERSECUTION OF THE QUAKERS.

CHAPTER XXXVII.

THE KING'S JUDGES.—REGICIDES.

CHAPTER XXXVIII.

THE INDIANS.

CHAPTER XXXIX.

ELIOT AND THE INDIANS.

CHAPTER XL.

KING PHILIP'S WAR.

CHAPTER XLI.

RECALL OF THE CHARTERS.

CHAPTER XLII.

THE KING'S COMMISSIONERS.

CHAPTER XLIII.

ANDROS.—THE REBELLION.

CHAPTER XLIV.

PURITAN LAWS.

CHAPTER XLV.

CHURCH MATTERS.

CHAPTER XLVI.

COLLEGES, SCHOOLS, AND BOOKS.

CHAPTER XLVII.

MANNERS AND CUSTOMS OF THE PEOPLE.

The

FIRST PAGE

of

AMERICAN HISTORY.

A.D. 986.

THE

NEW ENGLAND HISTORY.

CHAPTER I.

THE NORTHMEN IN NEW ENGLAND.

A.D. 986.

THE LAND OF THE NORTHMEN—ICELAND—GREENLAND—SKALDS AND SAGAMEN—EIRIK THE RED—BIORN'S VOYAGE TO ICELAND; TO GREENLAND—HE DISCOVERS AMERICA—WHAT LEIF DID—HE REACHES AMERICA, BUILDS HOUSES, FINDS GRAPES, NAMES IT VINLAND—THORVALD—HE DISCOVERS INDIANS—THORSTEIN GOES TO VINLAND AND DIES—THORFINN KARLSEFNE SAILS FOR VINLAND, A.D. 1006—INDIANS AGAIN—THEY FIGHT—FREYDIS—HELGI, FINNBOGI, AND FREYDIS MAKE A VOYAGE; THEY QUARREL—FREYDIS KILLS THEM—DIGHTON ROCK—CONCLUSION—AUTHORITIES.

THE first page of American History is nearly obliterated; it is in some degree mythical, and bears the marks of a wild and roving state of Society; yet it contains fact and truth as well as fiction, which the reader of History should know. In some degree I have re-presented the History in the language of the Sagas, and have prefaced it with a brief account of the interesting people who sailed out from Scandinavia.

The cold and silent North-land was, to the more civilized Greeks and Romans, a land of darkness and mystery; out of which came "men of a fair complexion, with yellow hair and tall in stature" (says Tacitus), who overran Italy, a century before the Christian Era, and made the recollection of the Cimbri fearful.

The Northmen cruized with their oared-ships in the Baltic Sea, and plundered whom they would, and were called by the suffering tribes Værengers (Væring-jar)—Sea-Rovers. Rurik, one of them, penetrated Russia (in the ninth century), and founded the first Czars at Novgorod; while other bands passed on southward and became the famous Body-guard of the Emperors at Constantinople, which sustained the tottering Empire.

The home of the Værengers and Northmen, was the rugged Scandinavian peninsula, now comprising Sweden and Norway.

Toward the end of the ninth century (A.D. 861), Iceland, lying out in the edge of the ice-ocean, was discovered by Naddod, and was visited by roving Vikings; and in the year 874, it was colonized by Ingolf, to whom many fled from Norway, to escape the tyrannies of Harold Haarfager, who ruled the Jarls and Kings with rods of iron. In his time, the Sagas say there was much sailing between Norway and Iceland.

In the ninth century the Piratical Expeditions of the Northmen were giving way to trading voyages, and many engaged in them from the love of adventure, and a wish for wealth:

"A fool is the Homebred Child,"

"Heimskr er heimalit barn," was a northern maxim which they believed: and their small ships pushed out into every sea, and dared unknown danger; they sailed without compass, guided by the stars and the magnet sagacity, which makes the Indian's path straight and wings the wild-drake to his northern nest.

It was not long, therefore, before the bold keel of the Northmen left a track of Sea-light (Moorild), between Iceland and Greenland, where settlements were made and continued for some centuries. Its Eastern and Western shores both appear to have been settled, and the great church at Strœmness was built, as well as others. About the year 1121, Bishop Eirik sailed thence to help the Christians in Vinland; and we catch another glimpse of that old land in the pages of the historian Torfæus, who mentions that in the year 1406, Gudride Andreasson was sent Bishop to Greenland, from Norway. From this time until the year 1721, nothing is known of it; then Hans Egede, pastor of Vaag, in Northern Norway, was moved with pity for those deserted Christians and savages, and after years of effort he at last sailed to Greenland, determined to spend his life, and a salary of £60 a year, to spread the blessings of the Gospel. No remains of whites were found there, and after fifteen years of hardship he was compelled to return to civilization, with shattered health and drooping spirits.

SKALDS AND SAGA-MEN.

The earliest History was of course unwritten, but has been preserved to us by the Skalds and Saga-men, the oral historians of that day. They were a class who supplied the place of books and journals, of preachers and singers; they were indispensable at the festivals of Kings and Jarls, and were welcomed in every hamlet and home, where, in long winter nights, they charmed the wandering listeners. From them are gathered the facts hereinafter given.

The Icelandic Skalds came to be the most famous; for that land, in that dark time was foremost in its love for literature and poetry; they went from Iceland to Norway, England and France, everywhere seeking praise and reward: they sang their own songs, and they chaunted those of others, for a good story was like gold. He was the most famous Saga-man who could furnish the best and most entertainment. The Skald stood before the Chief, whose deeds he was to recount; around him were the companions and followers of the leader. Now a wise Skald was courtier enough to embellish those deeds, and artful enough to weave up with them fancy and feeling, but he could not fabricate the facts, for it would have covered him and his patron with ridicule.

We may, therefore, rely in a great measure upon this unwritten history, which has reached us at last.

Let us now plunge into the Past, and try to discover an answer to the question:

"Who discovered America?"

EIRIK-THE-RED, son of "Thorvald hight-a-man," fled from Norway to Iceland, to escape vengeance for a murder done; there he lived for a time at Eirikstadt, near Vatshorn. But he lent to Thorgest his seat-posts;[1] and when he wanted them he could not get them back again; so there were disputes, and frays, and bitter fights. But Thorgest and his friends were too strong for Eirik, who was declared outlaw by the Thorsnes-thing. Eirik fitted up his ship to go, for there were other lands and other seas beside Iceland and the Ocean which rolled between it and Norway. He said to Styr Thorgrimson and the friends who bade him farewell among the Islands:

"I will go—I will go to the land which Ulf Krages saw when he was driven Westward in the Sea, the time when he found the rocks of Gunnbjorn."

EIRIK DISCOVERS GREENLAND.

So he went, and he promised to come back if he found the land; he found it, and the third summer he came back in his ship to Iceland, and told them of the new land he had found, which he called "Greenland;" because he said, "the people will go thither if it has a good name." And they did go, thirty-five ships (as they were called), fourteen of which arrived. In one of these was Herjulf, who settled in Greenland. This is briefly what happened fifteen winters before Christianity was established by law in Iceland, and was done in the year A.D. 985.

This Herjulf was a kinsman of the Norwegian Ingolf, who had colonized Iceland many winters ago (A.D. 874), and through him he had lands on the south-west point of the Island.

BIORN, his son, was "a very hopeful man." Biorn had

[1] Setstokka; these were tall columns attached to the seats of chiefs, on which were carved Thor and Odin, or other gods.

earned his own ship and had sailed to Norway, with such cargo as Iceland could yield. The love of the old land was strong in the hearts of the Northmen, and Biorn chaunted as he steered his ship toward the rising sun :

"There 's a flag on the mast, and it points to the North,
For Norway 's the land that I love,
I will steer back to North-land, the heavenly course,
Of the winds guiding sure from above."

Eastward steered Biorn toward the old land ; but after he had gone, westward went Herjulf, his father, with Eirik, as has been said ; and a Christian man in his ship sung a hymn, which went thus :

" Oh, thou who tryest holy men
Now guide me on my way,
Lord of the Earth's wide vault extend
Thy gracious hand to me."

Fourteen of Eirik's thirty-five vessels reached Greenland, and there Herjulf lived, and "was a very respectable man."

Biorn lay with his ship in one of those secure Friths, or Fiords, on the western coast of Norway (perhaps at Bergen), which never freeze ; he had sold and changed his skins and Eider, and was ready to sail back to his father and to Iceland. He said :

" To-morrow we will go." One of his men, whose eyebrows were gray with age, came to him and pointed toward the North. The Lysanigar or North-Light streaked the sky, and a faint tinge of copper flamed in its pale beams.

" We will not go to-morrow," he said, " for there 's blood in the sky, and there 'll be blood on the sea."

Biorn stood on the deck of his little vessel, till past midnight, and watched the fitful Aurora which streamed up into the zenith, portending storm. He said to himself, " Thor is mighty, but if the storm does not come, I will go to my father."

The next day the tempest came, and the little ship rode safe in the Fiord, and the sailors lay under cover, and listened to the howling of the wind, and to wonderful sea-tales.

One and another told of the fearful dangers of the whirling Mahlstrom, and these stories were full of fascination, for many ships and many men had sailed away and had not come back, and where were they ? Some of the crew had sailed in sight of the sucking vortex, and had heard the shrieking of the frightened whales, who had been swept down to destruction. They forgot the howling of the storm, they forgot the dangers of the sea, in the remembrance of those greater dangers ; but Biorn did not forget the purpose in hand, and he listened with one ear to the lull which told that the storm had broke.

The voyage to Iceland was a voyage of months, beaten and tossed in those inclement seas ; and when Biorn had found it and reached it ("to Eyrar in the summer"), he was told his father had gone with Eirik-the-Red, westward to Greenland. Biorn was moody, and his sailors asked him what he would do ? He said he would spend the winter with his father as his custom was. "And now I will bear to Greenland, though none of us have been there, if ye will give me your company."

To this they agreed, and for three days they sailed westward till Iceland was out of sight under the water, and then the fair wind fell, and strong north winds arose, and fogs, and they knew not where they were, and it continued many days. But at last the sun broke out, and again they bent their sails ; Biorn loosed a Raven, and as he rose in the sky and flew away, he watched his wings, and followed toward the land.

BIORN DISCOVERS NEW ENGLAND.

Through that day they kept their course, and then all eyes were strained upon the long low line of coast, and they asked Biorn if that was Greenland ? He said it could not be ; but he said, "Sail close to the land."

So they did, and found it covered with wood, with small hills. What land was it ?

They left the land and sailed two days before they saw another land, and then they asked Biorn if that was Greenland ? He said,

" No, for in Greenland they have very high ice-hills."

Here the sailors wished to land, pretending they wanted wood and water ; but Biorn said,

" Ye have no want of either of the two."

Then they turned the prow into the open sea, and sailed three days with a south-west wind, when again they came to land, which was high, and covered with mountains and ice-hills. The sailors said,

"Is this Greenland, and shall we land here ?"

Biorn watched the shore as they sailed along it, and said, " To me this land is little inviting, and I will not stop ;" and they discovered that it was an island.

Once more they struck out into the sea, and with the same south-west wind, sailed four days, when land again appeared, and the sailors said,

" Now, this is Greenland."

Biorn looked, and said, " According to what I have been told, this seems most like Greenland, and here will we steer for land." So they did, and landed in the evening under a ness,[1] where they found a boat, and near by a house, and just here lived Biorn's father, and from him the place was called Herjulfsness.

This was in the year after the colonizing of Greenland, and was A.D. 986.

Now Biorn had seen America, but he was not after continents—he was seeking his father whom he found ; nor does any glory attach to him as a discoverer, nor did he care the weight of a duck's feather for it. He was a brave, determined fellow, who did what he had in hand, and feared nought.

[1] A promontory.

WHAT LEIF DID.

Leif, eldest son of Eirik-the-Red, was another man, and he heard of the lands Biorn had seen, for there was much talk about them, and about voyages of discovery. So he came down to Herjulfsness to see Biorn, and to talk with him; and he bought his ship, determined to see and know what these new lands were, upon which Biorn had not set his foot. His father Eirik was the Jarl of the country, and he the next man to him. It was easy enough to victual his ship, for Greenland then produced much cattle and sheep; and it was easy enough to man it, for the Northmen loved adventure; and thirty-five men soon agreed to go, and some say Biorn was among them; but among them was a German, "Tyrker hight," who had come from a southern land, and had sung its praises, and of the golden wine, and luscious grape. Many came down to the ness to see the adventurers depart, and wives and women dropped some tears; but the men cheered, and the boys wished that they were men that they might go. Leif stood on the deck, and steered his ship southward; he waved his hand to his father, and shouted to him that he would return; his men turned their blue eyes upon Greenland's shores, and sang a farewell song, which ended with shouts of "Courage! courage! hurrah!"

They came first to the land that Biorn had seen last, and drew near it and anchored; they lowered the boats and went ashore, but found only a plain of flat stones lying between them and Ice-hills (Joklar Miklir); this was not inviting, and Leif said,

"Now will I give the land a name and call it 'Helluland.'"[1] This may have been what we call New-foundland?

They left it and found another shore, which was flat and covered with wood—with white sand all about them; and Leif said, "This shall be called Markland, for it is woody."

[1] From Hella—a flat stone.

Again they struck out into the Sea, and sailed two days with a north-east wind, and came to an Island, on which they landed and looked around them; there the dew on the grass was sweet, and they said: "We have come to a good land."

This may have been Nantucket.

They went to the ship and sailed westward, between the Island and the shore, over the shallows, so that as the tide ebbed their ship was left on the sands, and they ran to the shore where they discovered a river; with the return of the tide they returned to the ship, and floated her up the inlet, into what seemed a lake, and there they anchored and brought ashore their skin-cots, and made themselves booths. When Leif saw the glee of his men, and looked around at the fine woods and green pastures, his heart was high, and he said,

"This is a good land." He called together his men and took counsel with them, and said, "Let us here pass the winter, for the Rivers are full of Salmon, and the country is full of promise." So they set to work and built large houses, which remained many years, and were called Leif's-budir (or Booths), for his they were. Leif was a great and strong man, grave and well-favored, and he directed his affairs, not they him; and he was called "Leif-the-Lucky," because he did this, and brought things to pass. He divided his men into two parties to explore the country, and with one party he always went out. But one day Tyrker, the German, was missing, and Leif was much distressed, and swore in his rage, because the party had lost him, and then he went out to seek him. Tyrker soon appeared, and he talked German, and rolled his eyes around, and seemed out of his senses; but at last he said in Norsk, "I have not been far, but I have found something to tell of; I have found vines and grapes."

"But is that true, my fosterer?" quoth Leif.

"Surely it is, for I came from the land of vines and grapes."

The next day they found it true, and they gathered their boat full of them. Then they went to work to cut and hew timber for loading the ship, and so they passed the winter. Here they found but little frost, and the grass did not altogether wither, and the days and nights were more equal than in Greenland; the sun being in the sky on the shortest day from half-past seven in the morning to half-past four in the evening, which should indicate a north latitude of about 41°, 24′, 10″. But the winter was ended, and the ship loaded; then the strong Leif sailed away to Greenland, where he had earned both riches and respect.

When he went, he said, "Now, oh, land, will I give you a name worthy of you, and you shall be called VINLAND, from this day." And so it is called—the land about Mount-Hope, the land of King Philip of the Wampanoags.

There are those who will wonder at the charm which the Northmen found around the Narragansett-bay, and at the ecstacy of the German Tyrker, who discovered and ate the Fox-grapes of New England; but those who wonder have never passed a winter in Iceland, or in the "more serene" climate of Greenland, as Torfæus called it.

Leif sailed with his ship to Brattaahled, where Eirik, his father, yet lived, and his friends and neighbors crowded down to see the great timber-trees which he had brought, and to hear of the new Vinland he had found; and all over Greenland his sailors told the story of the voyage, in the long winter nights, and every one was a hero, and the fame of these things spread over the country.

That winter Eirik-the-red-headed died, being old, and Leif-the-Lucky, the grave and strong, became chief in his stead. Leif had done many things, and his father Eirik, had approved of him, but not of all the things he did, for he said, "You have brought injurious men here—Christian priests." Nevertheless, Leif persuaded his father to be baptized, and most of the people were then easily persuaded to become Christians too; this happened A.D. 1000, according to the History of Olaf Tryggvason.

THORVALD SAILS FOR VINLAND.

Then Thorvald, Leif's brother, wished to go on a voyage of discovery; for, he said, "Where there is much, there is more." Leif said to him,

"Thou canst go with my ship, brother, if thou wilt, to Vinland.

At this Thorvald was glad, for he despised the life of an idle man; and he took counsel of Leif, and engaged thirty of his men and sailed, and Leif said,

"Go—and may the Æsir (the gods) guide you."

The first winter, Thorvald spent in Leif's-booths, at Vinland, and caught many fish. But in the spring he went West and South in his boat, found the shores woody, with many Islands and much shallow water; but no men or beasts, and no works of man, except a sort of corn-shed. The next summer he sailed with his ship Eastward and Northward, and was caught in a great storm, and was driven ashore, and broke the keel of his ship. Much time was consumed in repairing the vessel, and they set up the keel on the point, and called it "Keelness." Then they sailed among the friths and points to the East, and shoved out a plank and went ashore into the country, and Thorvald said,

"Here is beautiful, here would I like to dwell."

When they returned to the shore they discovered canoes and men, all of whom they caught, except one. They killed the eight they caught. Then came out from the inside of the frith an innumerable crowd of skin-boats, filled with Skrælings (Indians), and Thorvald said, "We must put out the battle-screen, but fight little."

The Skrælings shot their arrows and then ran away. Thorvald inquired of his men, and found that none were hurt; then he said,

"I have an arrow under my arm, and the wound will be mortal; bury me on the beautiful point where I wished to dwell, and set up a cross, that it may be called Krossaness in all time to come." So they did, and then sailed back, and told the tidings to Leif at Greenland.

The third son of Eirik, Thorstein, who had married Gudrid, determined to go after the body of his brother; so he chose twenty-five great strong men for his crew, and took Gudrid his wife and sailed away; but they drove about in the sea all summer, and knew nothing where they were; and in the first week of winter they at last reached the western shore of Greenland. Thorstein-the-Black, who lived there, came down and invited Thorstein and Gudrid to come and stay with him. That winter many of Thorstein Eirikson's men died, and Grimhild, wife of Thorstein-the-Black, died, and at last Thorstein Eirikson himself died. Thorstein-the-Black took Gudrid from the chair upon his knees, and sat by her husband's body and comforted her. Then Thorstein, who was dead, sat himself up on the bench, and said,

"Where 's Gudrid?"

Three times he said that, but she answered not.

Then Thorstein-the-Black said, "What wilt thou, namesake?"

After a little he answered, "I would tell Gudrid her fortune, that she will be the better reconciled to my death, for I have now come to a good resting-place.

"I tell thee, Gudrid, that thou wilt be married to an Icelander, and have many children, powerful, sweet, and well-favored. Ye shall go to Norway, thence to Iceland, and after his death wilt thou go abroad to Rome, and come back again to Iceland to thy house, and thou wilt reside there and become a nun, and there wilt thou die."

When he had said this he fell back, and his corpse was set in order, and taken to his ship.

This mixture of the marvelous is consistent with the times, and with older accepted histories; and to most minds will not affect the genuineness of the credible incidents. It will rather be a proof of the genuineness of the Sagas.

About this time (A.D. 1006), came from Iceland Thorfinn Karlsefne, Thord's son, who lived at Höfda, in Höfdastrand, with two ships. He was an able seaman, and a merchant, and he traded with Leif—(Eirik in the Saga, but Eirik was dead). He spent the winter in Greenland, and married Gudrid (or Thurid), widow of Thorvald, Eirik's son, and they had a great yule, and a wedding-feast.

But there was much talk about "Vinland the Good," and Thorfinn determined to explore it, and so made ready his ships: a hundred and sixty persons went in them, among whom was FREYDIS, daughter of Eirik (married to a narrow-minded man, "Thorvard hight"), and Thorhall the hunter, who was a large man, "and strong, black, and like a giant, silent and foul-mouthed in his speech, and always egged on Eirik to the worst; he was a bad Christian." But he knew wood-craft, and was a leader.

When they had sailed two days they came to Helluland, then to Markland, where they killed a bear, and then to Keelness, and then they passed strands which they called Furdurstrands, and came to a land indented with coves, where they ran the ships to shore. But they sailed further westward, and landed on an island (Straumney), where were so many Eider-ducks, that one could hardly walk for the eggs. The country was very beautiful, and there they landed with their cattle.

During the winter they explored, and in the next summer the fishing was poor, and they were in danger of suffering hunger; then Thorhall, the bad Christian, disappeared, and when they found him he was lying on a rock, with his face to the sky, and they asked him, "What he did there?" and he said, "It was no business of theirs." But, the next day, when they caught a whale and had food, he said, "The Red-bearded (Thor) was more hopeful than your Christ; this have I got for the verses I sung of Thor my protector." When they heard this they threw the rest of the fish into the sea (for it had made them very sick), and sailed out and caught other fish.

After they had been there a time, they decided to make two parties; one to go Eastward, and one to go Westward. Thorhall, the hunter, took nine men and went East, and as he went he chaunted:

> "Let our trusty band,
> Haste to the Fatherland,
> Let our vessel brave,
> Plow the angry wave,
> While those few who love
> Vinland, here may rove,
> Or with idle toil,
> Stinking whales may boil,
> Here on Furdurstrand,
> Far from Fatherland."

Thus he sailed away, and they saw no more of him ever again, and some said his boat was driven ashore at Ireland, and his men made slaves. No man now knows.

Thorfinn and his company sailed Westward into the mouth of a river, and called the place Hóp; there they found fields of wheat (maize), and vines, and fish abundant; so that they dug holes in the sand, and when the tide went away they were full of fish—Sacred fish, Flounders (Helgir fiiskar), which tasted well. Rafn and others are disposed to think this place was Mount-hope Bay, but it is certain that if it were where Leif had built his booths, they would not have escaped mention.

One morning early, when they looked around, they saw many canoes, and poles were swung in them so that it sounded "like wind in a straw-stack."

Thorfinn said, "What may it mean?"

Snorri said, "Perhaps peace."

Then he took a white shield and went toward them, and they came toward him, and looked with wonder upon these white men with blue eyes and flowing beards. Thy were black and ill-favored, and had coarse hair, with large eyes and broad cheeks.

There was no snow that winter, and the cattle fed themselves on grass. In the spring the Indians came again and the sea was covered with canoes, and they exchanged an entire fur for a strip of red cloth ; and when the cloth began to fail, the Northmen cut it into smaller strips, "and still the Skrælings gave just as much for that as before."

For the Skrælings were not merchants, and the Norse were.

Then Thorfinn's bull ran out of the wood and bellowed, and the frightened Skrælings fled to their canoes. But when they came again, they came like a rushing torrent, and the poles were whirled the other way, and they howled very loud. They jumped from their ships (canoes) and went against the Northmen and fought. Thorfinn's people were confounded, and thought of nothing but running away, for it appeared to them that the Skrælings were about on every side, so they fell back along the river. Then Freydis said,

"Why do ye run—stout men as ye are—against these wretches? Give me weapons and I can fight better than any of ye."

She could not keep up with them for she was with child, so she seized the sword of a dead man who lay in the path, and bared her breasts and dashed the sword against them, which so frightened the Skrælings that they ran to their ships and rowed away.

Then the men praised her for her courage, but she scoffed them, and they wondered what it could have been that so pressed upon and frightened them, and believed it must have been a delusion. One of the Indians picked up an axe, and was delighted when he found it would cut wood, but when he broke it in trying to cut stone, he threw it away in disgust.

Finding the country unsafe, Thorfinn sailed back to Straumfjord, and found every thing they wanted to have. Thorfinn now determined to go in search of Thorhall-the-hunter; so he took one ship with a part of the people, and the rest (some say one hundred), he left behind with Biarni and Gudrid; whether they remained there and colonized the country no man certainly knows. During the autumn of the year 1007, Gudrid, wife of Thorfinn, bore him a son, who was called Snorri, from whom have descended Thorwalsden, the sculptor, and other noted men.

Snorri was the first white "native American" known in history, and should before this have been canonized.

Thorfinn sailed Eastward in search of Thorhall, passed Keelness, and then Northward and Westward, but found Thorhall nowhere, only wild woods over all as far as they could see. But time passed, and Thorfinn sailed away with Gudrid and his son to Iceland (A.D. 1011), and his mother thought at first he had made a bad match: afterward she changed her mind, for she found Gudrid was a distinguished woman. Many great men in Iceland are descended from Karlsefne and Gudrid, who are not here mentioned. So ends the saga of Thorfinn Karlsefne—"God be with us—Amen!"

Voyages to Vinland-the-Good, began to be profitable, and men talked much about them. Two brothers, Helgi and Finnbogi, had come from Norway to Greenland in 1011, and lay in the fiord. Then Freydis, Eirik's daughter, went from her home at Garde, and bade the brothers sail to Vinland, and go halves with her in the profit they might make. She went to the grave Leif, and begged him to give her the houses he had built; but he said as he had said,

"I will lend you the houses, but not give them."

So they fitted out two ships, and it was agreed that Freydis and the brothers should each have thirty fighting men, besides women; but Freydis broke the bargain, and hired five more. Helgi and Finnbogi reached Vinland first, and took their effects to Leif's houses, and when Freydis came, she said,

"Why bring ye in your things here?"

"Because we thought the bargain should be good between us," they answered.

"To me lent Leif the houses," quoth she, "not to you."

Then said Helgi, "In malice are we brothers easily excelled by thee;" which he had better not have said, for she was a woman.

They took away their goods, and built a separate house, and made things in order, and passed the winter in preparing timber for loading the ships. But the quarrel grew between the brothers and Freydis, so that none went from one house to the other, and there was an end to the sports.

Early one morning Freydis left her husband's bed, and putting on his cloak went, without shoes, to the brothers' house, and stood in the door for a little, in silence. Finnbogi lay there awake, and said,

"What wilt thou here, Freydis?"

"Get up and go with me," she said, "for I will speak with thee."

So he got up, and they went out together, and sat by a tree; then she said, "How art thou pleased here?"

"Well like I the country," he said, "but evil and unnecessary seems to me the discord that has sprung up between us."

"Thou sayest as it is," said Freydis; "but what I wish with you is to change ships, for ye have a larger ship than I, and then will I go hence."

"Then must I agree to it if it is your wish," said Finnbogi.

So they parted, Finnbogi to his bed, and she to hers. But Thorvard her husband woke and said, "Why are you wet? Why are your feet like ice?"

Then she broke out vehemently, and said, "I went to bargain with the brothers about the ship, and they beat me, and used me shamefully; now avenge my disgrace and thy own, or, miserable creature, I will leave thee and tell thy cowardice." He could not withstand her reproaches, and he bade his men get up quickly and take their arms; they fell upon the brothers sleeping, and bound them and led them out; but Freydis had each man killed as he came out; so all were killed, but no man would kill their women. Then said Freydis scornfully, "Give me an axe!" so was done; she took it, and stopped not till all were dead.

After this evil work Freydis was calm and satisfied, but she said to her people,

"Let no man tell of this when we come to Greenland, or I will take his life. Say that Helgi and Finnbogi stayed behind when we went away." But she forgot the Norse proverb, which runs thus,

"A secret can be kept by one, not by two; what three know is no secret."

She loaded the large ship with the best cargo, and had a quick voyage to Greenland, where the thing she had done was whispered about. Then Leif took three of the men and tortured them, and they told the story.

Leif said to Freydis,

"I like not to do to my sister what she has deserved, but I will predict that no good will come to thee or to thy posterity;" and from that day she was thought ill of and neglected; as was inevitable where a people have escaped the corruptions of what are called "Civilized Christian Courts."

Here we leave these early Sagas. They are as clear and consistent as any of the records of the day, and have in their details proofs of reality which could not well be invented. Some collateral evidences tend to sustain them.

THE DIGHTON ROCK. The Assonet, or "Dighton Writing Rock," is thus described by a Committee of the Rhode Island Historical Society, who visited it in 1830:—"It is situated six and a half miles south of Taunton, on the east side of Taunton River, a few feet from the shore, and on the west side of Assonet Neck, in the town of Berkley, County of Bristol, and Commonwealth of Massachusetts.

"It is a mass of well-characterized, fine-grained, graywacke. Its face measured at the base is eleven feet and a half, and in height it is little rising of five feet. The upper surface forms, with the horizon, an inclined plane of about sixty degrees. The whole of the face is covered to within a few inches of the ground with unknown hieroglyphics. There appears little or no method in the arrangement of them. The lines are from half an inch to an inch in width, and in depth sometimes one third of an inch, though generally very superficial."

There are no sure examples of Indians having recorded thus; and Professor Rafn thinks the Runic Th at once stamps its Scandinavian origin. Both he and Finn Magnusen believe that the name of Thorfinn is made out, and the number of his associates, CXXXI (160).[1]

This is found, too, in the country called Vinland-the-Good ; and beside it there are other marks at Tiverton and Portsmouth, which help to sustain the view. The rocks may go for what they are worth ; some think Rafn, Magnusen, and the R. I. Historical Society, are easily satisfied, and that time has had a peculiar effect on this rock, having rendered the hieroglyphics more (?) distinct. The strongest proof is in the Sagas, which are here briefly represented.

There is certainly no improbability, if there were no Sagas, that the hardy and adventurous Northmen should have struck the shore of America ; with them there is no reasonable doubt. The inscription at Dighton, is a slight confirmation. So is the following from Père Charlevoix's History of Nouvelle France, quoted by Pontopoddian. The Jesuit reports that he found in Newfoundland a different race from the Indians ; a degenerate people with beards and a white complexion : "Les cheveux blonds,

[1] Their 100 was 120, and with Thorhall's 9, this 131 would make 160, Thorfinn's whole number.

leur peau assez blanche, et ils ont de la barbe—etc. ; et pourroient faire croire, qu'ils sont une colonie d'Europeens qui ont degeneré par la misère et par le manque d' instruction."

Adam of Bremen, a German, who wrote in the eleventh century, also gives some account of Vinland, which he had from Sven Estridson, King of Denmark, nephew of Canute the Great, of England.[1]

I conclude then, that the Northmen did land on the shores of North America in the tenth century, and that they made temporary settlements ; but I think he must be an enthusiast, who fixes the places of their landing and living with so much precision, as some scholars are inclined to do.

I leave this interesting subject with the reader, trusting that he will have some entertainment in reading what is written. He may ask what authority there is for telling these things, in this old time of the world—and where he is to look for himself ? Many books are, therefore, recommended to his careful and attentive perusal ; some of them he will find in the Royal Library, at Copenhagen, a part of which he may read if he will in the old Norse, at least in Danish characters ; the rest in such languages as he can understand.

There is also a large and valuable collection in the Astor Library, New York, which is open to all.

AUTHORITIES THAT MAY BE STUDIED.

Somewhere toward the end of the twelfth century, Sæmund, a priest (born 1056), who had studied in France, wrote down some of the Poems, which are now known as Sæmund's, or the Elder Edda.

The later Edda, in prose, supposed to have been written in the

[1] Keyser—Religion of the Ns., p. 80.

thirteenth century, by Snorre Sturleson, was found in Iceland, by Arngrim Jonsson, in 1628. These may be called the Bible, or Holy-Books of the Northmen.

Ari Frode began in the early part of the twelfth century to write down past and present events; he is quoted by Snorre Sturleson in his Heimskringla (a history of the Northmen for three hundred years), written in the first half of the thirteenth century. Olaf Tryggvason's History, written in Latin by two monks, in the end of the twelfth century exists; and Professor Rafn, of Copenhagen, has translated the Flatöbogen manuscripts collected about 1390, in his Antiquitias Americanæ. Most of the remaining proofs of their early history are collected at Copenhagen, and from these works what we know is drawn.

The Sagas of Eirik-the-Red, and of Thorfinn-Karlsefne, are a part of the celebrated Flatöbogen MSS: a vellum containing copies of Sagas, executed between A.D. 1387, and 1395, found in the monastery of Flat-Island, in Iceland, and now preserved in the Royal Library of Copenhagen. The Saga of Eirik was probably written in Greenland, that of Thorfinn, in Iceland.

See Antiquitates Americanæ, by C. C. Rafn.

Mémoire sur la Découverte de l'Amérique au dixième Siècle, par Charles Christian Rafn. Copenhagen, 1843.

History of the Northmen, by Henry Wheaton. Philadelphia, 1831.

The Discovery of America by the Northmen, by North Ludlow Beamish. London, 1841.

Pontopoddian's Natural History of Norway. 1753.

Crantz's History of Greenland. London, 1767.

Frithiof's Saga, by Bishop Tegner. Stockholm, 1825.

The Religion of the Northmen—by Keyser. Translated by Barclay Pennock. New York, 1834.

CHAPTER II.

RISE OF THE PURITANS IN ENGLAND.

WICKLIFFE—HENRY VIII.—THE BIBLE A CONSTITUTION—SKEPTICISM—HUSS AND CALVIN—THE NAME "PURITAN"—THE CHARACTER OF AN OLD ENGLISH "PURITANE" OR NON-CONFORMIST.

FROM the time of WICKLIFFE,[1] in the fourteenth century, Puritanism may be said to have had life in England.[2] This great man could feel, think, act. He knew that power and security had made the Church fearfully corrupt. He saw that the "honors of the Church were given to unholy men; Priests do eat up the people as though it was bread." He saw that dignitaries had become "Bailiffs rather than Bishops;" that religious beggars—Monks and Friars—swarmed in every town and devoured the earth. His great soul was moved at these things, and he called for Purity, for Reform, in the Church of God. He was not alone: Rigge, Chancellor at Oxford, Brightwell, Reppington, and Hereford, were with him; and John of Gaunt—"time-honored Lancaster," son of Edward Third—stood by him, his staunch friend.

Wickliffe proceeded to Act: he demanded simplicity in worship. He asserted that "man can only be excommunicated by himself." He declared that the Pope and the Church had nothing to do with political and temporal rule. He boldly maintained, that "a Priest, yea, a Roman Pope, may be lawfully accused and brought to trial by Laymen." He translated the Bible into the vernacular, and held that it, not the Church, was the rule of faith. The two-headed Popedom (Urban in Rome, and

[1] Born, 1324; died, 1384. [2] Eliot's Passages in the History of Liberty.

Clement in Avignon, A.D. 1380), then distracted the Church; which in a degree protected this Puritan.

Protected by Lancaster, Wickliffe could not be burnt, nor could the Lollards, then the Puritans of England, be "harried out of England," as they were in James the First's day. Wickliffe was popular with the people, and the power of Royal and hereditary honor sustained him. The seed of Liberty is sown in the heart of man; Wickliffe watered it and made it to bud.

The day of the Great Reformation in England came. Little did HENRY THE EIGHTH care for the purity of the Church, or for Liberty of Conscience. His quarrel with Rome was as to power and patronage.

Whether Bluff Harry or Pious Paul should be Pope in England? Whether the capricious and tyrannical King should lord it in his own way, or after the way of some equally willful, but weaker, Pope or Council at Rome? In the struggle, the weaker went down, and England, cut loose from Rome, set up for herself, with Henry as her spiritual head. Absurd as this seems, it had been worse for her with Rome to rule her. But the struggle was not this time a losing one; perhaps it never is, for wherever there is movement, truth is developed and spread.

BIBLE THE CONSTITUTION.

Finding the old standards of Orthodoxy had become rotten, men looked for something that might not be altogether arbitrary and capricious. The Puritans, here and there since the days of Wickliffe, had appealed to the Bible, and asserted it as the standard, and the only one, in religious things. It was a sort of CONSTITUTION or Magna Charta, in place of the despotic and uncertain will of a Pope or Council, which might be good or bad, or right or wrong. Although the King did not for a moment allow any such claim to interfere with his will, yet that it was making its way, was clear, in that Vicar-General Cromwell, in the twenty-seventh year[1] of the King's reign, signified that the rites

[1] History of the Puritans, by Rev. H. W. Stowell.

and ceremonies of the Church should be reformed according to the Holy Scriptures.

Since Wickliffe's day, the Bible had been read and pondered by earnest men, and the appeal to God, as supreme over any and all earthly power and law, which pervades it, had carried strength and hope to those who had suffered and died victims of spiritual despotism. But what did the Bible teach, and what was the standard it set up? Bold men like Wickliffe, and Huss, and Luther, and Calvin, looked to see. They read and thought, and used their reason and experience, as men do now, and decided for themselves. Their decision was thundered in speech and action, and men gathered round them as particles to the strong magnet; for what truth they had, made them powerful, and their truth was fresh and clear, not smothered with the ceremonial and formalism of an old organization, which tends always to corruption and decay.

This Skepticism—this questioning of existing Gods and of past standards—is an old practice, coincident with the mental and spiritual action of man in all times; it is the spring from which flows among the mountains, the river which is to enrich both mental and spiritual growth. The hardy Enomaus, ages since, thus bearded Apollo in his temple: "What dost thou, wretch as thou art, at Delphi? muttering idle prophecies!"

The indictment of Socrates said:—"SOCRATES is guilty of crime, for not worshiping the gods whom the City worships, but introducing new divinities of his own." [1]

And we all know that Demetrius was shocked, because Paul, a wandering preacher from Tarsus, spoke against his Diana. That these Iconoclasts were then called "Infidels," is a matter of course. Such was the cry against Hooker and Hales, Stillingfleet, Cudworth, and Taylor; [2] such is likely to be the cry with the timid, the indolent, the unthinking, and the venal, against those who, faithful

[1] Grote's Greece. [2] Preface to Warburton's Divine Legation.

to themselves, go boldly forward, using the Past only to show them what the present is, and what the Future should be.

Huss was burnt; it was not from charity that Wickliffe, Luther, and Calvin escaped, for the Church was ready. The impulse to intellect given by Wickliffe was distinct through a century; and is not spent yet. Luther was a poet, and appealed to the intuitional rather than the logical faculty; but his voice penetrated the depths of man's nature, and shook the world. Calvin lived and acted in the intellectual consciousness, and his logic was clear, inflexible, and unmerciful. The essence of Calvinism was intellectual freedom and supremacy, for which, rather than for his theology, the world owes him thanks.

It may be well to say again, that the term Puritan was applied to men of high standing in the Church of England—men of the truest lives and loftiest talents; they held by the Spirit rather than the Letter, by the substance of the Church, not its forms.

Hooper, a distinguished divine of the Church of England, in the reign of Edward VI., had refused to be consecrated to the office of bishop, in what he deemed to be the superstitious robes of the Episcopal order. He had been an exile from England during the latter part of Henry the Eighth's reign, and his puritanism, his dislike of formal religion, had been deepened by his intercourse with the reformed churches on the continent.

The objection to ceremonies was not confined to the Puritans who left the Church. Jewel, Grindal, Sandys, Nowell, eminent Churchmen, were in favor of leaving off the surplice, and many of what were called Popish Ceremonies.[1]

But the term once honorable became one of reproach and ridicule, on the accession of Charles II. (1660), and was eagerly seized upon by profane and unscrupulous

[1] Young's note in Ch. of Ps. vol. 11.

men, to disgrace those who made any pretensions to piety, or to wish to reform abuses in either Church or State. It was not altogether undeserved, for the Puritans of the Commonwealth comprised many venal, corrupt, canting men, who were a disgrace to any party or Church ; and their folly and wickedness served to contaminate the cause they pretended to favor.

The ministers said,[1] "We protest before the Almightie God, that we acknowledge the Churches of England (as they be established by publique authoritie) to be true visible Churches of Christ : that we desire continuance of our Ministry in them above all earthly things ; and, 'Finally, whatsoever followeth is not set downe in an evill mind to deprave the Book of Common Prayer, Ordination, or Homilies ; but onely to show some reasons why we cannot subscribe to all things contayned in the same Booke.'"

The first part of the Book is taken up (226 pages) in Objecting to Translations "Generall and Perticul."

The second part (243 pages) is a detailed objection to the Applications of Scripture, etc., which no one now is forced to read.

The third part (166 pages) treats at large, and in sixteen various positions, the unlawfulness of Kneeling, and goes into "An examination of their Pretences, etc." of those who advocate it.

A superstitious reverence for the Prayer-book, the Surplice, the use of the Cross in Baptism, Kneeling at the Sacrament, was common and was encouraged ; and the Ceremonies of the Church, harmless enough in themselves, had reached an exaggerated importance. They had usurped the place of Christ, and, like the broad phylacteries of the Pharisees, covered a dead religion and a corrupt church. These trifles, therefore, the Puritans protested against loudly, persistently, and bitterly : they

[1] A Defence of the Ministers' Reasons for refusall of subscription to the Booke of Common Prayer, and of Conformitie, etc. Imprinted 1607.

were merely the standards around which they fought; while the real issues were Freedom, and Truth, and Righteousness.

"The Character of an old English Puritane or Non-Conformist," is thus begun to be described by "John Geree, M.A., and late preacher of the Word at Saint Faiths."[1]

"The Old English Puritane was such an one, that honored God above all, and under God gave every one his due. He highly esteemed order in the House of God: but would not under colour of that submit to superstitious rites. He reverenced Authority Keeping within its sphere. He made conscience of all Gode ordinances, though some he esteemed of more consequence. He was much in praier; with it he began and closed the day. He esteemed reading the Word and ordinances of God both in private and publike, but did not account reading to be preaching. The Word read he esteemed of more authority, but the Word preached of more efficacy." So the portrait is made out, and fortified by numberless references to Scripture by one of their preachers.

King James I. said of the same men, they were "pests in the Church and Commonwealth, Liars and Thieves."

The Non-Conformists claimed to be truly Church of England men, differing only respecting some ceremonies.[2]

Among the questions proposed to the Lord Prelates in 1587 was this one:

"By the Statute of 37 Henry VIII. c. 6, Every Person or Persons that cut out or maliciously cause to be cut out the tongue of any person, or shall maliciously cut off or cause to be cut off the ear or ears of any of his Majestie's Subjects, is to render trible damages to the partie, and to forfeit £10 sterling for every such offence:

[1] London, 1649.

[2] See "An account of the Principles and Practises of several Non-Conformists, wherein it appears that their religion is no other that what is Profest in the Church of England," etc. By Mr. John Corbet.—London 1682.

Whether then Our Lord Prelates and their officers, for cutting out faithful ministers' tongues, and closing up of their mouths, that they may not preach God's Word to the people, and cutting off some Laymen's ears, that they may not hear God's Word (and that maliciously against the Laws, etc.) are not Fellons, is a question worthy resolution."

The truth seems to be, that the Puritans represented the movement party in England, and the bitter persecutions they met with, were owing, not to their objections to surplices and ceremonials, but to their persistent protest and resistance to abuses in the Church; which men in place knew well would in the end destroy their places and limit or destroy their privileges. They were feared and hated as the Re-Formers of that day.

CHAPTER III.

THE PURITANS BECOME PILGRIMS.

THE STANDARD SET UP—PERSECUTION—EXPATRIATION FORBIDDEN—1602—JOHN ROBINSON AND HIS CHURCH—THE BOOK OF SPORTS—1607—THE PURITANS TRY TO FLY—ARE BETRAYED—ARE SEPARATED—THEY REACH HOLLAND—AT LEYDEN—1609—REASONS FOR LEAVING HOLLAND—CUSHMAN, CARVER, AND BREWSTER—THEY OBTAIN A GRANT FROM THE VIRGINIA COMPANY—THEY PREPARE TO GO—BARGAIN WITH LONDON MERCHANTS.

It seems to be a law of human nature that no evil is arrested till it becomes unbearable ; and then it is often too late. This is true of tyrannical usurpation.

Since the Law of the Six Articles (1539), till the accession of James I. (1603), nigh seventy years had passed, in which the Puritans had suffered buffetings, burnings, and persecutions in England. Men had been burnt in Henry the Eighth's reign for asserting the doctrine of Transubstantiation ; in Mary's reign for denying it ; and, again, in Elizabeth's for maintaining it. Conformity in doctrine and worship had been urged by the sword and faggot. Henry set up his headship, the Pope his, Elizabeth hers ; and Archbishop Whitgift had driven persecution home to the hearts of the people. James I. and his flatterer Bancroft, then asserted themselves as the "standard," and murder or exile was still the custom. Barrow, Greenwood, Penry, and a host more, were put to death, and yet some of these sturdy Englishmen would not yield the God-given right to think their own thoughts, and to worship their own God in their own way. In view of this freedom and this right, kings became to them as stubble, laws as parchment, country and home lost their charm, and even life itself was risked and lost. The world should thank them for their rebellion, for it reaps the harvest these "fanatics" sowed.

The love of father-land, with its homes, its childhood, its hallowed lives, and holy graves, was strong, but all these were overcome, even though voluntary expatriation had been made illegal and disgraceful by some of England's rulers.

John Robinson and his friends decided to go. Since the year 1602, this small body of Calvinists and Puritans had been wont to collect in the north of England, and listen to the earnest words of John Smith, Richard Clifton, and lastly, of John Robinson, their chosen pastor. They gathered themselves Sabbath after Sabbath with difficulty, walking for miles, and changing their places of meeting. They came together with doubt, and parted with fear, for they knew not when or where, the unjust laws and fierce soldiers might seize them.

Elizabeth had been no nursing mother to them, and James was a father bent upon their destruction. "Pests in the Church and Commonwealth, greater liars and perjurers than any border thieves," he called them.

In 1607 they contracted with a ship-master to carry them from Boston (in Lincolnshire) to Holland, where they could be tolerated. A part of them embarked—it was midnight; the captain betrayed them, and they were driven back to mockery, imprisonment, poverty, and punishment.[1] But they did not despair; again in 1608 a Dutch captain agreed to help them to get away from their country. They collected stealthily upon England's shore, in a desolate place between Grimbse and Hull. Most of the men were sent aboard in small boats, while the women and children, aground in a bark, waited the rising tide, ready to start; but busy tongues and spiteful, carried the news to the magistrates, and the "countrie was raised to take them." "Y^e^ Duchman seeing it (says Bradford), swore his countrie's oath, 'sacrement,' and having ye wind

1 Bradford's History. Young's Chronicles of Ps.

faire, weighed his anchor, hoysed sayles, and away."[1] The men were then forced to leave their families, and the women and children, with Robinson and a few others, were led back again to prison and persecution. Sore was the trial, and grievous their misery. Those in the ship had a sad and perilous voyage ; they were driven by the winds, and nigh shipwrecked on the ragged coast of Norway ; for seven days and nights they saw no sun, no moon, no stars ; and when the sailors lost heart, the Pilgrims cried, "Yet, Lord, thou canst save." They reached Holland, and in the following year the women and children were allowed to leave England (for who there could support them ?), and with Robinson they joined their friends at Amsterdam. In 1609 they removed to the fair and beautiful city of Leyden, where they were established for eleven years, and where the church increased to three hundred members.

"These English," said the Dutch to the quarrelsome Walloons, "have lived among us now these twelve years, and yet we never had any suit or accusation brought against them, but your strifes are continual."[2]

In Holland, the Pilgrims were honorable and industrious—they sought work with the Dutch and found it, and they took to new trades. Brewster was a man of property, not an idle "gentleman," and he learned to be a printer at the age of forty-five. Bradford, who had owned and farmed land in England, became a silk-dyer. They were good citizens it seemed ; good in Holland if not in England, and Robinson became noted as a scholar and preacher, one of the first there.[3]

Why then did they leave Holland ? Why again brave the perils of the sea ? Were they reckless and unsteady, as the churchmen charged ? Were they desperate and wilful, as the king asserted ? It is unmanly to assume

[1] Bradford's History of Plymouth Plantation, p. 13. M. H. C., 1856.
[2] Cotton's Account. [3] Cotton's Account.

bad motives, where nobler ones are at hand. Bradford enumerates some of their reasons; and they were:[1]

First, The country (Holland) was hard, and many discouraged: "Grim and grissled poverty was coming on them as an armed man."

Second, Old age was coming upon them, and no amelioration of their condition came with it.

Third, Licentiousness threatened their children, who, in another generation would become Dutchmen;[2] and there was fear that they would take the bit in their teeth. The Sabbath, too, was not well observed there.

Fourth, "A great hope and inward zeal of laying some good foundation for the propagating and advancing the Gospel of the Kingdom of Christ in those remote parts of the world," was strong with them.

So they sent Robert Cushman and John Carver, to England, with a petition, signed by nearly all the church, asking for privileges in the wilderness of the New World.[3] Sir Edward Sandys, a man of influence, befriended them; they were encouraged to settle in Virginia, but got little else, for James was then enforcing conformity, or "harrying the people." They returned to their friends disappointed, but not cast down; so in a short time (1619), Cushman and Brewster were sent to England to beg once more for liberty to live and worship in the wilderness.[4] At last they obtained a grant, not from the King, but from the Virginia, or London Company, and obliged to be content with this, they set about the preparation for their departure. This grant was never of the least service, for they were driven on the coast North of the Virginia patent, and settled themselves there with a charter from the God of the free!

[1] Young's Chronicles of Pilgrims, page 47. Brief narrative, do.

[2] Mauditt, 1774.

[3] See Robinson and Brewster's letter to Sir E. Sandys, in Prince. Young's Chronicles of Pilgrims.

[4] Cushman's letter in Young's Chronicles of Pilgrims, page 68.

Cushman and Brewster, both men of parts and of influence, applied themselves diligently in preparing the way for this untried and nigh desperate voyage. They sounded the Politicians; they enlisted the sympathy of friends and well-wishers; they approached the Merchants. Brewster was a stranger in London and in England, but, with Cushman, he was diligent and persevering. The dangers were great, but not desperate, and the difficulties were many, but not invincible. Their courage "was answerable" to the needs of the time. With "care, the use of good means, fortitude, and patience," and the help of Providence, all these might be borne or overcome.[1]

One thing was to be done—not the least important—viz., to provide themselves with stores, tools, and material aids for this new enterprise. The reports of Captain Smith, and the efforts of Gorges and others, had inspired a belief in the minds of some English Merchants, that the fisheries on the American coast might be made profitable—perhaps largely so. The Agents of the Church at Leyden were enabled, therefore, to enlist some London Merchants, and to have a Company ("The Merchant Adventurers") formed for the supply of the needed capital. The terms were deemed exceedingly severe—a share of ten pounds money being equal to a man's services—each share and man being entitled to draw an equal amount of the entire profits for seven (7) years.[2] But hard as these terms were, they did not preclude Civil and Religious rights, and the Puritans accepted them, although some of their number afterward severely blamed Mr. Cushman, and wished to repudiate the bargain. They enlisted their own property where they periled their lives, and so all became partners in a great business, which was to extend over seven years of time, and over the lands and seas of a new State. It is easy to see that this was no fantastic

[1] Chronicles of Ps., pp. 48–50.
[2] Chronicles of Ps., p. 83. Cheever's Journal, p. 131. Bradford's Hist., M. H. Coll., 1856.

imitation, as has been asserted,[1] of the early Christians, who had a community of goods, but a simple partnership, such as is now of daily occurrence.

So much being accomplished, Brewster and Cushman returned to their friends in Holland.

[1] Robertson's America.

The

VOYAGE TO NEW ENGLAND,

and

Settlement of

NEW PLYMOUTH.

A. D. 1620.

CHAPTER IV.

THE EMBARKATION.

DELFT-HAVEN—THE 22D OF JULY, 1620—THE SPEEDWELL—THE PARTING—ROBINSON'S ADDRESS—SOUTHAMPTON—THE MAYFLOWER—THE 5TH OF AUGUST, 1620—THEY SAIL—THEY PUT BACK—THEY SAIL AGAIN—THE SPEEDWELL PUTS BACK—THE MAYFLOWER SAILS ALONE—6TH OF SEPTEMBER, 1620.

DELFT-HAVEN is an unimportant sea-port, on the long line of the Dutch coast; yet it is worthy of remembrance, for it marks the march of Man toward the future, and toward Freedom. On the morning of the 22d of July, of the year 1620,[1] a few persons, on the quiet key, knew that a small bark of sixty tons, called the "Speeedwell," was prepared for a voyage; but whither and for what? She was no merchantman bound for gain, no privateer for plunder, no holiday sail for pleasure, no explorer for new continents. Some may have heard that she sought Religion and Freedom! Where were they to be found?

On the morning of the 22d of July, the living freight of this vessel gathered on her deck: men, women, and children, some old, but mostly young. They had come from Leyden, and with them came their pastor, John Robinson; they were English born and English bred, though they had now lived in this foreign land some twelve years; they did not forget the land of their birth, yet they thanked the Dutch for shelter, when they were driven out from their homes, and the places they loved so well. They had taken counsel of their hopes and of their fears—they had already met together, in their own words, "that we might afflict ourselves before our God," as in the days of

[1] Bradford's Journal in Prince.

Ezra[1]—" To seek of him a right way for us and for our children." They believed they had found the right way, and were now to go forward on it, leaving behind the larger part of their church, and their minister, for all could not then go. They were serious, and sad, yet most hopeful. The little children gazed upon the strange ships with wonder, those at the breast rested in quiet unconsciousness: none, young or old, knew all that was before them; and it was well they did not. The Dutch sailors rested from their steady labors to look upon this singular sight; some scoffed, but they were curious to see what this thing meant. Thus was gathered on the deck of the "Speedwell" this band of pilgrims, then at the other side of the wide ocean; strangers to the perils of the sea. They had collected together their little wealth, and their goods lay heaped in confusion upon the narrow deck; beds and chairs, pots and packages, chests and cradles, tools and implements, were mingled with casks of water and provisions, coils of cordage and other gear. A ready oath now and then escaped the impatient sailors, as the urgent business of the ship went on, for they were to sail that day.

THE PARTING ON THE DECK.

The Pilgrims stood in groups, and the conversation, if brief and low, was earnest. Then Robinson knelt down on the deck, and with him knelt his friends and companions; he stretched out his hands and cried to the Lord, and his words moved all hearts. We shall do well to remember some things that he said:

ROBINSON'S ADDRESS.

"Brethren, we are now quickly to part from one another, and whether I may ever live to see your faces on earth any more, the God of Heaven only knows; but whether the Lord has appointed that or no, I charge you before your God and his blessed Angels, that you follow me, no further than you have seen me follow the Lord Jesus Christ.

"If God reveal anything to you by any other instru-

[1] Ezra, viii., 21.

ment of his, be as ready to receive it as ever you were to receive any truth by my ministry ; for I am verily persuaded the Lord has more truth yet to break forth out of His holy Word. For my part I can not sufficiently bewail the condition of the Reformed Churches, who are come to a period in religion, and will go at present no further than the instruments of their reformation. The Lutherans can not be drawn to go beyond what Luther said ; whatever part of his will our God has revealed to Calvin, they will rather die than embrace it ; and the Calvinists you see stick fast where they were left by the great man of God, who yet saw not all things.

"This is a misery much to be lamented ; for though they were burning and shining lights in their times, yet they penetrated not into the whole council of God ; but were they now living, would be as willing to embrace further light as that which they first received ; I beseech you remember, it is an Article of your Church Covenant, 'That you shall be ready to receive whatever truth shall be made known to you from the written word of God.' Remember that and every other Article of your sacred Covenant. But I must herewithal exhort you to take heed what you receive as Truth ; examine it ; consider it, and compare it with those Scriptures of Truth before you receive it ; for it is not possible the Christian world should come so lately out of such thick Anti-Christian darkness ; and that perfection of Knowledge should break forth at once."[1] These noble and generous Counsels, far—far in advance of the sectarian bigotry of his and even of our days, were remembered and recorded by the grateful Winslow. But the time had come to part. Captain Reynolds gave the word, and with lusty arms and voices the white wings of the ship were spread. With many tears and embraces they parted ; in the words of Bradford, "they knew they were pilgrimes, and looked not

[1] Winslow's Narrative. See note in Morton's Memorial. Neal's History of Puritans. Mem. of John Robinson in Mass. Hist. Coll.

much on those things, but lift up their eyes to ye heavens, their dearest countrie, and quieted their spirits." [1]

It would be hard to say which were the most bereft, those who went, or those who staid. As they on the shore watched the departing bark with streaming eyes, they were borne up by a living faith, that Liberty and Righteousness should one day prevail. They sailed for Southampton, in England, where awaited them another small band, and the larger ship, the "Mayflower," which was to lead the way to a new world. After some disagreements and reproaches, between the Pilgrims and Mr. Cushman, and Mr. Weston, their agents in England, the final arrangements were now made; and on the 5th of August, 1620, the two ships, with some one hundred and twenty persons, stood out to sea.[2]

THE MAYFLOWER.

The "Mayflower" was a ship of a hundred and eighty tons; the "Speedwell" was about sixty tons. Smaller vessels had again and again explored the Ocean. Columbus's "Ships" were from fifteen to thirty tons burden, and without decks. Frobisher had traversed the watery waste, with a vessel of twenty-five tons; and Pring had coasted along the shores of New England in a bark of fifty tons. Those were manned by hardy seamen, to whom the tempest was a play-fellow; but these men, women, and children, knew nothing of the sea; they only knew that ships sailed, and too often did not return; they had seen the sea, even along the coasts of England and Holland, lashed into fury. To trust themselves upon it on an uncertain voyage, to a wilderness harbor, was no light matter. Yet they went out with courage and determination; and at once began to arrange themselves to their new circumstances.

They had hardly begun to do this, when signals from the "Speedwell" told that all was wrong, that evil threat-

[1] Bradford's History, p. 59. Young's Chronicles of Pilgrims, p. 89.

[2] Prince.

ened them. To turn back was the only alternative, and then to learn that the "Speedwell" was leaking badly, was the unwelcome news. To old England, then, they must once more steer, and that without delay, for the water made fast, so that when they arrived at Dartmouth, they believed that in three hours more, the ship "would have sunk right down."

After eight days of delay, they again sailed on the 21st of August; but before long the signals told of further trouble. Although God, in the language of a pious historian, "had sifted three kingdoms to get the pilgrim wheat of this enterprise;" it needed sifting once, if not twice more.[1] There were timid persons among the hundred and twenty, and now their small courage was spent; they were urgent to go back. Cushman wrote, Dartmouth, August 17, "Our viage hither hath been as full of crosses as ourselves of crookedness." He remained behind in England. The superstitious element was then rife in the land; and the habit of tracing every event to a special act of God, led some to fear that these delays and rebuffs signified, that God was displeased at their voyage; who could say he was not, who could prove that he was? The truth is that the "Speedwell" was over-masted, and the captain and crew were sick of their bargain (for a whole year). The nineteen timid Pilgrims had the fact of the leaky condition of the ship, and perhaps the voice of the captain on their side; so it was decided that the "Speedwell" should put back to England, and the rest of the passengers were transferred to the "Mayflower;" which, finally, on the 6th of September, set sail for America, solitary and alone.[2]

[1] "Indeed," wrote Cushman (1621), "it is our callamitie that we are yoked with some ill-conditioned people who will never doe good, but corrupt and abuse others," etc.

[2] Morton's Memorial, p. 32. Thacher's History of Plymouth, p. 16.

CHAPTER V.

THE VOYAGE.

THE SHIP BREAKS—THE IRON SCREW—SEA-SICKNESS—OCEANUS HOPKINS—THEY LOOK WESTWARD—THEY SEE LAND—9TH OF NOVEMBER—CAPE COD—THEY EXPLORE—MILES STANDISH—THEY SEE INDIANS—THEY SEE DEER—THEY FIND GRAVES—THEY FIND INDIAN CORN—WINTER COMES—INDIAN CRY AND ATTACK—FIRST SABBATH.

THE voyage of the pioneer ship was long, tempestuous, and monotonous, as what sea voyage is not? Yet, with a firm purpose, she opened a way through the buffeting ocean toward the setting sun. Already its rays came to them a little shorn, the autumn solstice was at hand, and winter not far away. In religious exercises, in hopeful conversation, the exiles passed the weary days; these were varied by storms, and once by a great danger. In the straining of the ship a strong timber threatened to break; then, among the lumber which they had brought, a great "iron screw was found, and the ship was saved." Their faces were turned westward, but who can wonder that a lingering look was cast behind, and that pleasant memories for a moment dimmed their recent sufferings, and present hopes? Men, women, and children suffered the "sickness of the sea," that sickness which is inexorable, which weakens the knees, enervates the heart, and paralyzes the brain. The sailors laughed and scoffed, but to them it seemed that death was nigh. Yet it was not; one only of the whole number, William Butten, died during the voyage, and one was born to take his place—the son of Stephen Hopkins, named Oceanus, the child of the sea.

Daily they turned their eyes westward, hoping for a sight of the new land. They had directed their course to the Hudson River, of which the Dutch navigators had made favorable reports. As the voyage lengthened, their longings for the land strengthened. They had been tossed on the sea now sixty-five days, when, on the 9th of November, the low line of the New World gladdened their eyes; they thanked God for the sight, and took courage. On the 11th of November they came to anchor within Cape Cod. Sixty-seven days they had passed in the ship, since their first departure on the 6th of September, and one hundred and twelve since the embarkation at Delft Haven on the 22d of July. They were weary—weary—many were sick, and the scurvy had attacked some. They might well rejoice that they had reached these shores. But they were yet far away from the mouth of the Hudson, and another voyage must be undergone to get to it.

Captain Jones opposed this, and saw breakers and dangers ahead. No doubt, he too was glad to bring the voyage to an end. Some have charged that the Dutch bribed him to deceive the Pilgrims. Bradford does not mention it, and the Dutch historians deny it.[1]

Pines, junipers, sassafras, and other sweet woods were growing on the shores; they found, too, "the greatest store of fowl that ever we saw."[2] Whales showed themselves, and one being fired at, the gun exploded, when the whale "gave a sniff and away, thanks be to God." Bleak and barren as the shore was, it seemed delightful after the long voyage, and they set about exploring. On Monday, the 13th of November, sixteen men went ashore, "with every man his musket, sword, and corslet," headed by Miles Standish. He had come of fighting blood—one of the Standishes having, long ago, put his sword "into Wat Tyler's belye." Those who have been on Cape Cod, and know of its stunted pines and heavy sand, will well understand how poor the prospect for a settlement must have been. They continued their explo-

[1] Bancroft, vol. i., p. 309. Gordon's New Jersey. Morton's Mem., p. 34. Grahame's History, vol. i, p. 226.

[2] Pilgrims' Journal.

rations, and it was not till the 15th of November that they saw signs of life; then they saw "five or six people, with a dogge, who were savages." They all ran away, "and whistled the dogge after them;" this touch of human nature, this whistling the dog, must have reassured the wanderers. Their boat, "their shallop," was sent ashore for repairs; and while these were going on, no exploration along the coast could be made; yet they were not idle.

No period in American History is more interesting than this, and no one can tell their story better than they have themselves done it. Whenever we can, let us read their record.

"They sent parties along the shore, and into the forests," following the trails of Indians; they knew nothing of the land, or its inhabitants and wild beasts; but they were not men whom small matters would discourage. Returning from a long search with inadequate provisions, "about ten a clocke," says one, "we came into a deepe valley, full of brush, woodgaile, and long grasse, through which we found little paths or tracks, and there we saw a deere, and found springs of fresh water, of which we were heartily glad, and set us downe and drunke our first New England water, with as much delight as ever we drunke drinke in all our lives."[1]

Again, they struck inland, and following a track, "well-nigh two foote broad," which they thought might lead to some village, or houses, they lighted their matches, to be ready for what might befall; but they now discovered that it was "only a path made to drive deere in when the Indians hunt, as we supposed." After a march of five or six miles, and no signs of people, they returned by another way, and on the plain, came to what looked like a grave, only larger. "Musing what it might be," they resolved to examine: they found "first a Matt, and under that a fayre Bow, and then another Matt, and under that a board about three quarters long, finely carved and paynted;

[1] Journal of Pilgrims.

also between the mats, we found Bowles, Trays, Dishes, and such like trinkets. At length we came to a faire new Matt, and under that two bundles—one bigger, the other lesse. We opend the greater and found in it a great quantity of fine and perfect Red Powder, and in it the Bones and Scull of a man. We opened the less bundle likewise, and found of the same powder in it, and the bones and head of a little child." "There was also by it a little bow."[1] These were the burial-places of savage and untutored men ; yet they told to the Pilgrims the old story of human suffering and human love ! Father and child lay here in the same grave.

"After this we digged in sundry like places, but found no more corne, nor any thing else but graves."[2]

THEY FIND CORN.

"Once, when examining one of the grave mounds, they found a little old basket, full of faire Indian Corne, and digging further, found a fine great basket full of very faire corne of this yeare, with some thirty-six goodly eares of corne, which was a very goodlie sight ; the basket was round, and narrow at the top ; it held about three or four bushels, which was as much as two of us could lift from the ground, and was very handsomely and cunningly made."

They delivered in the Corn to the common stock, to be saved for seed, "proposing, so soon as we could meet with any of the inhabitants of that place to make them large satisfaction."

They found at various times some ten bushels. This Corn they afterward mentioned to "Massasoit,"[3] desiring to pay it back to the owners, or to give them for it whatever they might rather need. On their expedition they led soldiers' lives, and partook of soldiers' fare. "This night" (they say) "We got three fat geese and six ducks to our supper, which we eat with soldier stomachs." But their long voyage had diminished their strength, and ex-

[1] Journal of Pilgrims. [2] Journal of Pilgrims, Nov. 30.

[3] Journal of Pilgrims. Young's Chron. of Pilgrims, p. 204.

posure now sowed the seeds of disease. While their boat was being repaired, they had been obliged to wade some distance in the cold water (three quarters of a mile to the shore), and so many of them "took the original of their death here."[1]

Winter had now set in with its cheerless skies and its bitter winds. December had come before their shallop could be repaired, "so as a party of explorers could examine the coast." Then Carver, Bradford, Winslow, Standish, and some ten more, started to find a place for settlement (6th Dec). The necessities of the case were urgent; they were much exposed where they were, both on board ship, and in their various efforts to land. The Captain, too, was impatient, and threatened to leave them. He no doubt pitied these simple souls, but could not be hindered by their plans. The Speedwell, which they had purchased, and intended to keep, had failed them, and they could not stay the Mayflower. On this, their most important and final search for a place of settlement, they were much exposed and in danger. The sea broke over them, covering them with spray. Edward Tilley "was like to have sounded (swooned) with cold." "The water froze on our clothes, and made them many times like coats of iron." For fifteen leagues the party sought in vain for a convenient harbor and a proper site. It seemed as though God was against them; they could not have landed at so unfavorable a point on the whole coast. They continue: "We espied some ten or twelve Indians, very busy about a black thing; what it was we could not tell, till afterward they saw us and ran to and fro, as if they had been carrying away something." This was the body of a Grampus, and the place was named "Grampus' Bay." On the 8th of December, all of a sudden they heard a great cry, and one of the Company came running in, shouting "Indians! Indians!" This was followed by a flight of arrows. But Captain Standish was ready,

[1] Journal of Pilgrims, Nov. 28. Mourts's Relation.

and quickly discharged his piece ; and then another and another, so that the Indians retreated, and, except for the fright, no harm was done. "The cry of our enemies was frightful" (so the Journal says). Their note was after this manner : "Woath wach haha hach woach," sounds which one may now utter with safety, if he can. "We took up eighteen of their arrows, which we had sent to England by Master Jones, some whereof were headed with brass, others with hart's horn, and others with eagle's claws."

The leader of the Indians was a "lusty man," who stood fire well, till at last, one taking good aim at him, "he gave an extraordinary cry, and away they all went." This spot was afterward known as "First Encounter." This was not the end. A storm of snow, rain, and wind came on, and they were puzzled to know which way to go ; but one of their sailors (who had been on the coast before) Master Robert Coffin,[1] seemed to know of a convenient harbor, to which they crowded sail, when the mast was shivered by the wind, and they were in danger of perishing. God seemed to be against them, but they would not give up ; their end was not yet to be. They gained the land, and found the place to be a small island (now Clarke's Island) secure from Indians ; and this being the last day of the week, they here dry their stuff, fix their pieces, rest themselves, return thanks for their many deliverances ; and next day keep their first Christian Sabbath ashore. This was the ninth of December, 1620.

[1] Mourts's Relation.

CHAPTER VI.

THE LANDING.

FOREFATHERS' DAY—FOREFATHERS' ROCK—THE HARBOR—THE LAND—THE MAYFLOWER SAILS TO PLYMOUTH HARBOR—THE COMPACT—THE NEW STATE BEGUN.

FOREFATHERS' DAY, 11th of December, 1620 (O. S.), 22d December (N. S.) "On Monday," says the Old Chronicler, "we sounded the harbor and found it a very good harbor for our shipping; we marched also into the land, and found divers corn-fields and little running brooks—a place very good for situation: so we returned to our ship againe with good news to the rest of our people, which did much comfort their hearts." This Monday is what we now know as Forefathers' day. It is hallowed time, and the ground they trod is holy ground. Forefathers' Rock, on which the Pilgrims landed, is now inclosed with a wharf. The upper part of it was drawn to the public square of Plymouth, and on the 4th of July 1834, was removed to the new Pilgrim Hall, where it now rests.

"This harbor," they said, "is a bay greater than Cape Cod, compassed with goodly land, and in the bay two fine islands (now Clark's Island, and probably Saquish peninsula), uninhabited, wherein are nothing but woods, oaks, pines, walnuts, beech, sassafras, vines, and other trees, which we know not. This bay is a most hopeful place, innumerable store of fowl and excellent food; and can not but be of fish in their seasons; skate, cod, turbot, and herring, we have tasted of; abundance of muscles, the greatest and best we ever saw; crabs and lobsters in their time, infinite. It is in fashion like a sickle or fish-hook.[1]

[1] Journal of Pilgrims. Young's Chronicles of Pilgrims.

The land for the crust of the earth is a spit's depth, excellent black mold, and fat in some places; and vines everywhere, cherry-trees, plum-trees, and many others which we know not. Many kinds of herbs we found here in the winter, as strawberry-leaves innumerable, sorrel, yarrow, carval, brook-lime, liverwort, water-cresses, great store of leeks and onions (callium canadense ?), and an excellent strong kind of flax or hemp. Here is sand, gravel, and excellent clay, no better in the world, excellent for pots, and will wash like soap, and great store of stone, though somewhat soft, and the best water that ever we drank, and the brooks now begin to be full of fish."

They had determined to look for the good, rather than the evil of their new portion; and they found it, and life was thus made easier. So December 20th, after due consideration, the high land was chosen, much of which was corn ground cleared; where, too, was a "very sweet brook" (now called Town-brook), "delicate springs," a fair harbor, a good hill for look-out and fort, and this was to be their rendezvous, the resting-place for the wanderers. Before they landed they signed their Compact, which will be given hereafter (chapter xv.) They landed at Plymouth on the 11th of December[1] (O. S.), (22d, N. S.), they arrived with their ship in the harbor of Plymouth on the 16th (27th, N. S.), and on the 25th (5th of January, N. S.), they began to build the first house.[2]

The student of history may well afford to remember the day, and mark the spot, where the Pilgrims landed. On the wild shore of a continent they planted the small seed of a new idea and a new empire: the Idea of individual liberty, and an Empire, in which, neither force nor fraud rule, as in the old world, but where the individual is supreme, and every man sovereign. The extent and duration of that kingdom, no man can yet measure. Nor can any altogether foresee its dangers.

[1] Add eleven days to the old style to get the new.

[2] Morton's Memorial, page 49.

CHAPTER VII.

WINTER SETTLEMENT OF PLYMOUTH.[1]

JOHN CARVER, GOVERNOR—THEY BUILD—THEY DIVIDE THEIR COMPANY—JANUARY 21ST, PUBLIC WORSHIP—STANDISH CHOSEN CAPTAIN—THEY MOUNT THEIR GUNS—PEREGRINE WHITE, FIRST-BORN OF NEW ENGLAND—LYONS—WOLVES—THUNDER—BILLINGTON NOT SIFTED—THEY MAKE GARDENS—SPRING.

JOHN CARVER was chosen governor, by election, for one year, a man of character, conduct, and property ; this was all the machinery of law they then needed.

On Monday (December 25th), a party went ashore to fell timber, to saw, to rive, to carry, and prepare for the important work of building ; and that day every man worked with a will, hopefully and heartily. A new home, a pleasant refuge, a future security was the aim of every one, and while they cheered one another, the axes rung out in harmony with their hopes ; their strokes were heavy as their hearts were light. The crowned oaks of the forest did homage and yielded their riches to found the infant State. On Thursday (the 28th), many went to work on the hill (Fort-hill, now Burial-hill), to prepare fortifications ; others measured and allotted the lands for building, for every person "half a pole in breadth by three in length" ($8\frac{1}{4}$ feet by $49\frac{1}{2}$ feet ?),in lots for families.

THEY DIVIDE THE COMPANY.

For convenience and economy, the whole company was divided into nineteen families ; fewer houses and less outlay would thus be required ; and it was agreed that every man should build his own house, so that more haste might be made, than when they worked in common. These houses were built in two lines, along what is now called Leyden-street. But

[1] Indian name of Plymouth was Umpame (Church).

their work was necessarily slow; the weather was not severely cold, but with much rain and storm; the journals reiterate "rain," "rain;" weather disastrous to health, for "a green Christmas makes a fat church-yard." There was little of public interest during these first few months; for the necessities of the position engrossed time and thought. But among a few recorded incidents, we note that on the 21st of January, they kept their public worship, for the first time on shore, and on the 17th of February, Standish was chosen their captain, and all were arranged in military orders. This may be called their first legislative act; the first communal life of men who believed in and were forced to act out the principle of self-government; every man could vote, and Francis Billington's voice counted the same as Governor Carver's. A minion, a saker, and two other guns were mounted on Fort-hill, where the structure for the fort had made progress. Births and deaths varied the monotony of existence there as elsewhere. Peregrine White, the first-born in New England, had appeared in November, and six persons had died in December, among whom was Dorothy, Bradford's wife, who was drowned. This was the beginning of a mortality, which carried dismay and destruction into the weakened ranks. We gather here and there a few facts and incidents, which will best illustrate their social and moral condition during their first winter.

LYONS.

Upon one occasion (January 12) two of their men, "having a great mastiff bitch," went some way after a deer, and forgetting themselves in their excitement, became lost, and wandered about all night, much to their discomfort and to the anxiety of their friends. They heard, in the night, as they thought, "two Lyons roaring exceedingly for a long time together, and a third that they thought was very nere them. Not knowing what to do, they resolved to climbe up in to a tree, as their safest refuge, though that would prove an intolerable cold lodging; so they stood at the tree's roote, that when the Lyons came they might take their opportunity of climbing up. The bitch they were faine to hold by the neck, for shee would have been gone to the Lyon; but it pleased God so to dispose, that the wilde beasts came not; so they walked up and down under the tree all night; it was an extreme cold night"[1]— pleasanter to tell of than to experience. It is curious to note how their long ears magnified the howling of the Foxes or Wolves into Lions, thus adding to their miseries.

Their Journal of January 19 says, "John Goodman was much frightened this day: he went abroad for a little walk, having lame feet, with his little spaniel. Suddenly two Great wolves ran after the dog; the dog ran to him and betwixt his legs for succor. He having nothing with him, threw a stick at one of them and hit him, and they presently ran both away, but came again. He got a plain board in his hand; and they sat both on their tails, grinning at him a good while; and went their way and left him."

Again, Saturday, the 3d March, "at one o'clock it thundered." "The birds sang most pleasantly before this. The thunder was strong, and in great claps, followed by rain very sadly till midnight."

"God not only sifted three Kingdoms to get the seed of this enterprise, but sifted that seed over again. Every person whom he would not have to go at that time, to plant the first Colony of New England, he sent back even from mid-ocean in the Speedwell;"[2] notwithstanding all this care, the seed was not cleansed; John Billington was among it, having "slipped in" in England; who now committed an offense, giving way to passion, and resorting to foul and wicked language, in a quarrel. He was the first offender against good order in the Colony, and afterward, in 1630, came to the distinction of being the first hanged, leaving descendants.

[1] Young's Chs. of Pilgrims. Pilgrims' Journal.

[2] Cheever's Journal of Pilgrims.

The Journal says, "The Governor with five more, go to the great ponds, and we begin to sow our Garden seeds." Again: "Monday and Tuesday, March 19th, 20th, proved fair days. We digged our grounds, and sowed our garden seeds." This indicates a warm and early spring. No fearful danger had threatened them from the Indians; they had suffered no alarm; indeed the place seemed strangely desolate. The Town-meeting, if such it can be called, held in February, to arrange the people into military order, had been interrupted by the appearance of two men at a distance; yet, as they knew savages were there, they knew that sooner or later they must meet them.

The spring came. On the 16th March, "a fayre warme day," birds began to appear, the hearts of the settlers warmed, and their blood flowed as the air once more began to speak of life, not death, and the snows began to run in murmuring rills toward the sea. They had had a grievous time through the winter; colds had been followed with consumption and death; but they had never dreamed of discouragement, and now this "fayre warme day" was a harbinger of Hope. Their winter was not all lost time; it was not an idle time. They had examined the country, had hunted for Game, and had tracked the deer through the snows. They had tried their new circumstances and were masters of them. Their houses had been built, and family arrangements completed. They had wintered with one another. On "Great Hill," their fortifications were begun, and now bristled with grim artillery—deep-voiced dogs of war—which, they trusted in God, might not be let loose upon the Indians, of whom they yet stood in dread.

CHAPTER VIII.

WELCOME.

SPRING—THE SHOUT—SAMOSET—THEY WATCH HIM—HIS DRESS—OTHER INDIANS WITH THEM—MASSASOIT—HE DRINKS RUM—THE ALLIANCE.

ON the 16th of March, one of those "fayre warm days," a party of grave and determined men gathered on the skirts of the settlement; Carver, Bradford, Winslow, Hopkins, and others among them. They felt the cheering influences of the day; dreary winter was past, and pregnant summer was before them; the first note of the frog, and the sound of the freed rivulet, were heard but not heeded, for they talked of their plans, and speculated as to the future. A strange sound in that solitary place came to their ears—who was it that shouted "WELCOME! WELCOME!"

A single dusky figure at the edge of the forest waved his hand, and came boldly toward them. They were startled, astonished, and then reassured, for he seemed friendly, and that hearty word "Welcome!" was full of kindliness. He came forward and greeted them, and seemed a friend. They responded with hospitality, and gave him "strong-water, bisket, butter, cheese, with pudding and a piece of mallard." 'Tis said, "The way to the heart is through the stomach"—his they reached. He told them, that he had learned some English from the fishermen—that the name of the coast was Patuxet—that an Englishman, one Hunt (who had been left in charge of a vessel by Captain Smith in 1614), on pretense of trading, had enticed twenty-seven Indians on board his vessel, had seized them, carried them off, and sold them for slaves, "like a wretched man (for £20 a man), that cares not what mischief he doth for his profit," that the Indians were exasperated, and would repay this mercantile act with savage cruelty; that the whites might have looked for extermination, but that a pestilence had some years before (1617 ?) swept the land of its people and they were weak;[1] this and more he told them. The Pilgrims, in their devout way, saw the finger of God in this desolation; he was working for them, no doubt. It was well that they saw God in their encouragements more than in their disasters.

SAMOSET.

The Indian boldly came, "all alone, and along the houses straight to the rendezvous; and refused to go away that night; and was ready to go aboard the ship, but the tide being out, and the wind unfavorable, it could not be done; so he was lodged in Stephen Hopkins' house, and we watched him," the chronicler says, "fearing evil, which did not come." He told them, too, how the Indians had killed three of Gorges' men, and of the huggery (fight) had between the Whites and the Indians. He was kind and friendly, so they bade him farewell in the morning, and gave him "a knife, a bracelet, and a ring."

This Indian was Samoset, who first had intelligent intercourse with the pilgrims; he was the solitary representative on that solitary shore, of the wild Red-man once master and owner of the land. Our hearts are drawn to him for his frank, fearless, and manly WELL-COME! a welcome which the white man has not well requited.

Uninteresting as the Indians are, we may well spend a few moments on him. "He was a man free in speech, a tall straight man, the haire of his head blacke, long behind only short before, none on his face at all; he was stark naked (this was the 16th of March), only a leather about his waist, with a fringe about a span long or a little more; he had a bow of 2 arrows, the one headed, the

[1] Hubbard's History. Thacher's Plymouth, p. 38.

other unheaded." Such was the appearance of an Indian Sagamore in those days.[1]

A few days after this he returned, and with him five other tall proper men and Squanto, who had been one of those Indian slaves; he had dwelt in Cornhill (London) with one John Slanie, a merchant, and now was to be, as the event proved, a valuable friend, interpreter, and ally to the whites. This intercourse was soon followed by a meeting between the Pilgrims and the great King Sachem of those parts.

MASSASOIT.

On the 22d of March the first interview took place between the Pilgrims and the Indians, with their great chief Massasoit, Squanto acting as interpreter. This was conducted becomingly on all sides, and according to the manner of the time. After Governor Carver had drunk some "strong water" (Rum) to the Sachem, Massasoit "drunk a great draught that made him sweat all the while after." The result of the Conference was an alliance, offensive and defensive, between the Governor and the Chief, applauded by the followers of both, and Massasoit was received as an ally of the dread King James. He is thus described by the Journalist:

"In his person he is a very lusty man, in his best years, an able body, grave of countenance, and spare of speech; in his attire, little or nothing differing from the rest of his followers, only in a great chain of white beads about his neck; and at it, behind his neck, hangs a little bag of tobacco, which he drank, and gave us to drink (smoke). His face was painted with a sad red (like Murrey) and oiled both head and face that he looked greasily." All his followers were likewise painted red, yellow, black, white, some crossed, "and other antic works," "some naked, and some with skins," "all strong, tall men in appearance."

Massasoit and his men seemed hungry, and were grateful for meat and kindness. The King was possessed with

[1] Pilgrims' Journal: Cheever, p. 58.

fear of the Guns, and motioned them away ; while he sat by the Governor he trembled, whether with fear or with the great draught of " strong water" they had given him we can not now know. The Pilgrims at first were fearful of him ; they could not be sure against treachery ; but they soon discovered that Massasoit had an enemy, " the Narrowhigansets" (a rival tribe) which he feared, and would fain have the strong white men on his side. It was his interest, therefore, to make friends, and time proved that it was his nature too.

His haunts were along the northern shores of Narragansetts' Bay, between Taunton and Providence, one of his principal seats being at Mount Hope. This interview was satisfactory ; they had looked one another in the face, the Strangers and the Savages, and had not perished.

CHAPTER IX.

DEATH.

MARCH, 1621—THE WOMEN SUFFER—THEY DIE—HOW THEY WERE BURIED—THE MAYFLOWER SAILS AWAY—NONE RETURN—GIPSEY LIFE—DEATH AND FREEDOM.

MARCH had come, and a new year was now bursting upon them ; but the Pilgrims, where were they ? Death had reaped the ripe harvest, and of the one hundred and two, scarce fifty now remained. Six had died in December, eight in January, seventeen in February, thirteen in March. Yet they had borne their sad afflictions with as much patience as any could, and they had no thought of retracing their steps. They had been exposed to a long and tempestuous voyage ; sea diet had weakened them ; the new untried winter had borne heavily upon them, and they had no warm houses, so that, "the searching sharpness of that purer climate had crept into the crannies of their crazed bodies, causing death." [1]

The beginnings of every new enterprise are hard ; inertia has to be overcome before motion begins, for a change of place, at once throws all into confusion, and time is needed for the law of gravitation to settle again the relations of matter ; beside matter, Mind must re-arrange itself.

THE WOMEN SUFFER.

Of the Pilgrims, the children probably suffered least, and the women most. Few women are idealists, and the facts of their lives, their homes, their friends, their churches, and all their accustomed ways, become a part of themselves ; these are supports, and, when taken away, they suffer as men

[1] Bradford's Journal. Thacher's Plymouth, p. 37.

do not. We find that the wives of Bradford, Winslow, Allerton, and Standish, all died in the first winter, and their short histories, their warm hopes, and their poignant sufferings, were ended. Notwithstanding the hardships to which these women knew they were to be subject, there is no record of a word of repining or doubt; strong affection carried them bravely across the wide ocean, and into sickness, suffering, and death.

Holmes, in his annals, tells that the dead were buried in the bank, at a little distance from the Plymouth rock, and lest the Indians should learn the weakened condition of the settlers, by counting the graves, they were leveled and sown with grass. The tale is one of sorrow, but one also of encouragement, for the living nevertheless trusted in God and themselves.

With the return of spring, came the sailing of the Mayflower. They had struggled through the winter, and the ship had always been in sight, a place of refuge and relief in any desperate emergency. While she lay in the bay, the Pilgrims had a hold upon friends, civilization, and Christianity; but let the ship once depart, and on the one hand there would be, the broad, deep, tempestuous sea, on the other, wide, unknown forests—peopled by savages and wild beasts. Port Royal was the nearest point where they could find white men, and that was away some five hundred miles. The future was before them with all its uncertainties—which they must march forward to meet; yet not one of the number returned in the ship! The sailing of the "Mayflower" surpasses in dignity, though not in desperation, the burning of his ships by Cortez. This small band of men, women, and children were grouped on the shore, watching her as she slowly set her sails, and crept out of the bay and from their sight; when the sun set in the western forest, she disappeared in the distant blue. A few Indians might have been hovering on the neighboring heights, watching the departure of the great sea-bird, but the last eyes that bade farewell to the "Mayflower" were those of woman.

GIPSEY LIFE.

But the sky was not inky, nor was their future desperate ; the sun still shone gloriously, the moon still bathed the earth with light, and the stars kept their ceaseless vigils. Spring here, as of old, followed winter, the murmuring of streams was heard, and the song of the turtle ; birds builded their nests, the tender grass sprang up under their feet, and the trees budded and burst forth into wondrous beauty. God was over all—their God—their friend—their protector here as in the Old World ; why should he not be, why not more their friend than ever before ? Life had not been altogether lovely to them in the past ; it had not been pleasant in England to be put into dungeons, or to have one's ears dug out, or to be plundered by low-bred policemen, or to be hunted like wild beasts into mountains and holes of the earth. Here there was freedom, room. He only can value this who has lost it ; yet no man lives, however low in the scale of civilization, who does not long for it, and will not suffer to get it ; will suffer danger, pain, and starvation rather than not be FREE. "Here," said one, "all are freeholders—rent-day does not trouble us."[1] Here, if anywhere, might not every one sit under his own vine ! Earth and sea had fruits, and they were free ; no monopolist, with subtle alchymy, gathered the earnings of men—no Church collected the unwilling tithes—no tax-gatherer waited on them with hungry coffers—no king, no pope, no soldier, challenged their gratitude for having taken their money to govern them ! They could govern themselves ! Social, religious, and political anomalies and technicalities had not yet become grievous burdens, bearing down soul and body to the earth. "Here," said Cushman, "we have great peace, plentie of the Gospel and many sweet delights and varietie of comforts."[2]

[1] Hilton, in Purchas's Pilgrims.

[2] "A Brief Review," London, 1774. Cushman's Reasons.

Here was free range ; the hunters' instincts could bourgeon and grow ; the deer that browsed, the fish that swam, and the fowl that flew, were free to all ; might be captives to each man's bow and spear. "Herring, cod, and ling," "Salt upon salt," "Beavers, otters, furs of price," "Mynes of gold and silver," "Woods of all sorts," "Eagles, gripes, whales, grampus, moos, deere," "Bears and beavers," "all in *season* mind you—for you can not gather cherries at Christmas in Kent." Who then would live at home. only to eat and drink and sleep and so die ?[1] or who would suffer persecution, scorn, and contumely, when the free wilderness was before him where to choose. They chose death here rather than sloth, degradation, or slavery elsewhere.

[1] Smith's Description of New England.

CHAPTER X.

NEW COMERS.

THE LAND FLOWING WITH MILK AND HONEY—VAIN EXPECTATIONS—SUFFERING—THE FORTUNE—ROBERT CUSHMAN—HIS REASONS—CANONICUS THREATENS—FIRST-FRUITS LOST—WEST COMES AS ADMIRAL—ROBERT GORGES AS GENERAL—MORELL AS CHAPLAIN—FAMINE AND INDIANS—SQUANTO STILL LIVES—MASSACRE IN VIRGINIA—THE LAST OF THE "FATHERS" COME—THEIR SHIPS ARE CAPTURED.

Too flattering accounts of the riches, and wonders, and delights, of the New World had been sent home—partly from a desire to tempt over others, but more from a wish to reassure friends at home, who had dissuaded them from this quixotic expedition. The new comers, therefore, trusted much to the resources of the land flowing with milk and honey," to the land filled with Vines and Grains, to the sea and shores abounding with fish.[1] They did not lay to heart the story of the foolish Virgins, and they too went out, having no oil in their lamps, no meal in their chests. "Indeed three things are the overthrow and bane of Plantations," said Winslow:

"1. The vain expectation of present profit.

"2. Ambition in the Governors, etc.

"3. The lawlessness of those that send over supplies of men unto them, not caring how they bee qualified."

These flattering stories brought improvident men, and there was blame on both sides. Suffering and starvation ensued. No "fowle" came in the summer, and the nets for fishing were insufficient. Indians too began to be insulting and threatening; even Massasoit was cool; the fort was therefore hastened.

A small bark, of some fifty tons, arrived at Plymouth

[1] Winslow's Good News. London, 1624.

on the 9th of November, 1621, bringing thirty-five new settlers, among whom were some who had been forced to put back with the Speedwell, on her final return to Southampton. By this bark, news was sent of a charter, granted to the Merchant Adventurers of London by the Plymouth Company, in the name of John Pierce, which was never used. Robert Cushman was one of the passengers in the Fortune ; he was an old and fast friend to the Pilgrims. Constrained to return with the unfortunate Speedwell, he took the first occasion for visiting that company of poor men, who looked upon him as a friend. But death had been busy ; Carver was gone, and more than half of those whom he had bade God-speed in the Mayflower, were under the earth, the grass growing on their leveled graves. Enough, however, yet lived, to welcome him to the land of the oppressed and the outcast.

A few extracts from Cushman's "Reasons for removing from England to America," may give some insight into the time when he lived. Cushman guards against the too common error of supposing, as the Virginia settlers had *not* done, that this was a land of Gold.[1]

He continues : "neither is there any land or possession now, like unto the possession which the Jews had in Canaan, being legally holy, and appropriated unto a holy people, the seed of Abraham, in which they dwelt securely and had their days prolonged—it being, by an immediate voice, said, that the Lord gave it to them as a land of rest after their weary travels, and a type of eternal rest in Heaven. But now there is no land of that sanctity, no land so appropriated, none typical, much less any that can be said to be given of God to any nation, as was Canaan, which they and their seed must dwell in, till God sendeth upon them sword or captivity. But now we are all, in all places, strangers and Pilgrims, travelers and Soujourners,

[1] Captain Smith describes the Virginia settlers, as made up of forty-eight needy "gentlemen," to four carpenters, who were come to do nothing else "but dig gold, make gold, refine gold, and load gold."

most properly; having no dwelling but in this earthly tabernacle, our dwelling is but a wandering, and our abiding but as a fleeting," etc., etc., more of which we are not called upon to read, it being *now* clear enough that America is a good and proper place to immigrate to, with rich land, if not holy. He well says, however, "The greatest let [hinderance] which is yet behind, is the sweet fellowship of friends!" but this was being removed, for friends were now on either hand.

The summer of this year had been unpropitious, and their crops were short. The Fortune had brought no store of provisions, and winter was coming upon them again, and thirty-five new settlers had come, with mouths to be filled, and untried courage to be strengthened. Added to this, an Indian messenger had appeared [1622] among them, and left a bundle of arrows, tied in a rattlesnake's skin. His going was as swift as his coming. Governor Bradford soon learned the language of this symbol—it was WAR! but he also knew that it was wise to resist beginnings, as so few do know; so he sent back the rattlesnake's skin, stuffed with powder and bullets, to Canonicus, chief of the Narragansetts—chief of five thousand warriors. This sufficed; courage, backed by these mysterious symbols, warned the powerful sachem to stop. But Bradford could not know this, and it stood the Colonists in hand to prepare for the worst. Their cannon, then, must be inclosed and protected; a stockade must be built around the town; their men be divided into parties and drilled; no precaution must be neglected. To be free, they must be strong and alert: such they were, and such they determined to be; and their descendants have not altogether forgotten their example.

THE "FIRST FRUITS" LOST.

Let us not forget the little Fortune. She had sailed for England, freighted with the "first fruits" to the Merchant Adventurers, consisting of some five hundred pounds' worth of Furs, Beaver skins, Clapboards, and Sassafras, and woods of various sorts. She had almost reached the English coast, when she was clutched by a French Privateer, taken to a French port, and after some detention, let to go to England, with an empty hold. So went the First-Fruits.

In this year (1622), some thirty-five sails went to the shores of New England for fish. The Plymouth Company in England, plead their monopoly against these, which was opposed by the Commons, but confirmed by the King. They sent out Francis West (June, 1623), as Admiral of New England, to protect their privileges.

He was followed by Sir Robert Gorges as Lieutenant-General of the country. Neither of them accomplished any thing; nor did Morrell, who came to establish Episcopacy, but went quietly away. Nature was too strong for them, the fish swam where they listed and men caught them where they could; no fleets or forts were there to hinder them, so conscience and honor laughed at the extravagant claims of the monopolists.

FAMINE AND INDIANS.

They were now in the spring of 1622, in the month of May, "at which time our store of victuals was wholly spent, having lived long before with a bare and short allowance."[1] Their crops were in the ground; the season for wild-fowl, for ducks and teal, was passed, and what now was before them? Tradition reports that the last pint of their corn being distributed, yielded five kernels to each person. Matters were bad enough surely, but they were not at their worst. Squanto, their interpreter and friend, had not been killed; he was alive, too much alive to his own importance, pluming himself upon his intimacy with the white folks. It seems he had made use of this to increase his consequence among the natives, and after the manner of an ignorant and child-like man, had talked big, and plotted, and counterplotted, and promised, and bragged, so that there was danger of destruction to the Colony; among other things he told Hobbamock, that the whites had the plague

[1] Winslow's Relation.

(which had destroyed so many of them), buried, and could at any moment let it loose upon them. Hobbamock asked of the Pilgrims if this was so? and discovering Squanto's cheat, he and Massasoit, too, were determined to kill him. It was only after much remonstrance and persuasion, that the messengers of the Sachem could be persuaded to return without carrying him back to die. It is likely that Squanto was cured of his bragging, and shorn of his borrowed glory thenceforward.

About this time a boat crossed the bay, and disappeared behind a headland. What did this portend? War with the French settlements might be possible; they soon learned that it contained an arrival of seven new colonists from a fishing-vessel, the Sparrow; a letter, too, from Captain Huddlestone (Hudston in Morton), told of the destruction of some four hundred colonists in Virginia (22d of March, 1622), by the exasperated Indians. Governor Bradford returned a friendly answer to Captain H.'s letter; and as there was no alternative, he dispatched Winslow to the fishing-ships, to purchase provisions for the sustenance of the colonists, until their crops could mature. Winslow found some thirty ships at the fishing stations, and was received with much kindness. He could purchase but few stores, yet these free-hearted and open-handed fishermen, freely gave what they could spare, and Winslow returned with a stock that furnished a scant supply till the harvest. Thus ended the second year of the Plymouth colony.

THE LAST OF THE FATHERS.

In the month of July, 1625, the ship Anne, followed soon after by the Little James, brought the rest of their long-expected friends, some sixty in number; wives and children of the early colonists were among them, and many dear old friends. These are counted among the "Forefathers," and rank with the Pilgrims of the Mayflower. But one, toward whom all hearts yearned, was not among them: John Robinson, their pastor, had died in March of this year. Opposition of one kind and another had prevented his coming to them, and now he was dead. He was but thirty-two years of age when the exiled church was re-formed at Amsterdam. He had long been the guide of the exiles, and was deservedly their leader and friend.

JOHN JENNY came in the James, "who was a godly, though otherwise, a plain man ; yet singular for publickness of spirit, setting himself to seek and promote the common good of the plantation of New Plimouth." To him be praise, and to his kind forever.

In this year, the most important event, was the sending of two ships laden with good dry fish and furs, "more than eight hundred pounds,"to the company in England. The ships sailed away lovingly, and had fair weather; yet when almost in sight of Plymouth, in England, one of them was seized by a Turk, the master and men sold for slaves, and the fine beaver-skins for fourpence apiece. This was discouraging, and the Pilgrims began to despair, and think that God was indeed wroth ; but such a conclusion was hardly to be accepted ; it was better to say that his judgments were inscrutable ; and so they said it.

In the larger of these ships (the Anne ?) went Miles Standish to negotiate affairs with the company ; the plague raged in London, and he could only put matters in a hopeful way. Among all the evil things, one good happened in this year, for James I., King of England, died, whose departure no man ought to have regretted. But Robert Cushman and John Robinson also died, whom men justly loved and reverenced.

In the year 1627, a ship bound for Virginia, was cast ashore to the north of Cape Cod, in Mannamoiet Bay; the Indians soon put the passengers into communication with the Pilgrims, who gave them assistance, extending their hospitality to some for more than a year, until they finally scattered; some to Virginia, some to other parts.

CHAPTER XI.

LANDS, CATTLE, ETC.

WORKING IN COMMON GIVEN UP—"DROWTH"—FAST—RAIN—THEY DIVIDE THE LANDS—THE UNDERTAKERS—CATTLE—HORSES—JOHN ALDEN'S BULL—WEALTH—THE DUTCH AT MANHADOES—WAMPUM—CONNECTICUT RIVER.

In the spring of 1623, the Pilgrims agreed that every man should cultivate for himself, and pay into the common stock only such portion of corn as was necessary to sustain the officers and fishermen.[1] Bradford distinctly says, that the plan of working in common and sharing alike, was not successful, and none were satisfied with it. So they began to set their corn, each man for himself, about the middle of April. In the first season, they planted twenty acres with corn, and dressed it with fish; in the second season, about sixty acres. Distress pursued them, for a "great drowth," which "it pleased God to send," almost destroyed their crops. "Now were our hopes overthrown and we discouraged, our joy being turned into mourning," said Winslow.[2] Parties went out summer and winter, for fish, and the best hunters scoured the woods for deer and game. Still they did not despair—they examined themselves, and fasted privately and publicly, hoping that God would be moved to mercy. The very next day after the fast, the heavens opened, and "distilled soft, sweet and moderate showers for fourteen days." A crowning and an especial mercy and answer which now "it pleased God" to grant.

In the year 1627 they made a division of lands, five acres by the water side, and four acres in breadth; although a single acre to a man had been allowed in 1624.

[1] Hubbard's History, p. 79.

[2] Good News, p. 44.

In the allotment of lands, there was a grant to the Indian, Hobbamock, who had taken the place, as interpreter of the lamented Squanto. He seems to have held by the Pilgrims and their God, in spite of enticements and obstacles, and to have died, "leaving some good hopes in their hearts that his soul went to rest."

There was much disappointment felt and expressed, from time to time, by the Adventurers in England, at the failure of the Pilgrims to send home good cargoes, and Mr. Weston charged them with weakness of judgment, rather than weakness of hands, and with spending their time in discoursing, arguing, and consulting, etc. The leading men of the Colony determined to be free of this. Sometime during 1627, Mr. Allerton went upon this business, to England, carrying with him nine bonds for £200 each; these were given individually by Governor Bradford, William Brewster, Miles Standish, Isaac Allerton, Samuel Fuller, Edward Winslow, John Jenny, John Alden, and John Howland,[1] who thus purchased the rights of the "Company of Merchant Adventurers," assumed the responsibilities of the Colony, and were known in that day as "The Undertakers."[2] He returned in 1628, and was engaged at various other times in the public business of the Colony. Sherley was the Agent for the Undertakers in England, and through the mismanagement of Allerton, their accounts became involved, and infinite trouble ensued. The claims of the English partners were finally compromised and paid in 1642. Governor Bradford and his associates had the monopoly of the trade of the Colony for six years; agreeing to pay for it, the above £1800, and the whole debts of the Colony, amounting to £2,400; and to bring them £50 a-year in hoes and shoes, to sell them corn at six shillings a bushel, and to bring over the balance of the

THE UNDERTAKERS.

[1] Bradford mentions but eight, and places Thomas Prince instead of Fuller and Jenny. To these parties were added, James Sherley, John Beauchamp, Richard Andrews, Timothy Hatherly, of London.

[2] Prince.

Church at Leyden, all of which they did. In the year 1628, having procured a patent for lands at Kennebeck, they established a trading-house there, near what is now Augusta. It was afterward seized by the French, and the trade was broken up (1635). In 1661, their rights there were sold to John Winslow and three partners for £400.[1]

CATTLE.

Edward Winslow, who had been sent to England upon business with the Company, returned in March, 1624, bringing with him an important accession to the Pilgrims—three heifers and one bull—the first neat cattle that came into New England.[2]

In the year 1627, division was made of the cattle (which had increased) into twelve lots, one lot to each party of thirteen: to Governor Bradford and his party, fell "an heifer of the last year, which was of the great white back cow, that was brought over in the 'Ann,' and two she-goats." In such manner to others. In May, 1627, it was further agreed, "That if any of the cattle should, by accident, miscarry, or be lost, or hurt, that the same should be taken note of by indifferent men, and judged whether the loss came by the negligence or default of those betrusted, and if they were found faulty, that such should be forced to make satisfaction for the companies' as also their partners' damage."

The first notice of horses occurs in 1644, when one belonging to the estate of Stephen Hopkins, was appraised at £6 sterling. It was a country for cattle, rather than horses, and it seems to have been a not uncommon thing, to ride on bulls. When John Alden went to Cape Cod, to marry Priscilla Mullins, he covered his bull with broadcloth, and rode on his back; when he returned he placed his wife there, and led the bull home by the ring in his nose.[3] One historian thinks, that had Isaac gone on a bull instead of a camel, Rebecca might not have said as

[1] Moore's Governors.
[2] Baylie's Mem.
[3] Thacher, p. 111.

she did, "I will go." Yet the bull is the handsomer beast. It is told that Alden at first went to ask the hand of Priscilla for his friend, Miles Standish; the father referred him to the daughter, who listened with attention; but fixing her eyes on Alden's handsome face, she said, "Prythee, John, why do you not speak for yourself?" Such frankness John could not resist in those "good old colony times."

Not long after, the Colony was in danger; wealth threatened its inhabitants, for in the year 1632, in consequence of the demand for cattle and corn, from the incoming colonists of "Massachusetts Bay," the Plymouth settlers began to grow rich, the prices of these things having so much advanced. In 1632 a cow came to be worth £20, which in 1640 fell to £5. More land became necessary for them, so that the town was being deserted, and men went out to look for and settle upon better farms. Duxbury grew into a town of importance, and a new church there drew away many from Plymouth, which was no ways agreeable to the settlers of the old town; and they hit upon the plan of granting lands at Green's Harbor (Marshfield), to such as should keep their houses in Plymouth.

THE DUTCH AT MANHADOES.

In this year, too (October, 1627), Mr. Isaac de Rozier, Secretary to the Dutch settlement at the Hudson River (Manhadoes), visited the Plymouth Colony, and laid the foundations of a trade, which promised to be mutually advantageous.[1] He seems to have been the first to introduce to their notice WAMPUM, or Wampumpeag, the Indian money. This was manufactured from shells of either the whelk (*buccinum*), or the quowhaug (*venus mercatoria*), and the process is thus described by a more recent traveler:[2] "It is made of the clam shell, consisting within of two colors, purple and white. It is first clipped to a proper size, which is that of a small paralelopiped, then drilled, and afterward ground to a

[1] Hubbard's History, p. 99. Bradford's Letters, Historical Collection.
[2] Burnaby's Travels, 1760.

round smooth surface and polished. The purple wampum is much more valuable than the white, a very small part of the shell being of that color." One fathom of their stringed money was rated at 5 shillings. With this money they were enabled to buy guns, powder, etc., much to the danger of the colonists, who made laws against such sales, without, however, being able to stop the cupidity of dealers.

CONNECTICUT RIVER.

The Plymouth people had been told by the Dutch of a river to the westward, which furnished good fish, whose banks were fat with soils, and fertile with pastures ; the Massachusetts men declining to join them in settling it, they fitted out an expedition by sea, led by Holmes, on their own account (1633). The Dutch would have stopped their progress at their fort of Good Hope (Hartford), and stood by their guns threatening to shoot. But the Plymouth men told them that they too must stand by their orders to go on, and so they did, and the Dutch did not shoot. They went a mile or so above the Dutch settlement, and planted their house at Windsor, buying the lands of the Indians.

CHAPTER XII.

WESTON'S COLONY.

THE CHARITY AND SWAN—BAD MEN COME—THEY STEAL CORN—SETTLE AT WICHAGUSCUSSET—THEY STEAL THE INDIANS' CORN—VOYAGE ROUND CAPE COD—SQUANTO DIES.

IT was toward the end of the month of June 1622 that the Pilgrims, watching from their Citadel on the Hill, saw two vessels bearing down from Cape Cod. Let us try to sympathize with their anxiety. The last arrival of seven colonists had brought a letter from Mr. Weston, one of the English Company, whom they had counted on as a fast friend, saying that their interest was no longer his. These ships proved to be the "Charity" and "Swan," having on board some sixty emigrants, sent out by Mr. Weston at his own expense, who were to found a Colony for his benefit. For their masters' sake they were kindly received by the Plymouth settlers; the sick were provided for, and cured by the Colony surgeon without cost, and their scanty stock of provisions was further subdivided. But there were among the new comers men that even Mr. Weston owned to be rude and profane fellows. Robert Cushman wrote from England, warning against these, solicitous that Squanto should explain to the Indians that they were not of the Plymouth Company, and were to be guarded against. They sent a coasting party upon a voyage of discovery, leaving of course a large part of the New Comers at Plymouth; but they were reckless, lazy, and wasteful; they stole the new green Corn, "and would not help us about the labor of it." Yet they were borne with, for the old kindnesses of Mr. Weston.[1]

Their coasting party returned, having decided to settle at Wichaguscusset, now called Weymouth, whither the party then went, leaving only the sick at Plymouth. But a short time had passed, when the Indians became loud in their complaints of these men ; there were those among them who cared nothing for the rule of Right. They stole the Indians' corn, and otherwise abused their confidence, and trifled with their friendship. Autumn came, and they were short of stores, when it seemed necessary for the Plymouth Colony to join with them in a trading Voyage, for the buying of corn and provisions, to save all from famine. The "Charity" had sailed in the end of Autumn for England, leaving the "Swan" for the use of the new Colony. Mr. Richard Green, Governor of the new settlement, suddenly died, and Captain Standish, who was to have succeeded him in command of the trading party, being taken sick, the Governor was obliged to take his place. This was the first voyage round Cape Cod. He succeeded in procuring a good stock of corn and beans, and some furs, so that the winter was got through with. This Voyage was brought to a sudden termination by the death of poor Squanto, who, in spite of his conceit and extravagance, had proved himself their fast friend. He bequeathed his ornaments to several of his English friends, and trusted that he might go to their God. His death was regretted, and he sincerely mourned.

[1] Winslow's Good News, p. 14.

CHAPTER XIII.

INDIAN EMBASSIES.

MASSASOIT RECEIVES THEM—HIS SPEECH—THE ATTACK UPON CORBITANT—MASSASOIT SICK—WINSLOW VISITS AND CURES HIM.

In the month of June or July,[1] 1621, an Embassy was dispatched to Massasoit, near what is now Bristol; Edward Winslow and Stephen Hopkins were selected to go, with Indian Squanto, for an interpreter. They carried with them a red cotton coat for the King himself, beads and jack-knives, for his chiefs; thus fortified with the persuasives of diplomacy, they set forth, and met with favor among the Indians on their way; Massasoit received them with friendship, and the great Sachem invited them to share his bed with his wife, which luxury they seem not to have enjoyed, for Winslow says, "they were worse weary of their lodging than their journey." On their journey, they had been obliged to lodge in the fields with the Indians, and on their return, came nigh famishing with hunger: added to this, the "savages barbarous singing, lice and fleas within doores, and muskeetoes without," made it a disagreeable mission. But Massasoit assured them that he would gladly continue the peace and friendship, "and for his men, they should no more pester us as they had done; also, that he would send to Paomet, and would help us with corne for seed."

Massasoit decked his kingly person in the red coat, and was much elated. He then collected his men about him, and "made a great speech;" the meaning whereof was thus: "Was not he Massasoit, commander of the country

[1] Bradford's Journal. Morton says 2d July.

about them? Was not such a town his, and the people in it? and such other towns (naming at least thirty places), and should they not bring their skins (to sell) to us (the English)?" and more, "so that as it was delightful, it was tedious unto us."

These touches of humor in Winslow are delightful unto us, and not tedious. Massasoit desired greatly that they should prolong their stay, but they wished to keep the Sabbath at home, and "feared they should be light-headed," for want of sleep, and the savages singing, etc.; so they exchanged courtesies and departed. They gained much knowledge, and were cautioned not to trust the Narragansetts—a rival and powerful tribe, who occupied what is now known as Rhode Island.

THEY ATTACK CORBITANT.

Not long after this, hearing that Squanto, their friend and interpreter, had been killed by Corbitant, a chief of these Narragansetts,[1] a party of ten (10) colonists armed themselves, and marched into the heart of the forest, surrounded the hut where they supposed the obnoxious chief to be, disarmed the Indians who came to the rescue, and made themselves felt and feared by this dangerous neighbor, who counted some five thousand fighting men! Happily for all, Squanto was not murdered, and war did not exist. Ten to five thousand! these were brave men; and this daring did much to give to the Indians that respect for the Plymouth men, which they seem to have entertained for no other.

MASSASOIT SICK.

In April, 1622, Massasoit was dangerously sick. He seems never to have failed in his friendship to the Pilgrims, nor they to have abused it. So soon as they heard of his sickness, Winslow, in company with Mr. John Hampden, started at once with such medicines as they had, and were of use in hastening his recovery. This was well, for their absence in his distress, had been made use of to poison his mind against

[1] Morton's Memoir, August 14, 1621.

them. Winslow, Hampden,[1] and Hobbamock, at first heard that Massasoit was dead, which news struck them "blank;" Hobbamock was troubled, and cried, "My loving Sachem, my loving Sachem! Many have I known, but never any like thee." Winslow went at once to Massasoit's house, which they found filled with Indians, "in the midst of their charms for him, making such a hellish noise, as it distempered us that were well, and therefore, unlike to ease him that was sick."[2] Massasoit could not see, but he grasped his hand saying, "Oh, Winsnow! Winsnow!" Winslow took hold of the case vigorously and intelligently; washed out the Sachem's mouth, and administered such help as he could; so that he soon mended, though near death then. At his request, Winslow practiced his skill upon other sick, and earned the gratitude of the chief; who cried, "Now I know that the English are my friends, and love me, and whilst they live, I will never forget this kindness."

[1] Mr. Baylies, in his Memoirs of Plymouth, assumes that this was the great Hampden, Vol. I., p. 410. I find no reason sufficient to sustain that opinion.

[2] Winslow's Good News.

CHAPTER XIV.

WAR.

PLOT DISCOVERED—WESTON'S PEOPLE HANG A MAN—ARE COMPLETELY DEMORALIZED—THE MASSACRE IN VIRGINIA—WAR DECLARED—STANDISH SEIZES THE CHIEFS—KILLS PECKSUOT AND WETAWAMAT—INDIANS PERISH OF FEAR AND WANT—ROBINSON'S REGRET—WESTON RUINED—MORTON'S COMPANY AT MT. WOLLASTON.

ONE of the fruits of this last journey to Massasoit, was the discovery of a plot of the Indians for the destruction of Weston's Colony, at Wessagusset.

On their return to Plymouth, Winslow found that Captain Standish had been decoyed from the colony by one of the Indians. Contrary winds drove him back, when the Indian was dismissed without exciting his suspicion.

Weston's Colony was so reduced, that one of their number in trying to gather clams, got fast in the mud, and had not strength to get himself out; he was found there dead; they were entirely incapable of success, being destitute both of principle and of business talent. It is told, that being forced by the Indians to take measures to restrain stealing they hanged one of the offenders, but took care to choose one whom they could spare, who was not likely to live long, rather than the most guilty. This is not true of them, but is reported as true of Captain Gorges and his colony.[1] (Note in Grahame's U. S., Vol. I., p. 235.)

The men of Wessagusset had utterly wasted their stores, and were driven to hire themselves to the Indians, that they might share their food, and stave off starvation; they ended by robbing them. Confusion, distrust, and exasperation ensued, and the Indians became bitter. Spring

[1] Morton's Memorial. Belknap's American Biography, Vol. II., p. 320.

came (1623), and they wanted seed corn; the Indians refused to deal with them, and there was evidence that they had determined to drive the colony from the country; we are at a loss to conceive why they should not.

Governor Bradford wrote to Saunders, the manager of Weston's Colony, warning him against violent dealing, and threatening future punishment, which checked their desperate projects. Early in March, Governor Bradford had received intelligence, that the exasperated Indians had determined to drive these base men from their shores, and that a wide-spread combination or conspiracy had been formed for the purpose, which was to include all the Palefaces.

This was fearful news, for the Indians in Virginia had felt the stings of contempt and injury; they had seen their lands passing away from them: they felt that self-preservation and revenge called for action; they knew the strength of the whites, so they used craft and secresy, in place of strength and courage; silently they laid their plans. On the 21st of March, 1622, they said to the whites, "Sooner shall the sky fall than peace be violated by us." On the 22d of March, they fell upon the unsuspecting villages, scattered along both sides of the James River. They spared none, not the young, not the old; the good and the bad fell together. In one hour nigh four hundred persons were cut off, and the Virginia settlement received a blow from which it did not recover for years.[1]

Nothing but the treachery of one of the Indians, who revealed the plot, saved the Virginians from total destruction. The whites thenceforth waged a ruthless and exterminating war upon the Indians, which was continued by law till the year 1632. The whites outsavaged the savages, and their cruelty was intense, for it was legal as well as revengeful. The colonists at Plymouth knew of this fearful massacre, and thought that self-preservation required a sudden and stunning blow.

[1] Bancroft, Vol. I., p. 182.

THEY DECLARE WAR.

On the 23d of March, 1623, being assembled in public court, the governor laid the evidences before them, when the unanimous voice declared for WAR.[1] 'Twas a sad business, for they knew Weston's men to be in the wrong. Right or wrong, having decided, to decide was to act. Captain Standish, with four others, watched his time, and having got the Chiefs of the conspiracy into a wigwam, gave the signal, sprang suddenly upon them, secured the door, and buried his knife in the heart of Pecksuot, one of the fiercest of the chiefs. The Indians died hard, after many wounds; and one Standish hanged. Hobbamock stood by and meddled not, but praised Standish greatly when the fight was done.

They returned to Plymouth with the head of Wetawamat, which was set up on a pole in the fort; one of the Indians who had been secured, was set at liberty with a defiant and threatening message; and the whole fight carried such terror among the Indians, that they fled from their homes, and wandering in swamps and forests, many perished through suffering and disease; among these were the Sachems Canacum, Aspinet, and Iyanough.[2] None but a woman durst come as a messenger, to these once peaceful pilgrims. Robinson wrote them, "how happy a thing had it been that you had converted some before you killed any." One can regret that they had not the courage and discretion to have turned their hands and arms against the settlers at Weston's Colony, and either compelled them to live decently, or else have exterminated them; rather than sanction a false issue, and rouse a hatred in the Indians against all white men and Christians.

The Colony at Wessagusset was utterly dissipated, some were hanged, some perished by the Indians, and the rest disappeared. Weston himself came, to find it destroyed and himself ruined; he received kindness only at the hands of the Pilgrims, whom he had been the means of injuring.

[1] Morton, p. 90. Winslow's Good News. [2] Chronicles of Pilgrims, p. 344.

This was the fate of a Colony composed of common men, and founded upon no higher law than the determination at whatever rate to make money.

MORTON'S COMPANY AT MT. WALLASTON.

In 1626, a settlement had been begun by Captain Wollaston (now Braintree), and with him had come one Thomas Morton. He was a man of parts, unscrupulous and crafty. He supplanted his captain and seduced the company. They set up a rollicking, jolly life of it, at Mount Wollaston, having strong drink, junkettings, May-poles (then a flagrant abomination), and other little varieties ; so that they became a scandal to their neighbors and to all good livers. Morton (page 137), speaks hardly of them, as no better than atheists, as "quaffing and drinking," "dancing and frisking," and even worse. But this kind of thing could not last, and Governor Endicott, coming over with authority from the Patentees, paid these roystering fellows a visit (1628), cut down their May-pole, and administered a sharp rebuke. This failed to bring them to a serious carriage, and Miles Standish was deputed to take Morton by force of arms ; which he did : and that time he was sent to England to answer for his misdeeds. He afterward returned, and fell under the displeasure of Governor Winthrop in 1631, who again sent him to England, where he published a sharp and scurrilous book, in which he calls Standish, Captain Shrimp, and Endicott, Captain Littleworth, and so he had his revenge. The assessment among the different settlements for this service, is given in Governor Bradford's letter-book, as amounting to £12, 7s., and this was not all that it cost.[1]

[1] Massachusetts Historical Collection, and Morton's Memorial, p. 136.

CHAPTER XV.

THE GOVERNMENT.

THE PATENT—COLUMBUS—DE GAMA—THE POPE DIVIDES THE WORLD—JOHN CABOT—GOSNOLD—THE LONDON COMPANY AND THE PLYMOUTH COMPANY—NEW ENGLAND, 1614—THE MERCHANT ADVENTURERS—PURITANS VAGABONDS AND FUGITIVES—THEY HAD NO PATENT—THE PATENT OF 1629-30—SIGNING THE COMPACT—DEMOCRACY—THE PROBLEM—RIGHTS AND DUTIES—SELF-GOVERNMENT—JOHN CARVER—WILLIAM BRADFORD—EDWARD WINSLOW—MILES STANDISH—ISAAC ALLERTON AND STEPHEN HOPKINS—FANATICISM—THE GOVERNOR AND COUNCIL—JURY TRIAL—THEIR CODE—NO CRIMES—POPULATION—THEIR LEGISLATURE—RELIGIOUS TEST—PLYMOUTH JOINED TO MASSACHUSETTS.

THE PATENT.

A GRANT from the Crown was believed to be of vital importance by the Pilgrims, that they might make a safe and permanent settlement. Political science had not shown, that the Title to land consists in the USE of it. In those days, the man who first set up a stake on a Continent, by so doing was believed to own it for his King. Such stakes and crosses were planted along the shores of America; they stood alone in their solitude for years, a perch for the Eagle, and a wonder to the roving savage; but in some sort were respected by nations and explorers.

In 1492, Columbus sailed on his wonderful voyage, and Spain claimed to own his discoveries, and assumed to give laws to the maritime world. Vasco de Gama, in the service of Portugal, turned the stormy Cape of Good Hope (1497) and claimed the sovereignty of Indian Seas, and the ownership of Oriental Continents. Pope Alexander VI., then a living, not a galvanized power, by an imaginary line through the Atlantic, extending from pole to pole, one hundred leagues west of the Azores, divided the unknown world, and granted all discoveries west of it to the kingdom of Spain, all east of it to Portugal.[1] But Henry VII. of England, not having the fear of damnation before his eyes, in 1496 (but four years after Columbus's voyage) commissioned John Cabot, a Venetian Merchant, and his three sons (of Bristol, England), to discover and occupy new countries in the name of the English king. Under this commission the northern Continent of America was discovered by him in 1497.

Bartholomew Gosnold, in 1602, the same year in which the Pilgrims were escaping to Holland, sailed across to Cape Cod, and, making a coasting voyage, returned with a good cargo, and a good report of the land. Two companies had been organized in England in 1606. First, the "LONDON COMPANY" of Merchants (or Virginia Company) who were to settle Virginia, ranging between 34° and 41° of latitude, under which Jamestown was settled in 1606–7. Second, the "PLYMOUTH COMPANY" in 1620,[2] composed of Merchants of Plymouth, Bristol, and the Western part of England, who had power over a country ranging from the 38th to the 45th degree. In 1614 the name of New England was applied to this territory by Captain John Smith.[3]

THE MERCHANT ADVENTURERS.

Under the patronage of the "London Company of Merchant Adventurers," the Plymouth settlers gained some sort of a grant of privileges from the "Virginia Company" first, afterward from the "Plymouth Company (1629–30). These Merchant Adventurers, according to Captain Smith, were composed of some seventy stockholders, comprising not only Merchants, but Handicrafts-men and others, who advanced about £7000, and were to receive returns from the Pilgrims, in the produce of the Colony, whatever it might be. Some of these looked to the profit of the ad-

[1] Robertson's America. London, 1816.

[2] Baylie's Mem. Hubbard, p. 85. Cheever's Journal of Pilgrims, p. 5. Haven's Introduction to Mass. Records.

[3] Wilson, p. 356. Bancroft, vol. i., p. 270.

venture, an very properly; otherwise the Pilgrims could not have sailed. This Contract between them and the Colony was to continue seven years; but it became so vexatious to both parties, that the Pilgrims were glad to purchase a release. (See ch. xi.)

The Pilgrims earnestly sought a Patent, liberty from the king of England, to go to a bleak and howling wilderness, there to suffer cold, hunger, sickness, and death, in order that they might at least lay the foundation of future homes for their descendants; they asked only to be LET ALONE, that they might gain a hard and honest living from the rugged soil, and to rule themselves as they could, and to worship their God as they saw fit—not as some other men thought proper. They had been "harried out of England," were not wanted there, and their request does not seem exorbitant. Yet it could not be granted; the "divine right" of the King and the Church did not coincide with the divine rights of the Puritans; and as the strong hand only could settle these things, and the King had the strong hand (for a time), his rights prevailed, and the Puritans were vagabonds and fugitives on the face of the earth.

The most they could get was a Grant from the Virginia Company to settle in the territory which that Company held from the King. This grant was questionable in many respects. Freedom of worship might be suffered, but it was not secured. The Mayflower touched the Continent far north of the limits of the Virginia patent, and the matter was therefore never brought to a test.

The Forefathers took possession, in their own right, of an unoccupied country, which, as soon as possible, they bought (and paid for) from the native inhabitants, who still claimed the right to roam and hunt over its surface—the right of Possession, not of Use. They endeavored to have the rights thus gained guarantied them by the English Government, but without success. The only charter which Bradford and the Settlers at Plymouth were at last able to get, was one from the Plymouth Company, securing them all the rights which that Company held from the Crown. This was given, January 13, 1629–30, in consideration that Bradford and his associates had now for nine years established and sustained themselves at their own charges, and by care and industry had approved themselves among men. It secured their rights to lands, between the Cohasset river on the North and the Narragansett river on the South, and also lands on the Kennebeck; privileges to make and execute laws; liberties to fish and to trade; and to make war in defense of these their rights.[1] At the restoration of Charles II., they feared its loss, and put it into the hands of Richard Bellingham and John Leverett for safe-keeping. In 1664, they enrolled all above sixteen years of age, "except timorous persons," into the militia, and required them to drill eight times a year.

New Plymouth remained a separate Government till after the Revolution in 1688, when, by King William's Charter, it was united to Massachusetts Bay. John Pierce obtained a Patent from the Plymouth Company, which he afterward sold to the "Merchant Adventurers" in London, but it was never of any use to the Pilgrims.

THE SIGNING THE COMPACT ON BOARD THE MAY-FLOWER.

Mutterings were heard from some of the smaller grains of this "choice seed," before it left the Mayflower. Some of the more ignorant sort said, "It is all very well; but when we get ashore, there is plenty of room, and one man will be as good as another; and if we have no voice in ordering matters, we can step out into the woods and order things to suit ourselves." Such was the talk which reached the ears of the leading men. Bradford, Brewster, and Carver were not only men of Justice, but men of SENSE, and they saw that to deny these men—though

[1] Prince's Chron. Baylie's Mem.

they were " Servants"—a voice in directing their own common affairs, would be not only unjust, but unwise. They foresaw the evils and dangers of division to the infant Colony, and they decided to anticipate them—not to wait, as most men do, till the people, stung to madness, rush into mischief.[1]

The whole body of the Settlers was therefore convened in the Cabin of the Mayflower, as she lay within Cape Cod. All were serious, wondering what was now to be done ; for it was evident that in taking this second great step, some important plan was afoot. Slowly and clearly the following simple Compact was then read :

"In the name of God, Amen. We whose names are underwritten, the loyal subjects of our dread Sovereign King James, by the grace of God, etc., having undertaken, for the Glory of God and advancement of the Christian faith, and honor of our King and Country, a voyage to plant the first Colony in the Northern parts of Virginia, do by these presents solemnly and mutually, in the presence of God, and one of another, Covenant and combine ourselves together into a Civil body politic, for our better ordering and preservation, and furtherance of the ends aforesaid ; and by virtue hereof, to enact, constitute, and frame such just and equal laws, ordinances, acts, constitutions, and offices, from time to time, as shall be thought most meet and convenient for the general good of the colony, unto which we promise all due submission and obedience.

In witness whereof we have hereunder subscribed our names, at Cape Cod, the 11th of November, in the year of the reign of our Sovereign lord, King James of England, France, and Ireland, the eighteenth, and of Scotland the fiftie-fourth, Anno Dom., 1620."[2]

[1] Mourt's Relation. London, 1622. Maudit, 1774.

[2] The names of those who organized this democracy, should live. This

Each man was asked to sign this instrument, and thus by granting to each his just right, all ground for disunion and revolution was removed. The Compact was signed by forty-one men, who with their families constituted the "One hundred and two,"[1] "the proper democracy" that arrived in New England. "This," says a historian, "was the birth of popular constitutional liberty." This was the birth of Individual Liberty, of Democracy! and thus were ORGANIZED the Rights of Man. Each man—master and servant—thenceforward was recognized as a man, felt the responsibility of a man, and voted as a man; his voice counted as One! The time had come in the history of the world, when in a civilized, organized commu-

is the list given by Prince, as signers of this "Compact," with the number in each of their families:

Mr. John Carver,†	8
William Bradford,	2
Mr. Edward Winslow,†	5
Mr. William Brewster,†	6
Mr. Isaac Allerton,†	6
Capt. Miles Standish,†	2

Name	No.	Name	No.
John Alden,	1	*John Crackston,*	2
Mr. Samuel Fuller,	2	John Billington,†	4
Mr. Christopher Martin,†	4	*Moses Fletcher,*	1
Mr. William Mullins,†	5	*John Goodman,*	1
Mr. William White,†	5	*Degory Priest,*	1
Mr. Richard Warren,	1	*Thomas Williams,*	1
John Howland,	0	Gilbert Winslow,	1
Mr. Stephen Hopkins,†	8	*Edward Margeson,*	1
Edward Tilly,	4	Peter Brown,	1
John Tilly,	3	*Richard Britteridge,*	1
Francis Cook,	2	George Soule,	0
Thomas Rogers,	2	*Richard Clarke,*	1
Thomas Tinker,†	3	Richard Gardiner,	1
John Ridgdale,†	2	*John Allerton,*	1
Edward Fuller,†	3	*Thomas English,*	1
John Turner,	3	Edward Dotey,	0
Francis Eaton,†	3	Edward Leister,	0
James Chilton,†	3		

The names in italics indicate those who died before the end of March; those indicated by the † brought their wives with them.

[1] Bradford's History, M. H. C., 1856.

nity, at Plymouth on the Massachusetts shore, this recognition of individual liberty was to be a RIGHT. A right which may be abused, which may occasion temporary disorders, but which must be asserted, and maintained, and admitted, and established, before a true communal life is possible—one which works together for the good of the individual, and therefore of the community; which neither seeks nor allows superior privileges to king, or priest, or aristocracy; but only the elevation and perfection of man whatever may be his condition or birth. No Society, no Community, no Nation can last, that does not act upon this as its central idea. Society, so far, has not been organized upon it, and so far society has gone to destruction. We have here the idea, and we have action under it; shall we be able to live up to it? It is the problem that is to be solved.

In the cabin of the "Mayflower" we have presented to us one of those small but significant events which influence the destiny of man through all succeeding history. On this 11th day of November, 1620 (22d November 1620 N. S.), serving men—villains—the slave class, were accepted as equals in political rights. Circumstances FORCED the superior to what may have seemed then an unwise admission. The men of birth and education among the pilgrims did not intend a Democracy, they had not faith in it; and the social distinction, between "Mr." and "Goodman" continued long after the *civil* had been ground to dust by the dynamic force of their unrecognized and undeveloped principle of religious right and duty. But the act was done, and could not be undone: the light from heaven was forced in upon men, and they saw. With Rights come Duties, and the rights once admitted and assumed, the duties must be done: time alone is needed, perhaps centuries, to ensure harmony between the two. But the duties of self-government can not be, and will not be assumed, so long as the rights are withheld: as well expect men to learn to swim without water, as to expect them to be self-governors without practice. Whatever king or class denies the intrinsic rights of self-government, sows broadcast the seeds of envy, hatred, injustice, degradation and confusion, and, sooner or later, of destruction. The wise king or governing class, will therefore urge this right of self-government upon the lower class, and will steadily sustain it: thus, and thus only, will the lower class everywhere be converted into true men and honest citizens.

THEIR GOVERNMENT.

Their government was of the utmost simplicity—technically it was nothing, for each man was free, and his own governor; there was room for self-development, and every one naturally gravitated to his place. It was fortunate that no Locke[1] was there, to draw up a full and scientific scheme of government; no Sieyes,[2] to construct a perfect Constitution; no lawyers or theorists, to destroy the simple arrangements of life.

JOHN CARVER had been named governor before they left the ship, believing, as they said, that "One Nehemiah was better than a whole Sanhedrim of mercenary Shemaiahs." Possessed of a good estate in England, he had spent it and himself in the service of what he believed to be true religion, and the interests of humanity.[3] He was a man of quiet dignity, and a reliable, honorable friend. His duties, of course, were those of a father living among, and working with and for his children; not those of a Despot, to rule his subjects—or a Politician, to beguile them by craft and lying words—not those of an Aristocrat, whose life is spent in keeping up the delusion, that he is the born governor of his fellow-men.

At the meeting, held March 23d, for the completion of their military arrangements (interrupted by Indians in February), he was chosen Governor for the year by all the people. A few days after this, in April, returning from work in the fields, to which labor he was not used, he was

[1] See that of Carolina. [2] Study the French Revolution. [3] Allen, Biog. Dict.

5*

seized with pains in the head, and died, and was buried in the best manner, "with the discharge of some volleys of shot by all that bore arms." Bradford was chosen Governor in his stead, which office he held almost uninterruptedly during his life.

WILLIAM BRADFORD was thirty-two years old when the Pilgrims landed at Plymouth. The little village of Ansterfield,[1] in Yorkshire, near Scrooby, in the North of England, was the home of this farmer boy. His nature was earnest, and true, and steady, and early in life the religious spirit in him was waked to action. Falling in with Robinson and his friends, he joined his lot to theirs, and in 1607 (then eighteen years old) was among them, in their efforts to escape from England to Holland. He stood by them with head, hands, heart, and purse through every difficulty, and shared every suffering. His property—not large—was discreetly used, not to forward the selfish purposes of William Bradford alone. Having no advantage of early education, he applied himself to learn what books can teach. He mastered several languages, and, somewhat of their literatures and history; was able to express himself readily and properly, and did not fear a disputant. When he died his library amounted to two hundred and seventy-five volumes; no small collection, when we remember the times, and his adverse accidents. From a sickly boy, Bradford, working in the open air, at his business of a farmer, grew to be a healthy, robust man. This is the key to his character; he had health! With it, a man may do and be much; without it he is no man. He laid his hand to the work and did it. In Holland he needed a new trade, and he learned to be a dyer; in America he was required to administer the affairs of a small nation, and he did it—calmly, and sagaciously, and bravely. On a time some young men declined to work on Christmas, having conscientious scruples, as they thought, superior to the necessities of the infant

[1] J. Hunter in Mass. Hist. Coll. 4th series.

state ; but, in the course of the day, finding their scruples rather burdensome, they indulged themselves in a game of ball. Bradford told them that their conscientious scruples might be urgent, but so were his, and he could not allow them to play while others were at work, and for their benefit.

When Lyford and Oldham (see ch. xvi.) plotted mischief, and proceeded toward action, the Governor met the case at the outset face to face ; he did not allow the mischief to come to a head, through any squeamish theories or fears. His business was to watch the interests of those who, engaged in other ways, had entrusted their public affairs to him. He did not wait for mischief to seek him, but, finding it, he put it out ; knowing that the "first step costs," he lived up to his knowledge. A man of nerve and public spirit, he was truly a Father to the Colony, and he died as a man should die, lamented and honored, though not quite in the fullness of years—A.D. 1659.

EDWARD WINSLOW[1] was one of the youngest of the men of mark among the Pilgrims, being twenty-six years old when he landed from the "Mayflower." A "gentleman born," he had traveled over Europe, and falling in with Robinson at Leyden, his truth and virtue found a response in the character of young Winslow ; who joined his Church, and was through life a friend of liberty and struggling manhood, not the blind and bigoted advocate of the privileges of his Class. His address and activity made him of the first value, and he was engaged in nearly all negotiations, with Indians, and with the Company and Government in England. He was a friend of the Parliament in their struggle with Charles I., and, returning to England from time to time, upon business of the colony, he was appointed, in 1655, one of the Commissioners to superintend the action of the fleet, sent by the Protector Cromwell to the West Indies. There he was attacked

[1] Born 1594.

with a fever, and lost his life. His wife died in the first winter after their arrival at Plymouth; and he afterward married Mrs. White—the mother of Peregrine, the first-born in New England. Winslow was a man of parts, and had the gift of speech. While in England, in 1635, he was imprisoned by Laud for having taught in the church, and for having, as a magistrate, performed the ceremony of Marriage; he believing it to be a civil contract, while Laud was urgent that it was a sacrament.

Winslow was the author of various pamphlets, mostly written in explanation and defense of New England; of which the following exist: "Good Newes from New-England," "Relation about Indians, etc.," "Hypocrisie unmasked," "A brief Narrative of the true Grounds or Cause of the first planting of New England," "The Danger of tolerating Levellers," "Glorious Progress of the Gospell among the Indians."

Three more of the Pilgrims deserve notice, because of their connection with the public affairs of the Colony.

MILES STANDISH was a Lancashire man, and came of fighting ancestors; so that in those fighting days, when history is a succession of wars, it was natural that he should have been a soldier, and have served in the Netherlands, the great battle-ground of Western Europe. He joined Robinson and his people at Leyden, and though he was never a member of the Church, his sympathies and connections made him their fast friend, while his character and courage rendered him so valuable, that Church Membership was not exacted of him. He was their captain, and fought with carnal weapons, and his name—"The Stalwart Standish"—has become a household word, because his heart was strong and his character fearless; not because his legs were long and his shoulders broad, for a ton of flesh will not make a man brave. Standish was a small man—so that Hubbard speaks sneeringly of him as a "small chimney soon fired."[1] But bold, impetuous, al-

[1] See Hubbard's History.

most rash, he went to his work, and by his daring filled his enemy with fear; he always conquered. He was by no means a man seeking to be embroiled; whenever he received orders from the Colonists he executed them, and then retired to his farm, and to his own labors. Being thirty-six years of age when he landed at Plymouth, he died at Duxbury, well in years, in 1656; and Morton says "fell asleep in the Lord," as is very common with "great men" in past and present times.

ISAAC ALLERTON and STEPHEN HOPKINS, were both men of character and courage; and were both intrusted with public business. Allerton was sent at various times to England, at first to good purpose; but at last he fell under the displeasure of the Colony—who distrusted his singleness of purpose, and found him dishonest. (Bradford.)

BREWSTER and ROBINSON, the minds which had a leading influence in the inception, development, and success of the Colony, are spoken of in the Chapter upon the Plymouth Church.

FANATICISM.

CARVER, BRADFORD, BREWSTER, STANDISH, WINSLOW, ALLERTON, HOPKINS, and ROBINSON, were all called "Fanatics" (and hated as such), when subject to oppression in England; they were all kind and good citizens in Holland, and became even conservative in America, where they could be free to make their own laws and to obey them; this fact is invariable, because founded upon a profound element of human nature. Let it not be forgotten, that oppression and injustice are sure to provoke violence and revolution, and that history shows that the last is always a certain consequence of the first. If we will but remember the years and centuries of scorn, ignominy, persecution, and suffering, bestowed upon the reforming party in the church, afterward called "Puritans," we shall not be surprised at any excesses into which they might have been betrayed, but the contrary.

THE GOVERNOR AND COUNCIL.

The Governor was chosen annually, by general suffrage, and in 1624, by request of Bradford, a Council of five (afterward, 1633, increased to seven Assistants), was also chosen. In this Council the Governor had but a double vote.[1]

Bradford was thirty-three years old when chosen Governor in 1621. He was annually chosen, so long as he lived, except when he urgently declined, as in 1633, 1636, and 1644, when Winslow was chosen; and in 1634 and 1638, when Thomas Prince was elected.[2]

Whoever was the man disposed to shirk his duties, we can not now know; but a curious law was passed in 1632: That whoever should refuse the office of Governor, being chosen thereto, should pay twenty pounds; and that of Magistrate, ten pounds.[3] Very curious, certainly; and we may suppose that that race is run out in Massachusetts, as well as in other States.

JURY-TRIAL.

As early as December 17, 1623, it was ordained by the court, that "all criminal facts, and all manner of trespass, and debts, between man and man, should be tried by the verdict of twelve honest men."[4] This distinctive peculiarity of northern civilization was then inaugurated at Plymouth: a practice which educates the jurymen and the whole people, into a knowledge of, and a loyalty to the laws, and so makes every man a lover of and doer of that justice, to which he is a party.

THEIR CODE.

Their laws were collected, and prefaced with a Declaration of Rights, in 1636. They were at various times revised and added to, and were printed in 1671. They called them "Their Great Fundamentals."[5]

In looking through the laws, passed from time to time in Plymouth, we find that generally they were such as the

[1] See "Body of Laws." Thacher's Plymouth, p. 78.

[2] Morton's Memorial. Allen's Biog. Dict.

[3] See Thacher's Plymouth, i., p. 123. Prince's Annals. J. Prescott Hall's New England Discourse. 1847.

[4] Plymouth Records; Hazard, vol. i.

[5] Memoirs of American Governors, by J. B. Moore, New York, 1846.

needs of the people called for, and that previous to 1632, they were but little more than the customs of the people.[1]

They provided for schools: "That twelve pounds should be raised for salary, etc.; that children should attend schools."

For ordering of persons and distributing the lands: That Freemen should be twenty-one years of age; sober and peaceable; orthodox in the fundamentals of religion. That Drunkards should be subject to fines and stocks, and be posted; and sellers forbid to sell to them.

That horse-racing should be forbid; so, too, walking about at nights.

That the Minister's salary should be paid by rate upon all the inhabitants. That Sabbath traveling should be forbid, and Sabbath work; also going to another town to church, and visiting on that day.

That every wolf's head should be worth, to an Indian, twelve shillings, or a "coat of duffels;" to a white man, twenty shillings.

That fowling, fishing, and hunting should be free.

Profane swearing was punished by "sitting in the stocks; lying, by the stocks, or by a fine."

Making a motion of marriage to any man's daughter, if made without obtaining leave, to be punished by fine or corporal punishment, at the discretion of the Court, so that it did not extend to life or limb. It was ordered, too, that short sleeves (for women) should not be worn, and that no sleeves should be more than half an ell wide (22½ inches)! Such a singular law seems to have been needed in that desolate country when they had insufficient food.

Card-playing was afterward forbid (1656), and sitting about too much at alehouses was to be reformed by the church[2] (1676).

Marriage was at a premium—for single persons were

[1] Book of Laws of New Plymouth, 1636. Revised, 1671.

[2] Thacher's Plymouth, p. 82. Do., p. 276.

forbid to live by themselves, or in any family without the consent of the select-men, and we can not believe that all young men and women enjoyed that. It is easy to see from the foregoing, how simple their arrangements were, and how naturally they grew out of their needs, their liberty, and their imperfect ideas of the model state.

NO CRIMES.

While all were earnest, and elevated by enthusiasm, by the hope of realizing their idea in their new home, and by the pressing necessities of the hour, offenses were few. Bound together by their principles, their sufferings, and their hopes, envyings and ambitions were saved. In old lands, stealing is the common vice—but here, where the partnership secured a share to EVERY one, why should any steal or cheat? The first offense was the use of vile speeches, and disobedience to the captain's order, by one Billington, who had "slipt in" in London. He was condemned to have his head and his heels tied together for an hour, but penitence secured his pardon. The next public offense was a duel with swords (June) between two serving-men! who copied the vices, not the virtues of "men of the world." There being plenty of room for every one, circumstances favored that virtue which their principles inculcated; and they were too busy to sin much. For the first ten years the population increased slowly, numbering but three hundred in all in 1630.

THEIR LEGISLATURE.

The legislative body, at first, was composed of the whole body of freemen, who were members of the church;[1] and it was not till the year 1639, that they established a House of Representatives.[2] Narrow as the restriction of civil rights to church members was, it is easy to explain it, by bearing it in mind that toleration, in any large sense, was hardly entertained by the most liberal religionists (see chapter on Toleration); by remembering that the one idea which inspired this emigration, and nerved these men for the

[1] Standish was not.

[2] Grahame, vol. i., p. 230.

bitterest sacrifices, was that they might be free from an ecclesiastical tyranny, which if it followed would endanger them; by recollecting, too, that the history they studied, and the guide they felt bound to follow, was the Jewish theocracy, ordained by God, as they doubted not, a model in Church and State for all time, and that under that dispensation, death was the punishment for smaller errors than dissent. These facts will explain and excuse, the religious tyranny which was afterward practiced in New England. But we shall see how the free idea with which they started, has gradually grown stronger and has overcome the evil customs of the time, and of the Pilgrims themselves.

This Church test of Citizenship prevailed till the year 1665,[1] when it was reluctantly yielded, at the requirement of his majesty's commissioners, and was entirely abandoned about the year 1686. As a matter of course it did not work well; the more unscrupulous the conscience, the easier it was and is to join the Church; and abandoned men, who wanted public preferment, could join the Church with loud professions, gain their ends, and make Church-membership a by-word. They do it to this day. Under the charter granted by William and Mary in 1691, Plymouth was incorporated with Massachusetts' Bay. The qualification for Electors was then fixed at a "freehold of 40 shillings per annum, or other property of the value of £40 sterling."[2] Plymouth Colony joined the Confederation in 1643; it persecuted the Quakers, but tenderly;[3] it took part in Philip's war—but these and other incidents will be related, in connection with the accounts of Massachusetts' Bay, and are not necessary here.

The final act of the Plymouth Court was the appointment of the last Wednesday of August, 1692, as a day of solemn fasting and humiliation, previous to their extinction as a separate State. This fast day was not at

[1] Thacher's Plymouth. [2] Thacher, p. 189.
[3] Prescott Hall's N. E. Discourse, 1847.

the usual season, but was beyond question duly observed by the Elders with prayers and tears, and by the younger portion in researches among the domestic nests, and in stolen enjoyment of the surrounding forests. The small seed dropped at Plymouth has grown into a noble tree, and the oppressed and the fugitive from other lands find shelter under its branches. Laus Deo.

CHAPTER XVI.

THEIR CHURCH.

THE FIRST SABBATH—CALVINISTS—PERSECUTION—THEIR CHURCH CONSTITUTION—LYFORD AND OLDHAM—THEIR MINISTERS—MR. ROGERS—RALPH SMITH—ROGER WILLIAMS—JOHN NORTON—JOHN RAYNOR—CHARLES CHAUNCEY—NO SACRAMENTS—LAY PREACHING—JOHN COTTON—WILLIAM BREWSTER—JOHN ROBINSON—PASTORS AND TEACHERS—RULING ELDERS—DEACONS—DEACONESSES—PROFESSORS—CHURCH TAX—SALARIES—PRAYERS—WOMEN SPEAKING—THE SUNDAY EXERCISES—CHURCH ADMISSIONS—CATECHIZINGS—FASTS—THE LORD'S SUPPER—MUSKETS—THE SABBATH—"THANKSGIVING"—HOW KEPT AND WHEN BEGUN—THE FIRST MEETING-HOUSE—HERESIES—SEPARATIONS—PROTESTANTISM—QUAKERS—THE DEVIL—THE INDIANS—RELIGIOUS DEMOCRACY.

THE Plymouth Church was an Idea put into its simplest form. It had no Ritual, no Cathedral, no Saints' days, no Organ music, no Processions or Splendors. None of these were there, on that dreary barren rocky coast.

THE FIRST SABBATH[1] of the Pilgrims was passed on the Island near Plymouth Rock, where their boat was stranded. There their Church was held, their prayers said ; their vault was the stormy sky ; their organ, the sweeping blast ; their sacrifice, a broken heart ; their priests, themselves ; their altars, their own hearts. The People were the Church. A few particulars, gathered from the past, will enable us to see how they realized their idea.

None will doubt that Puritanism was strongly attached to the intellectualism of John Calvin, which became and has continued to be the corner-stone of the New England Churches and Theology. Calvin brought God from the cloudy realm of spirit into the clear light of intellect. The Logical faculty in him aimed to compass the Infinite, and dared to attempt to express the inexpressible. In a degree the infinite was made finite, the incomprehensible comprehensible. In all things MIND asserted itself, and

[1] They liked the word Sabbath instead of Sunday, because the Jews used it.

in most it was triumphant ; it cleared away rubbish and the dark clouds of superstition, while it failed to express God. To such a body of brave inquirers, and independent thinkers, as had gathered at Plymouth, it was no easy matter to find a Teacher who was sufficient. Yet, for several centuries after Mind had asserted its freedom from the intellectual Slavery of the Church, and had cut loose from the dogmas and statements of Truth put out by Holy Councils of Rome, the Religious World held fast by those put forth by Paul, and John, and David, and Isaiah ; partly because they were the outpourings of earnest, burning, living souls, and partly because men dared not trust their own souls. The views and aspirations of these inspired men, priests and poets, were limited and comprehensible to many who feared to trust themselves alone in the vast and unexplored region of spirit; so they took the statements that they found already made, just as others accepted the statements of the Catholic Church, and were satisfied. But in the days of the "Pilgrim Fathers," few doubted that there was an expression of Truth, complete and final, and that whoever did not accept it, was sure of damnation.

So no church organization existed, which did not suffer and indulge in persecution for opinion's sake. Free as it was, the Plymouth Church certainly was not blameless, on this score ; yet they had lived in Holland, where religious worship was permitted, and there they had learned something.

Prince gives a summary of the religious tenets of the Plymouth church, which will suffice for us :[1]

1. It held that nothing is to be accounted true religion but what is taught in the Holy Scriptures.

2. That every man had the right of judging for himself; of testing his own belief by those Scriptures, and of worshiping God in the way that those Scriptures directed, and as it seemed right to him.

[1] CHRONOLOGY. Thacher's Plymouth.

This was a great step, from the Roman Catholic doctrine, surely ; it was putting in place of a church, with its Synods, and Councils, and Cardinals, who were to say from day to day what was and what was not true and necessary to salvation, a written Constitution ! and not only so, but it erected each man's conscience and intellect into a Court, to determine what that constitution meant ; each man for himself, each woman for herself. A leading, and earnest, and honest mind, like Robinson's, could give form and expression to his own lofty and pure ideas, and they met the wants of many minds, so that he became the standard around which friends gathered ; but in Theory, no man was bound to belong to Robinson's church, for one hour, whenever he snould hold different opinions. Persecution for a time will keep such a body of men together, for self-preservation, but it is of course, intellectually impossible for free-thinking minds to agree in opinion upon the vast variety of physical, historical, intellectual, and spiritual matters contained in the wonderful books of Jewish history and literature, in the lives of Jesus, and in the Epistles and writings of the Apostles. So much for their simple, yet broad platform.

LYFORD AND OLDHAM.

Mr. Cushman wrote from England, in 1624, that they had sent a carpenter, a saltman, and a preacher, "though not the most eminent."[1] The carpenter was a true man, who soon died : the saltman was a foolish fellow, who spoiled whatever he touched : the preacher was John Lyford, who seemed bowed to the earth with humility ; he at once began to exercise his gifts, though not the most eminent—people being hungry for "ordained" teaching. Lyford was really a Church of England man, and was forced upon the Colony by the Episcopal portion of the Merchant Adventurers in England.[2] He was well received by all, and Governor Bradford appointed him one of his Council. He seems to have

[1] Morton's Memorial, p. 111.

[2] The Landing at Cape Ann, by J. W. Thornton, Boston, 1854.

had no sympathy with those rigid, self-denying, Puritans, and Separatists ; or if he once had, it had become irksome ; and he found in John Oldham, a more genial companion. Oldham was a robust, active, daring, sensual, passionate, hearty materialist, and believed a good deal more in beaver-skins and roast-beef, than in the "five points ;" and he loved a game with the Indians of a Sunday afternoon, rather than a hard bench and a long sermon. To him Puritanism was a bore, and he liked a "jolly parson," rather than a sincere precisian. The "good old times" were good enough for him, and the Prayer-book and Homilies answered his needs. He was an actor rather than a thinker, and was quite ready to second anybody, in undermining these straitened Calvinists. With him Lyford intrigued, and together they sent off ridiculous and defamatory letters to England. Governor Bradford got wind of this (1624), boarded the ship at night, examined the letters, and finding what they were, retained them for future use. Growing bold, Oldham proceeded to set up a meeting in his own house, and to read the Prayer-book on Sundays, in a loud and dignified voice, sustained by Lyford ; things were coming to so dangerous a pass, that Bradford called the people together, and publicly accused the two ; they protested and denied, and Oldham blustered, but Bradford took out the letters and read them to the assembly, and so they were confounded. Lyford confessed himself a reprobate, and with tears, prayed for pardon. It was granted ; but he was not staunch ; and being a second time convicted, he was deposed and banished. He was a bitter enemy of the Colony, henceforth, until he died in Virginia. Oldham being forced to go, went to Nantasket, and was engaged there and at Cape Ann, trading with the Indians, until he lost his life among them, having a hatchet sunk into his head.[1] (1636.)

THEIR MINISTERS.

Lyford was succeeded by a Mr. ROGERS as Minister, who "proved crazed in the brain,"

[1] Morton's Memorial. Cheever's Journal, p. 327, etc.

and was sent back to England; and in the year 1629, eight years after the settlement of the Colony, RALPH SMITH, one of four ministers who came over to Salem, was found at Nantasket (now Hull) in a desolate and destitute condition; him they eagerly seized and took care of, and availed themselves of his gifts (which were very "low") for some five or six years.

Then young ROGER WILLIAMS, "brilliant but unstable," as some thought, ministered to them some three years, till he concluded to go to Salem in 1634, to which the Church consented.

JOHN NORTON, who afterward was at Boston, was their next Minister, but he remained only a short time.

At last "it pleased the Lord" to send them JOHN RAYNOR, "an able and a godly man," whose labors they enjoyed many years.

CHARLES CHAUNCEY, afterward President of the College at Cambridge, was his assistant for some three years [1638], but declined settling. He had views about Baptism, and so had the Church, and they did not agree: Chauncey held to "dipping," and the Church did not.

John Raynor continued with them till 1654, some eighteen years. "Unhappy differences," and "unsettledness"—many being "leavened with prejudice against a learned ministry," and "sectaries" becoming epidemic—were believed to have caused his departure, which was much regretted.

THEY HAD NO SACRAMENTS.

In the long intervals between "consecrated ministrations," the Church was not without Gospel teaching, but it had not the Sacraments. Elder Brewster was able to teach twice every Sabbath, powerfully and profitably, and without stipend, which he steadily declined; "doing more in this respect in a year," so John Cotton declares, "than many that have their hundreds per annum do in all their lives." It seems there is one brilliant exception to the Indian axiom, "Poor pay, poor preach." Brewster had a singular good gift in Prayer too, "yet seldom lengthy or prolix," in the exercise of it, which, in those days, as in these, was a virtue much to be commended. Without the afflatus of Ordination, he was so much better than most of their ministers with it, that the Colonists felt a sensible relief and pleasure in getting again his sterling sense and untortured truth.

The absence of Sacraments was early regretted. The Church record says, "The more is our grief, for we used to have the Lord's Supper every Sabbath, and Baptism as often as there was occasion," etc.

LAY PREACHING.

We discover that Winslow (and others too) from time to time "exercised his gift to help the edification of his brethren," when better could not be had.[1] Laud had him up for this when he was in England—for this and for marrying, and he not a Minister. Winslow replied, that he himself had been married by the Magistrate in Holland, and that so far as he could see, the Scripture was not against it; and besides, it must be that or nothing, or worse, for they had had no Clergyman in the Colony for several years. But this did not satisfy Laud, and Winslow was clapped into prison, and lay there some four months.

Mr. John Cotton came to them as their Minister in 1666, and remained till 1697, over thirty years, and until after the union of the Colony with Massachusetts Bay.

Elder Brewster and John Robinson deserve our attention.

William Brewster was nigh sixty years old when he came to New England in the Mayflower. In the church, while at Leyden, he had been a Ruling Elder, and was a staunch supporter of it in New England. In the constrained absence of Mr. Robinson, their pastor, Elder Brewster occupied the place of Lay Preacher to the Colony, and was worthy of the honor of being the first minister of New England. He had been at Cambridge

[1] Hubbard, p. 63.

University, and afterward in the service of Davidson at the Court of Queen Elizabeth. On the disgrace of his master he had returned to Lincolnshire, had done much service to religion, had held the first meetings of his friends, and organized a Church in his own house at Scrooby, Nottinghamshire.[1] He was foremost among those who essayed to sail from Boston, England, and in Holland had laid his hand to the daily tasks of life, as well as spent his soul in trying to benefit his fellows. Brewster declined to administer the Sacrament, having never been ordained, so that the Plymouth Colony were for some years without them, yet always growing in strength and virtue.[2] He was the regular and stated Preacher of the Church until about 1629, working for his bread with his own hands, and so bringing himself as near as possible to the early Christian practices. We can not doubt that the words of such a man had weight, and that for years the Pilgrims found him an acceptable successor to Robinson. Governor Bradford bears honorable testimony to his tender and compassionate nature, which neither his religious tenets, nor adversity, nor injustice, could render harsh or sullen. It is pleasant to know that the death of such a man was in a green old age, and that he went quietly to his future without a pang, nigh eighty years of honor on his head. He laid himself down amid loving and tried friends, who could not but be glad that he "so sweetly departed this life unto a better."

It was in April, 1644, that his pilgrimage here was ended.

John Robinson, their Moses, who led them out of England, and from the oppressions which years had not softened, was not permitted to join them in their promised land. At the sailing of the "Speedwell" and "Mayflower" he remained behind with the larger part of his

[1] Hunter in Mass. Hist. Coll., 4th series. See Chronicles of Pilgrims.

[2] Belknap's Am. Biog., vol. ii., p. 257. Cheever's Journal. Bradford's Journal.

people at Leyden; like Moses from the top of Pisgah, looking into the promised land, but not entering it. He was in the prime of life, about forty-four years of age, when the Pilgrims sailed—a life remarkable for its courage, constancy and truth. When quite young, the base, time-serving policy of leaders in the English Church was a thorn in his side, a corruption in his dish, a skeleton in his chamber—seeing clearly, and feeling keenly, whither this tended, one can not wonder that it should have poisoned the sweet fountains of his nature, and that then the waters flowed harsh and bitter. Time was needed to show to him too that the god-like in man can never be wholly corrupted—that in spite of fearful and insidious temptations, a ray of the divine nature still illumined the English Church, and saved it and the English nation from degradation and contempt. As he grew older, his humanity increased, and his vision grew stronger, so that he bloomed into that rare flower among men, and rarer among theologians—one who with large charity and faith, desiring liberty himself, denied it not to others—who found truth for himself, and doubted not that others found it. He was a man of Ideas, rather than of Action. He may be called the planter of New England, for he sowed such seed as germinated at Plymouth, and has been borne upon the winds and the waters to every part of America. His love of liberty led him to choose and cherish the congregational practice of Church discipline; and at a time too when the Brownists had brought it into disgrace. Out of this self-government in the Church grew self-government in the State, democracy and the representative system.

The extract from his address to the Pilgrims (heretofore quoted, ch. iv.) shows the calm yet vigorous character of his mind. With good practical talent, he combined scholarly tastes and acquirements, to such a degree that in Holland, in 1613, he was chosen to defend Calvinism against Episcopus and the Arminians, at the University of Leyden, and as his friends believed, "completely foiled the enemy." Hubbard, in his History, speaks of him thus: "A man of good learning, of polished wit, and ingenious disposition, and courteous behavior, yet not without too great tinctures of the sensorious spirit of their rigid separation."[1]

"He was at first a Puritan only, and officiated a while in the national church,"[2] in the neighborhood of Norwich, England. While there, his mind was perplexed respecting his duty in relation to the church. So much was his perception and judgment overborne by the opinions and conduct of "good men," in whom he had much confidence, that it was long before his own mind could act; and he says, so much was the light of truth "dimmed and overclouded with the contradictions of these men, that had not the truth been in my heart, as a burning fire shut up in my bones, I had never broken these bonds of flesh and blood." About 1604, it is believed he joined the Separatists at Scrooby. When they escaped from England (ch. iii.), they found that Mr. Smith's society at Amsterdam, which had removed from England some time earlier than Robinson and his friends, was troubled with contentions; so Robinson's congregation sought quiet at Leyden, in 1609.

At that time, regarding the ministry of the Church of England as a "false ministry," he was reordained by his own church; thus endeavoring to restore things to that state which he thought existed among the early Christians. Believing the truth of his doctrines, and earnestly wishing to benefit his fellow-men, and finding himself restricted both by the language of the Dutch, and their unwillingness, he seconded the spontaneous movement which led to a free settlement in America.

Among his recorded principles we find the following: "He maintained the spirituality, and self-government of

[1] Hubbard's History of New England, page 42.
[2] Ashton's Memoir, Mass. Hist. Coll., 4th Series.

the Church of Christ, but allowed the interference of the magistrate to compel attendance on public worship, though not to dictate opinion." He said also: "Religion is not always sown and reaped in one age," as the whole light is not received in one day. His descendants have learned, what he had not, that forced attendance upon Sunday services, is as pernicious as forced opinions, and that safety for Church or State consists only with freedom.

He opposed the administration of the sacraments by Brewster, and in his letter to him, quoted Rom. xii., 7, 8, and 1 Tim. v., 17, against it. Possibly his expectation to join them at Plymouth, influenced his opinions, but it is more likely, that large and liberal as he was, the odor of sanctity that hung about the priesthood was yet dear to him.

We must now leave him: "He fell sick Saturday morning, February 22d, 1625, next day he taught us twice, in the week grew weaker every day, and departed this life on the first of March. All his friends came freely to him, and if prayers, tears or means could have saved his life, he had not gone hence."[1]

DIED AT LEYDEN.

Robinson and his friends began by being Puritans, remaining in the English Church hoping its reform; but they found they could do more without than within it, and at last separated from it, were driven from it, and were known as "Brownists" (a term of reproach), afterward as "Independents," and then as "Congregationalists."

The Church at Plymouth never saw the face of Robinson in New England. That excellent man—who, in an age of bigotry and religious intolerance, could believe the further revelation of truth; could say, as he did, that Luther and Calvin did not know all things;[2] could be modest enough to believe that he himself had not penetrated "the whole council of God;" who, after suffering indignity, persecution, and expatriation at the hands of

[1] Eliot's Biog. Dict. [2] Winslow, in Young's Chr. of Ps.

the English Church, came again to have charity for it, and even to admit that it might be a Church of God—this scholar and gentleman, only looked into the promised land: his bones lie on the other side of Jordan, neither bearing nor needing sculptured marbles and flattering epitaphs.[1] Yet he had this satisfaction, that he was loved and honored by his own people in life and in death. Enemies, and over-cautious friends among the "Adventurers" in London, hindered Robinson's coming, till death cut him down before his work was done. Some there feared that Robinson's purity and strictness might be in the way of the emigration from England,[2] and they therefore opposed his coming. But his Truth has blossomed on the rocky shores, in the sheltered valleys, and on the breezy hills of New England, and borne a great harvest.

PASTORS AND TEACHERS.

The Holy writings furnished the Puritans, as they held, sufficient authority for all they did. Did not Paul the Apostle, in his letter to the Ephesians, expressly mention both Pastors and Teachers? (ch. iv., 5, 11.) Was not lay Preaching, too, permitted? "For they that were scattered abroad," the Epistle said, "went everywhere, preaching the word; and some of them were of Cyprus and Cyrene; and the hand of the Lord was with them."[3] And in Corinth, too, it was clear that one furnished a Psalm, another a doctrine, a fourth a revelation, a fifth an interpretation.[4] Now, they reasoned, if it was right to do it in the Apostles' days, when Christians were persecuted, why not now, when it seemed persecution was no ways slack?

The Officers of the Church, and the conduct of affairs, were ordered by the Members, and, if possible, upon Scripture authority. The officers were a PASTOR and a TEACHER (sometimes united in one person), who were to Preach, administer the Sacraments, and rule the

[1] It is not certain where he lies buried; George Sumner thinks in St. Peter's Church, Leyden.

[2] Cotton's Acct., Mass. Hist. Coll., v. 4.

[3] Acts, ch. xi., 5, 20.

[4] 1 Corinthians, ch. xiv., v. 26.

Church; of *Ruling Elders* to assist the Pastor; and of *Deacons*, who were to hold and distribute the money, and to assist at the Lord's Supper. For these they quoted chapter and verse.[1]

In the Amsterdam Church, an ancient widow or Deaconess existed, "who with a little birchen rod, kept little children in great awe."[2]

Thomas Morton says: "There is amongst these people a Deakonesse, made of the sisters, that uses her guifts at home in an assembly of her sexe, etc."

He says again: "I cannot chuse but conclude, that these Separatists have special gifts, for they are given to envy and malice, extremely."

PROFESSORS. The Church, consisting of the Professors rather than the "Society" (which was made up of all who paid towards its support), took the lead in selecting and calling the Preachers. In getting the sense of the Church, votes were called for by the lifting of hands, or sometimes by calling upon one and another to speak; or by general assent after some had expressed a particular one; but they never called for a negative vote; as Cotton quaintly says, "it would be the using of hammer or axe in temple work."

The Church seems to have paid liberally (by tax on all the inhabitants)[3]—Mr. Cotton's salary having been £80 in 1668; payable, one third in wheat or butter; one third in rye, barley, or peas; and one third in Indian corn; the prices for which were fixed as follows: wheat, 4*s.* 6*d.*, barley, 4*s.*, rye, 3*s.* 6*d.*, corn, 3*s.*, peas, 3*s.*, butter, 6*d.*[4]

As the average pay of Clergymen in New England now is about four hundred dollars, this was liberal for those days.

But can we, who speak and write, and print with steam-fingered presses—can we appreciate the luxury of being able to pray without a book, and to preach as long and as

[1] Thacher, p. 265. Eph., iv., 11. [2] Gov. Bradford. Cheever, p. 214.
[3] Book of Laws, ch. 13. Thacher, p. 274. [4] Thacher, p. 125.

many sermons as they chose, and "to speak in meeting," whoever would—each man his gospel, or his revelation, or his interpretation, and no James, by the Grace of God, to "Harry them," and no Laud to hang them, for doing it?

"Brown bread and the Gospel is good fare," they said to one another.[1] Cushman writes: "But we have here great peace, plentie of the Gospell, and many sweet delights and variety of comforts." Indeed there is reason to believe, not only that men spoke as the spirit moved them, but that women, and even children, exhorted in the public assemblies; for by-and-by[2] [1744] Josiah Cotton presented a written request, that the Church should be assembled, to consider as to the propriety of women doing so, contrary to the Apostolic direction. It seems from this, that the sex aspired to their "rights," even in the infancy of the Church and the country, and at least spoke!

Some may admire, some may despise, the extreme simplicity, and democratic inattention to "law and order," which pervaded their early worship. Any one, it seems, could speak in meeting, and not be censured. Governor Winthrop, in his Journal, dated October 25th, 1632, says:[3] "The Governor, with Mr. Wilson, Pastor of Boston, and others, went on foot to Plymouth from Massagascus. The Governor of Plymouth, Mr. William Bradford, a very decent, grave man, with Mr. Brewster, the Elder, and some others, came forth and met them without the Town, and conducted them to the Governor's house, where they were kindly entertained and feasted every day at several houses. On the Lord's day there was a Sacrament, which they did partake in; and in the afternoon, Mr. Roger Williams, according to custom, propounded a question, to which the Pastor, Mr. Smith, spoke briefly; then Mr. Williams prophesied,[4] and afterward the Governor of Plymouth spoke to the question; after him the elder;

[1] A Brief Review of the Rise and Progress of N. E. London, 1774.

[2] Thacher, p. 283. [3] Savage's Winthrop, p. 92. [4] Preached.

then some two or three more of the Congregation. Then the Elder desired the Governor of Massachusetts and Mr. Wilson to speak to it, which they did. When this was ended, the Deacon, Mr. Fuller, put the Congregation in mind of their duty of contribution ; whereupon the Governor and all the rest went down to the Deacon's seat, and put into the box, and then returned."

The following brief Notes of their Religious practices will not be uninteresting :

At first, all candidates for admission to the Church, were required to make a public statement of their belief and experiences ; but it being found that "divers of low voice, who were also bashful," were hindered by this, it was not required of them, or of women ; and their testimony was accepted in writing, which was read before the assembled church.

About the year 1681, the practice of reading the lines for singing, was begun ; which is now called "Deaconing the Psalm." It was supposed to have grown out of the necessities of some who could not read, but who could and would sing.

CATECHIZINGS of the boys and girls early prevailed in the Church and out of it ; Perkins's Catechism was at first used, afterward the Assembly's. Private family meetings, for spiritual exercises, were introduced later. (1707.)

FASTS were always resorted to in any sore affliction, such as droughts or sickness, and as Cotton and others state, in some cases with signal success. It was found, too, by-and-by (1676), that some of the brethren were prone to sit about at public houses "with vain company and drinking ;" painful as it was, they had to be taken in hand. So easy was it for the regenerate even to fall into danger and the snare.

Women also, church members, mothers, in that poor and desolate country, were led away by a propensity as wide-spread as it is lamentable, to make parade of their hair, and to deck themselves with ribbons and other such finery, clearly inexpedient, if not wicked; and it was ordered that they should not do it, nor should they wear sleeves more than twenty-two and a half inches wide. In this way did the early society try to stem a gigantic evil.

THE LORD'S SUPPER was received sitting at the table. It was with them as with the early Christians, a "Communion," not a mystery; but, unlike the early Christians, it never degenerated into a feast for eating and drinking.

Twelve persons were enjoined to bring their muskets to meeting every Lord's-day, with their swords, in case that need should require them.[1]

The SABBATH was a great and Holy day to them, and more especially God's time, than Monday and other days. The reverence of the Sabbath was so intense, that not even physical suffering and their greatest necessities could induce them to sacrifice the observance of their first Sunday on Clark's Island; which was thenceforth holy ground, and was reserved to furnish wood and pasture for the town's poor; until the times of Andros, when Counsellor Clark coveted it and obtained a grant, but never got possession of it.

THANKSGIVING.

The Sabbath was their only Holy-day, until THANKSGIVING came to be the Annual Festival. Before stating the small and accidental origin of this Institution, let us, in order to understand its present importance, leave the past and come down to this present time. (1853.) In this year we learn that the passengers on the great railway which leads into New England, numbered during Thanksgiving-week, twenty-five thousand two hundred and ninety-two and a half![2] this half being the odd child. This great army of people were leaving the sweet security of streets, their own fire-sides, and going out, not into the wilderness, but into the bleak and wintry weather to enjoy the fruits of the earth, to thank God for all things, and not the least, for this great Thursday—the Thanksgiving of the year. It is a proper

[1] Plymouth Colony Records. [2] New York Tribune.

thing for these children of New England to do. Pleasant memories of childhood and youth are clustered around this November time, and by a kind of magic the Past is made Present.

The corn is garnered, the crops gathered, the work is done ; the Earth has put on her rest, and the husbandman is in harmony with her. Again are heard the notes of preparation : on Sunday, the sounding proclamation is listened to with attentive ears ; how "the year has been crowned with goodness," how "peace is upon our borders, and plenteousness in our palaces," how "the clouds drop fatness," and how "servile labor and vain recreation" are by law forbidden. The week is full of bustle, consecrated to the mystic rites of fire-worshipers ; the body becomes great—almost god-like. For it, are elaborated "the great chicken-pie," tarts and custards, and seed-cakes, adorned with unintelligible characters—clearly not Hebrew. Fires are burning, the hearth is swept, clean caps are donned, and all is expectation. Fathers and mothers, sisters, cousins, children, and even dogs are ready to welcome to the old homesteads which adorn New England, this crowd of returning children. Thursday is well-spent (even with some excesses), for all good and kindly feelings are called into vivid action ; hatred, malice, and uncharitableness are banished ! The day then is a holy-day, and as such is to be cherished and preserved. It is one of the "peculiar institutions" of New England, fast making its way into South Carolina.

When and by whom was the festival instituted ?

It is easy to answer. In 1623, two centuries and a half ago, Winslow, writing to England, mentions that after the gathering of the harvest, the Governor (Bradford) sent out a company for game, that they might furnish themselves more dainty and abundant materials for a feast, and rejoice together after they had gathered the fruits of their "labors."[1] So they got their game, and

[1] Morton's Mem., p. 100.

they cooked it, and they ate of it, and they feasted Massasoit and ninety of his Indians, and they thanked God with all their hearts for the good world and the good things in it. So they kept their first thanksgiving. Governor Bradford said, "Nor has there been any general want of food among us since to this day" (from 1623 to 1646.)

THE FIRST MEETING-HOUSE.

The religious services of the Plymouth Church were held in the Fort—upon the roof or deck of which were mounted the great guns; and it was in 1648 that a "meeting-house" was built. They held that a Church was a body of Christians, and the place where they met was a "meeting-house;" so they called it by that name. Wherever holy men met, there God was sure to be, and there he could be worshiped; so they held, and so they practiced. Their churches were therefore likely to be rude; and it is certain that around them did not gather that wealth of memories, that magic of association, that mystery of sentiment which hangs upon every arch and angle and nook of the time-eaten, moss-covered, century-shadowed country churches of Old England.

HERESIES.

The dangers at that incipient stage, from division and weakness were great; for minds were seething and fermenting. Roger Williams had started his heresies at Plymouth, much to their distress. Mr. Chauncey's Anabaptist tendencies had been hard to bear. And, alas! in 1637, the dreaded Antinomians appeared in New England, and several young people were near being carried away "into the paths of darkness;" and John Weeks and his wife did go, and were cast out of the Church, for "their abominable opinions," as the Church held them to be. Notwithstanding this, sometime after, Samuel Hicks fell to questioning about "Baptizing of Infants, Singing of Psalms, the Ministry, the Sabbath," etc.; and though the Church gave him large answers in writing, he could not desist, but went on and on, till the issue was as Cotton says, "this poor unsettled man fell yet further and further, and at last he became a Quaker" (!)[1]

But the Church of Plymouth could not always have Halcyon days, though the wisdom and moderation of Bradford and Brewster secured it against disaster. Division, disintegration, being one of the inevitable operations of nature ; in order that reunion, reformation, man forever be going on, the poor Church at Plymouth was separated from time to time, much to the sorrow of those remaining, so that, before the close of the century, four (4) new congregations had grown to life, from the blood of her throbbing heart. First, was Duxborough ; second, Green's-Harbor, now Marshfield ; third, Eastham ; fourth, Plympton.

PROTESTANTISM asserts the right of the Individual, in opposition to the authority of the class—the Priesthood. It tends to separation, to the isolation of each man, to anarchy in creeds and worship. This must be—each one's right to his own mind and conscience must be insisted on, at whatever cost, equally with the right to his body. Whenever this shall be frankly and fully established, this state of denial and opposition will pass away, and an AFFIRMATIVE religious condition will ensue, which will be the central fire of the new and true Catholic Church, yet to come. In those days the cry of "Quaker" was the cry of mad dog, equivalent to Unitarian or Transcendentalist, or Freethinker now. Few Quakers lived long enough in New England to prove that they were not children of the devil. From 1650 to 1660 New England was much "infested" with them ; and it must be admitted that the followers of the profound spiritualist, George Fox, and the calm, wise "Friend," William Penn, did not always deport themselves with propriety. At this day even it would be indiscreet for men or women to go naked about the streets ; it would not be harmonious or

[1] Thacher's Plymouth.

quieting to have the Church exercises rudely interrupted by rash persons, crying " Woe! woe! woe!" and " bearing their testimony" when it was not asked or paid for. When we remember, that with many now, with nearly all then, heretical opinions were believed to lead a man straight to hell and its horrors, we can not wonder that the coming of the Quakers into Plymouth caused a shudder. Mary Dyer appeared, but she was not murdered there; they sent her out of the jurisdiction, and they never enforced sanguinary laws against this sect, as was done elsewhere. They dismissed General Cudworth and Thomas Hatherly from being Magistrates, because they had entertained Quakers; but the Plymouth Church is free from blood. Then there was Laud in England, always a distant but dreadful vision—a poor little unhappy man, with his own troubles, and many of them too, but one whom distance and fear exaggerated into a monster as terrible as Job's—which made all his bones to shake.

LAUD'S "Commission," intended to rule the churches in New England, which would have made " the country no better than slaves" (1635), proved unsuccessful, the Lord protecting the "poor church at Plymouth in an especial manner, marvelous in one's eyes," as Secretary Morton states. It never left England, or reached New England. The old woman in Edinburg, who threw her stool at the head of the Priest, who presumed to read the Prayer-book, initiated a diversion in their favor, and Hampden and Cromwell, at the head of the Independents, the free-thinkers and free-actors in England, were beginning about this time to furnish Laud, Strafford, and Charles with occupation at home; and so the Colonies for this time escaped. But this fearful Commission, though they escaped it for that time, struck chill and dread to every heart. Power was granted by it to some ten or twelve persons, part of whom were Papists, headed by Laud, who knew neither fear nor pity, to revoke all charters and grants, to appoint new Governors, make new laws, and establish new courts, even ecclesiastical ones, and the Colonists knew well what the Courts of Star Chamber and High Commission were. Over and above all these was the Devil himself, constantly watching, never sleeping, going about like a roaring lion (roaring silently !) seeking to devour all good people. Now and then he was visible—so they thought—and certainly was hand and glove with the stupid Indian pow-wows.

THE DEVIL.

Morton, in his Memorial, says, "Behold how Satan labored to hinder the Gospel from coming into New England. It was in this way: before the Indians came to make friendship with the English, they collected together all the powaws in the country, who for three days together did curse and execrate them, with their conjurations, and this they did in a dark dismal swamp."[1] For three days together they carried on this protracted meeting, in a very disagreeable place certainly ; yet the Devil had to give way, as he always does, to the light and truth, which Brewster and Bradford carried in their hearts. This Devil held a very important place in the history and Theology of New England ; as indeed he has through all the darkness of the past. As Typho, he disturbed the world in Egypt, as Ahriman in Persia, as Siva in India ; and just in proportion to what we call the strength of Heathenism, has the positive quality of Evil, and its power, been exalted into an equality or superiority to that of God, who is positive Good.

With the Indians, the early Plymouth Church did but little. The Pilgrims were fighting the elements for physical life, they were struggling against foes in England, and divisions at home, and had no strength for the work of Christianizing Indians. Robinson regretted this; and when Standish killed some of them, that the conspiracy growing out of the wickedness of Weston's colony might

[1] Morton's Mem., p. 63.

be suppressed, he wrote, "How much better it would have been to have converted some first."

They supposed, at first, that the Indians had no religion, their rites were so few. It was found afterward, that their root ideas were the same as the whites, and that an idea of a God, a Supreme, was also an integral part of their souls. When Winslow explained to Corbitant what "grace before meat" meant, and what the Pilgrim idea of God was, Corbitant said, "Just so we believe"—but they could make no meaning of the more ingenious statements of theology, and they doubted the seventh commandment as Winslow explained it—for "to be tied to one wife might be very inconvenient;"[1] which has been a common belief with all nations except the Germanic.

At last, in the beginning of the seventeenth century, we see a Church with no priest, with no hierarchy, with no forms, with no past (except the Jewish); none like it since that at Corinth, so entirely free to work out its own ideas into life and action. It was a Religious Democracy! Its doctrines and practices were the outcome of the time, and were decided upon or discarded by the votes of the members as men. In theory, the Majority ruled in the Plymouth Church. It is a noticeable thing in the history of man, and has had its influence in New England, both in Church and State. The day had come when a few brave men could take this step, in the advance toward freedom, and not be swallowed up and lost; the day had come when democracy was possible in the Church, foretelling its coming in the State; a day yet certain to be, when the State shall assimilate to the Church, and the true religious spirit pervading all men of all classes, may leaven even politicians, when Church and State shall be as One.

[1] Winslow's Visit to Massasoit.

The Settlement

of

MASSACHUSETTS BAY.

A. D. 1628.

CHAPTER XVII.

MASSACHUSETTS BAY.

ROGER CONANT—THE PATRIARCH OF DORCHESTER—JOHN ENDICOTT—WHITE MEN DISCOVERED—THOMAS WALFORD—WILLIAM BLACKSTONE—DAVID THOMSON—SAMUEL MAVERICK—CHARLESTOWN—THE ROYAL CHARTER—CRADOCK—OLD SETTLERS JEALOUS—TOBACCO—NEEDS OF A NEW COLONY—JOHN HIGGINSON'S COMPANY—NOT SEPARATISTS—ORDINATION—CHURCH COVENANT—THE BROWNS.

ROGER CONANT, a brave and determined man, not liking the proceedings at Plymouth during the Lyford troubles, left that Colony, and in his pinnace sailed across the bay to Nantasket, in 1624 ; and the next year removed to Cape Ann, where he found a few fishermen,[1] living there to cure fish during the absence of the vessels.

Some English merchants, wishing to station men to follow the business of fishing continuously, Conant was appointed their agent, and by his direction the settlers moved farther down the bay to Naumkeag (now Salem.)[2]

The Adventurers in England became discouraged, but Conant sustained his men, and, few as they were, they remained sentinels of Puritanism on the northern shore. To the eye of faith, mountains are chrystal and oceans nothing ; and old John White, the "patriarch of Dorchester" (England), saw these watchmen across the Atlantic. Zealous to spread the Gospel, and to establish his way, which was not tolerated in England, he set himself to interest others in the little Colony at Salem. Dudley, Johnson, Eaton, Saltonstall, Pyncheon, Bellingham, and others, men of substance and "gentlemen born," agreed to co-operate with him. So they purchased

[1] Hubbard (1625).

[2] White's Brief Relation. Young's Chronicles of the Pilgrims. Bancroft's Hist., vol. i., p. 339.

of the "Plymouth Company or Council for New England" (March 19, 1627–8), a strip of land, in width three miles, north of the Merrimack, and three miles south of the Charles River, and extending from ocean to ocean; and they were not likely to be crowded.

JOHN ENDICOTT.

But who should lead the new adventure? John Endicott was just the man, and he agreed to go. Firm, rugged, and hopeful, he took his wife and children, and went into the New World at the head of the company, numbering nigh one hundred souls.[1] (Sailed June 20, 1628, arrived Sept. 6.)

The forests were just beginning to dress themselves in their autumn brilliancy, when Endicott stepped from his boat to receive the welcome of Roger Conant.[2] Glad enough were the "sentinels" once more to press the hands and look into the faces of civilized men. Their hearts and cabins were open.

To build more houses, to explore the country, to treat the Indians well, and not to plant tobacco, were Endicott's orders.[3] His parties pierced the forests and coasted the shores. They were startled at Charlestown Neck, when they came upon the house and home of a solitary white man; for there Thomas Walford, an English blacksmith, had taken up his abode. On the promontory (now Boston) they found another, William Blackstone, who had come there to indulge his solitary humor. He was an English clergyman, fond of books and horticulture, and from him the settlers afterward purchased all the promontory, except his garden. He was a Puritan and liberalist, but he declined a Church connection. "No, no," he said; "I have not fled from the Lords bishops to be subject to the Lords brethren!" So he

[1] Johnson's Wonder-working Providence. Belknap's Biog. Prince, p. 249. Hubbard's History. Havens's Introduction.

[2] Memoir of John Endicott, by Charles M. Endicott: Salem, 1847.

[3] The savages were believed to be subjects of *saving* grace. Cradock's Letter in Young's Chronicles.

afterward moved away to the banks of the Pautucket, where he died (1675). David Thomson was at Thomson's Island, and Samuel Maverick was found on Nottles (or Noddles) Island, in Boston Harbor.

An excess of individuality marks the Teutonic races. These men could stand ALONE, and in no other way; they did not gather into cities because they were weak, or because they were social; but went out from men because they were strong, and could brook no restraint, not even that of society or family. This quality, when properly attempered, makes men kings, and nations great; it explores unknown and dreaded continents, and colonizes savage countries.

In June (1629), a party under the lead of Thomas Graves removed westward, and began a settlement called Charlestown.

THE CHARTER.

After much expenditure of time and money, on the fourth of March, 1629, a Royal Charter for the "Massachusetts Bay Company" had been obtained.[1] Matthew Cradock was chosen Governor in England, and John Endicott for New England. The ship which carried news of the Charter to the new world, carried also full instructions to Endicott, reiterating those already mentioned; commending to him the ministers Higginson, Skelton, and Bright, also the Browns; Waterman, a venison hunter, and Wilson, a surgeon; authorizing him to use force when necessary, and to expel the incorrigible; appointing that all should cease their labor at "three of the clock in the afternoon of Saturday, to prepare for the Sabbath," and urging kindness and honorable dealing toward the Indians.[1]

To allay the jealousies of the old settlers (Conant and his friends)—who naturally enough feared that they should sink into insignificance, and "that we seek to make slaves of them"—it was directed that they should be incorporated into the new Society, and enjoy all its privileges. It seems

[1] Prince, N. E. Chron., p. 247. [2] Young's Chron., p. 141. Hazard, vol. i.

too, that the first planters had an earnest desire to raise tobacco: Endicott was, therefore, directed to allow it for the present; though it was, as the letter strongly says: "A Trade by this whole Companie generally disavowed, and utterly disclaymed by some of the greatest Adventurers amongst us, who absolutely declared themselves unwilling to have Hand in this Plantacion, if wee intend to cherish or permit the planting thereof." In a subsequent letter this is reiterated thus: "We esspecially desire you to take care that noe Tobacco bee planted by any of the new Planters, under your Government, unless it bee some small quantity for meer necessity and for Physick for Preservation of their Health, and that the same bee taken privately by Antient Men and none other." One other point is thus urged upon Endicott: "And wee heartily pray you that all be kept to Labor, in their several employments. As the only means to reduce them to a civill, yea a godly life, and to keepe Youth from falling into many enormities which by nature wee are all too much inclyned unto." It was also directed that a Register should be kept "of what is done by all and every in each Familye," so that "noe idle Drone be permitted to live amongst us."

Some idea of the needs of a new country, which we can now hardly appreciate, may be got from this memorandum. Among the articles shipped for the uses of the colonists, we find enumerated—chalk, bricks, sea-coal, iron, lead, armor, drums, powder, cannon, soap, clothing of great variety, etc., etc.; and upon the Records of the Company a memorandum of things to be sent, which runs thus:

"Ministers,

"Patent under Seal,

"Seal,

"Men for making Pitch and Salt,

"Vine-dressers,

"Wheat, Rye, Barley, Currant-plants, Tame Turkeys,

* * * Brass-ladles, Spoons, Oil'd skins of leather,

Madder seeds," etc., etc. Such a list shows our complex condition, and the innumerable things needed to make up a civilized community—beginning with Ministers and ending with Madder seeds!

In the year 1629, nigh four hundred English Puritans arrived at Salem (let it be remembered that these were still members of the Church of England, though Nonconformists), among them four ministers. Higginson and Skelton were settled at Salem, and Smith afterward at Plymouth. Bright, the fourth, was a Conformist, and remained not in the new country. When they left England they forgot their sufferings and persecutions, and exclaimed —not "Farewell, Babylon! farewell, Rome!" but—"Farewell, dear England."[1]

Higginson and his companions found, in the great new country, room, and "A good company more of honest Christians," with their horses, kine, and sheep;[2] they found also some half score of houses ready built, and more in progress, they found much forests, but also many acres of land, which had been cleared by the Indians, planted in corn; plenty of wild turkeys, partridges, and other game; the sea stored with fish of many kinds; even the air was good to them, "A sup of it being better than a whole draft of old England's ale!" but the greatest comfort was that, "the true religion and holy ordinances of Almighty God" were taught among them; plenty of preaching, diligent catechizing, and strict exercise might be fully enjoyed; there was no let or hindrance. Among their discomforts were "musketoes, rattle-snakes, and Indians."[3]

These New England settlers were Puritans; but not Separatists, like those at Plymouth; they still belonged to the Church of England and declined the services of Smith, because he was a Separatist. But Governor Endicott had had some correspondence with Governor Bradford of Plymouth, to learn their views and usages as to

[1] Mather. [2] Forty cows, as many goats, a horse, and six or seven mares. Young's Chr., p. 260. [3] Young's Chronicles, p. 259.

outward worship, which he approved.[1] So when the Ministers came, the business was to set the Church in order.

For this purpose, the 6th of August, 1629, was kept, a day of fasting and high solemnity. Mr. Skelton, the pastor, laid his hands on the head of Mr. Higginson, the teacher, and so blessed him, Mr. Higginson did the same to Mr. Skelton; this was done though they had been ordained in England. In the afternoon Governor Bradford arrived, and gave them the right hand of fellowship. The Church entered into a Covenant one with another, brief, clear, and decided. One thing was made plain; that they had determined to stand where Bishop Hooper had stood before them—not upon a Creed, or a Council, or a Tradition, but "that the Holy Scriptures solely, and the Apostolic Church is to be followed, and no man's authority, be he Augustine, Tertullian, or even Cherubim or Seraphim!"[2]

"JOHN and SAMUEL BROWN, Gents," did not like the look of things. They asked, "Why is not the Book of Common Prayer used?" "Why is not the order of exercises the same as in the English Church?" "Why a new ordination?" "Why this?" and "Why that?"—to the disgust of the Governor and Ministers. The Browns pressed their point, and insisted upon the Prayer-book being read, which the settlers did not love; and at last Endicott called them before him. Being men of high spirit and bold speech (Lawyers and Merchants in England), they charged that the Colonists were "Separatists," if not even "Anabaptists," and that they must look to it. The ministers stoutly denied this, and claimed to be Church of England men, though Nonconformists. The Browns would not be quiet, so Endicott sent them back with the ships they came in, and got the matter out of New England.[3] Then for a time the Church had rest.

[1] Hubbard, p. 115. Hutchinson, vol. i., p. 11.

[2] Prince, 189, 191. Mather, vol. vi. Cheever, 294. Young's Chr. p. 61.

[3] Young's Chr., p. 288. Morton's Memorial.

CHAPTER XVIII.

THE CHARTER TRANSFERRED TO NEW ENGLAND.

CROMWELL, HAMPDEN, AND VANE—THE CHARTER—TRADING CORPORATION—QUESTION DISCUSSED—AGREEMENT OF SALTONSTALL, WINTHROP, ETC.—TRANSFER DECIDED ON—JOHN WINTHROP CHOSEN GOVERNOR—EFFECT OF THE TRANSFER.

THE good news from New England stimulated the Puritans and liberalists all over Old England. Charles I. and Laud were carrying things with a high hand. The Star Chamber and Ecclesiastical Courts were rampant, and the King determined to govern without a Parliament, and make England happy in spite of herself. Some of the first men of England believed that liberty must flee. Cromwell, Hampden, and Vane seriously considered the propriety of emigrating to New England; and other men of property and breeding believed that in England, religious and political rights were untenable. The insignificance of the Colony was, no doubt, the reason that Charles allowed it the privileges of a Royal Charter (4th March, 1629), the securing of which gave a new impulse to the desires and plans of the Puritans; and he and his ministers were willing to be rid of men who had both talents and conscience. This Charter empowered the Company (not the colonists) to transport persons, to establish ordinances, to settle Government (not contrary to English laws), to elect officers, to punish criminals, etc. It was a trading corporation, with the powers of Government. It did not guaranty religious liberty, nor did it contemplate it; and it was not till 1662[1] that the English King granted that, or that the Massachusetts Charter was made to favor freedom of worship; nor was it till after that time [1691]

[1] Bancroft, vol. i., p. 344. Hutchinson's Coll.

that it was enjoyed in the Massachusetts Colony. There was nothing to hinder the Puritans from carrying out their principles into practices ; this the Browns and some others saw, and that they would proceed to do it ; not so much upon a foregone determination, but because it was inevitable, from the absence of a hierarchy, or army, or other control ; and because it was inherent in the doctrine of "Private Judgment," which they claimed to follow.

But the point of interest which now claims attention, is of the first importance. The Charter secured to the Company certain rights. Now the question was asked, "Why not transfer the corporate body to New England ?" This was a novel and startling proposition, and might be pregnant of much. But, why not ? The question was started, and would not rest; and soon it engrossed all others. Finally it was brought before the Corporation. The Records of the Company, held at Mr. Goff's house, in London, on the 28th August, 1629, at which were present twenty-five members, state that, in full Court, two committees were appointed, of three each, one of which was to present the next day, arguments against, and the other in favor of settling the chief Government of the Company in New England.

This matter had been brought up for private and serious consideration, a month before, by Mathew Cradock, Governor of the Company ; and a few days before this action of the 28th of August, an agreement had been signed at Cambridge by Saltonstall, Winthrop, Dudley, Johnson, Humphrey, Nowell, Pincheon, Sharpe, Vassall, and some others, that they would embark with their families for New England, to inhabit there—*provided*, the Government and the Charter should be legally transferred and established in the Plantation. This proposed act certainly was a bold and important step ; the consequences might well be, as they have been, momentous. Its technical legality has been seriously doubted and denied. That the intention of the King was to make a trading corporation in England, there is no doubt ; but whether the meetings of the Company could not as well be held in New England as in Old England ? If they could, then such men as those named above, were ready to trust their lives there, and dying, leave their children in the new Continent.[1] On the 29th of August, 1629, the Company held a full meeting to hear the arguments, and to decide this question. After discussion and argument on both sides, the Deputy (Mr. Goff), put the question, when by the erection of hands, "it appeared by the general consent of the Company, that the Government and Patent should be settled in New England, and accordingly an order to be drawn up to that effect."[2]

ELECTION OF GOVERNOR.

Having signed articles of agreement, which were to govern matters between the settlers on the one hand, and the Joint-stock Adventurers at home, on the other, the Company met on the 20th of October, 1629, to elect a new Governor and Officers, from among those who were to go to New England. Mr. John Winthrop, out of four others mentioned, was chosen by a general vote, as one every way worthy, both for "integrity and sufficiency," for this first and most exalted post ; which he was pleased to accept, and took the oath. Mr. John Humphrey, or Humfry, was chosen Lieutenant-Governor, with eighteen Assistants, who were to form the Council. Dudley was afterward chosen in place of Mr. Humphrey.

What was to be the effect of this transfer of the Government from Old to New England, no one could altogether foresee. One result, and one of the greatest was, that it converted the Colonists slowly and imperceptibly from Englishmen to Americans ; and strengthened in them a sturdy independence and individuality, so inseparable from Teutonic nations.[3]

[1] See Grahame's History United States. Hutchinson's History Massachusetts, vol. i., p. 13.

[2] Young's Chronicles, p. 88. Gervinus: Introduction, p. 27.

Some of the best and purest of the gentlemen of Enland, only waited for this decision to confirm their wishes, and the emigration in the year following (1630), was some fifteen hundred. They came to possess the earth and civilize it, and they brought with them much good and little evil.

CHAPTER XIX.

THE SETTLEMENT OF BOSTON.

JOHN WINTHROP—HIS JOURNAL—HIS SHIPS SET SAIL—ENGLAND DID NOT REGRET—THEY REACH NEW ENGLAND—LAND AT NAUMKEAG—SUFFERING AND HOPE—CHARLES' RIVER—BOSTON—STARVATION—LADY ARBELLA JOHNSON—THOMAS MORTON IS CAPTURED AND SENT AWAY—BOAT LOST—SIR CHRISTOPHER GARDINER—PHILIP RATCLIFF—NIGHT FRIGHTS—WINTHROP LOST.

JOHN WINTHROP, the Father of Boston, was among those who came in 1630. His Journal, valuable alike to the historian and to the reader, opens:

"Anno Domini, 1630, March 29th, Monday" "Easter Monday, Riding at the Cowes, near the Isle of Wight, in the Arbella, a ship of Three hundred and fifty tons." This vessel was so named in honor of the Lady Arbella Johnson, daughter of the noble house of Lincoln; who, with her husband, was a passenger in the ship.

On that day, the 29th of March, 1630, they weighed anchor, spread their sails from Cowes, and sailed down the channel to Yarmouth; where they were joined by their consorts, the Talbot, the Jewel, and the Ambrose. Finally, on Thursday, the 8th of April, the ships sailed from Yarmouth, where the feet of those Pilgrims pressed the soil of their dear Old England for the last time. Sadness was in their hearts and tears in their eyes, for they loved the Land of their fathers; and they could not forget the tender associations of youth, nor the holier associations of manhood, when thus leaving it forever. But as the hart panteth, for the water-brooks, so their souls longed for Liberty and God, and they went out full of Hope. With a fair wind they passed the Needles, drew steadily away from those venerable shores; passed St. Albans, Portland,

Dartmouth, the Eddystone, with its fiery eye, watching for ships over the broad sea. The Lizard, and at last the Scilly Islands disappeared, went down day by day in the blue distance, and were left with the past, till on Sunday, the 11th, their little fleet, of nine sail, stood out bravely into the stormy Atlantic. They were prepared to buffet the winds and the waves, they knew whither they were bound, and they did not conceal from themselves their dangers and hardships. They had nerved their hearts, cleared their decks, and prepared their cannons and powder-chests; they had drilled their men and instructed their women, should pirates or enemies threaten. They had fasted and prayed, and then they went forth from the Past, where was knowledge and certainty, to the dim and shadowy Future; they trusted in themselves, and they trusted in the Lord of Hosts, and were strong.

England did not regret their departure, she did not know her best men! What nation does? To materialists and politicians, these men seemed to be visionaries and idealists; impracticable, and in the way. Yet this class is always the life of a nation. We can look BACK upon them and surfeit them with praise; but can not easily see them walking amongst us, and so learn to cherish not kill the Prophets. Through a varied but stormy passage, with much cold, they kept on their way, till on Tuesday, the 8th of June, there came a wild pigeon into their ship,[1] harbinger of land; which showed itself about three o'clock in the afternoon, to the North-west about ten leagues. Here they took many Codfish and Mackerel and refreshed their palates, after their long voyage of seventy days.

THEY REACH NEW ENGLAND.

On Saturday (12th June) they drew near their port—Salem—and shot off two pieces of ordnance as a signal of their coming. Shortly after they came to anchor, and their eyes dwelt upon the promised land. About two o'clock, Mr. Endi-

[1] Winthrop's Journal.

cott the Governor, and Mr. Skelton the Minister, with Captain Levett, came aboard, to give them a hearty welcome ; for they had common hopes and fears, were united in faith and practice, and pioneer-life brings out hospitality, heartiness, and good fellowship. So Winthrop, who had been chosen Governor in England, went on shore with Endicott, accompanied by some of the assistants and the women, to Nahumkeck (or Naumkeag), where they "supped with a good venison pasty aud good beer, and at night returned to their ship." In the mean time, many of the people on the ship went ashore at Cape Ann, "and gathered store of fine raspberries ;" and at evening an Indian came aboard, who spent the night and startled them by his dress and manners. He was their first savage, the wild man of the wilderness. So passed the first day on this New England shore.

Winthrop's arrival with friends and stores was none too soon. He found the colonists reduced to their last provisions ; many weak and sick ; some eighty having died in the winter before. The presence of new faces inspired their tired hearts with hope, and again the struggling Colony moved onward. Its beginning, so weak, might yet end in peace, plenty, and power. Who could tell ?[1] In the eleven ships starting with Winthrop, there were some seven hundred persons. It was necessary, therefore, to look into the resources of the country, to discover where it would be best to "set down." Salem was well, but might there not be better ? A party of explorers went up the bay (now Boston Harbor, June 14th, 1630), "made by a great company of islands, whose high cliffs shoulder out the sea ;"[2] and decided at last upon a spot on the Charles River (Newton or Cambridge), as a proper place to build a city. But the people were weak, and sick with fevers and scurvy, and they could not build a city. They lay in tents along the Charles River, and

[1] Winthrop's Journal ; Young's Chronicles, p. 311

[2] Dudley's Letter to the Countess of Lincoln. Hutchinson's History.

many of the poorer people suffered; till at last they planted themselves where they could, some at Charlestown, some at Medford, others at Watertown, Roxbury, Lynn, Dorchester, and a few on the neck now called Boston, which name they had intended to give their principal place; for this simple and good reason, namely: Among the Boston men who came to New England, were Mr. Cotton, Mr. Dudley, Mr. Bellingham, Mr. Leverett, Mr. Coddington, and Mr. Hough, and Boston was a prominent town in Lincolnshire, 116 miles north of London.

BOSTON.

So Shawmut or Trimountain was named Boston, which name it bears to this day; and the 17th of September (1630), is agreed upon as the date of its settlement. They set themselves to work in earnest to build houses, for the time was short till winter; but their trials were great; the dead-weight had to be overcome. Some cut down trees, some hewed and shaped the timbers; all hands were turned to account. Yet they labored under great disadvantages; wanting every thing, tools, materials, carts, and, above all, carpenters: for the carpenter is not inferior to the priest or poet. But they went forward, and though many sickened and died, and over a hundred, discouraged with so dreary an outlook, went back in the ships to England, the brave and stout-hearted staid and builded. They contracted with Captain Pierce, that he should return from England with all speed, and bring provisions and stores. But great suffering came upon them, and tradition loves to tell how Winthrop was dividing his last peck of meal with a starving man, when the white wings of a ship on the line of the ocean brought light and life to the wayfarers. Whether true or not, it is credible of noble human nature, such as Winthrop had. They had fasted in body, and had appointed a day of fasting in spirit; but the arrival of Captain Pierce changed it into Thanksgiving.[1] (5th February.)

[1] Hutchinson. vol. i., p. 23.

The ships having gone, the food decreasing, and the mortality increasing, they held fasts and prayed the Lord.[1] But he would not yet be placated; for Mr. Gager, a surgeon, a "right godly man," died (Sept., 1630); Mr. Higginson, one of the Ministers of Salem, died; the Lady Arbella Johnson also died; and at last died Mr. Johnson himself, one of the Undertakers, and one of their foremost men. From the time of their setting sail, in April, 1630, till December of the same year, there died about two hundred of their number.[2] 'Twas a fearful affliction; "so low had the Lord brought them!" For it was in this spirit that afflictions were borne; the right spirit too, provided it does not lead to fatalism, despair, and death.

LADY ARBELLA JOHNSON.

A halo of poetry lingers around the memory of Lady Arbella Johnson, wife of that well-known and well-loved Mr. Johnson, who spent his money and his talents in the service of the new Colony. The settlers had a respect for rank and birth, and at this period they did indicate breeding and superiority. The colonists loved her, and were proud of her aristocratic birth. The Lady Arbella was a daughter of the noble house of Lincoln. High born and fair, she came to the wilderness, a beautiful flower driven by the wild winds from her sheltered garden to this desolate shore. But she was generous, and strong in her love and sympathy for those with whom she lived. She shared in the excitements and privations incident to life in the wilderness, and though one of the first buried there, has left a memory that is embalmed in the hearts of the gentle and good.

What with famine, sickness, deaths, Church organizations and State settlements, building of houses and allotting of lands, hunting of deer and catching of fish, making friends of the Indians and trading for corn, thanksgiving for the past and prayers for the future—life was not dull, nor were the bodies, minds, and souls of

[1] Dudley's Letter to Countess of Lincoln. [2] Prince's Chronology.

the people idle. Other and more exciting incidents occasionally happened.

THOMAS MORTON, who had settled at "Merry-Mount," would live in his free, reckless way, fearing neither man nor God, as the Pilgrims thought; he would sell guns and fire-water to the Indians; he did not hesitate to "shoot hail-shot" into them, because they refused to bring him a canoe to cross the river. By doing such things he was discrediting all the whites, and giving the Indians both a cause and the means to be dangerous. The whole community were exercised, and, seizing Morton, they set him in the bilboes, burned his house to the ground in sight of the Indians, and sent him away prisoner to England.[1]

So, too, the story (December, 1630) went from mouth to mouth, how a company of six men and a girl, going in a boat to Plymouth, were driven out to sea by a storm, and losing their "Killock-stone," could not bring themselves to anchor; the next morning they were out of sight of land, and the cold increasing, there was nothing for them to do but to lie down and die; but one of the men, having heart and courage, kept looking for land, and spying it, he set the sail, and they were driven ashore about fifty miles from Plymouth; and meeting there with some Indians, got help toward Plymouth, where they were kindly cared for. Three of them died, however, and one Garvard, "was a godly man." All the other boats but this, "God had preserved."[2]

Sir CHRISTOPHER GARDINER too, calling himself a Knight of the Sepulcher, gave occasion for much gossip and scandal; for, instead of being a Knight, "he had two wives living in London," both of whom had written the Governor, one of them desiring his return and amendment, while the other only wished his destruction. He was an agent of Gorges, and sent by him to look into matters pertaining to his grants. When the men went to

[1] Dudley's Letter. [2] Dudley's Letter. Winthrop's Journal.

his house, some seven miles away to fetch him, he took his gun and disappeared in the woods; but, sad to tell, there was living with him one called his kinswoman, who was believed to be any thing but what she should be, "living with him after the Italian method." She, refusing to confess any more than she saw fit, much distressed the whole people, and, as no better way was hit upon for disposing of her, she was sent back "to the two wives in Old England, that they might search her further."[1]

So difficult was it to get away from the wickedness of Satan, who, even in this virgin land, and among these Puritan people, would thrust himself in where his company was no ways wanted. It was discovered that Gardiner was a papist, which was worse than all; and the Indians, having found him, came in to ask if they might kill him; but it was thought best to ship him away to England, where, with his three wives, and his "Italian method," and his popery, he would not poison Massachusetts. In 1631, Philip Ratcliff, agent for Governor Cradock, indulging in freedom of speech, pronounced harsh judgments on some of the authorities; also against the Churches. This could not be borne, and he was condemned to lose his ears. They were cut off. He was afterward whipped and banished, which processes did not serve to increase his love for the colonists. He hated them bitterly, and did them mischief in England.

And in March, 1631, one of the men of Watertown, having lost his calf, and hearing the wolves howling in the night, got up, and shot off his musket several times to frighten wolves; but the wind carrying the report to "Rocksbury," much frightened the people, so that they roused up themselves and beat-up their drum, and sent off to Boston for more help, for what could it mean? No doubt the Indians were coming! But next morning the calf was found safe, the wolves and the people being well frightened. The former had disappeared, and the latter

[1] Winthrop's Journal.

went "merrily to breakfast." This was a good joke, and one and another was quaintly rallied, how "great fear and trembling had come upon him, making all his bones to shake."[1] (Job, ch. iv., v. 14.)

And one afternoon the Governor (Winthrop) being out at his farm at Mistick, took his gun for a short walk; but it becoming suddenly dark, he could not find his way back, and was obliged to make up a fire, and spend the night in the woods, walking up and down, and "singing Psalms." He came safe home again the next morning, much to the delight of his servants, who had spent the night in hallooing, and shooting off guns, hoping that he might hear them.

These are among some of the unimportant incidents, which serve to show what the first life in the new world was.

[1] Dudley's Letter. Winthrop's Journal.

CHAPTER XX.

SETTLEMENTS AT THE TIME OF WINTHROP'S COMING.

THE NEW ENGLAND COAST—THE FRENCH AT ACADIA—MARYLAND—PLYMOUTH TRADING-HOUSE CAPTURED.

THE Settlements, when Winthrop arrived, were few and small.[1] Sir John Popham had attempted one in 1607 at Sagadehoc, near the mouth of the Kennebeck in Maine, but it proved a failure. Weston's, at Wessagusset, (now Weymouth) begun in 1622, had dispersed, as had that of Gorges, begun at the same place in 1623. Thomp-

[1] The "PLYMOUTH COUNCIL FOR NEW ENGLAND" were appointed by the King (Nov. 3), 1620, with powers to make grants and settlements in America, 1635. They seem to have granted with little care, as follows:

9 March, 1621–2, To Captain John Mason, from Salem River to Merrimack River, called Mariana.

10 Aug., 1622, To Mason and Ferdinando Gorges, between Merrimack and Sagadehock Rivers, called Laconia.

13 Dec., 1622, To Robert Gorges, 10 miles by 30 miles square on Mass. Bay. (No use was ever made of this.)

19 March, 1627–8, To the "Massachusetts Company," between 3 miles south of the Charles, and three miles north of the Merrimack Rivers. (Settlements were attempted upon the above grants.)

1630. To the Earl of Warwick (what is now Connecticut), afterward purchased by Lords Say and others. (Title questioned.)

7 Nov., 1629, To John Mason, between Merrimack and Piscataqua Rivers.

1631. To Mason and Gorges, a re-grant of portions of what was granted before.

1635–6. To the Marquis of Hamilton, some part of Connecticut.

April, 1635. To John Mason, from Naumkeag to Piscataqua River (New Hampshire.)

1635. To Ferdinando Gorges, between Kennebeck and New Hampshire, (B.)

1635. The Great Patent was surrendered to the Crown.

son's settlement, with the Hiltons, at the mouth of the Piscataqua, New Hampshire, begun in 1623, had come to nothing. There was a small settlement at Cape Ann (Gloucester) and one at Nantasket (Hull) ; both begun in 1624. Winisimet (Chelsea) was begun in 1627, and Naumkeag (Salem) in 1627. Wollaston's Company, who were at Quincey in 1625, held on for some time after the arrival of Endicott in 1628, under the lead of Thomas Morton. Roger Clap, and a few others, had been set ashore (May, 1630) by the Captain of the ship "Mary and John," and had worked up to the Dorchester fields, where they had begun a settlement.

The Plymouth Settlement had sustained itself. It may be well to remember, that none of the settlements, inspired merely with an eye to trade, had been able to sustain themselves against all obstacles and reverses. Both the Plymouth and Massachusetts Bay settlers were strong in the hope of establishing their religious opinions and worship ; and they struck their roots deep and grew vigorously, if slowly.

The French had been hovering over the coast since they had been routed from Lacady (Nova Scotia—Acadia) in 1613, by Sir Samuel Argall, but with small results.[1] During the war between England and France, in 1628, Port Royal had fallen into the hands of the English, and in the next year, Quebec was taken by them ; the brave Champlain welcoming the English as saviors from starvation. In 1632 news came of the selling of Canada and Lacady, by Charles I. (in 1629) to the King of France. Thus Richelieu came to possess "one of the finest provinces of the known world for fishery, masts, and harbors,"[2] while Charles was busy about church ceremonies and court tailoring.

[1] In 1603, Henry IV. of France had granted to De Monts the territory of L'Acadie—extending from 40° to 46° of north latitude, with power to subdue and Christianize the inhabitants.

[2] Prince's Annals. Hutchinson, vol. i., p. 28. Bancroft, vol. i., p. 325. Belknap's Biography and Annals ; De Monts.

Other news, too, came to the colonists, how the king had granted to Lord Baltimore, a "papist," a large seignory, to be called Maryland, with power, and prerogatives greater than ever before bestowed. These were grievous tidings, foreshadows of evil. But mingled with them, came the sound of the great Gustavus's guns, who fought in Germany for the Protestant faith, and overran Pomerania, Bavaria, and Swabia, beating the conqueror Tilly in a hundred battles. The Calvinists and Protestants gave thanks and praised the Lord;[1] till at last, at the fatal battle of Lutzen (Nov. 6, 1632), the star of the Swedish king set in blood, and the faces of the Protestants were darkened.

The French, however, gave the planters but little trouble, till a party of them (June 1632),[2] in a small vessel, came down to the trading-house of the Plymouth Company, at Penobscot; and finding most of their men away, after many "congees" and soft phrases, borrowing the guns which were racked there meanwhile, they took violent possession of some £400 or £500 of beaver and goods, and sailed away, leaving their respects only for the master. Prince says they were led on by a false Scot ("I suppose a Papist"), to do this very impolite deed. The French commander afterward took and kept possession of the place, giving the Plymouth men "bills for the goods," who did not recover the place.[3]

The French were unable in the end, to cope with these religious English, though they held Canada and Nova Scotia for more than a century, and strung a chain of forts and stations westward, along the Lakes to the valley of the Mississippi.[4]

[1] Winthrop, vol. i., p, 90. [2] Prince's Chron.

[3] Hubbard's History, p. 162.

[4] See Chapter on the French in America, vol. ii.

CHAPTER XXI.

FORTIFIED TOWN.

NEWTOWN—CAMBRIDGE—EMIGRATION—THE SHIPS STAYED—CHARTER RECALLED—NUMBERS WHO CAME—INDIAN CORN—WINTER—CLIMATE.

THERE were reasons enough why the Massachusetts settlers should build an inclosed and fortified town. They consulted together and decided to do it ; for what might they not have to fear from Indians and enemies ? So in the winter of 1630–31, they began their houses at Newtown (Cambridge). Deputy-Governor Dudley framed and finished his house there, and Governor Winthrop began his ; but time brought changes, and Winthrop took down his frame and set it up at Boston ; which was a disappointment, and the beginning of heart-burnings between Dudley and Winthrop, that in the end came to a heat. Winthrop's good sense led him to think that Boston promontory possessed advantages, and that it was unwise to waste their little strength in fortifications. They afterward renewed their plan and palisaded Newtown, fearing the Indians.

The tide of emigration seemed to flow and ebb ; through 1630 it was at the flood ; in 1631 it nearly ceased. Climate and the sufferings of settlers were against free emigration ; and besides, Morton, Ratcliff, and Gardiner were busy in England against the Colonists. In 1631 only ninety persons came over. But again, in 1632, the current set westward ; the colonists not having been molested, and Laud's pesterings in England increasing in virulence, many ships then prepared to start, and some of England's best men were about deserting her; among them the Lords Say, Seal, and Rich, John Hampden, Saltonstall, Pym, Cromwell, and the younger Vane; when, on the 21st February, 1633, the king in council issued an order to stay the ships, and directed Mr. Cradock to cause the Charter to be returned. It might have been well for the king if he had helped them to go; he hindered, but did not press the matter, and the emigration was not all stayed; but before the year 1640 the prospect of reform in England, caused men to stay there, "in hopes of a new world."

NUMBERS WHO HAD COME OVER.

By the year 1640 (when the flush of emigration ceased) some four thousand families and twenty thousand persons, had come into New England, as was supposed.[1] False and narrow men were among them, but the quality generally was good. The persons wanted were: first, merchants skilled in commerce; second, seamen; third, husbandmen; fourth, all manual occupations, "only printers of cards and dice-makers I could wish to forbear."[2] Drones and broken-down gentlemen and scheming adventurers, were not wanted in this new land, and the temptations at first were not sufficient to bring them over. No doubt the troubles of getting under way were hard to bear, but nothing can stand against a bold determination. Once or twice they suffered for want of food, but the bays and rivers were full of fish and fowl, and their resources were soon ample. INDIAN CORN was their staple grain. They found some cleared fields, where the Indians had raised it, and from them they learned the simple methods of cultivation; for some years, they had only their hands and their hoes with which to tear up the stubborn Massachusetts soil, but the bounty of God is great, and this grain yielded abundantly even with such scant tillage. Now and then (1632) a wet and dark and cold summer cut it short; when a long dreary winter opened before them, like the Valley of

[1] Hutchinson, vol. i., p. 93. This is probably an over-estimate.

[2] Good News from New England: Mass. Hist. Coll. 4th Series.

the Shadow of Death; spring, and heaven, and sunshine, and joy, were on the other side, but how should they reach them? Few of them turned back; they trusted in their hands and hearts and went forward on their way.

An idea prevailed there, that WINTER broke up on the 10th day of February, and that for years he had held himself to this day—unlocking then his icy jaws. Every tenth year, too, was very mild; so the Indians said.[1] All the early writers found it necessary to show how good the climate was.

Upon this matter of climate, a strange hallucination exists—most persons being quite certain, that somewhere there exists a climate whose heat is freshness, and whose frost is mildness; whose winds are balmy breezes, whose dews are dropping honey; where the fever of life is tempered, the throbbing of the tender nerves stilled; where sleep is sweet, and waking cheery; where health overflows, and knowledge and control are unnecessary; where happiness is a satiety, and life only a present pleasure and a future hope. With such expectations, no one finds his own climate exactly what is needed for perfect development, and of course all his short-comings are laid on its broad shoulders.

The early writers of New England did not take such a view of their climate. They needed settlers and friends, and their climate seemed almost perfect. Wood had been "carefully hatched," yet had pleurisy and disease sapped his life in England; while in New England, "scarce did I know what belonged to a day's sickness."[2] A short account by another hand, will well enough illustrate the different eyes of observers. A Church of England man says: "In New England, the transitions from heat to cold are short and sudden, and the extremes of both very sensible. We are sometimes frying, and at others freezing; and as men often die at their labor in the field, by heat, so some in winter are froze to death with the cold."

[1] Wood's N. E. Prospect, p. 4.

[2] Page 11.

"As from my lands (in Rhode Island) I can see the Atlantic Ocean, I have seen it froze as far as the human eye could reach; and 'tis common in a beautiful salt lake that fronts my farm, to have the ice three feet thick every winter."[1]

The Puritan saw the good, the Churchman the evil, of the country.

[1] America Dissected. 1752. By James Macsparren, "a Clergyman there."

CHAPTER XXII.

WINTHROP, DUDLEY, VANE, AND ENDICOTT.

WINTHROP—HE AND DUDLEY QUARREL—ROTATION IN OFFICE—THE REPRESENTATIVE SYSTEM—DUDLEY—JOHN HAYNES—THE QUARREL REVIVES—VANE CHOSEN GOVERNOR, 1636—DANGER OF ELECTION RIOTS—VANE DEFEATED—SIR HARRY VANE—VANE ADVOCATES TOLERATION—MRS. HUTCHINSON—VANE RETURNS TO ENGLAND—TAKES THE REPUBLICAN SIDE—HE AND CROMWELL QUARREL—VANE'S CHARACTER—IS BEHEADED—ENDICOTT.

JOHN WINTHROP was the model man of Boston. He was rich, well educated, gentlemanly; he was dignified and pure-minded. He was in the prime of life and in the fullness of his powers, when he came to Massachusetts in 1630—being forty-three years old. He had some knowledge of the Law, and had been chosen Governor by the Company in England. Possessed of an estate worth some £700 a year, he was able to devote his time and talents to the service of the State; and having a mild and generous disposition, was disinclined to harshness and severity, and disposed at the outset to leave society to work out its own shape—such seeming to him the wiser course. But this did not suit the more rigorous views of such as Dudley and Endicott, who were for compelling uniformity. With his accustomed pliancy, Winthrop yielded too much, and gave way to others, in the persecutions which were carried on against Roger Williams, Mrs. Hutchinson, and Minister Wheelwright. But his kindness of heart rarely deserted him, and he wrote privately to Williams to sustain and encourage him, after he had fled.[1] Winthrop was a conservative, and feared to trust the people far; which will in some degree serve to explain his readiness to acqui-

[1] See Chap. xxv.

esce in measures which his heart condemned. Yet he was by no means incapable of anger, nor always weak in an emergency. In his dispute with Dudley, he got into a round passion, and used as high words as Dudley did; but he was magnanimous and generous, and ready to forgive and forget. The avidity with which the people left him, in 1636, to seize upon young Sir Harry Vane, to elevate him to the post of Governor, mortified and disturbed him; but he waited his time, regained his place in the popular favor, and through life was the first man in Massachusetts. His private life was charming, and his letters to his wife, who remained for a time in England, are full of the tenderest sympathy and love. But she died, and he afterward [1647] married Martha Coytemore, the relict of Thomas Coytemore.[1]

[1] The inventory of the property of the rich widow, is worth preserving, as a sign of those times:

Item	£	s.	d.
"A parcell of books, £7 8*s.* 8*d.*, a feather bed and boulster, £3, together,	£10	8	8
"A bed steed, trundle bed, with roapes and mats,	1	10	0
"2 pr. striped curtens, and valance, and green rug,	2	10	0
"1 feather bed, flock, boulster, pillow, blankets, red rug, and trundle bed,	1	15	0
"A pr. brass hollow andirons, fire-shovell, tongs, and creepers,	1	15	0
"A ciprus chest, £2 10*s.*, 7 pr. Holland sheets, £10,	12	10	0
"3 diaper table cloathes, 3½ duss. napkins, 2 cold. clothes, and a damask napkin,	7	10	0
"4 pr. Holland pillow bears, 3 cold. clothes, 1 duss. napkins, 2 towels,	3	5	0
"3½ duss. napkins, £1 12*s.* 6*d.*, 2 pr. sheets and 1 pr. pillow beers, £1 6*s.*,	2	18	6
"1 pr. striped silke curtens and valence, 5 windo curtens, 2 windo cloths, 1 cold. cloth, and chimney do.,	5	0	0
"1 green cloth carpet, 1 cold. do., 1 chimney, do., and a little table cloth,	3	10	0
"1 silk red and green quilt, £2 10*s.*, a little Turkey carpet, £1 6*s.*,	3	16	0
"A suite of red tabie, £3, 54¾ oz. of plate, at 4*s.* 6d., being half—whole, £12 6*s.* 4*d.*,	15	6	4
"A parcel of cheney plates and saucers, £1, 1 trunk, 2 flaskets, 4 cases, 12*s.*,	1	12	0
"A meridian compass, and etc., etc.,	1	14	0

Winthrop was subject to many griefs, first in the loss of his wife, then of his children, and then of his property, through unfaithful agents; he died at the early age of sixty-two. He left us the most faithful and valuable history of that early time, extending from 1630 to 1648. It is well, and in great part, fairly written, and is a fitting monument of his own life. The following sketch of his character, by Cotton Mather, will show how fulsome the praise of the pulpit was:

"Our *New England* shall tell and boast of her WINTHROP, a *lawgiver* as patient as *Lycurgus*, but not admitting any of *his* criminal disorders; as devout as *Numa*, but not liable to any of *his* heathenish madnesses; a *Governour* in whom the excellencies of *Christianity* made a most improving addition unto the *virtues*, wherein even without *those* he would have made a *parallel* for the great men of *Greece*, or of *Rome*, which the pen of a *Plutarch* has eternized." The emphasis to this character is here preserved, as it is left to us, in the Magnalia. (Vol. i., p. 109.)

Winthrop and Dudley were for some years the two leading men in the settlement. This grew out of their superior wealth, education, and talents. The first had been chosen Governor, and the other Deputy, which places they held until 1634; when Dudley was advanced to be Governor. Winthrop was the calmer man of the two, from temperament as well as from his discipline; but Dudley was a positive man, downright and upright, and did not always look with patience upon the cautious, if not temporizing ways of Winthrop.

"An old coverlet tent, 26½ lbs. powder, at 20*d*. per lb.,	£2	18	2
"2 brasse skellets, 2 spits, 1 jack, 1 stewpan, £2 6*s*., halfe the farther Mill, £100,	102	6	0
"Land beside all apportioned to yᵉ child, £12 10*s*., a tapestry coverlet, £1 6*s*.,	13	16	0
"12 leather chayres, £1 10*s*., 2 ould coverlets, etc.,	4	11	0
And so on in detail, amounting in all to	£620	10	8

In April, 1632, Dudley had resigned his office in displeasure, and in May (1), the Governor and Assistants met at Boston to consider of it; they all maintained that he could not do it, except by consent of the power that put him there, which he did not agree to. But the meeting went on to discuss Dudley's bargains; selling seven and a half bushels of corn to receive ten for it at harvest, was held by the Governor and others to be usurious; this Dudley resented sharply; then came up the matter of Dudley's house, which Winthrop had cautioned him, about adorning and wainscotting so much, in the beginning of a new Colony. This was before dinner, and there were high words. After it, a hot discussion was held about the propriety of allowing the whole body of freemen to vote in the election of Governor.[1] And on the 8th of May, it was agreed by the General Court, that the Governor and Assistants should be chosen anew every year, by the General Court. At this time, Winthrop and Dudley were reconciled, and "things were carried on very lovingly," and the "people" carried themselves with much silence and modesty. But the differences between Winthrop and Dudley were not so ended. Dudley brought his discontent with Winthrop (who he thought took too much upon himself), before the Ministers convened at Charlestown, August 6, 1632. After prayer, the Deputy stated his grievances, some of which, the Ministers allowed against Winthrop. But after dinner, when Dudley charged that he had exceeded his authority, the Governor claimed that the Patent gave him whatever belonged to a Governor by Common-law, or the Statutes, etc.; then the Deputy began to be in a passion, "and told the Governor that if he were so round he would be round too. The Governor bade him be round if he would. So the Deputy rose up in great fury and passion, and the Governor grew very hot also, as they both

WINTHROP AND DUDLEY'S QUARREL.

[1] Winthrop's Journal.

fell into bitterness; but by mediation of the mediators they were soon pacified."[1]

In May, 1634, Dudley was chosen Governor, "rotation in office" beginning to assert itself as the rule. At this Court, too, it was voted that Towns might send delegates to three of the four General Courts—the whole body of freemen only being required to vote at the election; thus arose out of their necessity the Representative system.

THOMAS DUDLEY had reached the ripe age of fifty-four when he came to New England, in 1630. He was well in years to undertake such a strange and arduous service as the planting of a new Colony. But he was a robust man, had been a soldier; and stimulated by the principles of the Puritans, he took hold of the new enterprise with vigor and determination. In England he had been the business-man of the Earl of Northampton, and had restored order to his disordered estates, and ease to his damaged finances. Dudley was a man of rugged honesty and blunt manners, impatient of control or opposition; he never stooped to conciliate others, but drove on his own way, and was what might be called a hard, prejudiced man; but he was incapable of deceit or meanness, and was worth a thousand time-serving politicians, in the infancy of that new State. He was at various times intrusted with the highest interests of the Colony. He sternly opposed Mrs. Hutchinson, and was ready to sacrifice his Minister, Mr. Cotton, rather than yield to those who claimed religious toleration. Being a man of property, he was much respected, but not loved by his fellow-citizens. He lived to the ripe age of seventy-seven, and died in 1653.

To continue the "rotation," John Haynes was chosen Governor in 1635. He was followed by Sir Harry Vane, 1636, who had shortly before came to the country. When Winthrop was succeeded by Dudley, he did not altogether escape censure; the fact that Winthrop was then examined is well, for no man need be so great, that what-

[1] Winthrop's Journal.

ever he does is presumed to be right, because he does it. But Winthrop left his post with dignity and untarnished integrity; and he might have torn his books of accounts, as Scipio Africanus did, and said, "A flourishing Colony has been led out and settled under my direction. I have spent myself and my fortune in its service. Waste no more time in harangues, but give thanks to God."[1]

The old differences between Winthrop and Dudley smoldered, breaking out from time to time into flame and faction. Sir Harry Vane and Hugh Peters (who came over in Oct. 1635) brought them and the authorities together, when it seemed the difficulty resolved itself into the over-leniency of Winthrop, and over-severity of Dudley. The matter was fully discussed, and put to vote, and the vote was against Winthrop. Winthrop expressed himself convinced, and promised to exercise more strictness hereafter. Their differences were satisfactorily settled, and they lived "lovingly together" after that, Winthrop continuing (after 1636) to be chosen Governor till his death, March 26th, 1649.[2]

In 1635 came over Sir Harry Vane, the Minister Mr. John Cotton, and Mrs. Anne Hutchinson, three of the most remarkable persons in the early days of New England, between whom there was a strong sympathy, especially in religious tendencies. The advent of Vane was looked upon with great favor; for he was a man of birth, wealth, and decided talent, with strong religious ideas tending to Puritanism, and reform in Church and State. His manners and conversation commended him to the people in the Colony, and he was at once elected Governor in May, 1636. For a few months things went on well, till Mrs. Hutchinson, "the masterpiece of woman's wit," as the orthodox Johnson called her, developed her doctrines, and found friends and supporters in Vane and Cotton. A powerful party was formed against her, and against Vane and Cot-

VANE CHOSEN GOVERNOR.

[1] Hutchinson, vol. i., p. 40.

[2] Mather's Magnalia.

ton, while nearly the whole of Boston town, where Cotton was Minister, were staunch in his support. Mrs. Hutchinson went down before the tempest, and was banished, as was the Minister Wheelwright, her brother-in-law.[1]

The people in Boston resented this severity, and at the General Court in May, 1637, sent up their petition regarding liberties, which Vane the Governor proposed to read before going to election. Winthrop, then Deputy, objected, because it would consume time, and lead to discussion ; but Vane persisted, and both parties grew hot. Wilson, the Minister, mounted into a tree, and harangued the people, who were pretty nearly divided between the new and the old ; but many came from a distance, and wished to have done, and so go home, and they cried out, "Election ! election !" and there was great danger of a riot that day. Vane carried himself stiffly, and was stung with this change in the breeze of popularity. Deputy Winthrop declared that if he, Vane, did not order the election, he, Winthrop, would ; whereupon he did, and Winthrop was elected Governor. This defeat mortified Vane, and it was not long before he returned to England.

SIR HARRY VANE.

It is a singular fact in the history of New England, that, among the pioneers, were such men as Henry Vane, well-born, well-bred, and in his case able to command at home a splendid career. New England may well claim him as one who spoke and acted there the doctrines of Civil and Religious Liberty ; doctrines in advance of the time, but which have since established themselves through the whole land. When in 1635 Vane came to Boston, he was but twenty-three years old, and though his father held a high position at Court, and Vane was in the midst of that gay life, he was then a Puritan. But, more than that, at that early age, he held to the principles of Universal Toleration, and full liberty to all religious sects.

[1] See ch. xxxi.

Knowing him as a person of high birth, and as holding the principles of the Puritans against the will of his father, the settlers in Massachusetts Bay welcomed him among them with open arms. As they knew him better, they liked him better ; he was soon the most popular man of Boston, and in the next year was elected Governor, over the heads of the older men, such as Winthrop and Dudley, which they might naturally look upon as a freak of popular favor quite uncalled for. The administration of Governor Vane was at first peaceable and regular enough ; but an opportunity only was needed to develop the seeds of jealousy and distrust. The first question arose upon the displaying of the King's flag at the King's fort in the harbor. The Ministers and most of the Council opposed it, for it contained the Cross, symbol of the idolatrous popish church ; and only Vane and Dudley favored its being raised. Vane assumed the responsibility, and ordered the colors to be raised. Vane seems to have favored the plan of kindness and conciliation towards the Indians, and to have concerted with Roger Williams to continue peace. But the quarrel was already begun, which never was quieted, and which finally culminated in the destructive King Philip's war.

But it was in the famous Antinomian Controversy with Mrs. Hutchinson (see ch. xxxi. vol. i.,) that Vane was wrecked. He and Cotton both sustained her in some of her principal views. They were opposed by the whole body of the Clergy, and by most of the older Magistrates, and by a majority of the people ; and although Boston supported Vane and Cotton, Vane went down before the violence of the opposition, and Cotton yielded. Winthrop being chosen Governor, a singular law was passed (1637) forbidding any new comer to inhabit in the Jurisdiction, unless he should be allowed by some one of the Magistrates. Winthrop felt obliged to defend this law publicly. Vane wrote against it, and took the broadest ground for freedom—positions equal to those of Roger

Williams and John Milton. But party-spirit ran high, and even Winthrop then was bitter, though afterward his magnanimous temper led him to do justice to Vane.

Vane shortly after this sailed for England, believing his opportunities for usefulness in the Colony at an end. But it was not until the meeting of the Long Parliament (Nov. 1640), that he was able to bring his talents or principles to bear in England. Then he enlisted among the opponents of the arbitrary plans of Charles I., Strafford, and Laud ; and was among the most earnest and talented of that earnest and talented band in which Pym, Eliot, and Hampden, were conspicuous. During his public career, he lost no opportunity for showing his interest in the Colonies, and to him Roger Williams expressed his thanks for the favor shown him in England. When the civil war broke out, Vane took a leading part in all negotiations and public matters ; always on the republican side. At last, when it was clear to Cromwell that Charles would be restored by the votes of the Parliament, he turned it out of doors—applied the "Pride's Purge," as it was called. Although Vane opposed the king, he did not hesitate to oppose this action also, and for a time he took no part in public affairs. After the death of the king, Cromwell induced him to use his talents for the service of the government ; where he was indefatigable, until he and Cromwell quarreled (1653). It is not necessary to follow him step by step to his death on the scaffold.

The character of Vane was pervaded by a profound religious sensibility, which has given rise to the most extravagant charges. His tendencies were toward Calvinism, but he seems to have been a Spiritualist, who subordinated ordinances and forms to the purer instincts of the soul ; when under the influence of those lofty impressions, his style and manner were liable to misconstruction, and by common-place minds he was called an enthusiast and a fanatic. His memory has been traduced by royalist historians, and, as with Cromwell, it is safe for us not to depend upon them. One of the best of them (Hallam) thus speaks of Vane:

"The Royalists have spoken of Vane with extreme dislike; yet it should be remembered that he was not only incorrupt, but disinterested; inflexible in conforming his public conduct to his principles; and averse to every sanguinary and oppressive measure; qualities not very common in revolutionary chiefs." (See Upham's Life of Vane.)

He perished on the scaffold, after the Restoration of Charles II., being then, June 1662, fifty-two years old. He died a victim of the enemies of liberty, but as a royalist present said: "He died like a prince;" certainly like a brave man as he was, and as princes sometimes are not. Standing on the scaffold, he said: "Bless the Lord, I am far from being affrighted at death. Ten thousand deaths rather than defile my conscience, the chastity and purity of which I value beyond all the world."[1]

Winthrop died in 1649: Dudley, in 1653: then, till his death (1665), the honors of Governor fell upon the rugged, but kind old Endicott: then on Sir Richard Bellingham till 1672; on John Leverett, till 1678; on Simon Bradstreet, till the shipwreck of the Charters (about 1685).[2]

"Governor Endicott was, undoubtedly, the finest specimen of the genuine Puritan character to be found among the early Governors; he was quick of temper, with strong religious feelings moulded in the sterner features of Calvinism; resolute to uphold with the sword what he had received as Gospel truth; and fearing no enemy so much as a gainsaying spirit. Cordially disliking the English Church, he banished the Browns and the prayer-book; and, averse to all ceremonies and symbols, the cross in the king's colors was an abomination he could not away with. He cut down the May-pole at Merry-mount, published his detestation of long hair in a formal proclamation, and set

[1] Mather's Magnalia, vol. i., p. 125 [2] Ibid., vol. i., p. 127.

in the pillory and on the gallows, the returning Quakers. Inferior to Winthrop in learning—in comprehensiveness, to Vane—in tolerance, even to Dudley—he excelled them all in the keen eye to discern the fit moment for action, and in the quick resolve to profit by it, and in the hand always ready to strike." (Hubbard's Remarks in Belknap's American Biography.)

CHAPTER XXIII.

THE GOVERNMENT.

THEOCRACY—THE MINISTERS—PRIEST AND KING—THE LAW OF ORDER—DEMOCRACY—WHO OWNED THE LAND—JOINT STOCK—COMMON STOCK—GOVERNOR AND ASSISTANTS—FIRST COURT—CHURCH-MEMBERS, FREEMEN—TAXES—THE FIRST LEGISLATURE—TWO HOUSES—THE SOW BUSINESS—FOUR COURTS—THE BALLOT—WRITTEN LAWS—"BODY OF LIBERTIES"—MUNICIPAL GOVERNMENT—TOWN MEETINGS—"SELECT-MEN"—MILITARY AFFAIRS—"TRAINING-DAY."

THE first intention of government, in the Massachusetts and New Haven Colonies, was to establish a Theocracy, to insure the rule of the saints; and the first legislation was, in a good degree, intended to promote religion. This idea was not peculiar to them; they looked to the Mosaic code, and found the model which they intended to follow; but they slowly came to learn that it was a going backward. But this idea gave to the clergy a mighty influence in the Colony, and stamped the character of the State.

The colonists appealed to God—to the highest law; and who should know that so well as the clergy? The Ministers were above the average in education and moral worth; yet we shall see how regard for their order, jealousy lest it should be weakened, and a deference to the customs of the Jews, changed them at times from kindly men into bloody persecutors; how they became unjust, ungenerous in religious matters, and how they urged the persecutions against Williams, and Wheelwright, and Mrs. Hutchinson, and Gorton, and imbrued their hands in the blood of the Quakers, and of those poor people termed Salem witches; and how this vitiated their intellects and poisoned their sympathies. They were in a false position, and were themselves the victims of the mistaken notion, that they alone knew the counsel of God.

History shows us, that when the world was young, Priest and King were united in the same person; and that, so soon as the offices were separated, a struggle for power went on between the two—the one attempting to legislate for the soul, the other for the body; till, with here and there a rare exception, they joined hands to sustain one another, and thus keep their feet on the necks of the poor, the ignorant, and the laborious. Nowhere has the power and duty of Self-Government in Church or State been forced back by Priest or King upon the people. Wherever man has made head against despotism, and asserted the rights of the individual, against the Camp, the Court, or the Church, it has been through struggle, destruction, and death; through Revolution, not through Conservatism. But, nevertheless, the rights of the individual (Self-Government, Democracy), have slowly made their way, as they must continue to do. Thus Cranmer, and Hooker, and Jewel asserted their independence of the Pope; thus the Puritans stood up against the English Church; thus Roger Williams refused to yield to the Churches in the Bay; and thus now—thanks to their rebellious fathers—is it the unquestioned right of every man in New England to decide for himself in all matters of Church or State, and, having decided, to ACT. It seems clear that this is the inevitable outcome of manhood, and that there can be no other way of working toward a sound and satisfactory future.

It was a great thing in the march of freedom, that this fertile and varied country was opened, just when Luther and the Reformers had fulminated their ideas, against the old superstitions and dying despotism of Rome; for there were here no rigid customs to be overcome, no foregone conclusions to impede a progress to future freedom, sure, if slow.

THE LAW OF ORDER.

We have seen at Plymouth how the better men, on board the Mayflower, were constrained, unwillingly, to grant civil rights to their servants. We shall see how the people (the Church-members) in Massachusetts came to take and keep powers which even Winthrop (the most liberal of the Magistrates) believed to be dangerous; and how the people (the mob) have taken the powers from the Church-members alone, and now exercise them in common; and yet Massachusetts has not gone to anarchy! For there is a law, higher than man's, which forbids that; it is God's law of ORDER. They did not there contemplate a government by all the people, and in their answers to the proposals of Lord Say and others,[1] they say, it is clear from Nature and Scripture, "that there are two ranks of men—one 'gentlemen,' and the other 'freeholders;' and that the principal business of Governing should belong to the former." The Reverend Cotton, the leading mind at one time in the Bay, in his letter to Lord Say (1636), stated clearly:—"Democracy, I do not conceive that ever God did ordeyne as a fitt Government, eyther for Church or Commonwealth. If the people be governors, who shall be governed?"

WHO OWNED THE LAND.

It is a question of some consequence to ask, and to answer: "Who owned the land? In whom was the title vested?" The Charter granted by King Charles (March 4, 1629), through the intercession of Lord Dorchester, distinctly gave it to the patentees called the Massachusetts Company:—"To be holden by them, their heirs and assignees, in free and common soccage, as of the manor of East Greenwich: paying, in lieu of all services, one fifth of the gold and silver that should be found."

This was the conventional way of conveying wild lands to the subject; and was then held and believed to be a good and sufficient title. The Company therefore considered themselves the owners of this land, fully competent to sell or regrant it, at pleasure. It should be remembered, that the Puritans took pains also to purchase a title from the Indian occupants.

[1] See Hutchinson's Appendix, vol. i.

THE JOINT-STOCK.

To carry out the plans of the Massachusetts Company, it was necessary to have money, and various of those interested in England, had subscribed to a Joint-stock for that purpose. This Joint-stock Company were to have the trade in Beaver for seven years, to reimburse their expenditures, and they were to pay half the expenses of Fortifications and of Ministers. The business of this Company afterward went into the control of some ten of the principal men interested, who were called "The Undertakers." These were John Winthrop, Sir Richard Saltonstall, Isaac Johnson, Thomas Dudley, John Revell, Mathew Cradock, Nathaniel Wright, Theophilus Eaton, Thomas Goff, and James Young. They were to transport passengers at five pounds each, and freights at four pounds per ton. They were also to furnish goods to planters at twenty-five per cent. advance. Beside this, a "COMMON STOCK" was raised (February, 1630) by subscription, among the friends of the enterprise, which was to be applied to the payment of Ministers, to the transporting of poor families, to the building of churches, etc.; and for every fifty pounds so subscribed and paid, two hundred acres of land were allowed in the Colony.[1]

The King's Charter provided for the election of a Governor and Assistants, called Magistrates, by the members of the Company, or the Freemen. This body was to be the Law-maker and Executive; and the formation of a Legislature, or a body of delegates from the people, was not contemplated.

There seems to have been, at first, a doubt as to the relative powers of the Governors, Endicott and Winthrop; and it was not until August that Winthrop began to exercise authority. Then the form of an election was gone through with in Massachusetts, when Winthrop was chosen Governor, Dudley, Deputy-Governor, and Bradstreet, Secretary.

[1] Drake's History of Boston, p. 76. Company's Records. Young's Chronicles.

The FIRST COURT was held on the 23d of August, 1630, at Charlestown, at which were present, Winthrop, Dudley, Saltonstall, Rossiter, Nowell, Sharp, Pyncheon, and Bradstreet. They took order as to the support of Ministers, the building of houses, the sending for Morton at Mount Wollaston, and the wages of mechanics, which were fixed at two shillings a day.[1]

Such was the first Colonial Legislation, and such was the first Legislative body. No heralds, no wigs, no processions, no trumpets, no cannon, no gilding, and no feathers were necessary to impose upon the senses, or give majesty and authority to law! This body consisted of the Governor and Assistants, and for the first three years they assumed and exercised all power. But at the first General Court held in Boston, October 19th, 1630, it was decided that the Freemen were to choose the "Assistants," and the Assistants were to choose the "Governor and Deputy," from among themselves.[2]

At the General Court in May, 1632, the practice was made more democratic, and the whole body of Freemen decided to participate in the election of Governor and Deputy, as well as of Assistants.[3] So by rapid steps the people took the power into their own hands, much to the dislike of the Assistants and governing class.

CHURCH MEMBERS, FREEMEN.

At the Court of Election, May 18th, 1631, it was ordered that once every year a General Court should be held for the election of Assistants, and that no man was to be admitted to the rights of freemen who did not belong to some Church in the Colony.[4] This continued until 1665, and was finally discontinued early in 1691.

The question of the right of the "Company" to lay Taxes, came up on the refusal of some of the Watertown

[1] Winthrop and Savage in W. See Colony Records. Hubbard's History, p. 146.

[2] Hazard's State Papers. Prince's Chronology. Hubbard's Hist., p. 147.

[3] Winthrop's Journal. Hubbard's History, p. 148.

people to pay an assessment. They were cited before the Court; when they confessed their error; and the following position was laid down: "That this Government was in the nature of a Parliament, and that no Assistant could be chosen but by the freemen, who had power likewise to remove the Assistants, and put in others."[1]

THE FIRST LEGISLATURE.

On the 1st of April, 1634, notice was sent to the towns, that the freemen should appoint two from each town, to meet and consider affairs at the General Court, to be held on the 14th of May, following. As the numbers increased, all could not join in making laws, and this plan came in the progress of things. They were not to make new laws, but only to reform those which were amiss, and to prefer grievances to the Assistants. Twenty-four persons met on the day appointed.[2] This assembly soon began to exceed the powers granted by Winthrop, and became competent to make, as well as to mend laws. This year, Dudley was chosen Governor, in place of Winthrop.

In Massachusetts until 1644, the General Court, consisting of the Magistrates and the Deputies, sat and determined matters together. But as the towns increased in number, it was evident that the Magistrates would be outvoted, and they pressed for separate houses, so that no legislation should be valid, unless it was agreed to by both houses. This was carried into effect;[3] and in all New England now we see the "Commons and Peers" modified into "Deputies and Council," which has now become "Representatives and Senate."

As early as 1632,[4] the towns sent deputies to advise with the Governor about public affairs; but in 1634, the Representative system was fully established, as has been said. The powers of the Assembly and of the Magistrates were not well defined; and it was not till 1643, that the negative

[1] Winthrop's Journal, February 17, 1631.

[2] See the Colony Records, and Winthrop. [3] Hutchinson, vol. i., p. 449.

[4] F. C. Gray's Essay. M. W. C., 3d series, vol. 8.

voice of the Magistrates was established. This grew out of a quarrel about a sow, which Winthrop mentions as the "sow business," and which kept the Court and the Colony in a contest from 1636 to 1643. The Deputies favored one side, and the Governor and Magistrates the other, and this excited the Democratic spirit, so that some of the towns urged that the negative voice of the Magistrates (or Upper House) should be revoked. But the Magistrates held their own.

In Connecticut and Rhode Island the Magistrates were more dependent upon the people, and the usage was more Democratic than in Massachusetts.

The following extract will indicate the way they then did public business:

The General Court (or Assembly) met in 7th month, 1666, and took it into consideration, how the King might be pacified for his displeasure at the failure of his Commissioners. The Records state that they spent the forenoon in prayer, for short prayers were not then in fashion. "These prayed:

Mr. Wilson, Mr. Whiting,
Mr. Mather, Mr. Cobitt,
Mr. Symmes, Mr. Mitchell."

And then they had a discussion, which resulted in an address to his Majesty, which was loyal, not slavish. The Massachusetts Courts always adjourned to attend the weekly "Thursday Lecture." In Connecticut, the sessions of the Legislature (in 1713) lasted ten or twelve days. The salary of the Governor was £200; and the whole cost of the Government was less than £800 a year.[1]

Four Courts were appointed to be holden in each year, at one of which, only, the whole body of freemen were to be present for the election of Magistrates. The Ballot also was introduced, in place of a show of hands; and it was decided that the consent of the people was necessary for levying taxes.

[1] Trumbull's History, vol. i., 477.

CONSTITUTION. In the next year [1635] it was decided to have a body of written laws, as a sort of Magna Charta, or Constitution; they were established in 1641. Ninety-eight sections, called "the Body of Liberties" (compiled by Rev. Nathaniel Ward, who had in England been a "practicer in the courts of the common law"), were adopted, which continued over thirty years.[1] Ecclesiastical and Admiralty Courts (always dangerous) were dispensed with.

MUNICIPAL GOVERNMENT. The prime strength of New England, and of the whole Republic, was, and is, in the Municipal Governments, and in the HOMES. At a meeting of leading men, called by Governor Vane, in 1635, among other things decided was this insignificant one, thus noted: "That trivial things should be ended in Towns." This is exactly the reverse of what is practiced by Monarchists and men with Aristocratic instincts, who draw to themselves EVERY sort of ordering, denying that the people are capable of self-government. They are sufficiently answered by the experience of New England, also by the experience of a town of emancipated slaves in Russia,[2] and by the common sense of men, which tells us, that nine of ten men can order their own affairs better than any other will do it, and that experience will correct their errors. The leaders in Massachusetts were not corrupted by the long possession of power, and thus were willing to put back upon the people the settlement of smaller matters.

Each town of New England was, and is, a small Republic. The formation of towns was promoted by the dread of, and danger from, Indians, and also by the demand for churches and schools. People, therefore, did not scatter wide upon large plantations, but collected in towns and

[1] See ch. xliv. Documents of the Constitution, by Francis Bowen, Cambridge, 1854.

[2] See Haxthausen's Travels in Russia.

villages, with their farms lying out around them. A sensible writer of this day well says:[1]

"Accordingly, whenever land was granted to settlers, it was in adjacent tracts, not generally more than two hundred acres each; and it was an indispensable condition to the license for settlement, that a learned and faithful minister should be provided to dispense the Word of Life. To secure constant attendance at meeting, and to prevent danger from Indians by dispersion, the Court ordained that no dwelling should be located more than a mile from the meeting-house. This clustering system prevailed until after the extirpation of the Indian tribes, and the establishment of passable roads. Thus New England grew up a congeries of towns."

The first agreement of the Massachusetts Bay settlers was, that each subscriber to the "Stock" for outfit, should be entitled to two hundred acres of land; and that each settler should have fifty acres at any rate. But new towns made their own arrangements and divisions.

The TOWN-MEETINGS were held annually (commonly in the spring), when it was expected that every voter would be present to take his part in the direction of affairs; this was looked upon as a prime duty; and it was held that a man who would not use his liberty and do his duty, was no good citizen. In Haverhill, the roll of voters was called, and the absentees were fined eighteen pence; and so it was elsewhere. At first they met in the Church; but in course of time, every town provided itself with a Town-house, in which to conduct its meetings and hold its courts. The meeting came to order, and a grave and good citizen was chosen Moderator. Then all town business was brought up in order. Motions were made, briefly debated in a business manner, and voted upon. Matters passed at one meeting were often reversed at a subsequent one, and the minutes read, "Ondone next meeting." They granted Lands, established and repaired Mills,

[1] F. H. Underwood, in Putnam's Magazine, 1855.

Roads ("Paths"), and Ferries. They took order as to clearing Common-lands, paying the Schoolmaster, raising the salary of the Minister, and they elected Deputies to the General Court or Assembly. In every town, some "Prudentiall men" (from three to seven), called afterward "Select-men," were appointed to administer all affairs of the town, between the meetings. They held small Courts, and decided petty offenses, and acted as referees in disputes about bounds, etc. This is the way these States grew up, and their growth has been true and strong.

The General Court, consisting of the Governor and Magistrates and the Deputies, attended to those matters which concerned all the Towns, and which could only be settled by the towns in Convention. The Town Meetings provided for those things which concerned the welfare of the inhabitants of the towns. The Family arranged its affairs for the good of all its members ; and, lastly, each Individual governed himself with reference to his own will, and the needs of the community. So completely was Government diffused by this natural and perfect system ; and at this day the Governors of some of our States have no veto, and no power of appointment to office.

The danger we have now to apprehend is from the increasing patronage and power of the General Government at Washington, which within a few years has been rapidly centralizing. If the States of New England are willing to pay uncounted millions of taxes, in the shape of Custom duties ; if they can no longer make their own roads and bridges, and forts, and can no longer protect their own borders with their own soldiers, then Despotism is upon her, and the days of her liberties are numbered. Whenever the people see this danger, they will stand firmly upon their State Rights, demand direct taxation, and the danger will be strangled.

Military Affairs were second only to the establishment of Religion in the minds of the best men in Massachusetts. They early set about building fortifications, and provided themselves with cannon and other munitions of war. Every town had its own train-band, and every man was expected to be a soldier. The towns were required to keep on hand a supply of powder and shot, and to see that their citizen soldiery were exercised to arms.

The presence of bands of Indians made it necessary for every man to be familiar with the use of arms, which might also become necessary for defense against civilized oppression. Yet the singular sagacity and sense of some of the leading men in Massachusetts is shown in various ways ; in this among others, that in 1637, when some of the "gentlemen" of the Bay wished to be incorporated as a military company, they were refused, in view of the Pretorian Guard, and "how dangerous it might be to erect a standing authority of military men, which might easily in time overthrow the civil power." The company then formed was the "Ancient and Honorable Artillery." If "Training day" had not become a sort of popinjay show, it would be useful and desirable, and whenever it shall be restored to its proper uses, it will be respectable.

The militia law was full and complete in Connecticut (1650).

Every person above the age of sixteen years was to provide himself with a good serviceable gun or musket, which was to be in "Continuall readiness."

The soldiers were to be trained at least six times yearly.

Soldiers were to choose their officers, subject to confirmation of the Court.

Every town also was to keep on hand a supply of powder (3 pounds to each soldier) and lead.

All capable of bearing arms were obliged to appear "to train." The Captain began and ended the exercises with prayer, "and at three o'clock we had a very noble dinner, to which all the clergy were invited." [1]

[1] John Dunton's Journal. M. H. C., vol. 12, second series.

In 1630, at Cambridge, a field was set apart for a "Training field," which continued so as late as 1813. The people proposed that the Trained bands might choose their own officers ; but Winthrop gave them satisfactory reasons against it for that time ; they afterwards succeeded in doing it. When the fortification on Cornhill (Boston) was building, the people from each town came and worked on it—Charlestown first, then Roxbury, then Dorchester, etc. In 1635 a special Commission for military affairs, with full powers, even of life and death, was appointed, consisting of Winthrop, Humphrey, Haynes, Endicott, Coddington, Pyncheon, Nowell, Bellingham, and Bradstreet. In 1639 the two regiments in the Bay mustered one thousand able-bodied, well-armed men.

"We learn," says Winthrop, "at one training (1641) there were 1200 men on duty at Boston, yet not one drunk, though there was plenty of wine and strong beer in the town."

In giving in the number of the militia to the Commissioners in 1665, the secretary of Massachusetts speaks of 5000 foot soldiers and 400 horse ; though, as all were enrolled, this number did not include the aged and infirm.

The soldiers had plate armor, and Joseph Leverett, during King Philip's war, enumerated as necessary "blunderbusses and hand granadoes, and armour, and if it may be, at least armourers to mend arms."

In 1643 the Commissioners for the United Colonies advised, "That every man may keep by him a good gun and sword, one pound of powder, with four pounds of shot, with match or flints suitable, to be ready upon all occasions, etc." "They are all very diligent in training of their soldiers," Lechford writes, "and military exercises, and all except magistrates bear arms, or pay to be excused." In 1653 the Commissioners appointed Captain Leverett Commander-in-chief for the United Colonies.

The wages of a common soldier, on duty, were not to be over 6 shillings a week.

The state of manners and morals may be indicated by the following extracts from the articles of war agreed upon by the General Court during King Philip's war :

1st. "Let no man presume to blaspheme the holy and blessed Trinity, God the Father, God the Son, and God the Holy Ghost, upon pain to have his tongue bored with a hot iron.

12th. " Drunkenness in an officer shall be punished with loss of place, and in a private at discretion.

18th. " If any shall negligently lose, or sinfully play away their arms at dice, or cards, or otherwise, they shall be kept as prisoners or scavengers, etc."

CHAPTER XXIV.

TOLERATION.

LAW OF THE SIX ARTICLES—BOSSUET—THE SCOTCH—THE PRESBYTERIANS—CARTWRIGHT—LOCKE—LAW OF QUEEN ELIZABETH—CRANMER AND THE BIBLE—LIBERTY GAINS—PURITANS AND JAMES I.—HAMPTON-COURT CONFERENCE—PURITANISM DID NOT DIE—CHARLES I.—LAUD.

THE Puritans in New England repudiated the idea of toleration: they were so firmly convinced of the truth of their doctrines, that any man who would not embrace them was deemed worthy of punishment. Few anywhere comprehended the liberty contained in the teachings of Jesus, and believing that the Mosaic code was God-given—without fault—they at first proceeded to extirpate heretics with unsparing rigor. They were most sincere in this impracticable plan, which was often applied without personal animosity; even toward Roger Williams. Governor Winthrop remained his fast friend for life, and between Williams and Cotton, through all their controversies, was an honorable respect.

The leading Minister, Mr. Cotton, wrote: "It was toleration that made the world anti-Christian, and the Church never took hurt by the punishment of heretics."[1] Few seemed to consider, that the attempt to make all men think alike, would put swords into the hands and murder into the hearts of sects, till they first destroyed one another, and then individuals themselves.

Although most of the Puritans opposed freedom of worship in New England, the doctrines they held, and for which they suffered and expatriated themselves, contained seeds of both religious and political liberty, as we shall see.

[1] Bloody Tenet.

Those who love to point to the Puritans of New England as peculiarly intolerant, are probably ignorant of the state of public opinion at that day. It may be interesting briefly to refer to it.

Toleration in religious matters had not yet existed in the sixteenth century. In the Low Countries and Holland, it was an accident rather than a principle, the result of indifference more than intention. With Reformers, men who claimed liberty for themselves, it was rare that it meant liberty for other men; they claimed the right of enforcing their doctrines with the sword, and of punishing heresy with death!

The law of the Six Articles, passed in Henry the Eighth's reign (1539), was intended to "settle" disputed matters; it established "Transubstantiation," "Celibacy of Priests," "Auricular Confession," etc., as TRUTHS. Parliament thanked the King, and enacted that whoever spoke, preached, or wrote against them, should be burned, and his estates be forfeited. A plentiful holocaust ensued, and the King's coffers were replenished. Archbishop Tindal had appealed, not to the Pope, or to Councils, or to the King, but to the Bible. So did Latimer; so did the Ridleys; so did Cranmer; so did Bradford: yet none of them believed in full toleration; they had not reached it. They accepted what was behind them, but feared what was in advance; were tolerant up to their own position, no farther.

BOSSUET, the Catholic, maintained, with all the force of his eloquence, that the State was bound to extirpate false religions. At the same time, the Scotch Commissioners in London, in the name of their Church, remonstrated against "sinful and ungodly toleration." The English Presbyterian clergy protested against the scheme of Cromwell, and declared that they "detested and abhorred toleration." "My judgment," said the moderate Baxter, "I have freely made known. I abhor unlimited liberty, or toleration for all." "Toleration," said Jonathan Edwards, "is the grand will of the Devil, his masterpiece; it is the most compendious, ready, and sure way to destroy all religion." And the simple Cobbler of Agawam (Rev. Mr. Ward, 1647) said: "He that is willing to tolerate any religion, or discrepant way of religion, besides his own, unless it be in matters merely indifferent, either doubts of his own or is not sincere in it."[1] He also said (1645): "To authorize an untruth by a toleration of State, is to build a sconce against the walls of heaven, to batter God out of his chair."

CARTWRIGHT, who was a leader of the more moderate Puritans in England, and had suffered for his labors in trying to bring about a further reformation, seems not to have comprehended the principle of liberty of conscience. He said: "The Magistrates ought to enforce the attendance of Papists and Atheists, in the services of the Church; to punish them if they did not profit by the teaching they might hear; to increase the punishment if they gave signs of contempt; and if at last they proved utterly impenitent, *to cut them off*, that they might not corrupt and infect others."[2]

Cartwright said (see his second reply): "Hereticks ought to be put to deathe now. If this be bloudie and extreme, I am contente to be soe counted, with the holie Ghoste." "I denie that upon repentance there oughte to followe any pardon of deathe."

Baylie, one of the Scottish Commissioners,[3] said reproachfully: "The great shot of Cromwell and Vane is to have a liberty for all religions without any exceptions."

Dr. Increase Mather, in his election sermon (May, 1677), said: "The Lord keep us from being bewitched with the whore's cup, lest, whilst we seem to detest and reject her with open face of profession, we do not bring her in by the back-door of Toleration."

[1] Knowles's Life of Roger Williams, p. 77. "Simple Cobbler of Agawam:" 1647. [2] Reply to Whitgift, cited by Stowell.

[3] See Brooks's Lives of the Puritans.

Even in 1690, when Locke—one of the most liberal and enlightened men of England—wrote his Letters on Toleration, he hesitated about granting freedom to Papists, and denied it to Atheists.

In Queen Elizabeth's day a law was passed, enacting that any person above the age of sixteen, who refused to attend Church for a month, should be imprisoned; if he obstinately persisted, he should be banished the kingdom; and if he returned he should suffer death."[1]

These references will serve to show that extreme legislation against religious liberty was not peculiar to the Puritans of New England.

THE BIBLE.

But about the year 1540, by the King's most gracious leave, Archbishop Cranmer issued his edition of the Bible. Copies of it, though rare, were scattered over England, and men read its words, or heard them spoken. The great truths which Jesus taught, and the withering rebukes and denunciations of the Prophets against false priests and wicked rulers, shed light and gave strength to the people. Chained to the desk, as the book was that it might not be stolen, men, women, and children gathered round any one who could read, and, using their own reason and understanding, tried to know what this standard did teach: this gave an immense impulse to intellectual action. The life of the Carpenter's son touched their souls, warmed their sympathies, and enlisted their action. Here was a Man, poor, despised, and neglected; but he had been loyal to the truth, had lived up to it, and had died on the Cross a martyr to truth and courage; a victim to the hatred which Church and State are sure to extend to Reformers. Over all this manhood was cast the mystic hue of miracle; and the deepest earthly interest was awed into wonder by the belief that this was God himself incarnated in an earthly form. The burning, often bitter words, of the Poets, of Amos, of Ezekiel, more than all, of Isaiah, told

[1] Grahame, vol. i, p. 214.

them that no sin, no wrong-doing could escape its punishment; that God's law was supreme, and no man, no King, no Priest, no Nation could disobey and live; that no "powers that be" are of God, unless they are based upon Justice and Truth; that wicked rulers and wicked priests ought to be destroyed; that formal worship, new-moons, and fasts, and sacrifices, are an abomination to God; that God was no respecter of persons; but that before him, poor and rich, weak and mighty, fared alike.

Such teachings, scattered through these writings, took strong hold upon the hearts of earnest men, and led to action. Texts were printed on the souls, texts which told of the wickedness of oppressors, and the vengeance which visited them; which showed how men went gladly to death rather than obey wicked laws; which assured them that God was the friend of the righteous, though man might be his foe.

Through many years this growth went on, and was not confined to the common people. Archbishop Grindal wrote to Queen Elizabeth—"I can do nothing against the truth but for the truth. I consider, also, that he who acts against his conscience, resting upon the laws of God, builds for Hell."[1]

Religious liberty and the rights of conscience were steadily gaining strength, though at times it seemed as if they were crushed, never to rise again. The "Law of the Six Articles," made burnings and murders legal; and they went on. Under Queen Mary (called "Bloody" by Protestants, for no reason which would not apply the title to Henry and Elizabeth), it became lawful to burn such as denied the supremacy of the Pope, and asserted that of the King—and the burnings went on. In Queen Elizabeth's day (1571), the "Thirty-nine Articles" of the Church of England, were passed, and only some two hundred and forty, out of nine thousand four hundred

[1] Strype's Life, cited by Stowell, p. 212.

Priests, who held livings under Mary, resigned their livings, rather than subscribe the Articles.[1] The "Act of Uniformity" was proclaimed in 1574, and large numbers of the laity forsook the parish churches, with some of the clergy. The burnings, banishments, and persecutions still went on. Many extreme Puritans, and some of the best citizens and men of England, were forced to fly to the Low Countries.

THE PURITANS AND JAMES I.

The afflicted Puritans hoped much from the accession of King James I. (1603.) He had declared his attachment to Puritan doctrine and discipline, had twice sworn to the "Covenant," in Scotland,[2] and had praised God that he was born to be King of such a Church. The English people—and the Puritans above all—learned that "no fool is perfect unless he knows Latin," and that no hatred is so bitter as that of the Renegade. In January, 1603-4, was held the "Hampton Court Conference," a kind of Theological Convention, which was once more to "settle" things. This pedantic King presided; four Doctors appeared in behalf of the Puritans; various Bishops and dignitaries in behalf of the Church: the wishes of the Puritans were presented—were answered by the Bishops; the King then took up his parable, and with much Latin, and many coarse jests, put the Puritans to silence; he likened himself to Christ, declared that he would have but one opinion and one discipline; that he would be the father and guide of the Church, and that if the Puritans would not conform, "he would harry them out of the country."[3]

The Bishops and dignitaries applauded greatly, for it was one of James's maxims—"No King, no Bishop;" and they joined hands to keep their power and revenues. Bancroft, one of the Bishops, thanked God on his knees —"for such a King as since Christ's time had not been

[1] Stowell's Puritans, p. 116. [2] Prince's Chronology.

[3] Prince's Chronology. Bancroft's History, vol. i., p. 296.

seen." The Doctors went home with sadness on their faces, and grief in their hearts. The proclamation of Conformity followed (March, 1604), and more than one thousand five hundred ministers were suspended, or silenced, and were treated with harshness ; but not one Bishopric was vacated. Decent Puritanism was borne down and had to succumb, die, or fly. The severities and urgencies of the King and Church, drove them out to seek refuge in Holland, in America, anywhere, to escape the hounds of a cruel law. Even this relief was afterward denied them, for in America, it was feared they might grow too strong, and a proclamation (Charles I.) ordained that none might go without the King's license. But the "love of Liberty" is strong, and Puritanism did not die. The rigid and painful Archbishop Laud, found it a file which broke his teeth. It had then leavened up into the high-born and educated classes of England. Hampden, Eliot, Pym, Vane, Cromwell, and other names well known to fame, were with them. Freedom in Church led by the hand its twin brother, Freedom in State,[1] and they had grown in strength, though exposed to the tender mercies of the wolf, and the bitter blasts of the storm.

Charles I. determined to rule as a despot in State, and Laud to lay every man upon the Procrustean bed of his own narrow theology. The persecutions, and burnings, and imprisonments then went on. But slowly coming, the crisis at last arrived, and the wind, which others had sown and they fanned, came upon Charles and Laud, a whirlwind. Hampden went to jail rather than pay an unjust tax of twenty shillings ; Eliot lay in prison ; Leighton was in irons in Newgate ; Prynne's ears were dug out ; but all could not save Charles and Laud from the vengeance of an indignant people ; not even the talent of Strafford availed ; down they went before the tempest they had raised—first Wentworth, then Laud, and then Charles himself (1649), victims of their own folly, infidel-

[1] Laud's Letters to Strafford.

ity, and love of despotism. Liberty raised its head, and for a time Puritanism triumphed.

Kings, Bishops, and Courtiers, discovered that they, too, had a joint in their necks, and the lesson then taught, the world has never forgot.

CHAPTER XXV.

ROGER WILLIAMS AND RHODE ISLAND.

THIRTY-TWO YEARS OLD—HIS OPINIONS—PREACHES AT SALEM—AT PLYMOUTH—THE INDIANS—TROUBLE AT SALEM—THE STRUGGLE BEGINS—PROGRESSIVES AND CONSERVATIVES—THE FREEMAN'S OATH—ENDICOTT CUTS THE CROSS—PRESBYTERY—FREEDOM OF WORSHIP—DANGEROUS OPINIONS—THE STRUGGLE GOES ON—ENDICOTT IMPRISONED—WILLIAMS IS BANISHED—RUINED—HE FLIES—PROVIDENCE—INDIAN GRANTS—UNIFORMITY—MRS. HUTCHINSON—NEW EMIGRANTS—AQUETNECK—DANGERS—CANONICUS—MASSACHUSETTS UNGRATEFUL—CONSTITUTION—VERIN—LIBERTY OF CONSCIENCE—DEMOCRACY—PROVIDENCE CHARTER—GORTON—WILLIAMS GOES TO ENGLAND—RETURNS—UNION—KING'S DEATH—CODDINGTON—WILLIAMS IN ENGLAND—PRESIDENT—CHARTER RENEWED—BAPTIST—CONTROVERSIES—GEORGE FOX—INDIANS SOLD—WORK—WILLIAMS DIES—HIS WRITINGS—CIVIL LIBERTY—RELIGIOUS LIBERTY—WILLIAMS'S CHARACTER.

When Roger Williams reached Nantasket, with Captain Pierce in the ship Lyon, on the fifth of February, 1631, he thanked God he had reached a country where there were neither lords nor bishops; where if a man had ideas, he could put them into words at least, and as he hoped into practice.

He was then a bright young man (some thirty-two years old) with quick-flowing blood. He walked into Boston town with a free step, and wondered what the future of that new colony, as well as his own, was to be. Nobody knew, and nobody cared where he was born, nor is it of much moment now. He was of Welsh birth and blood (from Carmarthen); and a "godly minister," with great activity.[1] Much as the colonists valued godly ministers, the arrival of the good ship Lyon just then, with two hundred tons of meal and other things of prime necessity, was of more pressing interest than he. The colonists during the winter had suffered great distresses, and the poorer sort of people who

[1] Winthrop, vol. i., p. 41.

lay long in tents, were afflicted with scurvy, and longed for the juice of lemons, then aboard the ship. But young Williams at once made his way, and with some decision gave it as his opinion, that the English was not a true Church, and that the congregation at Boston ought to make a public declaration of repentance for having communed with it in England. Many of the Colonists thought so too ; but the times, as they thought, were not ripe for such decided doctrines. But to Williams, if it was right to think it, then it was right to act it. He was no politician : so he refused to join their Church, and careful people opened their eyes at the rash young man, and wondered where he expected to preach. But besides this he had another opinion quite at variance with one held by nearly all the world. It was : "That the magistrate should restrain and punish crime, but that he had no right to interfere in matters of conscience or to punish heresy."[1] He said, the public, or the magistrate, may decide what is due from man to man, but when the magistrate attempts to prescribe a man's duties to God, he is out of his place and there can be no safety ; for it is clear, that if the magistrate (or king) have the power, he may decree one set of opinions or beliefs to-day and another to-morrow ; as has been done in England by different kings and queens, and by different Councils in the Roman Church, and "all would be heaps of confusion."[2] But, however logical he might seem, careful people said, it would not do to let everybody think and teach just what they chose ; for if they did the world would certainly come to an end : at least God and his Truth could not be sustained.

But farther he said : "Why lay such stress upon your patent from King James of England ? Your patent is but a parchment—James has no more right to give away or sell Massasoit's lands, and cut and carve the country,

[1] "Breaches of the First Table"—the first four Commandments—these offenses were called.

[2] See "Hireling Ministry."

than Massasoit has to sell James's, or to send his Indians to colonize Warwickshire."

The Colonists had tried very hard to get the patent, and it was the usual way, and they wanted the land, and it had a better look to hold it with a patent than without it, and more than all, it protected them against England, and the grasping taxation of the Court, Camp, and Church. So they stuck to it, and put logic and Williams out of their way.[1]

With such novel and unpopular opinions, what was Williams to do? Luckily for him, young ministers were not so common in New England then as now, and moreover, Endicott at Salem—who was a royal man (though he did strike Goodman Dexter, provoked to do it "by his carriadge" and such "daring of me")[2]—had a sympathy for his bravery and his opinions, and the Salem people, after Mr. Higginson's death, invited Williams to come and preach for them, which he did (April 1631). This caused a commotion, and the Court took the matter up, and wrote to Mr. Endicott—objecting, and "marvelled they would choose him without advising with the Council; and withal desiring him that they would forbear to proceed till they had conferred about it."[3]

The Salem people, however, liking Williams, chose to hear him preach, and having for some time ruled their own affairs, under the direction of Endicott, did not enough stand in awe of the new authorities. But Williams went up to Boston, and took the oath to the civil government; and on the same day (18th May, 1631) the Court passed the celebrated order that none but Church Members should be admitted to the freedom of the body politic.[4]

[1] The New Englanders bought their lands from the Indians. Knowles's Life. Mather's Magnalia. Dwight's Travels. Williams's Reply to Cotton.

[2] Endicott's Letter to Winthrop, in Memoir, p. 41.

[3] Winthrop's Journal.

[4] Elton's Life of Roger Williams. This continued till 1665. Note to Savage's Winthrop, vol. ii., p. 171.

HE WENT TO PLYMOUTH.

The dissatisfaction with Williams and the Salem Church, grew warmer, with the advance of summer, and the displeasure of the magistrates was so great, that Williams decided to go to Plymouth, and assist the minister Smith—whose gifts were not great.[1]

We have seen how the Sunday was enjoyed while Williams was there, in the sketch of the Plymouth Church (ch. xvi.). The people there having already separated from the English Church were not afraid, so Williams was well received, and Governor Bradford says his teaching was approved.[2] But the active mind and body of the man were at work, and the careful Brewster was watchful of so very outspoken a man. During these two years Williams began his intimacy with the Indians, and friendships were commenced, which resulted in his preservation and the salvation of the Colonies. "My soul's desire," he said, "was to do the natives good." The subtle Indians saw it, and stood by him. "God was pleased," so he said, "to give me a painful, patient spirit to lodge with them in their filthy smoky holes, to gain their tongue," etc. In this way he came to know Massasoit, Canonicus, and Miantonomo, bold men, chiefs of the powerful Narragansetts. So things continued till August, 1633, when, upon the death of Mr. Skelton, Williams returned to Salem.[3] The people there liked him and wanted him. Endicott received him with rough, hearty cordiality, and the people with sincere welcome. The magistrates at Boston wrote, requesting them not to settle him, but they would do it, and in August of the following year, he was instituted in the Church.[4]

From this time there went on a struggle between Williams and the Government. John Endicott was one of the Assistants, who stood by Williams, and the Court was not quite ready to carry matters to extremity. On a day

[1] August, 1631.
[2] Prince, p. 377. Winthrop.
[3] Nov. 1633. Mem. J. Endicott, p. 49.
[4] Gammel's Life, p. 37.

when Endicott was at Boston, the Minister, Mr. Cotton took occasion to preach upon the subject of vails, which were worn by women in the Church. After the sermon Endicott spoke (as was the custom), and took the ground, that as they were the sign of submission, and were Scriptural,[1] they ought to be continued. Williams sustained Endicott, and this question became of great interest. Sermons were preached and rebutted, and at last Cotton came down to Salem, and preached against them, and the women inclined to his view.

PROGRESSIVES AND CONSERVATIVES.

In every society there are Progressives and Conservatives, those who wish to go forward, and those who wish to move slowly, if at all. Williams certainly belonged to the former class, and there seemed no sufficient reason to him to forbear speaking his truth, and attempting to put it into practice. There will be occasions enough in any society for this difference to show itself. Williams had put forth his views in a book, claiming that they could have no right to lands under this grant from the King, "nor otherwise, except they compounded with the natives," the Doctrine and the style of which much offended "the Magistrates and Ministers." Endicott was written to, and it was decided to censure Williams for his "Errour and presumption." Williams wrote that he had no purpose to have stirred further in the matter, and offered the book to be burned, and so the difference was ended for the present.

But in 1633 trouble seemed brewing in England against the Colonists. Charles, Laud, and Wentworth, hated Puritans and Reformers, and the Privy Council ordered the Colony Charter home to be "regulated." Cradock wrote for it in 1634, and in 1635 "quo warranto" was issued. The Court decided to reply to Cradock's letter, but not to send the Charter. Great dread of the threatened "Commission," for regulating the plantations, spread

[1] 1 Corinthians, xi. 5.

through the Colony, and resistance was seriously contemplated, and to "avoid and protract" was decided on.

In this state of things the FREEMAN'S OATH was offered to the people, which bound them to allegiance to the Colony rather than to England. Williams could not be quiet in this seething world ; nor could Endicott. Both of them saw the inevitable tendencies of the Roman Catholic Church to despotism ; and feeling that such a church was dangerous to their infant liberties, they decided that the symbol under which the Pope and Laud marched should not be their symbol ; so Endicott cut the cross out of the King's colors.[1] This made trouble ; and Endicott, at the next Court, was "sadly admonished," and disabled from office for a year. Williams held peculiar views respecting oaths, and cited the Scripture command—"Swear not at all." And as the freeman's oath clashed with the oath to the King already taken, Williams spoke against it, and dissuaded some from accepting it.[2]

He early foresaw, too, the dangers to be feared from the too great influence of the Clergy in the State, and refused to attend their stated meetings, lest they might grow to be a sort of Presbytery ; and he boldly asserted the startling doctrine that "no one should be bound to maintain a worship against his own consent."[3]

It is clear that to them he held novel and dangerous opinions, and that his activity aggravated the Ministers and Magistrates ; so they sent for him to come to Boston, to see what could be done. He was willing to go, for he feared nothing so much as indifference and stupidity. He felt himself strong in his opinions, though they were unpopular ; and his earnestness, and honesty, and straightforwardness had made him dear to the Salem people, in spite of his opinions ; for character, not doctrine, is always the essence of manhood. So he took his staff in his

[1] Hubbard, p. 255. [2] Gammell, p. 67.

[3] Hubbard says "he had a fly-blown imagination," p. 189.

hand and went. The Magistrates gave him a hearing, and the Ministers sat by. He was true to himself that day, and spoke for Liberty of Conscience and Worship, and for the separation of Church and State; and though the Ministers confuted him "clearly" (as Winthrop thought), and though Endicott "gave place to the truth,"[1] Williams maintained his position. The question was not ended, and in July, 1635 (Haynes then Governor), he was brought before the Court to answer for these things—"divers dangerous opinions."

First, that the Magistrate ought not to punish the breach of the First Table, otherwise than in such cases as disturbed the civil peace. Second, that he ought not to tender an oath to an unregenerate man. Third, that a man ought not to pray with the unregenerate, though wife, child, etc. Fourth, that a man ought not to give thanks after the sacrament or after meat, etc.[2] Thus the grounds of the quarrel are stated by Winthrop, in the terms of the day. As we now judge, the real question at issue was, the right of the Civil Government to interfere in matters of religion.

On the one side were—the usage of the world, the governor and the magistrates, the clergy, the majority of the people; on the other side was—Roger Williams, a man of blameless life, distinguished talents, and determined courage. He stood alone[3] in the universe of God, with no weapon but his tongue, and no power but truth, and though he might—must go down, yet he feared nothing.

Uniformity, the ministers said, is the necessary thing. Williams replied: so the Pope says, and so said Henry VIII. and Bloody Mary, and having the power, they tried to enforce it. But, said the Ministers, if the magistrates can not intermeddle to hinder a Church from running off

[1] Winthrop, vol. i., p. 158.

[2] Winthrop, vol. i., p. 163; Morton's Mem., p. 155.

[3] The Salem Church finally deserted him.

to heresy, what is to become of true religion? Williams said: If, with a fair field, truth is not equal to error, then Satan must be stronger than God—which I do not believe. The Ministers urged, that the people needed guides, that they were not yet able to decide for themselves. Nor will they ever be, if you keep them in leading-strings, answered Williams. No, he continued, when you force the conscience of men, you invade the prerogative of God; by no dungeons, or whippings, or burnings, can you compel a man to see the truth as you do. It has been tried—thousands have perished in the name of Jesus Christ, the Prince of Peace.[1] Yourselves, even have been driven from England, at the peril of your lives, because you could not worship God as Laud decreed; and now I am in peril because I hold and teach what you do not believe to be true. If you use force against me you will do violence to your best instincts; you may imprison, you may kill me, but you can not destroy a grain of God's truth.

It was useless. The Ministers thought that he who should obstinately maintain such opinions (before cited) should be removed,[2] and he was sent back to Salem, that he and the Church might consider and give satisfaction or else expect "the Sentence."

A few days after, the Salem people preferred a petition to the Court about some land, "but because they had chosen Mr. Williams they were refused," etc.[3] So the Salem people must go without their lands or dismiss Mr. Williams. Now they loved Mr. Williams, but they wanted the land, and money-loving Christians began to think the matter had a serious look, if it was to interfere with their lands; but, at first, the Church was incensed at this legal tyranny, and sent letters of admonition to the other Churches, which only made matters worse; for their deputies were deprived of their seats in the General Court, and tough old Endicott was imprisoned for a day.[4]

[1] Bloody Tenet.

[2] Knowles's Life, p. 71.

[3] Winthrop, vol. i., p. 163.

[4] Knowles, p. 71. Winthrop, vol. i., p. 166.

At last in October, 1635, Williams was again convented, all the Ministers of the Bay being desired to be present. He justified his letters, and maintained all his opinions; and though Mr. Hooker was "chosen to dispute with him," yet he said: "What I believe, I believe, and I can not change until I am convinced. What I think and believe, that I will speak." So the Court next morning sentenced him: "To depart out of our jurisdiction within six weeks, all the Ministers, save one, approving the sentence."[1] Nov. 3d, 1635.

HE IS BANISHED.

In consideration of his family, and the approach of Winter, he was allowed to remain in his house till Spring.[2]

Williams was now a ruined and disgraced man; somewhat exasperated too, for his Church at last deserted him and disclaimed his errors, and wrote an humble submission to the Magistrates. The time, no doubt, will come when men of Property will join hands with men of Principle; but it was too soon for such a God-like fact, in Salem, in the year of our Lord 1635, by several centuries.

Powerless and sick, Williams was not without comfort. In the language of Job, he denied that he was wicked, and said, "Though I die I will maintain my integrity." Some twenty of his Salem friends yet stood by him, and resorted to his house to solace him, and to listen to his teachings. Winthrop (not then governor) wrote him privately, expressing sympathy, and advising him to go to the Narragansett country, where no white men had yet asserted jurisdiction.[3]

[1] Winthrop, vol. i., pp. 171, 173. Knowles, p. 51.

[2] The sentence ran thus: "Whereas, Mr. Roger Williams, one of the Elders of the Church at Salem, hath broached and divulged dyvers newe and dangerous opinions against the aucthoritie of magistrates, also write l' ses of defamçon, both of the magistrates and churches here and that before any conviccon and yet maintaineth the same without retraccon. It is therefore ordered that the said Mr. Williams shall dep'te out of this Jurisdicçon within sixe weeks nowe next ensuing, wch if hee neglect to p'forme, it shall be lawful for the Gov'nr and two of the magistrates to sende him to some place out of this Jurisdicçon, not to returne any more, without licence from the Cou[rs]."

[3] Williams's Letter to Mason. M. H. C., vol. i.

We can not well appreciate the bitterness felt by the clergy toward him; though at the present day religious hatreds are not quite unknown; and it is difficult to see how they could resist Williams's position; for Cotton and Hooker were men of mind, and the clergy were up to the average of men in sense and morality. Yet long after time had softened the rancor of the struggle, Mather called Williams, the "Korah of New England," and declared, that he had "a windmill in his head;" while Hubbard, of Ipswich (died 1704), was glad to say, that he had a "fly-blown imagination," with a "heady and turbulent spirit." It must be remembered, that it is not uncommon for religious controversy to debauch the intellect and to paralyze the affections, and that Williams was himself injured by it.

Thus matters stood in January, 1635–6; Williams still in his own house, and the people coming to him and listening to his damnable opinions. Then the Magistrates fearing the founding of an "infectious" colony on their borders, sent for him to come to Boston, intending to ship him to England;[1] but he refusing to come, Captain Underhill was sent to fetch him, in a small sloop. He heard of this, and in the dead of winter,[2] fled alone through the forest. "Bread and bed I knew not for fourteen weeks," he said; he fled from Christians to savages, through snow, through darkness, through forests, till he reached the kind-hearted, but stupid Indian and heathen Massasoit.

RHODE ISLAND.

1635-6.

Here begins the History of Rhode Island, and for forty years, the history of the State and the Man are one. The "heart's desire" of Williams, to do the Indians good, was now returned to him many fold. Massasoit, Chief of the

[1] Winthrop, vol. i., p. 175. [2] January, 1635–6.

Wampanoags, was his friend. So were Canonicus and Miantonomo, Chiefs of the Narragansetts, who numbered four thousand fighting men. The Indians were his friends, and fortunately knew nothing of "breaches of the first table," or the delicate dangers of the Freeman's Oath; but they were open to the influences of kindness and justice.

Williams planted his corn at Seekonk, for he knew that the basis of every good State and Society, is Agriculture; but learning that this might be in the limits of the Plymouth claim,[1] he removed on lands purchased by him (not stolen), from the Narragansetts.[2]

As he floated in his canoe down the river Pautucket, and drew near the future site of the beautiful city of Providence, the Indians shouted to him,

"Wha-cheer, friend, Wha-cheer?"[3] and grasped his hand with ready sympathy, as he stepped ashore.

On the hill, the forests just clothed in their full leafage, bowed their heads to this fugitive—the Hero of a great idea, and whispered "FREEDOM." Where they bourgeoned, the huts of the first settlers were built, and where Providence now stands,[4] the standard of Religious Liberty was first planted; there it has stood, and there it will stand. Hither came some twenty of Williams's friends (and his wife and two children), who had stood by him through all disasters, and who were now to begin a new State. Every man put his hand to the work, and Williams planted with corn "Whatcheer and Saxifrax Hills," so that the grateful Earth yielded to them her fruits, as richly as to those of Orthodox faith; and the place became a refuge for "persons distressed for conscience."[5]

Hither came all sorts of distressed people—Free-thinkers, Anabaptists, Visionaries, men with one idea, or with

[1] Letter from Governor Winslow.

[2] See Deed in Rhode Island Hist. Coll., vol. iv. Knowles, p. 106.

[3] "What Cheer," a Poem by Judge Durfee.

[4] Called by the Indians, Moshassuk.

[5] Those who first came were William Harris, John Smith, Joshua Verin, Thomas Angell, and Francis Wickes. Knowles, p. 3.

many; and slow-minded, sensible people, shook their heads at the hopelessness of combining them into a State. Discord, confusion, and anarchy, are sure to come, they said; for a while they may come, said Williams; let them, if it must be; time will prove the truth of my doctrine: that the civil power has no jurisdiction over the conscience. Time has done it.

But a few years had elapsed, when Williams was able to write as follows, to Sir Harry Vane, (1654): "We have not only been long free (against whose cruel oppressions God raised up your noble spirit in Parliament), but we have, sitten quiet and dry from the streams of blood spilt by that war in our native country. We have not felt the new chains of the Presbyterian tyrants, nor in this Colony have we been consumed with the over-zealous fire of the (so-called) Godly Christian magistrates. Sir, we have not known what Excise means. We have almost forgot what tythes are, yea, or taxes either, to Church or Commonwealth."[1] Circumstances forced open the eyes of other men to this principle of religious freedom. Governor Haynes, who had pronounced Williams's sentence, and who was afterward Governor of Hartford, found it desirable to leave the "Bay" with Hooker; and he admitted to Williams, "that the most wise God had provided this part of His world for a refuge for ALL SORTS of consciences." Thus the leaven worked.

But there were eyes then and afterward which could not be made to see, such as Cotton Mather (a man of great industry, but of deep and passionate vanity); he said that the Rhode Island Colony was "a colluvies (a sink) of Antinomians, Famalists, Anabaptists, Anti-Sabbatarians, Arminians, Socinians, Quakers, Ranters, and every thing but Roman Catholics, and true Christians—bono terra, malo gens: 'A good land and a wicked people.'" Still, in the language of that day, the Lord permitted the Colony to increase and prosper.

[1] Knowles's Life, p. 270.

Williams built himself a house, near the once-famous spring called by his name (now in the heart of Providence —Bowen-street); but his first planting, at Seekonk, had been abandoned, and he was an impoverished man; so much so that in his letter to Mason, he says: "It pleased the Father of Spirits, to touch many hearts dear to him, with many relentings; amongst which, that great and pious soul, Mr. Winslow, melted, and kindly visited me at Providence, and put a piece of gold in the hands of my wife, for our supply."

The grant of lands, from Canonicus and Miantonomo, was large and valuable, and Williams might have lived as Lord-proprietor; for he asserts, and we may believe his positive testimony, that the land was obtained by his own money, and through the regard of the Indians for him; though it was not thousands nor tens of thousands of money, could have bought of Canonicus an English entrance into the bay.[1] But with whatever other faults, Williams was not greedy for lands or power, and he generously conveyed to twelve of his Associates, equal rights to the lands, by Deed, in 1638, confirmed afterward in 1661. For this he received thirty pounds, which was paid out of the proceeds of a tax of thirty shillings, levied upon each new settler who occupied portions of the land.

But uniformity of opinion seemed as far away, after Williams's banishment, as before. Mrs. Hutchinson had arrived in Boston, in 1636, "holding views." She had a free gift of speech, and having the sympathy of Governor Vane, and the Reverend Mr. Cotton, she soon stirred up the Theological Waters. There was nothing to be done but to banish her, too; for they had not learned that Truth is the only weapon that can pierce Error, and that if Mrs. Hutchinson spoke the truth, no amount of persecution could silence it; and that if she had been let alone, she would have found her place, and the public quiet

[1] See Deed in Knowles, p. 107. Rhode Island Hist. Coll., vol. ix., March, 1638. Backus, vol. i., p. 94. Bancroft, i., p. 380.

would not have suffered. In August, 1637, the Ministers collected at Cambridge, to see what could be done ; they were overwhelmnd with fear, for they found that no less than eighty-two damnable heresies had crept in.[1]

With Mrs. Hutchinson,[2] forcibly or freely, came great numbers from Massachusetts, and they found a warm welcome and a ready hand with Roger Williams. Through him, the Indians were induced to sell the beautiful Island of Aquitneck, or Aquiday, or Rhode Island (now a very un-Puritan place), where they prospered so well, that they were willing to forget the fires from which they had fled. "It was not price nor money," said Williams, "that could have purchased Rhode Island : Rhode Island was obtained by Love—by the Love and favor which that Honorable Gentleman, Sir Harry Vane, and myself, had with that great Sachem, Miantonomo."

The Island was bought in the name of Mr. William Coddington,[3] the leading man in the new settlement ; and it became another place of refuge for men with free thoughts.

Williams was indefatigable in his endeavors to continue peace between Massasoit, Canonicus, and Miantonomo, and was successful. They granted what he asked, for they perceived his justice, which no man, of whatever color, can possibly withstand ; and he never denied them what they asked. The old Chief Canonicus loved him as his own son ; and Williams went safely among them, when most exasperated and frenzied at the encroachments and insolences of the whites. He bore a charmed life. On the west of Williams's settlement were the bold and warlike Pequots. In 1634, they murdered Captain Stone (an Indian trader who probably deserved it), and in 1636, John Oldham was killed at Block Island. Endicott was sent down [August, 1636] to punish and revenge these things, which only exasperated the Indians, and brought about a league against the whites.[4]

[1] Knowles, p. 141. (See ch. xxxi., xxxii.)

[2] 1638: Winthrop. [3] March, 1637–8. [4] Chapter xxix.

Governor Vane wrote to Williams about the dangers of the conspiracy; so Williams alone, in his canoe, hastened across the Bay to the haunts of Canonicus and Miantonomo, cutting through a stormy wind. He was none too soon, for there were the Pequot diplomats, urging the dark dangers which hung over the natives, reiterating the encroachments of the whites, the chicanery, and insolence, and cruelty which some had practiced, and appealing to their pride of possession and of Race.

For three days and nights, Williams, in the Sachem's house, mixed with the bloody Pequot embassadors, and pushed his dangerous mission; and at last his old friendship and superior skill prevailed; Canonicus and Miantonomo refused the Pequot league, and remained in friendship with the whites. Winthrop was in favor of passing a vote of thanks to Williams for what he had done; but Dudley (a born bigot, though an upright man) could not allow any recognition of merit in a man who held such doctrines.[1]

The Massachusetts Bay Colony, in spite of Winthrop's respect for Williams, was determined to cut off the heretics; so they forbad all dealings; and when John Greene (who, as Savage quaintly observes, "seems not to have attracted the wrath of heaven to shorten his days," because of his religious opinions) wrote a letter, charging the Magistrates with having usurped powers, the Court passed an order [1638] to apprehend ANY of the Providence folk, found in their jurisdiction, and to send them out of the bounds, unless they would disclaim such opinions. This act cut them off from the trade of Boston, and they were at times in straits, so that Williams says: "My time was spent, day and night, at home and abroad, on the land and water, at the hoe and at the oar, for bread."

The action of the Orthodox Colonies seemed now vindictive, and it must have severely tried the forbearance of Williams and his friends; for, notwithstanding the labors

[1] Williams's Letter to Mason. Elton's Life, p. 54.

of Williams to protect them from the Indians, when in 1643, the Confederacy[1] (of Plymouth, Massachusetts Bay, Connecticut, and New Haven) was formed for mutual protection against these very Indians, Providence and Rhode Island were rigorously excluded—first for one reason and then for another; and rumors even reached them, that the Confederation entertained the idea of taking action against them, as Heretics, dangerous to the safety of the religious colonists.[2]

Hutchinson says: "After all that has been said of the action or tenets of this person, while he was in the Massachusetts Bay, it ought forever be remembered to his honor, that for forty years after, instead of showing any revengeful resentment against the Colony from which he had been banished, he seems to have been continually employed in acts of kindness and benevolence."[3]

Religious Liberty produced its proper fruits in the mind of Roger Williams; he declared ("Bloody Tenet"), "Kings and Magistrates must be considered invested with no more power than the people betrust them with." "The sovereign power of all civil authority is founded in the consent of the people."

THE CONSTITUTION.

The Constitution of the new State was a model of brevity and simplicity; for Constitutions become manacles and fetters when not founded upon broad and simple truths. It ran thus: "We, whose names are hereunder written, being desirous to inhabit in the Town of Providence, do promise to submit ourselves in active or passive obedience to all such orders, or agreements, as shall be made for public good of the body, in an orderly way, by the major consent of the present inhabitants, masters of families, incorporated together into a Township, and such others whom they shall admit unto the same—only in civil things."[4] This Covenant was signed

[1] Confederation, 1643, continued till 1686. [2] Williams's Letter to Mason.
[3] Hutchinson's History of Massachusetts Bay, vol. i., p. 38.
[4] Knowles, p. 120.

by the citizens, and this was all that was found necessary in a true and simple state of society. Their affairs were conducted by the whole body, assembled in Town-meeting, until 1640. No power was delegated until then. So jealous were they of their religious rights, that when Joshua Verin "refused to let his wife go so oft as she was called for to Mr. Williams's—they required to have him censured."[1]

Verin plead, that the Scriptures gave him the right, to prevent his wife from going to Church ; and though "one Arnold," a witty man, spoke for him, it was voted that, "for breach of covenant in restraining liberty of conscience, he shall be withheld the liberty of voting, until he declare the contrary."[2]

Here was an early, practical, and successful assertion of "Woman's rights ;" not yet thoroughly understood.

In the disputes which broke out in Providence (1640), about "metes and bounds" of lands, they reiterated that they "still held forth liberty of conscience ;" and in 1641, the Court ordered that no man should be "accounted a delinquent for doctrine," and that the law should be perpetuated. In 1640, the Arbitrators reported : "We agree, as formerly hath been the liberties of the Town, so still to hold forth liberty of conscience." An act passed 1641, says, "It was ordered and unanimously agreed that the Government which this body politic doth attend unto in this Island, is a Democracy, etc."

During the terrible days in Massachusetts, when Quakers were whipped and hanged (ch. xxxvii.), (1656 to 1658).[3] Williams was steady, and remained staunch to his principles. When the Commissioners sent requests, urging the banishment of Quakers, the Rhode Island Assembly promptly declined, and said, "We find, moreover, that in those places where these people are most of all supposed to

[1] Winthrop's Journal.

[2] Annals of Providence. Winthrop, i., p. 283. Staple's Hist., p. 23.

[3] Charles II. sent an order that they should desist.

declare themselves freely, and are only opposed by arguments of discourse, there they least of all desire to come.[1]"

Three times the United Colonies required the Rhode Island Plantations to join in the persecution, but three times she staunchly refused.[2]

PROVIDENCE SECURES A CHARTER.

Troubles grew up (1642) between the Authorities at the Bay, and Samuel Gorton, a bold and positive man—who held to Liberty of Conscience as strongly as Williams did—who had settled at Showomet, afterward called Warwick, within the limits of the present town of Cranston.[3] (Ch. xxxiii.) Four of his company having acknowledged the Jurisdiction of Massachusetts Bay, and the politic Magistrates there being inclined to take advantage of this, to get possession of the country, and to put down heresy, Williams and his friends thought it a safe precaution against their stronger neighbors, to secure a Charter from England. It was decided that Williams was the man to go to England, for he was the friend of Vane, and known to Cromwell. As he was not allowed to enter Boston, he sailed from New York, in June, 1643. In England, he found all in a flame, civil war raging, Hampden just killed, Charles fled from London, and Parliament in possession of the city and the power. Parliament was favorable to the Colonies, and inclined to freedom ; so with the powerful aid of Vane, he was successful in getting from the Commissioners of Plantations, a liberal Charter, which was dated March 14th, 1643–4.[4]

He returned with a strong letter, also, to the Massachusetts Magistrates, which secured him a landing at Boston (September, 1644), but did not abate their resistance ; for now, with their Charter, these Schismatics seemed more dangerous to them than before. The Colonies around the Narragansett Bay, were at this time beset with dangers from without as well as from within ; Ply-

[1] Hutchinson's History. Elton's Life, p. 127.
[2] Knowles, p. 295.
[3] Knowles, p. 183.
[4] Hist. Coll., vol. ii., p. 121.

mouth laid claim to Aquetneck, and sent one of her Magistrates, Mr. Brown, to forbid others to exercise jurisdiction. Massachusetts claimed to own Providence, and the parts adjacent ; and Connecticut sent in her claims on the west ; so that Rhode Island was nigh suffering the fate afterward meted to Poland ; but the firmness and judgment of Williams, backed by his friends, sustained the infant Colonies.[1]

The news of Williams's return preceded him, and quickened the pulses of the people. They met him at Seekonk. A fleet of canoes crowded the river, and when the brave man came down to meet them, cheer after cheer thrilled his heart, and brought tears into his eyes. He embraced them in silent gratitude, and his satisfaction was such as patriots and single-hearted philanthropists only can feel. No lines of soldiers paid him a drilled homage, no parks of cannon belched forth noise and smoke, no shopkeepers hung out banners inscribed with patronage and praise ; but the sincere gratitude and esteem of the whole people gave him such a reception, as Kings might long for and Gods envy.

CODDINGTON and his friends, on Rhode Island, had founded themselves (1638) as a separate Colony at Portsmouth, upon the idea of intellectual and spiritual liberty ; and Coddington was chosen Judge, after the fashion of the Israelites ; their Constitution, established March (1640), stated That the Government was a "Democracie or popular Government." That it was the power of the "Majority of the freemen to make Laws ;" that no man should be made criminal "for Doctrines ;" in fine, they recognized and appealed to the good rather than the bad in human nature, and chose for their seal and motto, a bundle of Arrows, and AMOR VINCET OMNIA : Love overcomes all things. Love is the fulfilling of the law.[2]

[1] Winthrop. Knowles, p. 47.

[2] Bancroft, vol. i., p. 393. Providence Records. Hutchinson, vol. i., p. 73. Rhode Island Colony Records, Providence, 1856.

The obtaining the Charter was followed by a Union of the Plantations (Providence, Portsmouth, Newport, and Warwick; called at first "The Providence Plantations") around Narragansett Bay (1647). It provided for an Annual President and Legislative Assembly; and the code of laws concludes, "All men may walk as their conscience persuades them, every one in the name of his God." The Union was renewed in 1654,[1] and at the first general election held at Warwick (September, 1654), Williams was chosen President of the Plantations.

UNION OF THE "PROVIDENCE PLANTATIONS."

The struggle in England, between the King and the people, excited intense interest in the Colonies, and from time to time great news reached them. Williams wrote thus to John Winthrop, the younger, at Nameag, dated Narragansett, 26, 3, 1649:

"SIR: Tidings are high from England, many ships from many parts say, and a Bristol ship came to the Isle of Shoals within few days confirms, that the king and many great lords and parliament men are beheaded; London was shut up on the day of execution, not a door to be opened," etc. "The States of Holland and the Prince of Orange (forced by them) consented to proceedings; It is said, Mr. Peters preached (after the fashion of England) the funeral sermon to the king after sentence, out of the terrible denunciation to the king of Babylon—Is. xiv., 18, etc., 'All the kings of the nations, all of them lie in their glory, every one in his own house. But thou art cast out of the grave like an abominable branch—the raiment of those that are slain thrust through with a sword, that go down to the stones of the pit; as a carcass trodden under feet. Because thou hast destroyed thy land,'" etc. This was great news in New England.

All his life Williams labored for peace, peace; plead for it (see Letter to Mass. Magistrates, Elton, p. 118) with Indians and with whites. But his hopes and plans were

[1] Elton, p. 115.

endangered by the action of Coddington; and the safety of the Narragansett Plantations was in peril.

WILLIAM CODDINGTON was the father of Aquetneck. He had been a Magistrate in Massachusetts, a merchant, a man of substance and of courage. He was among the few who strenuously advocated freedom of conscience and worship. He stood by Vane and Mrs. Hutchinson in the great Antinomian Controversy, and went down with them. He was a man of such character and wealth, that Winthrop and others made efforts to induce him to stay with them at Boston; but he chose to sacrifice his business, and his estate at Braintree, and go with his friends to make a new settlement.

In forming their new State they decided to be governed by the Word of God; and Coddington was appointed JUDGE. But this did not work well, and in 1640, it was changed to Governor, Lieutenant-Governor, etc., etc., in the regular worldly fashion. Coddington was chosen Governor till the Union; and administered justice with discretion. He went to England in 1651, obtained a charter for Rhode Island, and was appointed Governor of the Island; but it excited jealousy, and with reason—lest their laws and liberties should be encroached upon, and the opinion was so strong against him, that he was forced to resign, when a new union was formed. For a time he had no hand in public affairs; but in 1674–75 he was again chosen Governor. In his later years he held the doctrines of the Quakers, and was always a warm advocate of liberty of conscience.

Coddington was of the king's party, in the struggle which was going on between Charles I. and the Parliament of England; and the new charter he had procured in England constituted him Governor for life. This caused much anxiety; and again Williams, with John Clarke (a noble man) was obliged to go to England (November, 1651); where he procured the recall of Coddington's charter, and the confirmation of the one first obtained. To procure the means of going, "he sold his trading-house at Narragansett," which yielded him a good profit—for in his estimation, true patriotism was better than large profits.

While Williams was in England (1652) negotiating for the renewal of the charter, the Court wrote to him from Providence, that it might tend to good order, "if it might be the pleasure of that honorable State, to invest, appoint, and empower yourself to come over as Governor of this Colony."

It was not done, and so the choice of a chief officer devolved upon the people of the colony. We can but rejoice that this was so, and that no such bad precedent crippled the free action of the people.[1]

He enjoyed, while there, the society of such men as Milton, Marvell, Vane; and had frequent interviews with Cromwell. These were men who could comprehend the doctrine of freedom of conscience, and strengthen his head and his heart. He said in a letter to Winthrop (July, 1664), respecting Cromwell's idea that liberty of conscience should be maintained in all American Plantations: "Sir, a great man in America told me that he thought New England would not bear it."[2] Great men have been saying such things, since the foundation of society, and distrusting the instincts and reason of men; they do it now, but they are not the greatest.

During this visit he also had a singular correspondence with his old Master's daughter—Lord Coke's—then Mistress Anne Sadlier of Stoudon, Puckridge. Williams was earnest and logical, but gentlemanly; the lady cool and bitter. She was for the King, and read "the Bible—the King's Book ('Icon,' not written by him), Hooker's Polity, Andrews' Sermons, Jeremy Taylor, and Dr. Jackson upon the Creed, and wanted no new lights." She had no doubt that God had begun his judgments upon Milton here, and that "his punishment will be hereafter in hell." Also, that Jeremy Taylor's plea for liberty of Prophesy-

[1] Staples's Annals, page 86. [2] Knowles, page 264.

ing, "and you (Williams) would make a good fire;" also, "that such as you (Williams) will rise devils." All which is interesting, showing the temper of the times, but is not profitable for present reading.

When Williams returned from England in 1654, he brought a letter from the Lord Protector's Council, which allowed him in future to embark or to land in any of the Colonies; so he was not molested. After his return he was elected President of the united Settlements, and, in the short time he served, came into collision with William Harris, who claimed that there should be "No lords—no masters." The feud between him and Williams, was of some standing, and became bitter, so that Williams would not even write his name, but designated him as "W. Har." Williams held the office of President for two years, when he was superseded by Benedict Arnold, then an honorable name.

THE CHARTER RENEWED.

On the accession of the dissolute but good-natured Charles II., it was thought best to secure a renewal of their Charter, and Dr. Clarke, (one of the best of men of Aquiday, or Rhode Island) was their agent to get it. Charles granted it, to the surprise of his Ministers, and against their wishes, July, 1663. "It was the freest that ever bore the signature of a King, and was the astonishment of the age.[1] It contained this clause: "No person within the said Colony, at any time hereafter, shall be in any wise molested, punished, disquieted, or called in question for any differences of opinion in matters of religion, who do not actually disturb the peace of said Colony." It also provided, expressly, for Representation by the Freemen. Under this liberal charter, which she seemed to "bear" very well, notwithstanding the fears of a "great man in the Bay," Rhode Island continued to flourish till the year 1843, never losing sight of Williams's cardinal principle, and only limited in a physical greatness worthy of

[1] Gammel, p. 182. Knowles, p. 319. Williams's letter to Mason.

this free principle, by her territorial bounds. This Charter was seized by Andros, 1687, but was never legally forfeited (ch. xliv. vol. i.). The Colonial Legislature provided that Freeholders and their eldest sons only should be freemen, which worked well for a time, but in this century has given rise to serious disturbance.[1] The condition of the people there was good ; better than in England. In the report made by the Governor of Rhode Island to Charles II., they say, "We leave every man to walk in religion as God shall persuade his heart, and as for beggars and vagabonds we have none amongst us." Another observer said, "The worst cottages of New England are lofted ; there are no beggars, and not three persons are put to death annually for civil offences."

At this period Evelyn, in his Journal, writes as follows: "Went to Uppingham, the shire town of Rutland ; pretty, and well built of stone, which is a rarity in that part of England, where most of the rural villages are built of MUD, and the people living as wretchedly as the most impoverished parts of France, which they much resemble, being idle and sluttish. The country (especially Leicestershire) being much in common ; the Gentry Free-drinkers."

During King Philip's war (which began in June, 1675, and ended in August, 1676), Rhode Island was exposed to attacks from the Indians, but Williams was as fearless as ever ; he trusted to his long life of justice, and was safe. They said, "But as for you, brother Williams, you are a good man—not a hair of your head shall be touched." He remained at home as usual, and though 76 years old, accepted the post as Captain in the Militia, drilled them well, and held them ready for active service. The war occasioned great alarm and distress over all the plantations, and many of the inhabitants fled to Newport for safety. But the Indians attacked Providence in March (26th), 1676, which was of course weakly protected,

[1] Hildreth, vol. ii.

and burnt some twenty-nine houses, and fear and danger were not ended till the death of Philip in August, 1676. (See ch. xli.)

WILLIAMS BECOMES BAPTIST.

About the year 1638–9, Williams was re-baptized by immersion, as Winthrop[1] states, by "one Holliman, a poor man, late of Salem;" and that he was persuaded to it by "the wife of one Scott," the sister of the great Heresiarch of that day, Mrs. Hutchinson. This was the beginning of the first Baptist Church in America. "Anabaptist" was the mad-dog, infidel cry of those days; and had become so, partly because the sect had developed the doctrine of Freedom of Conscience, and partly because of the atrocities and excesses of the "Rustic war" of Munster. The Anabaptists of Munster seem to have been as much misunderstood and vilified as any other Reformers. In the "Rustic war" provoked by tyranny and cruelty [1535], many Anabaptists (twice baptized) joined; but the ferocity and desperation of the time can not justly be charged to them; rather upon those who goaded the people to resistance. At various times the Anabaptists have admitted that Magistracy was proper, and they seem to have anticipated Roger Williams in his doctrine of Freedom of Conscience; which will account for the vilification and misrepresentation of the Royalist writers of that day.[2]

It is not necessary to go into any elaborate defense of this step of Williams, when we remember that the first and second Presidents of Harvard College, Dunster and Chauncey, held the same views, and that Baptists now have church accommodation in the United States for over 3,000,000 persons, and are as well-behaved and law-abiding as any citizens. But at that time it was charged, that Williams and the Anabaptists repudiated all laws and

[1] Winthrop. March, 1638–9.

[2] Note in Knowles's Life of Williams. See, also, Confessions of Seven Churches, in London, 1646. Appendix to Neal's Puritans. See Winchell's Discourses.

Magistrates, and were going straightway to destruction. Williams continued with the Baptists some three or four months, and after that, according to Richard Scott, he belonged to no Church organization. In this he was not unlike many remarkable men of the past and present times, such as Milton and Cromwell. From having considered the English Church a wicked one—from having refused to associate with it or with the New England Churches, unless they repudiated it, and to pray with unregenerate people—he came to be willing to preach in any Church, and to consort in religious practices with any people.

At last he settled upon this, "That every one should have liberty to worship God according to the rights of their own consiences; but otherwise not owning any Churches or ordinances of God anywhere upon earth."[1]

WILLIAMS HAS CONTROVERSIES.

It is common, and to some extent excusable, in looking at remarkable men, especially so if they have been champions of great ideas, to see them only from one point of view, and to glorify them, to the injury of truth and the rising generation. It is safest, it is most manly, to see men fairly, as they are, whoever they are, whether alive or dead. There are tender souls who feel that after death, the good alone lives, and should only be spoken of; and in a degree this is true. But when we look at any man, let us endeavor to take courage from his virtues, and warning from his weaknesses or wickednesses, so we shall learn to be equal to present demands, and fit for coming times.

In his controversy with Harris, Williams showed himself capable of bitterness and severity, equal to any; so, too, in his clashing with Gorton. The Rhode Island Plantations had refused, again and again, to join in the persecution of Quakers; but Williams none the less disliked their principles, and champed the bit till he could charge upon them. There were at least three reasons for this: he loved a theological skirmish; he believed he

[1] Morton's Mem., p. 154.

could prove their principles wrong; and he wished to clear his Colony from the charge, that because it tolerated the Quakers, it therefore admitted the truth of their doctrines. So, when George Fox, their remarkable Apostle, came to Newport [1672], Williams sent down to him a challenge, to discuss publicly, "fourteen propositions, to wit," which it is not necessary to repeat.

It did not reach Newport till after Fox had left; and it was suspected that the friends of Williams might have prolonged its voyage from Providence to Newport intentionally; but Williams was willing to charge, that the "Fox slily slipped away," and Fox had no hesitation in charging Williams with lying. The discussion, however, was held between Williams, for himself, and John Stubs, John Burnyeat, and William Edmundson, for the Quakers, and continued three days at Newport, and one at Providence. Williams went down in his boat, thirty miles; he says: "God graciously assisting me in rowing all day with my old bones, so that I got to Newport toward midnight, before the morning appointed;" and he was then 73 years old. The great discussion brought together all the people, and the meeting-house was crowded. Both parties, at the outset, were confirmed in their convictions, and both parties went in to win, rather than to be enlightened. The whole thing, of course, was confusion, subtle thrusting and parrying; and resulted in hatreds, and two pernicious Religious books: one by Williams, called "George Fox digged out of his Burrowes;" the other by Fox and Burnyeat, called "New England's Firebrand quenched;" in which all show up themselves and one another.

Acting upon the plan of presenting whatever, good and bad, may illustrate the character of a remarkable man, and the times in which he worked, we come to the sale of Indians following the Philip's war. In August, 1676, a Town-meeting was held at Providence, and, as the record has it, it was judged that certain Indian prisoners ought to be delivered as slaves, or servants for a term of years, to those "who stayed, and went not away." A Committee was appointed, who adjudged the division, and Advertisement was put out to—

"Inhabitants wanting to have Indians at the price they sell at Rhode Island or elsewhere"—all under five years to serve till thirty, above five and under ten till twenty-eight, etc.

To this notice was signed the name of Roger Williams, and four others.[1]

All regret, and some are surprised, that Williams should have had a hand in this transaction; he is to be judged, but not harshly; there were many excusing circumstances, which it is not necessary to present.

It is better to admit the probability that, Idealist as Williams was, he was not always equal to himself, and did not appreciate either the folly or wrong of this proceeding, in a social or economic point of view. He had the authority of the Jews for selling their captives, and exasperated at the fierce onslaught of the Indians, his long-continued kindness and justice toward them was provoked into a desire to punish, as well as to render them powerless. The result could only be wanton destruction to the slaves, and a weakened moral sense in the community.

The life of this man was nigh spent; he had had faith in the doctrine of Religious Liberty, had suffered and labored for it, and had sustained it, and now after a long and active life, he saw it, as he fully believed, fully established. Yet he did not sit down in sloth. When past seventy-seven years of age, he continued to go among the Narragansetts to preach; and his interest in the Colony did not relax. He might have been rich; as his son said, "If a covetous man had that opportunity as he had, most of this town would have been his tenants."[2] But he freely gave away and parted with his property, so that he

[1] Knowles's Life, p. 348.

[2] See his son's letter in Knowles's Life, p. 10.

had to ask help to print some discourses. And now with more than four-score years on his head, he went down to his grave, deserving more honor than if he had gathered to himself the wealth of the Indies, leaving a heritage to this nation, richer than gold—the possession of Religious and Civil Freedom.

At the age of eighty-four (1683),[1] he died, and was buried on his own land, where he had first set his foot in that wilderness, forty-seven years before; and was remembered by the people many days. No stone now marks his grave.

HIS WRITINGS.

It is well to notice that Williams's activity impelled him to work as well as to think, and that the ACT with him followed the thought, as the thunder does the lightning. Whatever his hand found to do, he did it with a will, and no work to him was mean. We can not therefore look to him as a book-maker, but as a man who wrote his thoughts in life rather than words. A short account, however, of his writings will not fail to interest.

In 1643, "The Key to the Indians' Language," was published in England.[2]

It contains accounts of the manners and usages of the Indians, and is valuable. Upon one point he confirms the evidence of Winslow; he says, "He that questions whether God made the world, the Indians will teach him: I must acknowledge I have received in my converse with them, many confirmations of those two points: 1. That God is; 2. That he is a rewarder of all them that diligently seek him."

In 1644, "The Bloody Tenent of Persecution," was published.

The grand doctrine of which is, that the obligation to love and obey God, binds the heart of every man; but each is responsible to God alone, for his religious opinions and rites.

[1] Between January and May; in Knowles's Life, p. 354.

[2] See R. I. Hist. Coll., vol. i.

In 1652, "Experiments of Spiritual Life and Health," appeared.

It was dedicated to Lady Vane, and prefixed with a letter to his wife in which he says: "I send thee, tho' in winter, a handful of flowers made up in a little posy for thyself and our dear children, to look and smell on when I, as the grass of the field, shall be gone and withered."

In 1652, also appeared his reply to Mr. Cotton's pamphlet upon the Bloody Tenent—the title to which is a sample of the times, and is as follows:

THE BLOODY TENENT
yet
MORE BLOODY
by
MR. COTTON'S ENDEAVOURS TO WASH IT WHITE IN THE BLOOD OF THE LAMBE.

Of whose precious Blood spilt in the Blood of his Servants, and

Of the Blood of Millions spilt in former and later Wars for Conscience' Sake,

That

Moſt bloody Tenent of Persecution for Cause of Conscience, upon a Second Trial, is found now more apparently and notoriously guilty.
etc., etc.

By R. WILLIAMS, of Providence in N. E.

LONDON: etc.,
1652.

"The Bloody Tenent" grew out of a protest against religious persecution, written in Newgate with MILK upon sheets of paper, which were smuggled to the prisoner by the woman who supplied him with food. This paper was transcribed by a friend, and sent to Mr. Cotton of Boston, who answered it.

Then Williams wrote the "Bloody Tenent of Persecution," and dedicated it "To the Right Honorable both Houses of the High Court of Parliament." It is a bold, clear, and manly argument against the persecution of men for Conscience' Sake. He believed what men (with exceptions) now all believe,

"That the blood of so many hundred thousand souls of Protestants and Papists spilt in the wars of present and former ages for their respective Consciences is not required or accepted by Jesus Christ, the Prince of Peace."

That human laws upon Conscience invade the prerogative of God, and that they are null, and no man is bound to obey them.

That the Early Christians held what we hold ; as Tertullian expresses it,

"It is the natural civil right of every man to worship whatever he pleases ; it is inconsistent with the nature of Religion to propagate it by force, for it must be received by voluntary consent, and not by coercion.[1]

That the duty of the Magistrate, in relation to religion, consists in the impartial protection of all citizens in the exercise of their religious privileges, whenever these do not degenerate into an active disturbance of the public good.

That laws, making men ineligible to office, or making any distinction, because of Religion, would be tyrannical and pernicious.

In 1652 also appeared "The Hireling Ministry none of Christ's," in which he does not oppose the payment of Clergymen, but the LEGAL establishment of Churches and Compulsory support of Ministers by tithes or taxation.[2]

In "George Fox digged out of his Burrowes," he indulged in the style of contemptuous bitterness, then common in religious controversies, and both he and Fox

[1] Knowles's Life of Williams, p. 364.

[2] Elton, p. 88.

suffered in their reputations, and in their own integrity; and it is well for them that these books are forgotten.

The greatness of Williams consisted in First, The clearness with which he recognized a Principle.

Second, The fidelity with which he accepted it; and

Third, In the courage and patience he displayed in putting it into action. He was no infidel—as so many persons termed religious are. Whatever was true he had faith in it, and he neither feared to say it, nor to act it; and this is his crowning glory.

He said—and mark his logical honesty, so rare and so noble—"I desire not that Liberty to myself, which I would not freely and impartially weigh out to all the Consciences of the world beside. All those consciences—yea, the very consciences of the Papists, Jews, etc., ought freely to be permitted their several respective worships, their ministers of worship, and what way of maintaining them they freely chose."

Williams was the first to announce, maintain, and establish Freedom to all men in opinion and worship, whether Hindoos, Jews, Papists, Atheists, Turks, or Christians.

In 1644 the Bloody Tenet was published, while Jeremy Taylor's "Liberty of Prophesying" was issued in 1647; and Bishop Heber admits that the last claims Liberty for Christians ONLY.

In 1634 Lord Baltimore settled Maryland, and established freedom of religious worship for Christians only; and the Assembly of Maryland in 1649 enacted, "that no persons professing to believe in Jesus Christ shall be molested; while any one speaking reproachfully against the blessed Virgin or the Apostles, shall forfeit five pounds."[1]

But two years before that [in 1647] the first General Assembly in Rhode Island, following the principle of Roger Williams, concluded their code of laws in this way:

[1] Chalmers's Political Annals. Cited by Knowles, p. 371.

"Otherwise than thus what is herein forbidden, all men may walk as their consciences persuade them, every one in the name of God." Williams's idea of Religious Liberty bore its legitimate fruits—Civil Liberty and Democracy—the supremacy of the people. He said more than two centuries ago in the wilderness of Rhode Island, "Kings and Magistrates must be considered invested with no more rights than the people intrust them with." "The Sovereign power of all civil authority is founded in the consent of the people." [1]

CIVIL LIBERTY A CONSEQUENCE OF RELIGIOUS LIBERTY.

The Conservatives and the timid and Class-Legislators then (as now) said—"but, Mr. Williams, the people are not ready for this, even if true ; we shall have schisms and anarchy, and the world will go to destruction !" Williams replied, I do not fear the truth ; the world is always ready for that, and you, and people like you, who dare not speak it, and act it, are the real mischief-makers ; wise as you are, you do not know the whole counsel of God, and you will do well to speak out what you do know ; trust the God which is in the soul of every man, and so put every man upon his own responsibility, to learn the truth and to do it.

But they could not, or would not, accept such honest daring. They felt bitterly, and accused him of being worse than the Quakers and Anabaptists, and of advocating "No Government." Williams, therefore, deliberately placed on the Town-record of Providence, his protest against this charge.

He said : "I affirm that (in case of a ship at sea), none of the Papists, Protestants, Jews, or Turks, be forced to come to the ship's prayers or worships ; but I never denied that the commander of the ship ought to command the ship's course ; and compel the seamen to perform their duty, the passengers to pay their freights, etc."[2]

When some one-sided man circulated a tract saying, that it was tyranny to execute judgment, even "against

[1] See Bloody Tenet.

[2] Gammell's Life, p. 165.

transgressors of public or private weal," Williams met him face to face, the champion of decent law and order; thus that calumny is set at rest.

Their Constitution, as has been said, was the first that secured entire religious liberty, to which Rhode Island has remained faithful; no act of religious intolerance having disgraced her statute-books. It is well to notice two charges which have been made; one by Chalmers,[1] that Roman Catholics were disfranchised. Such a provision appears in an edition of Laws subsequent to 1719; but the Honorable Samuel Eddy, has sufficiently shown, that it was a spurious insertion, at variance with the Charter, the Laws, and the Spirit of the people of Rhode Island.[2] Francis Brimly has said also, that in 1665, the Quakers were outlawed. This is thus disposed of. The King required an oath or agreement; the Quakers refused it, because it bound them to serve in the militia; and so they were disfranchised, not by an act of Rhode Island. The next year this was modified, and one of their number was elected Deputy Governor.[3]

WILLIAMS'S CHARACTER.

The rapidity of his blood, and his highly organized nervous system, are the key to Williams's character; for his quickness of insight, and his fervid imagination, though they led him to see and maintain the noblest truths, they also led him to advocate opinions, which may be called fantastic; such as the "gift of tongues" and "power of prophecy," in the true ministry. He was at times hasty, rash, changeable, and pertinacious, but he was also generous, brave, prompt, and disinterested; a man to respect and love. He was a free-thinker, a free-speaker, and a free-actor, both in religious and civil things; in the largest sense, a free-man; and the world has come to his principles. Few men are inspired by God, with so large a perception of truth, and so

[1] Political Annals.

[2] See Walsh's Appeal. Gammell's Life, p. 209. Elton's, p. 135.

[3] Knowles, p. 324.

strong a faith in it, and the memory of Roger Williams, fidelity to his principles, and respect for the State he founded, so loyal to Liberty, should be cherished by every man, who has faith in Truth, Freedom, and the Future.[1]

[1] For List of Governors of Rhode Island, from 1647, see ch. ii., vol. ii.

CHAPTER XXVI.

MAINE AND NEW HAMPSHIRE.

GORGES—POPHAM—CHALONG—SAGADEHOC—SETTLEMENTS ATTEMPTED—CAPTAIN MASON—LACONIA—PROVINCE OF MAINE—THE PLOW PATENT—CLEAVES AND VINES—MASSACHUSETTS TAKES POSSESSION—KING'S COMMISSIONERS—CONFUSION—THE MASSACHUSETTS PURCHASE—NEW HAMPSHIRE—PRING—THOMPSON AND THE HILTONS—DOVER—STRAWBERRY-BANK — BURDET—UNDERHILL—WHEELWRIGHT—ANNEXATION—CONTROVERSY—CUTT, FIRST PRESIDENT—ROYAL PROVINCE—SWAMP-LAW—TRADE—INDEPENDENCE.

Sir Ferdinando Gorges, like Raleigh, was a naval commander ; like him, he was fond of adventure ; sanguine and indefatigable, and capable of intrigue. When Captain Weymouth returned to England from an unsuccessful effort to discover a North-west passage to India, in 1605, he brought with him some New England Indians ; three of whom were taken into the family of Gorges, then Commander at Plymouth. The information gained from them, stimulated his genius, and excited in Gorges the idea of establishing Colonies ; thus pushing both his fortune and fame in the New World. When King James I. granted the two patents for colonizing Virginia, Gorges and Sir John Popham (Chief Justice of England), were the two leading men in the Northern or Plymouth Company ; and it was through their influence, that Henry Chalong was sent out on a voyage of discovery, in 1606. But in 1607, it was determined to make a settlement, and a hundred men, with George Popham, as President, and Raleigh Gilbert, as Admiral, were sent out (May 31, 1607). They touched the Continent at the Sagadehoc, or Kennebeck river ; and immediately giving thanks to God, as the custom was, set to work to get up houses, and to organize for furring and fishing ; but in the spring of 1608, Popham, the President, died, and Sir John Popham died in Enland, and Gilbert's brother died, so that he had to return, and the settlement came to an end; the country being branded as intolerably cold.[1] Gorges was not easily discouraged; he sent out Richard Vines, who, during his short stay, made some discoveries. He was followed by Henry Harley (1614), who accomplished nothing toward a settlement; the Expedition sent by Gorges and Dr. Sutliff, in 1615, had no better success. Captain Dermer, too, met with ill-success; he ranged the coast from Maine to Virginia, and was the first who passed the whole length of Long Island Sound (1619). But he died of wounds received from the Indians; and Gorges was nigh discouraged, and almost determined to have nothing more to do with these courses.

About 1622, Gorges struck hands with Captain John Mason, and they procured a grant from the Plymouth Company of a large tract, between the Merrimack and the Sagadehoc, extending to the river Canada (or St. Lawrence), which district they called Laconia; out of which it was hoped great things would grow. But Gorges spent large sums of money, for which he got no returns; yet he persisted in his plans, and, to carry them out, petitioned for the revocation of the Grand Charter of the Plymouth Company, through whom other grants had been made (ch. xx.). The intention then was, to recall all smaller grants, and to establish one general government from St. Croix to Maryland. The Company relinquished their Charter in 1635, and in 1637 the King appointed Gorges (then more than three-score years old) Governor-General; which honor he was not able to exercise. In 1639, the Crown confirmed him in his grant. His cousin, Thomas Gorges, came over in 1640, and remained about three years, endeavoring to make a state out of "Chancellor, Treasurer, Marshal, Marshal's Court," etc., etc., rather than out of men.

This territory was to be called the Province or County

[1] Hubbard, p. 224. Belknap's Biography. Gorges.

of Maine—in compliment to the Queen, who held a province of the same name in France;—and Gorges and his heirs were to be lords proprietors.[1] He was elated, and proceeded to organize an elaborate form of government and a settlement; the cardinal idea of which was, that the settlers were to go there, and he was to govern them; but it did not work.

In 1643, the troubles in England between the King and Commons grew violent, and in that year Alexander Rigby bought the old grant called Lygonia or "Plow Patent," and appointed George Cleaves his deputy-president. Governor Thomas Gorges about that time returned to England, and left Vines in his place. Between Cleaves and Vines there was of course a conflict of jurisdiction, and Cleaves appealed for aid to Massachusetts; and both parties agreed to leave their claims (1645) to the decision of the Massachusetts Magistrates, who decided—that they could not decide the matter. But the next year the Commissioners for American plantations in England decided in favor of Rigby; and Vines left the country. In 1647, at last, at the age of seventy-four, Sir Ferdinando Gorges died, and with him died all his plans for kingdoms and power in Maine.

In 1651, Massachusetts, finding that her patent, which included lands lying three miles north of the head waters of the Merrimack, took in all the lower part of Maine, began to extend her jurisdiction, and as most of the settlers favored her authority, it was pretty well established till the time of the Restoration (1660).

Upon the Restoration of Charles II., the heir of Gorges claimed his rights to Maine. His agent in the province was Edward Godfrey. Those claims were confirmed by the Committee of Parliament, and in 1664 he obtained an order from the King to the Governor of Massachusetts to restore him his province.

In 1664, the King's Commissioners came over, and pro-

[1] Hazard's Coll.

ceeded through the Colonies, and among the rest to Maine; where they appointed various officers without the concurrence of Massachusetts: so that for some years Maine was distracted with parties, and was in confusion.

In 1668, Massachusetts sent four Commissioners to York, who resumed and re-established the jurisdiction of Massachusetts, with which the majority of the people were best pleased; and in 1669 the Deputies from Maine again took their seats in the Massachusetts Court.

Her jurisdiction was, however, disputed by the heirs of Mason and Gorges, and it was not finally set at rest till the year 1677, by the purchase of their claims from them, by Massachusetts, for twelve hundred and fifty pounds sterling. By King William's Charter of 1691, Maine was incorporated with Massachusetts.[1]

NEW HAMPSHIRE.

Martin Pring, in 1603, in coasting along New England, with the "Speedwell" and "Discovery" (the last a bark of twenty-six tons), seems to have touched New Hampshire, and to have entered the Piscataqua river. But no settlements were attempted till the arrival of David Thompson and the Hiltons, sent by Mason and Gorges (the Laconia Company) in 1623.[2]

They had been fishmongers in London, and were to make much money by preparing fish for market. The Hiltons set up stages on the river at Dover, and Thompson near the mouth of the river at Little Harbor. In 1631, Williams and Chadburn, men of ability, with a number of planters and traders, came over and established themselves at Strawberry-bank, now the flourishing city of Portsmouth. Under the direction of Chadburn, the "Great House" was built, the beginning of a manor or Lordship, which was afterward assigned to Captain Mason, and was called Mason-Hall.

[1] Belknap's Biography. Gorges. Lucas's Charters. The History of the State of Maine, by William D. Williamson: Hallowell, 1839.

[2] Hubbard, p. 214. Hutchinson, vol. i., p. 103. Adams's Annals of Portsmouth, 1825.

Captain Wiggan and the Rev. Leveridge came over in 1633, and were a valuable accession. But the Rev. Burdet seems not to have left a good name ; he undermined Wiggan and assumed his place of Governor. In his turn, Burdet was undermined by Captain Underhill, who had been obliged to leave Massachusetts. Underhill had considered himself one of the elect—having received assurance "over a pipe of that good creature, Tobacco,"[1] as he said ; and that he should hold on to that assurance, "although he should fall into sin." But he was thrust out of the Bay, because he was a fellow who would speak his mind, and who was strongly suspected of loving other good creatures—having confessed that he "had had his will of the Cooper's wife ;" so, going to Piscataqua, and being an active man and a soldier, he was chosen Governor, and Burdet left. Their town they called DOVER.

In 1629 [May 17], Rev. John Wheelwright and others bought of the Indians the lands lying between the Piscataqua and the Merrimack. Whatever their deed was, it was disputed, and not recognized by the heirs of Mason.[2]

After the expulsion of Mrs. Hutchinson from Massachusetts, Wheelwright was obliged to leave there, and with his friends, settled as a body politic on the south side of the great Bay, up Piscataqua river, and called their place EXETER. The increase there was very slow—the Massachusetts plantations being more attractive to the larger number of settlers. Meanwhile that Colony were discovering, that the bounds of their Grant extended north beyond these new settlements ; and in 1641, their Court passed an order (with the consent of the settlers at Dover and Strawberry-bank, on the Piscataqua), "That from thenceforth, the said people inhabiting there, are and shall be accepted and reputed under the Government of the Massachusetts,"[3] etc. Mason had died, and confusion

[1] Winthrop, vol. i. [2] Adams's Annals of Portsmouth.
[3] Hutchinson, vol. i., p. 109. Winthrop, vol. ii., p. 38.

ensued, so that the settlers were mostly glad of the transfer.

A long controversy ensued between Mason's heirs and Massachusetts as to the right of Jurisdiction.

The History of New Hampshire and Maine at this period, was much the same. In 1660, at the time of the Restoration, the heirs of Mason applied to the Attorney-General in England, who decided that they had a good title to New Hampshire. The Commissioners who came over in 1664, attempted to re-establish them ; but as the settlers favored Massachusetts, she resumed her government when they left. Mason's heirs renewed their claim in 1675, and in 1679, it was solemnly decided against the claim of the Massachusetts Colony, although their grant technically included all lands extending to three miles north of the waters of the Merrimack river.

John Cutt was the first President in New Hampshire, and thenceforward to the American Revolution, New Hampshire was treated as a Royal province—the Governors and Lieutenant-Governors being appointed by the King, and the laws made by the people, being subject to his revision.[1]

The King claimed all the Forests ; and no persons but his officers were allowed to cut the grand pine-trees which covered the hill-sides, and crowned her mountain tops. But the people were free, and there was no standing army in New Hampshire, to shoot them down, and the "loggers and raftsmen" took the liberty which the king claimed as a divine right. They asserted "Swamp Law," and cut their share. They persistently resisted Governor Cranfield's high-handed plans for taxing and governing them ; and he at last begged to be allowed to remove "from these unreasonable people."

In this Colony, trade was mostly in the exchange of lumber, beef, fish, oil, and live-stock, for rum, sugar, molasses, and coffee, with the West Indies.

[1] See vol. ii., ch. ii.

Ship-building was an important occupation; and ships, of from two hundred to three hundred tons, were constructed, to the number of ten or twelve annually. Great quantities of pine-tree masts and spars were prepared for England, and shipped off annually.

It was not insisted on, that New Hampshire was settled as a religious Colony; and under the Wentworths Episcopacy was favored.

One of the New Hampshire Ministers, reproached the people [1691] that they had left the first purpose of their ancestors, who came to this howling wilderness, to enjoy without molestation the exercise of their pure principles of religion; when one of his congregation interrupted him, saying: "Sir, you entirely mistake the matter. Our Ancestors did not come here on account of their religion, but to fish and trade;" which was true.

A long step now takes us to the time of the American Revolution.

Then a Provincial Congress assembled at Exeter, in New Hampshire, on the 21st of December [1775], to devise measures to secure the public good. They agreed upon an Executive and a Legislature, to consist of a Council and a House of Representatives, which alarmed some people, who remonstrated strongly, lest it should look like dissolving the Union with Great Britain. But the Patriots said: "When the Union becomes a tyranny, it had better be dissolved." So that Union was then dissolved, and New Hampshire joined the United States.

CHAPTER XXVII.

THE SETTLEMENT OF NEW HAVEN.

DAVENPORT, AND EATON, AND HOPKINS—1638—QUINNIPIAC—HENRY WHITFIELD—GUILFORD—MILFORD—STAMFORD—BRANFORD—COMMERCE—THE GREAT SHIP LOST—THEOPHILUS EATON—HOPKINS—JOHN DAVENPORT—FIRST SABBATH—THE STATE—CHARTER—UNION—THE DUTCH.

THE fierce clash about religions in Old England from 1630 to 1640, was like the confusion of tongues in the old times at Babel; it scattered men to the four winds of heaven, and colonized New England. Mather likened the Puritans to the "peculiar people whom the great God had carried into a wilderness to establish a theocracy, he himself being their Lord of Hosts."

In the Hector (20th June, 1637), arrived at Boston, the Rev. John Davenport, and with him came Theophilus Eaton—his old schoolmate—and Edward Hopkins, rich London merchants. Winthrop and his associates welcomed them heartily to the New World.

They reported matters to be growing worse rather than better, for godly, free-thinking men in England, and the country was getting to be no better than Turkey or Rome. Many persons—their friends—were sure to follow, and they looked about for a favorable position, where would be room to welcome them. The Massachusetts Magistrates were exceedingly desirous, because of their character and property, that they should remain near Boston; but they, hearing that west of the Connecticut Plantations, were good situations, sent to purchase some which lay to the southwest, toward the Hudson River, which was done.

By this means they gained much fresh virgin soil, and as they hoped, were beyond the reach of the new Governor-General, who was then much talked of. In March, 1638, the Ministers, Davenport and Pruden, with many more, went round by water to Quinnipiac, to settle there, and began, around the bay which runs up between the two brave old trap-rocks (called "East and West Rocks"), the town—which has grown up to be the most beautiful city in America—now called New Haven. A company, mostly young men, joined them from the southerly parts of England—Kentish, Suffolk, and Surrey men, under the ministry of the Rev. Henry Whitfield, among whom was young William Leete ; afterward Governor of the United Colonies of New Haven and Connecticut. These, under the lead of Whitfield (1639), settled at Guilford, a pleasant place some sixteen miles east of New Haven ; the Indian name of which was Menunkatuck. The land was purchased for the uses of the town, from the Sachem-squaw, and was held in trust by the Rev. Henry Whitfield, Robert Kitchell, Wm. Leete, William Chittenden, John Bishop, and John Caffinge ; and consisted of the lands between Stoney Creek (Rutawoo) and East (Aigicomock) Rivers. The Church was formed in 1643, when the lands were divided ; and Whitfield was their first minister. He was rich, and built the "Stone House," now standing and in good condition, which was used at times for a fort. He afterward removed to England, and was succeeded by his son-in-law, the Rev. John Higginson.

Milford was begun by Peter Pruden, and his friends ; Stamford, by a company from Weathersfield ; and Branford, by another emigration from that town, where there were many church quarrels. These all clustered about New Haven, and enjoyed the satisfaction of seeking and cultivating new virgin lands.

The New Haven settlers were men of trade and money, they built great houses and hoped to thrive by Commerce rather than Husbandry, but their first undertakings were unsuccessful, and they suffered many losses ; "the Lord," for some reason, "being against them ;" so that in five or six years, their stock was much wasted, and they near the bottom.[1] But they determined to make one more effort, against what seemed destiny; so they built a great ship, of which "the godly Mr. Lamberton went Master," freighted her with corn, and furs, and plate, and much property for England. In her went Mr. Grigson, and sundry other considerable persons, godly people, too. But it was all to no purpose, for she was "walt-sided," ill-built, and ill-laden; they cut out the ice in the harbor with saws so that she could get to sea, and she was never heard of afterward. The loss was grievous, and was clearly enough the result of mismanagement, rather than any displeasure the Lord may have had with their trading. The loss was not only of their goods—which for a time paralyzed their trade—but of, at least, ten precious Christians; who, as Cotton said, went to heaven in a chariot of water, rather than of fire as Elijah did.

As the older men died or removed, the younger ones were more ready to bend their backs to the labors of Agriculture, and as the Colony was not able to remove to a more promising location, it began to thrive, as it has continued to do from that day to this.

Their principal man, THEOPHILUS EATON, had been a Turkey merchant in England, where he gained wealth; and for a time he was agent for the King, in Denmark. When his friend and fellow townsman, the Rev. Davenport, was forced to abandon England, he decided to come to the strange land with him. Many inducements were held up for them to settle near Boston; but as the best lands there were taken up, and as they had commerce in view, they decided to go elsewhere, and purchased at Quinnipiac. Through twenty years Eaton was annually chosen governor, which is good proof of his ability and justice. One good thing of his is preserved to us: he said, "Some account it a great matter to *die well*, but I am sure it is a great matter to LIVE well." Much the greater of the two indeed.

[1] Hubbard, p. 321.

The New England divines were prone to try their hands at poetry, and it is a matter of serious consideration, why their good intentions should have so signally failed in the execution. They put upon Eaton's tomb these lines:

> "Eaton so meek, so fam'd, so just,
> The Phœnix of our world, here hides his dust;
> His name forget New England never must."

EDWARD HOPKINS, his son-in-law, was also a successful merchant in England. He settled at Hartford, and was, with Haynes, Governor of Connecticut, till his return to England, where he was in favor with Cromwell, and was appointed Warden of the fleet; but he was the fast friend of New England, and left large bequests to the Colonies, when he died in 1657.

JOHN DAVENPORT, their Minister, was in the prime of life, and in the full vigor of his intellect, when he came to settle at New Haven, being then 41 years old. He had been a distinguished preacher in the English Church, and had been forced to leave for Holland under the iron discipline of Laud. He was a man of strong and decided views, and was among the most urgent of those who held to the Rule of the Saints. He refused to participate in the indiscriminate baptism of children in Holland; and in New England was exceeding strict as to the repentance of those admitted to church membership. He was a scholar, a gentleman, an excellent preacher, and one of the most intrepid of the New England divines. It was his mind which shaped the infant legislation of New Haven. On the 1[illegible]th of April (1638) the band of Pilgrims were collected under a spreading oak (near the corner of George and College-streets); around them was the budding forest, in which the spring birds were just beginning to sound their notes; and under its shelter were raised the frail tents of the wanderers. It was Sunday—"the Lord's day," and the voice of Davenport rose in the calmness of the spring morning—and every man stood up in the presence of God—as he gave forth his first prayer in the wilderness. During thirty years Davenport was their Minister, and was among the first in New England.

THE STATE. During the first year, little "Government" was needed or exercised. Each man was a lord to himself. On the 4th of June (163[illegible]) the settlers met in Mr. Newman's barn, and bound themselves by a sort of Constitution. Afterward, on the 29th of October, the "Seven Pillars," chosen to govern the Church, convened the Freemen who were church members, and they chose Mr. Eaton for Governor, and seven Magistrates or Assistants. They decided to make the Bible their law-book ; but, by and by, new towns were made, and new laws were needed, and they had the good sense to make them.

Their State was founded upon their Church, thus expressed in their first compact, signed by one hundred and eleven persons : "That Church members only shall be free Burgesses, and that they only shall chose Magistrates and officers among themselves, to have the power of transacting all publique civil affairs of this plantation, of making and repealing laws, dividing of inheritances, deciding of differences that may arise, and doing all things or businesses of like nature."

New Haven did a brave and manly thing in sheltering the Regicides (see vol. i., ch. xxxvii.), and the name of John Davenport should be held in honor there and elsewhere.

After the Connecticut Charter was obtained [in 1662] by Governor John Winthrop, it was proposed that New Haven should unite with Connecticut. This was opposed by many, and strongly by Rev. Mr. Davenport, because he believed in a Government of Church members as practiced in New Haven, which rule did not prevail in Connecticut. But circumstances, and their many natural sympathies, made a union inevitable, and it took place in May, 1665. John Winthrop was chosen Governor of the two united Colonies.[1]

THE DUTCH.

The New Haven and Connecticut people were constantly on the verge of a quarrel with the Dutch at Manhadoes (New York). They were always at variance about their bounds, for this good reason, because there were none; but in 1650 it was agreed between them, that the line of division should begin at Greenwich bay, some four miles west of Stamford.[2] Irving tells us how the Dutch did not like the smell of onions, so the Yankees planted their rows a *little* further west every year, and the Dutchmen retired with tears in their eyes, and so the New England men got the most land.

This story is ingenious, if not true.

[1] Trumbull's Hist. Connect., vol. i., p. 289. [2] Hazard, vol. ii.

CHAPTER XXVIII.

THE SETTLEMENT OF CONNECTICUT.

QUONEHTACUT RIVER—HOLMES BEGINS WINDSOR—JOHN HOOKER—WEATHERSFIELD—IMMIGRATION—EARL OF WARWICK'S GRANT—SAYBROOK—HARTFORD—SPRINGFIELD—JOHN HAYNES—ROGER LUDLOW—FENWICK—WILLIAM PYNCHEON—JOHN WINTHROP—THE UNION—CONDITION OF THE COLONY.

As early as April, 1631, Wahgumacut came to Boston from the Connecticut River,[1] and offered the white men corn and beans, if they would come and settle in his country.[2] He may have been a good man, but if he had been a wise Indian he would have distrusted the fire-water, the guns, and the energy of the whites. They were too weak to accept his offer then, but the report of the rich and beautiful valleys and plains, which lie along that river from Bellow's Falls to Haddam, floated in the air. In 1633 the Plymouth folks prepared a house, and shipped it round, for the beginning of a trading-post, and for securing a purchase made from Attawauhutt, and to prevent the inroad of those (by no means dull) Dutch from the Hudson, who had already got a footing, called Good Hope, nigh what is now Hartford. The small Plymouth enterprise was led by William Holmes, who paid no heed to the threats of the Dutch fort, but sailed past them, threatening to shoot back; and pitched his tents at Windsor.[3]

Now the land about Boston was not rich, and after three or four years of cultivation, it became spent; even manuring it with fish would not keep it in heart, as it will not any land; and many began to be uneasy at the

[1] Spelled by Winthrop "Quonehtacut."

[2] Prince's Chronology.

[3] Morton's Mem., p. 174.

prospects in the future; for a fertile country is the foundation of all prosperity. They too had heard of the rich valleys of the Connecticut, and at the September Court (1634) the principal topic, was the intention of the Rev. Mr. Hooker (who came over in 1633), with many of the inhabitants of Newtown—his congregation—to go to those better lands. In this year, too, some of the inhabitants of Watertown seem to have removed to Weathersfield.[1]

The Newtown people had heard much good of the new lands, and desiring what was best, and moved by that instinct which drives men forward to the utmost verge, and suspecting "that two such stars as Mr. Cotton and Mr. Hooker could not continue in one orb;"[2] for these and other reasons, they desired to go. But whether they should have leave from the rest? Considering the weakness of the Colony, and their own peril, and their present advantages, and that it was "as the removing of a candlestick, a great judgment," and so on, ought they have leave to go? The Court putting it to vote, after much discussion, there was found to be fifteen for it to ten against it.[3] This difference grew to a dissension, so that a fast became necessary; and a sermon from Mr. Cotton, preached from Haggai, 11th chapter, 4th verse, "Yet now be strong, oh Zerubbabel," etc., tended to quiet the matter for a time. In this discourse, Cotton held that the ultimate resolution of matters ought to be in the whole body of the people, yet that the Magistracy and the Ministry ought to have a negative voice; so there were three powers in the State, the People, the Ministers, and the Magistrates: such seemed to be Mr. Cotton's elements for the making of a State.

But in 1635, some of Newtown and Watertown gained leave to go whither they would, provided they continued under the government; so in October (15th, 1635, according to Winthrop) the first emigration from the hardly

[1] Preface to Hinman's Early Settlers of Connecticut.

[2] Hubbard's History, p. 173.

[3] Winthrop's Journal.

settled vicinity of Boston (Dorchester) took place, consisting of some sixty men, women, and children, with cows, horses, and swine. They settled at Windsor, and pushed out the Plymouth people.

SAYBROOK. The Earl of Warwick seems to have held the first grant of Connecticut (1630), from whom it passed to the Lords Say and Brook, and others, who for many years were intent upon establishing a new Colony, and becoming lords proprietors.[1]

Under their commission, John Winthrop the younger came over in 1635, and in November[2] he sent a bark of some thirty tons, with twenty men and munitions, to take possession of the mouth of the river, and commence the fort and town afterward called Saybrook.

HOOKER EMIGRATES. In the last of May, of the next year (1636), the principal Emigration took place. It consisted of a hundred persons, led by the fervent Hooker, and the large-minded John Haynes, who had been Governor of Massachusetts, in the preceding year. Most of the Pilgrims went on foot, but Mrs. Hooker was carried in a "horse-litter." The season was charming, the forests were at their flush, and the birds sang in glad surprise, at this singular exodus into the almost unseen wilderness. What brave people there were in those days! The settlers "set down" at various points on the river; the Roxbury people, led by William Pyncheon, at Springfield (Agawam); Mr. Ludlow and the Dorchester folk, at Windsor (Mattaneaug); Mr. Hooker, Mr. Stone, and Mr. Haynes, with the Cambridge Church, at Hartford (Suckiaug), and some of the Watertown men were below, at Weathersfield (Pauquiaug).

JOHN HAYNES, the principal settler of Connecticut, came to Massachusetts in 1633. He was a man of greater wealth than Winthrop, being possessed in England of an estate of a thousand pounds a year, and he was a man of equal talents and of a larger nature; he was at once made an

[1] Hutchinson, vol. i., p. 64. [2] Winthrop's Journal, vol. i., p. 173.

Assistant, and in 1635, was chosen Governor, when he declared that he would not be chargeable to the people for an allowance. He joined Mr. Hooker's congregation at Newtown, and both he and Hooker grew in popularity and influence. The petition of Hooker's congregation, to be allowed to remove to Connecticut, at first refused, was afterward granted, and it was shrewdly surmised that the rising popularity of these two leaders had something to do with the ultimate consent.[1]

Haynes was the leading man at Hartford, and with Ludlow, had most to do in shaping the infant State. It is well to note that Church Membership was not made a test of Citizenship, as it was in Massachusetts. Haynes had gone through a severe experience, in the trial and banishment of Roger Williams, and it is probable that his sense of justice, his generosity of character, and his better statesmanship, were all shocked by it. It is quite certain, that he continued to be upon the most friendly terms with Williams.

His wise management, integrity, and liberality, endeared him to the people, and he was chosen Governor every alternate year (which was all their Constitution allowed), until the day of his death, which happened in 1654.

Roger Ludlow was one of the principal men in Connecticut. He was from a good family in England, was full of talent, impetuosity, and ambition. Failing to be chosen Governor in Massachusetts, in 1634—which he felt was due to him in the natural rotation—he protested that the people were imposed on, and that the elections were arranged and managed by the Assistants, which is not improbable. But his complaints injured him in public estimation, and he was left out of the Magistracy also. He then removed to Connecticut, where, for nineteen years, his talent and activity were of great value. He was every year Magistrate or Deputy Governor, and found more room for his active talent than in Massachusetts. He com-

[1] Trumbull's History.

piled the Connecticut Code, often called "Ludlow's Code," which is a remarkable and valuable collection of laws. It was first printed in 1672.

In 1639, he removed to Fairfield, which was then a border-town, and much in danger from the jealousies of the Dutch, at Manhadoes. In 1653, the Commissioners of the New England Colonies, agreed to make war upon the Dutch at Manhadoes, but Massachusetts refused to stand by Connecticut, which greatly exasperated Ludlow and his friends; so the town of Fairfield determined to make war themselves, and chose Ludlow commander; but the New Haven Court interfered, and punished some of the recruiting leaders. Ludlow was aggravated, and shortly sailed away to Virginia; where it is supposed he died.

Colonel George Fenwick, who came out for the Lord's Say and Brook (in 1639), was perplexed to know how to manage these people, who, ascertaining that they were beyond the bounds of the Massachusetts patent, had established the most liberal political society that the world had ever seen. At last the inhabitants purchased the title of the Lords (December, 1644), and Mr. Fenwick was chosen one of the Assistants. The Colony went on in its own way, until the Restoration of Charles II. John Winthrop was then sent to England, and succeeded in gaining a wonderfully free Charter, which was and is remarkable, securing as it did, freedom in Church and State. (1662.)

Mr. Pyncheon, and his friends at Springfield, were found to be within the Massachusetts limits, and were received back again in 1641; Mr. Pyncheon being appointed to hold Court there.[1]

WILLIAM PYNCHEON was the leading settler of Roxbury, where he continued till 1636; in that year, when there was such a scattering of the people, he led a party to the Connecticut River, and settled at Springfield. There he was the Magistrate, and first man, there he built himself a fine house for those days, which stood for many years, and

[1] Hutchinson, vol. i., p. 100.

there he traded with the Indians and grew rich. He was a man of cultivated mind, and of active piety, and was held in great respect in the Colony, till he wrote and published a book (1650) called, "The Meritorious Price of Man's Redemption;" altogether too liberal for the Magistrates of the Bay, who censured him severely and without scruple, and directed his book to be burned by the hangman. Conceiving himself to be ill-treated by persons in authority, with his son-in-law, Captain Smith, and the Rev. Mr. Moxon, he left for England (1652), and never returned. His descendants have owned property in Springfield, and have held places of honor to this day.

John Winthrop of Connecticut, possessed the sterling sense and manly sincerity of his father, John Winthrop of Massachusetts. The younger Winthrop had every advantage of travel and education, and was one of the few early settlers, who had had a university education (at Cambridge in England), yet was not a minister. He was the favorite of his father, who died too soon to see the manhood and honor to which his son arrived. He did not sit down under the skirts of his father, at Massachusetts Bay; but procuring the agency of Lord Say and Company, he established a new Colony, and built a fort at Saybrook, on the Connecticut river. It is a singular fact, that possessed as he was, of scholarly and scientific tastes, he took resolutely hold of the material life of a new colony, and worked to shape it well, for the superior structure which was to be built upon it. He seemed to appreciate what so many scholars and divines forget, the prime value of a good material base. From 1659 to 1676 he was chosen Governor of Connecticut, and in that position seems to have given universal satisfaction; if he had vices or enemies, they are forgotten. He was too large a man to engage in the persecution of Quakers, which he everywhere opposed; and if he believed at all in the rank superstition of witchcraft, then so common, it was as a query, not as a fact. His leisure time was devoted to science, and his contributions to the Royal Society of London, of which he was an early member, were highly valued. Indeed, Boyle and other scientific men, at one time, had a plan for joining him in the New World, for the investigation of natural knowledge.

UNION OF NEW HAVEN AND CONNECTICUT.

The Colony of Connecticut had managed its own affairs for a long time without a Charter (which, after all, was but a piece of sheepskin), in its own way, and well. The Charter, which Winthrop was able to secure in 1662, included in its limits the Colony of New Haven, which, up to this time, had had its own Governor and laws. When the Committee from Connecticut proposed to Governor Leete of New Haven, that a Union should be formed, he submitted the question to the Freemen; which awakened a great interest, and a strong opposition, from some of the principal men, such as Minister Davenport. The discussion of this question was continued with much heat, through some three years, and the Colony of New Haven was divided into two parties, one for, and one against a Union. Some of the inhabitants put themselves under the protection of Connecticut, and refused to pay taxes to New Haven; and there was danger of bloodshed in Guilford, in an attempt to make forced collections. The wisdom of Governor Leete, who lived there, alone prevented it.

The King's Commissioners, who came over in 1664, decided that the Connecticut Charter included New Haven, and as the authority of the Magistrates in New Haven was daily becoming weaker, it was at last agreed that a Union should take place, which was consummated in May, 1665.

Since the year 1701, the General Court, or Legislature, has met alternately at Hartford and New Haven.

Governor Leete (or Leate), in his reply to the English Commissioners in 1680, says, "We have two General Courts, and two Courts of Assistants for the trial of capi-

[1] Trumbull's Hist. Conn., vol. i. For loss of Charter, see ch. xlii.

tal offenses." "We have four principal towns, Hartford, New London, New Haven, and Fairfield."

"The commodities of the country are provisions, lumber, and horses.

"We have no need of Virginia trade, as most people plant so much tobacco as they need.

"The value of our annual imports amounts, probably, to £9,000.

"In 1671, the number of men was . . . 2,050.
" 1679, " " . . . 2,507.

"The property of the whole Corporation doth not amount to £110,788 sterling.

"The people are strict Congregationalists. There are four or five Seven-day-men, and about as many Quakers.

"We have twenty-six towns and twenty-one churches. The stipend of the clergy is from £50 to £100. Wages are from 2*s.* to 2*s.* 6*d.* per day, for laborers. Wheat is 4*s.* a bushel; pork 3*d.*, beef 2¼*d.* a pound.

"Beggars and vagabonds are not suffered, but are bound out to service."[1]

Connecticut never indulged in the religious persecutions which stain the History of nearly every other State of that day. She early established and sustained schools and colleges.[2] Her people have, from the outset, been industrious and honest. Crime has not abounded; while talent, and character, and courage, and cleanliness, have been common through all her History. Her people now produce as much as any people, and waste less. The need for money, and the difficulty of getting it, has bred in her borders a small army of base Office-seekers, who are her only curse.

[1] M. H. C., vol. iv. Chalmers's Pol. Annnals. Beside these, a small property qualification (£20) was required of voters. Hildreth, vol. ii., p. 460.

[2] See chap. xlvi.

CHAPTER XXIX.

THE PEQUOT WAR.

MURDER OF STONE AND OLDHAM—GALLOP RUNS DOWN THE PINNACE—DESTROYS THE INDIANS—CANONICUS SENDS MESSENGERS—ENDICOTT'S EXPEDITION—ATTACKS BLOCK ISLAND AND PEQUOT HARBOR—UNION OF INDIANS—ROGER WILLIAMS—ATTACK ON THE PEQUOT FORT—SACHEM'S HEAD—SASSACUS—THE FAIRFIELD SWAMP FIGHT—CAPTIVES SOLD—PEQUOTS ENDED.

THE rivalries and contentions of the Narragansetts and Pequots, the two most powerful tribes in New England, were incessant, and kept the whites in constant alarm. Now and then a collision would happen between some white trader and the Indians, in one of which[1] Stone, an Englishman, had been killed.

In 1636, John Gallop discovered some mischief. He was coming from the Connecticut, in July, in a small vessel of twenty tons, manned by himself, his two boys, and one other, when, seeing a pinnace near Block Island, he drew toward it, and hailed; but received no answer, and soon discovered that the deck was filled with Indians. This excited suspicion, and especially as the Indians put up sail, and tried to get away; but Gallop, with his one man and two little boys, having two pieces, two pistols, and only duck shot, headed them, fired into them; and although the Indians stood ready with guns, pikes, and swords, he drove them under hatches. The wind being

[1] Captain Underhill reports, that the Indians charged, that the whites had enticed their Sachem abroad, and then refused to give him up, except for a ransom of a bushel of wampum. When they had collected it and sent it aboard, their Sachem was sent back to them, but killed dead, and that his son, for that, had slain Captain Stone, finding him in the cabin, drunk. M. H. C., 3d series, vol. vi.

fresh, Gallop turned upon the pinnace, and going stem-on, nearly upset her, which so frightened the Indians, that six of them jumped overboard and were drowned. There being too many Indians for him to venture to board her, he came stem-on again, and getting fast to her, shot into her, so as to make havoc with such as were in the hold; none of the Indians appearing, he cleared his vessel and stood off, when four or five Indians more jumped into the sea and were drowned. Gallop now boarded the pinnace (there being but four left in her), when one of the Indians surrendered, whom Gallop bound, and then the second. The other two kept their swords in the hold, and would not come up. Gallop knowing that where two Indians are together, they could untie one another, was puzzled to know what to do with the second one whom he had bound. He resolved his doubts, and made short work of it, by throwing them both into the sea. This courage and ferocity of Gallop were remarkable; and there are few instances in bush or border warfare, equal to it. Fourteen men were opposed to two, and twelve of the fourteen were destroyed. The whites must even then have come to hold an Indian very cheap, thus to attack such a force, and thus to dispose of prisoners. Gallop found the body of John Oldham under an old seine, with his head cleft, his arms and legs much cut; he committed it to the sea. Finding no traces of Oldham's companions (his two sons and two Indians), and that he could not get at the two Indians hidden in the hold, he took what goods and sails remained, and towed the pinnace away; but night coming on, the wind rose, so he was obliged to let her go, and she was driven to the Narragansett shore.

CANONICUS SENDS MESSENGERS.

The two Indians who had been with Oldham, and one other, came messengers from Canonicus, bearing a letter to Governor Vane—written by Roger Williams, who lived at Providence, was familiar with the Indian languages, and friendly with the natives—saying that they were sorely grieved at the business, and that Miantonomo had gone, with seventeen canoes, and a great force, to take revenge. Upon examining these Indians, the Governor became satisfied that nearly all the Sachems of the Narragansetts, except Canonicus and Miantonomo, had been concerned in this affair; and so he wrote, that he expected them to send back the two boys, and to take proper revenge upon the Islanders. The boys were soon sent back, and afterward one of the suspected Indians was sent. The Colonists did not let the matter rest here, but, in August, sent Lieutenant Edward Gibbons and John Higginson to treat with Canonicus. He received them with great state, entertained them royally, with boiled chestnuts and blackberry pudding, but was wise and wary, and careful not to bind himself with conditions.[1]

ENDICOTT'S EXPEDITION.

It was evident that trouble was brewing, and that the Pequots were getting fierce, perhaps desperate. This the Massachusetts people discovered, and the Governor and Council decided that punishment should be done for Oldham's death; not that they loved Oldham, but that a stop must be put to such things; so in August, Captain John Endicott was sent, with a force of some ninety men, volunteers, with directions to attack Block Island, and to put to death all the men, but to spare the squaws and children. They landed and marched over Block Island, but could discover no Indians; so they burned their houses and corn, and sailed across to the Pequot Harbor, where they held a parley with the Pequots, but could get no speech with their Sachem Sassacus. The Indians gathered in numbers, but finally were ordered to withdraw, for it was evident their parleying meant nothing. Endicott marched his forces into their country, killing and wounding some, burning wigwams, and spoiling canoes. Then he marched back to his vessels, and sailed for Boston. This attack seems to have served to exasperate the Indians still more than be-

[1] Winthrop, Journal, August, 1636. Hubbard's Indian Wars.

fore, and not to have intimidated them. The Pequots now spared no pains to gain over the Narragansetts, and were artful in their persuasions, that all should make common cause against these English intruders, who were gradually taking up their corn and hunting-lands, monopolizing the rivers, and spreading themselves along the Coasts. It was a seductive thought to be rid of these white men (before whom they were powerless), who had made them, once Chiefs and Kings in the land, now dependants and slaves, hardly free in their own camps and wigwams. Once free to roam over the boundless plains and forests—hunting where they would, planting or plundering where they would, fighting or killing, or being killed, when they would, they were now called to account for any brawl or breach of the peace, wherein these white men were often the aggressors. They were held liable for any losses which these whites might incur, of tools, goods, or the like. They who had gotten their lands for a song, and had seduced their allegiance by arts and strength, now cited these Red men to appear at their Courts, and show reasons, make reparations, conclude treaties such as they (the whites) might require, no matter how unpalatable to the proud hearts and undisciplined habits of the Indian. The time had come, when by Union and Effort this might be ended, when the Cause might be removed. This talk was sweet to the Narragansetts; but revenge was sweeter. Might not the Narragansetts now join these few but powerful white men, and satisfy their old hatreds against their rivals, the Pequots, by a bitter, swift, and comprehensive destruction? This was a present and immediate good; the other, too, was good, but it was further off. Child-like and Indian-like, they listened to the present, heeded not the future, and sided with the whites against the Pequots. It was during this doubt and danger, that Roger Williams, forgetting the severities of the whites, went alone among the Indians, and for three days and three nights worked against the Pequot messengers, to hinder the league (ch. xxv.) But the Pequots were roused, and the whites were roused, and mischief was inevitable.

ATTACK ON THE PEQUOT FORT.

The Connecticut Colony was nearest to the danger, and she raised one hundred and ten men, who, under the command of Captain John Mason, after receiving the blessing of Minister Hooker, sailed out of Hartford to the sound of fife and drum. Down the peaceful Connecticut they wended their way, until they found in the wild country, their Indian ally Uncas, Chief of the Mohegans, in waiting with his hundred dusky warriors. They rendezvoused at Saybrook, and then proceeded eastward to the Mystic river, were was the strongest fort of the Pequots. Before day [May 26, 1637] they attacked it with fury, and took the Pequots by surprise, asleep; being well armed, they made an onslaught, and drove back the Indians, killing many. At last Mason broke into the palisades, and set fire to the wigwams, and then a dreadful destruction began. After the wigwams were fired the Indians ran, "and indeed," said Captain Mason, "such a dreadful terror did the Almighty let fall upon their spirits, that they would fly from us, and run into the very flames, where many of them perished." Many of the frightened and flying Indians [about one hundred and fifty] were shot, and many rushed into the fire; among them women and children, and old men, some one hundred and fifty more.[1]

SACHEM'S HEAD.

The power of the Pequots was broken from that hour.[2] Captains Stoughton and Mason[3] followed up this attack, and sailed to the West, with eighty men, in pursuit of Sassacus. At a

[1] Winthrop, vol. i., p. 225. Hutchinson, vol. i., p. 80. Hubbard Hist.

[2] A brief History of the Pequot War, by Major John Mason, Boston, 1736.

[3] Mason had been a soldier in Netherlands under Sir Thomas Fairfax. When the wars between the King and Parliament broke out, Fairfax wrote to him to return. But Mason remained in New England.

point east of New Haven he caught two of their Sachems, and cut off their heads, leaving them on poles, a prey to the ravens ; and the point (now a well-known watering-place) has been famous as "Sachem's Head," since that day. Sassacus and the remnant of his tribe fled west to the Mohawks ; but Mason, following them, surrounded the remnant of the tribe, entrenched in a swamp to the west near Fairfield. Through a day and night the fight went on, the Indians of course being the losers, and in the morning most of them had escaped or were killed, and some two hundred women and children were left prisoners. With these, and the booty of trays, kettles, and wampum, Mason marched back again. Sassacus and twenty of his men were treacherously slain by the Mohawks, and his hair was sent as a trophy to the whites. They had now slain and taken in all about seven hundred Indians. It was a fearful destruction, and was ended by a division of the prisoners between Connecticut and Massachusetts. Fifteen of the boys and two of the women were sent to the Island of Providence, and sold as slaves by the Massachusetts authorities ; the rest were distributed in various quarters ; and that was the way an old nation was ended.[1]

[1] Winthrop, vol. i. Hutchinson, vol. i., p. 80.

CHAPTER XXX.

THE DEATH OF MIANTONOMO.

PLOTS—MIANTONOMO GOES TO BOSTON—SEEKS REVENGE—ATTACKS UNCAS—IS DEFEATED AND SEIZED—IS CARRIED TO HARTFORD—MAGISTRATES AND MINISTERS PRONOUNCE HIS DOOM—HE IS KILLED—WHY?

THE result of this extreme destruction of the Pequots, was a restless dread among the next powerful tribe—the Narragansetts, whose Chief was Miantonomo, a tall, handsome, and sagacious man. The Narragansetts anticipated evil, particularly as they knew that Uncas and the Mohegans (on the west, between the Thames and the Connecticut rivers), were favorites of the English, and under their protection. Letters were sent to Boston, that Miantonomo was plotting against them; that the whites had it from various Indians, and that if Massachusetts would send one hundred and twenty men to Saybrook, Connecticut would send as many, and war should be begun. But the Massachusetts Magistrates were not willing to launch into a war upon the vague reports of rival or malignant Indians, such as Uncas was; so they sent to Miantonomo to come to Boston. He came, and dared his accusers to meet him face to face; he declared that his accusers deserved death, and that this mischief was made by Uncas; he said he would go and settle it with him, or he would meet him in Boston. He put his hand into that of the Governor, and satisfied him of his honesty. But Miantonomo went back wounded and indignant; he knew and they knew, that many a time he had befriended the whites, and had refused to join the Pequots. Many of the Indians had had their

MIANTONOMO DESIRES REVENGE.

arms, which they had fairly bought and paid for, taken away; and in Boston, Miantonomo was treated with indignity, and was refused a seat at the Magistrates' table. But the expectation of this conspiracy, through some years pervaded all men in the Colonies, so that a man could not hallo at night, to frighten the wolves, but the towns were roused with the suspicion that the Indians were torturing somebody; and it was the easiest thing to work upon the minds of the scattered inhabitants. The proofs of a conspiracy were at that time declared to be insufficient, and now they seem unworthy of any but cowards, or such as owed Miantonomo a grudge; as Uncas, and some among the Colonists did. Miantonomo dared not revenge his insults upon the English, but he watched his chance against Uncas; and when Uncas quarreled with his ally, Sequasson (July, 1643), Miantonomo invaded his territory with a thousand warriors. He had given notice of his intention to Winthrop, then Governor, and was not forbidden.

MIANTONOMO IS TAKEN.

Uncas was surprised, but hastily gathered some five hundred of his warriors together, to withstand the invaders. Advancing in front of his men, he challenged Miantonomo to single battle, which he declined, feeling his superiority in numbers; then Uncas fell flat on his face, and his men poured in a volley of arrows, and charged the Narragansetts with their tomahawks and the war whoop; they were astounded, and broke in dismay. Miantonomo found it impossible to rally them, and he himself was seized and given up by two of his own men, who hoped thus to save their lives. That hope was vain, for Uncas brained them on the spot. Then the haughty Chief stood silent before his captor, and Uncas taunted him, and said: "Ha, ha! why do you not beg for life." Miantonomo answered—"Kill me, I have no fear." But Uncas feared to kill him, for he was the greatest King of all, superior by far to Uncas; so he carried him prisoner to Hartford, and asked leave of the Magistrates to kill him. They knew not what to answer, and he was kept prisoner until the meeting of the Commissioners of the United Colonies at Boston. (September 16th, 1643.) Now Miantonomo had been the friend of the whites, and had sold them lands, and fed them (though they were heretics, such as Roger Williams and Samuel Gorton, but he knew it not), and he might justly look, as he thought, for fairness and justice from the English. The Commissioners were in great doubt, for they declared "it would not be safe to set him at liberty, neither had we sufficient ground for us to put him to death." In this difficulty they called in five of the fifty assembled Ministers, who soon decided the matter, and quoted Agag, and sundry other cruel doings of the Jews, toward unarmed enemies, and pronounced his doom—Death. Then word was sent to Hartford, that he should be delivered to Uncas, for death, but not for torture.

MIANTONOMO IS KILLED.

In the mellow autumn weather, when the brilliant leafage clothed the departing year, Miantonomo was led out to die. He was marched, bound with cords, along the east bank of the river, between files of Uncas's Indians, with a few white musketeers, sent to sanction the bloody act. He walked with a dignified step, not knowing his fate; and as his face turned toward his own land and his own people, it was lighted once more with the hope of life and freedom. A few hours carried him beyond the bounds of the Connecticut Colony, and into the territories of Uncas; then the brother of Uncas, marching behind him, sunk a hatchet into his brain, and the soul of the great sachem was free; his blood and his body lay along the sandy plain of the Connecticut.

It seems a wicked, wanton, cruel deed, and deserves no apology. It was advised by five clergymen, and consented to by some of the wisest and best of men, such as Winthrop, Winslow, Fenwick, and Eaton: they, too, were the victims of a dark suspicion, and an unworthy fear. Governor Stephen Hopkins says: "This was the end of

Miantonomo, the most potent Indian prince the people of New England ever had any concern with; and this was the reward he received for assisting them, seven years before, in their war with the Pequots. Surely a Rhode Island man may be permitted to mourn his unhappy fate, and to drop a tear on the ashes of Miantonomo, who with his uncle, Canonicus, were the best friends and greatest benefactors the Colony ever had; they kindly received and protected the first settlers of it, when they were in distress, and were strangers and exiles, and all mankind else were their enemies; and by this kindness to them, drew upon themselves the resentment of the neighboring colonies, and hastened the untimely end of the young king." Miantonomo was dead, but his blood was like dragon's teeth, which sprang up armed men; who, thirty years later, under King Philip, worked a fearful revenge.[1]

[1] Winthrop, vol. ii., p. 130. Hazard, vol. xi., p. 11. Hubbard, p. 450. 2d Hist. Coll., p. 202.

CHAPTER XXXI.

MRS. HUTCHINSON.

POSITIONS OF VANE, COTTON, AND MRS. HUTCHINSON—HER BIRTH AND RISE—ANTINOMIANISM AND FAMILISM—WEEKLY MEETINGS FOR WOMEN—THE COVENANTS OF WORKS AND OF GRACE—THE NEW AND THE OLD—STATEMENTS OF DOCTRINE—THE QUARREL BEGINS—THE MINISTERS ENLIST—WHEELWRIGHT AND MRS. HUTCHINSON BROUGHT BEFORE THE COURT—HUGH PETERS—THE QUARREL GROWS WARM—VANE DEFEATED.

No person in the Massachusetts Colony created so profound a sensation in so short a time, as Mrs. Ann Hutchinson, who had come over with Mr. Cotton and Sir Harry Vane in 1635; and between whom there was a ready sympathy. Mr. Cotton says of her, "that she was well beloved, and all the faithful embraced her conference, and blessed God for her fruitful discourses." Others, who had no sympathy with her opinions, speak well of her knowledge and talents.[1]

A few words may help us to understand the positions which Mr. Vane, Mr. Cotton, and Mrs. Hutchinson came to hold in Boston. Vane was at once chosen Governor, to the neglect of older and more conservative men, such as Winthrop and Dudley. Cotton, by his talent, took a first rank in the Church, and was made Minister in Boston; and Mrs. Hutchinson's claims, endorsed by two such men, placed her in a peculiar and influential position.

Mrs. Hutchinson stands in New England History, as the representative name for a profound and bitter struggle. She was born in England; the daughter of Mr. Marbury, a preacher in Lincolnshire; and was the wife of William Hutchinson, who came to Massachusetts as a merchant. When she first began to entertain and to spread her re-

[1] Hubbard, p. 283. Winthrop. Weld.

ligious views is not certain; but on board ship, it is known that her theories excited attention, and the alarm of one clergyman, the Rev. Mr. Symmes. In that time, when spiritual independence was asserting itself in England, it is not strange that a woman like Mrs. Hutchinson should think and speak for herself. There were two words then in use, which expressed a vague but frightful danger—the one was, "ANTINOMIANISM," and the other, "FAMILISM." Few defined them in their own minds, but they were words of power, and could be used with effect to cry down obnoxious theories or principles, as "Infidel," "Abolitionist," "Socialist," "Revolutionist," etc., have been used since.

"Antinomianism" had come into notice in Germany, about a century before this time, and meant, "Against Law," that is, simply that the Gospel (Christ) had superseded the Law (Moses). Expressed in that way, there can be no objection to it; but it had come to signify a very different thing in the minds of the people. Under cover of the name, base men had sheltered themselves, and excesses had been committed, which had been eagerly seized upon by the Conservative—the "Church and State" —party, to discredit and disgrace the Antinomians and their doctrine, and now the word had come to mean a cover for any kind of license or wickedness.

"Familism" was another word which had been adopted by a German sect, who called themselves "The Family of Love." They held that Love was the fulfilling of the law, and that among true believers a deep and all-absorbing feeling of love towards one another and towards God, was superior to any or all forms and creeds.

Familism was originated by Henry Nichols, a Westphalian in Holland, in 1555, and he claimed, that he had a commission to teach men that the Essence of Religion consisted in Divine Love. Other tenets no doubt grew to this pure and lofty idea, and his followers became objectionable, being charged with laxity of morals; but this was not essential to secure them persecution and misrepresentation. It was enough that they separated themselves as more holy, and did not go in the "old way."[1]

But it is easy to see how these simple doctrines might be abused by deluded or deluding men; and that when they presumed to set up their immediate revelations, to set public opinion and law at defiance, there must have been a fierce struggle, and the weaker must go to the wall.

"Antinomianism" and "Familism" had much to do with the quarrel, which rose around Mrs. Hutchinson, and it is probable, that had there been no such words, the matter might have been ended in peace and soberness. These words produced misapprehension first; then charges were made, and denied, and then heat and anger took possession of most minds. The Intellect of New England was active in religious things, and Sermons and Lectures were the staple of conversation. It was common for the listeners on Lord's day to take notes, and during the week to meet once, or oftener, and discuss the doctrines advanced.

The vigorous and daring mind of Mrs. Hutchinson conceived the idea of supplying a want, and she began to hold weekly meetings for the WOMEN. Notwithstanding the disgrace which has been heaped upon her by contemporary writers, it is easy to see her the center of an interested auditory, and to believe that her eloquence and earnestness greatly moved her hearers. She at once collected all the best women in the town, and from the country round about, to the number of seventy, and her meetings rivaled even "the Great and Thursday Lecture." Sustained by Governor Vane, by the great Mr. Cotton, and by her brother-in-law, the Rev. John Wheelwright, it is plain enough that she might have presumed upon her position and talents, and have ventured to pronounce unwise and unwarrantable judgments. Mrs. Hutchinson

[1] See Mosheim. Note to Morton's Mem. Neal's Puritans.

introduced new watchwords, "The Covenant of Works," and "The Covenant of Grace." Under these she and her friends classified the ministers of the Bay. In the former class were understood to be those who relied upon a formal and methodical piety, and a rigid observance of religious duties, as evidence of acceptance with God; while in the latter, those who held to and preached the higher "Covenant of Grace," were included. It is plain that the precisians, pretty sure to be the larger class, would be severely criticised, and that they would severely resent it. Phrases were bandied between the two parties; "Justification" and "Sanctification" were in all mouths; children even jeered one another, and confusion seemed imminent. There was no stemming the tide of discussion which swept on. Mingled with these Religious questions was also a political one; whether the "New," led by Vane, should rule, or whether the "Old," headed by Winthrop, should prevail. Mrs. Hutchinson and Vane had with them nearly the whole of the people of Boston, and the sympathy of Cotton; while Winthrop's strength lay in the great body of Magistrates and Ministers.

Things proceeded so far, that Stephen Greensmith was had before the Court, and fined heavily for having said, that all Ministers, except Mr. Cotton, Mr. Wheelwright, and Mr. Hooker, taught a Covenant of Works.

The Church in Boston was greatly impressed with the teachings of Mr. Cotton, and was remarkably united.

The Rev. Wheelwright (brother-in-law to Mrs. Hutchinson), held opinions the same or like to hers, the principal of which, briefly stated, were:

1st, "That the person of the Holy Ghost dwells in a sanctified person."

2d, "That no Sanctification can help to evidence to us our Justification."[1]

These propositions are bald and meaningless enough now, and were a sort of re-statement of the doctrine of

[1] Winthrop, vol. i., p. 200.

Justification by Faith, but then they served as the standard, around which the world struggled. The New-Comers, fresh from Theological skirmishing, stood by Mrs. Hutchinson, and the Old Settlers rested stubbornly on their Church-and-State, wishing no change. Vane and Cotton led one party, Winthrop and Minister Wilson the other. The town and country were distracted with subtleties, and whoever had brains or words enough, fashioned some new statement, and "Justification and Sanctification," "Covenant of Works," and "Covenant of Grace," were heard at every hearth-stone.

The other Ministers of the Bay came into Boston to confer with Mr. Cotton and Mr. Wheelwright about these things; yet with little result. Many of the Church in Boston, wished to have Mr. Wheelwright called to be a teacher there. Winthrop opposed it, and as Mr. Cotton and Mr. Wilson were already there, it was not carried; but during that discussion the heat increased, so that as Hutchinson says,[1] "the fear of God and the love of our neighbor seemed to be laid by;" at which the Holy Ghost may well have been surprised, if that were possible. To increase the flame, Mr. Wheelwright preached a sermon, inveighing against those who walked in a Covenant of Works;[2] which contained also some expressions, that were seized upon as tending to sedition; for it must be remembered, that the doctrine of the indwelling of the Holy Ghost in the believer opened the way, indirectly, to this position—that each man was a law unto himself, and could walk safely in his own light, and as the "Law and Order" party insisted, was in danger of going into complete anarchy and destruction.

Wheelwright and Mrs. Hutchinson were called before the Magistrates, and examined upon these matters; and Wheelwright was ordered to remove out of the jurisdiction. Mrs. Hutchinson met her examination fearlessly, and with great tact and presence of mind; but at last

[1] History.

[2] January, 1636.

made some exposition of revelations in her own soul—"vented her mind," as they reported it; in which she clearly stated, that God had revealed it to her, that she should come to New England, "and that there I should be persecuted, and suffer much trouble," etc. Mr. Cotton was then set to examine her, which it was hard for him to do, and bitter for her to endure; for she had been his friend and follower.

Vane, the Governor, protested against these proceedings, and finding how things were going, proposed to resign his post, which the Church in Boston remonstrated against: they also sent a remonstrance to the Court for their proceedings against Mr. Wheelwright. The contest grew more serious, sermons were preached, discussions were held, tongues, public and private, ran to all extremes. Hugh Peters publicly reproved Vane, and accused him of making mischief. Vane assembled the Court, and declared the necessity of his departure for England, for various reasons; but the Court refused to listen, and so he staid till his year expired. The Reverends Cotton and Wilson disagreed, and discussed with Christian asperity; letters were written and replied to; churches were disturbed in their exercises by public questions, which were answered and replicated, and so the fight waged toward the destruction of both Church and State, there so woven together. Mr. Wheelwright and Mrs. Hutchinson went onward in the "damnable courses," and many people in the congregation of Boston, got up and went out of meeting, so soon as Mr. Wilson began his exercises, and there was ill-blood and confusion. So the Magistrates decided that the case was desperate, and "the last remedy was to be applyed, and that without further delay."

This thing went on in October, through November, December, and so till the elections in May; when parties were so divided, that the public business could not proceed, and a division ensued which nearly resulted in a tumult and blows; but the majority finally elected Winthrop Governor, and left Vane out of all place. The Halberds, who had acted as a guard of honor upon the Governor, now laid down their arms, and Boston refused to the new Governor the usual honors. The election was ended, but Vane afterward refused to sit with the Magistrates in the Church, and went down to the Mount to keep the fast with Mr. Wheelwright. Winthrop (see Journal) thought this wrangle of words ought not to have been, and that being, it ought to be composed. But there were jealousies and envies lying beneath it, and minds were fermenting; the deepest part of man's nature—the spiritual—being stirred, and there being no possible power of expressing these aspirations and distinctions in words, there could be only fierce contention, or mutual forbearance, and full liberty of opinion; for which the time had not arrived.

The point which most weakened Wheelwright and his party with the people, was the threat which they made, of appealing the matter to England; and almost to a man, even then, the people looked upon that as a sort of treason. Winthrop and his party took advantage of this, and it became a patriotic duty to defeat those who talked of appeal to England, rather than to sustain freedom of discussion in the persons of Mr. Wheelwright and Mrs. Hutchinson. We shall see in the next chapter how the matter ended.

CHAPTER XXXII.

THE GREAT CAMBRIDGE SYNOD.

THE PRESS—THE MINISTERS GATHER—THE EIGHTY-TWO ERRORS—WHEELWRIGHT AND OTHERS BANISHED—MRS. HUTCHINSON TRIED AND BANISHED—SEVENTY-FIVE DISARMED—MRS. HUTCHINSON CAST OUT BY THE CHURCH—THE CONSERVATIVES WIN—JOHN COTTON—AN OLD FOOL—A SCHOLAR—MRS. HUTCHINSON'S FRIENDS—WOMEN PUT DOWN—WELD'S "RISE, REIGN, AND RUIN"—MRS. HUTCHINSON IS KILLED—ABORTIONS.

THE press groaned, and pamphlet after pamphlet was issued, so that in the end few knew how the matters growing out of Mrs. Hutchinson stood, or where the difference was. Even the dangers of the Pequot war were not enough to allay the excitement; nor could fast-days do it, although they were tried.

The crisis seemed so imminent, and dangerous doctrines became so numerous, it was decided that a grand Synod or Council of all the Ministers should assemble at Newtown (Cambridge), to get matters once more into shape. So from every part of New England (except Providence), they threaded the wilderness, gathering to the Council. Davenport and Hooker, Wilson and Cotton, Weld and Wheelwright, and great numbers more, were there. (August, 1637.) Mr. Hooker and Mr. Bulkley were chosen moderators; and after prayer by Rev. Mr. Shepard, the confusion began. Three long weeks were "spent in disputing," and then EIGHTY-TWO opinions were condemned —"some as blasphemous, others erroneous, and all unsafe; by all the assembly, except Mr. Cotton."[1]

Antinomians and Familists condemned by the Synod of Elders, etc.: London, 1644. The same as T. Weld's "Short Story of the Rise, Reign, and Ruin of the Antinomians," etc.: 1644.

Among the eighty-two errors condemned (Synod, Aug. 30, 1637) are such as these :

Error 9. The whole letter of the Scripture holds for a covenant of works.

Error 15. There is no inherent righteousness in the saints, or grace ; and graces are not in the souls of beleevers, but in Christ only.

Error 19. That all graces, even in the truely regenerate, are mortall and fading.

Error 34. We are not to pray against all sinne, because the old man is in us, and must be, and why should we pray against that which cannot be avoided ?

Error 49. We are not bound to keep a constant course of prayer in our families, or privately, unlesse the Spirit stirre us up thereunto.

Error 60. A man may not prove his election by his vocation, but his vocation by his election.

Error 72. It is a fundamentall and soule-damning errour to make sanctification an evidence of justification.

It was believed that the Synod would have put matters to rest, but such was not the case ; for Mr. Wheelwright and Mrs. Hutchinson were as firm in their opinions as before. The Court decided to disfranchise Aspinwall and Coggeshall, deputies from Boston, who had been foremost in the remonstrance in favor of Wheelwright. He also was disfranchised, and banished. Through all this war of words and principles, Mrs. Hutchinson seems to have kept on her way, holding her meetings and spreading her opinions ; but now Vane was gone to England, and Mr. Cotton was evidently settling back to his old associations, and the Court thought Mrs. Hutchinson should be stopped. So they cited her to appear (Nov., 1637), and after many "speeches to and fro," she was banished the Colony, but allowed to remain in her own private house through the winter. Capt. Underhill, and some five more of those who had subscribed the remonstrance in favor of Wheelwright, were disfranchised ; and those who would not acknowledge their fault (some seventy-five persons), were disarmed, with much trouble.

In March, 1638, it was decided to deal with Mrs. Hutchinson in a Church way, and she was afflicted with infinite discussion, but upon some points—such as the truth of the doctrine of the Resurrection of the Body (which, Roger Williams says, the Indians disputed), the sacredness of the Sabbath, and others—she maintained her own; and as she could not be brought "to see her Sin," as they termed it, the Church, with one consent, cast her out.

That a whole State should come to bitter hostility, almost to mutual destruction, for differences of opinion upon such subordinate and abstract theories, is incredible of the sense of that people. This explanation of it is elsewhere suggested, viz.:

The struggle was begun in New England between the Old and the New, between the Conservatives and the Reformers, rather than with the individual, Ann Hutchinson; and these doctrines were simply the bones about which they concluded to fight. The Conservatives, headed by Winthrop, won the battle.

Through all the wranglings, and especially at their beginning, Mr. Cotton was claimed by the New-Lights, for he was powerful among the Ministers, and with the people. Yet the Old Party were loth to let him go, and by much persuasion, and partly because of his own flexibility, and by means of vague expositions, he was kept in his place. He was, however, in danger, and was borne hard upon by Dudley and Hugh Peters, blunt orthodox leaders; but the influence of Winthrop was in his favor, so he was spared. In a sermon preached some ten years after, his principles appear to have been almost the same as those of Mrs. Hutchinson.

John Cotton.—No young man at the Cambridge University of England, was more prominent for learning and genius than John Cotton, who afterward became famous among the New England Churches; at first his tastes and ambitions were directed to literature and scholarship; but by and by his spirit was troubled with the fire of God, and his earnest wish then was, to lead away the hopes of men from baser things to the things of the Spirit; to a desire for holiness rather than happiness.

He became a minister, and was settled at Boston, England, where his preaching was acceptable. But he was not a man to conform to evils and abuses, in the Church or out of it; and he was reported to the ecclesiastical authorities, and for a time suspended. But this first blast of persecution passed, and he remained in his parish some twenty years, and grew stronger and more decided in his Nonconformity. At last, the persecuting Court of High Commission cited him to appear before it, and answer for his misbeliefs. When the Archbishop of Canterbury ordered proceedings against him, the Earl of Dorset interceded, till he found matters were got to such a pass that he sent Mr. Cotton word, "That if he had been guilty of *drunkenness or uncleanness*, or any such *lesser fault* he could have obtained his pardon; but inasmuch as he had been guilty of *Nonconformity* and *Puritanism* the crime was unpardonable; and, therefore," said he, "you must fly for your safety."[1]

Cotton was not of the kind to seek martyrdom; he put on a disguise, and sought and reached New England (1633) where he was warmly welcomed—for his fame, his talents, and his learning made him acceptable. He received the first position in New England at that time, and was through his life Minister of the first church in Boston. There can be little question of that superiority, which even his cotemporaries admitted. Yet, with all his talent and learning, he seems to have preserved the mildness and modesty of his character.

One day some wild, graceless young fellows saw him coming down the street, and one of them said,

[1] Backus's History, vol. i., p. 55.

"There comes old Cotton—I 'll go and put a trick upon him." So he went, and said in his ear:

"Cotton, though art an old fool!"

The Minister was greatly astounded, for it was probably the first time that such a thing had been intimated to him. He was silent for a moment, and then replied:

"I confess I am so; the Lord make both me and thee wiser than we are, even wise unto salvation." He then waited quietly until the young scapegrace hastily retreated.

Cotton seems to have been more scholarly than most of the New England divines, and open to good influences. He was well read in Latin, Greek, and Hebrew, and passed most of his days in the study of books; he was averse to the rough life of the woodsmen, and to the exasperation of theological controversy. He continued the fast friend of Mrs. Hutchinson; and her followers, with his influence, to back up her talent, were strong; but it is probable that they pushed Mr. Cotton too far, and that he himself was willing to remain in good-fellowship with the Churches, rather than to be driven away again, as Wheelwright and Mrs. Hutchinson were. So he drew off from the intimacy which had existed, and joined the Ministers in condemnation of their heresies. Both parties blamed him, for he sided fully with neither. He was violently assaulted by the clergy, for giving any countenance to heresy, and for not standing by his "order;" and he was bitterly reproached by Mrs. Hutchinson's friends, for joining with those who appealed to the civil power to crush freedom of discussion, when in England he had felt its weight, and inveighed strongly against it. Few men are strong enough to stand alone, or to suffer injustice and contempt for opinion's sake. Cotton temporized and compromised, and succumbed. He suffered in his own estimation for doing so, and in the confidence and esteem of his fellow-men. But his talents, his virtues, and his friends saved him, and he lived and died honored and respected.

He preached against forced taxes and tythes for the support of the clergy, and in favor of the "Voluntary System," which has worked so well in New England.

Cotton's "Milk for Babes," was for a long time the catechism upon which the children of New England were fed. Various of his other works remain, but are now read only by the patient student or the curious investigator.

As a preacher, he was in the first rank; his voice was sonorous and musical, and his manner was calm, but clear and direct. No minister in New England was more beloved by his people, and when he died, no man's loss was more severely felt.

He died in 1652, aged 57.

After Mrs. Hutchinson's Excommunication, her spirits revived—for she had been much dejected—and she gloried in her sufferings.

We can well see, how her woman's nature must have been shocked at the harsh and bitter controversy, so full of injustice and misrepresentation, into which she seemed driven; nor can we doubt that she was betrayed by her own enthusiasm, and the exasperation of her enemies, into some extremes, which were a surprise to herself. It was certainly charged upon her that she was a Familist, and that she taught doctrines which made no distinction between vice and virtue, and which led to all kinds of immorality and to the rapid ruin of society. The answer to this is, that Coddington, Clark, Aspinwall, and her friends, who went to Rhode Island [1638], established themselves as a State—a "Democracie"—with Liberty of Conscience, and that society flourished there as well as, if not better than in the Bay. Such, too, was the case at Piscataqua, whither Wheelwright led another party of their friends; and he lived long enough to live down the surprising charges made against him and human nature—which can exist only with "Order" and with "Freedom."

Vane and the Movement party, were put down and turned out of power. The women too, who, under Mrs.

Hutchinson, had begun to aspire to a voice in church matters at least, were also put down. The Synod Resolved :

"That though women might meet (some few together) to pray and edify one another ; yet such a set assembly (as was then in practice in Boston) where sixty or more did meet every week, and one woman (in a prophetical way, by resolving questions of doctrine, and expounding Scripture) took upon her the whole exercise, was agreed to be disorderly, and without rule."

Thomas Weld, in his "Rise, Reign, and Ruin of the Antinomians," etc., speaks of Mrs. Hutchinson in this strain :

"But the last, and worst of all, which most suddenly diffused the venom of these opinions into the very veins and vitals of the people in the country, was Mistress Hutchinson's double weekly Lecture, which she kept under pretence of repeating Sermons," etc. He continues: "Now—oh! their boldness, pride, insolency, and alienations from their old and dearest friends, the disturbances, divisions, contentions, they raised amongst us, both in Church and State, and in families—setting division betwixt man and wife !

"Now the faithful ministers of Christ must have dung cast upon their faces, and be no better than legal preachers, Baal's priests, Popish factors, Scribes, Pharisees, and opposers of Christ himself!" And so on ; and it must be borne in mind that he was one of the ministers, and wrote as he and they felt—bitterly.

MRS. HUTCHINSON IS KILLED.

Mrs. Hutchinson joined her friends at Rhode Island, where her powerful mind influenced all who came near her. Her husband having died in 1642—Randall Holden[1] says : "Fearing that Aquidneck would be brought under the dominion of the Massachusetts when what might she not suffer ?"—she removed westward into the edge of the Dutch Country

[1] Letter from Randall Holden. R. I. H. C., vol. ii.

(New York), where she and her family (sixteen persons), all her children, except one daughter who was carried into captivity, were killed by the Indians. So she perished in the prime of her years—she who was fitted to adorn and enlighten any society, by the elevation of her character and the superiority of her intellect. Another noble person seems to us to have been wasted.

But death was no protection to her. Few who had opposed her, doubted that God had forgotten his majesty, and had instigated the Indians to punish her for her heresies. Mr. Hooker, who was a kind man, "the light of the Western Churches," said, "The expression of Providence against this wretched woman, hath proceeded from the Lord's miraculous mercy, and his bare arm hath been discovered."

The hatred of the times, is shown in that a malformed birth from Mary Dyer,[1] one of Mrs. Hutchinson's friends, was talked of through the settlement, as a "fearful monster," and elaborately described by Winthrop, who was a gentleman and a Christian. So, too, an abortion of Mrs. Hutchinson, no doubt caused by the anxiety and care she had undergone, was minutely inquired into, and minutely described by the Reverend Mr. Cotton, "in open assembly upon a lecture day;" and these things were believed to be God's ways to condemn the errors of Antinomianism, and of Mrs. Hutchinson.[2]

The Magistrates proceeded so far as to examine the midwife, and to dig the child up out of its grave, after it was much corrupted, to make the matter sure.

[1] The description of Mary Dyer's child is curious. The father and mother, they took pains to state, were of "the highest forme of our refined Familists." "It had no head, but a face, which stood so low upon the breast, that the ears (which were like Apes'), grew upon the shoulders. The breast and back were full of sharp prickles. It had upon each foot three claws, with talons, like a young fowle. Upon the back it had two holes like mouths. It had no forehead, but in the place thereof, above the eyes, four hornes," etc.

[2] Winthrop's Journal. Hubbard's History. Hutchinson's History. Bancroft's History. Weld's "Rise, Reign, and Ruin."

CHAPTER XXXIII.

SAMUEL GORTON.

AT BOSTON—AT PLYMOUTH—AT RHODE ISLAND—AT SHOWOMET—USURPATION OF MASSACHUSETTS—GORTON TAKEN PRISONER—HE OUGHT TO DIE—IS PUT IN IRONS—HIS CATTLE SEIZED—HE IS SET AT LIBERTY—HIS RELIGIOUS OPINIONS.

SAMUEL GORTON arrived in Boston in 1636. He had a quick, active mind ; given to religious things ; with a fanciful turn, tending to spiritualize all things. Enthusiastic, extravagant, and mystical, he was incapable of rest. It was inevitable that his activity should impel him to interest himself in, if not to interfere with, the course of things. The discussion of religious matters being a necessity of life in Massachusetts, Gorton's speculations and views—subtle and bold—made him a marked man. Boston soon become uncomfortable to him, for the Ministers were ready and determined against men or women, who threatened to damage their authority, or that of the nascent State ; and nothing was more dreaded then than new opinions. The Ministers felt sure they were right, and Gorton, too, was urgent for his theories ; but the Churches and Ministers had the power. Gorton left Boston and went to Plymouth ; there he met with much the same treatment as at Boston ; and afterward, at Rhode Island, he and Coddington came to open quarrel. The cause of the quarrel, as some say, being about some swine ;[1] it proceeded to violence in open Court ; Coddington crying out, " You that are for the King, lay hold on Gorton ;" he answering, " You that are for the King, lay hold on Coddington !" But the victory was with Coddington,

[1] Lechford. Savage, in Winthrop, ii., 59.

Gorton being banished, and, as some assert, whipped! Banished men, and men with individual and peculiar opinions, and weak Indians, all drew toward Roger Williams, at Providence ; he was the star toward which the eyes of wanderers ever turned. Here Gorton remained for a time, but afterward, making a purchase from Miantonomo and two other Sachems, of lands on Narragansett Bay (at Showomet, now Cranston), he established himself there, with such as chose to enjoy his way of thinking.[1] But four of his company afterward (1642) complained to the Magistrates of Massachusetts, that they could not consort with Gorton and his company, and offered themselves and their lands to the protection of that Colony.

They were accepted, partly to protect them, but more because the opinions and practices of Gorton's company were offensive, and "because the place was likely *to be of use to us,* and we thought it not wisdom to let it slip ;" so Gorton was summoned to answer at the Court at Boston. He agreed to leave the matters in dispute, to be settled by arbitrators, which was refused. At last, a body of forty soldiers was sent down for him, and after some skirmishing—nobody being killed—he and some of the others were brought to Boston. The Indians had been sounded, and through Benedict Arnold (one of Gorton's opposers), two Sachems alleged that Miantonomo had forced them to sell their lands to Gorton. The Colony Commissioners took measures to convert the Indians to Christianity ; they agreeing to speak reverently of the Englishmen's God, not to swear oaths, not to work on Sundays (they said abstinence from that was no trial), not to kill, to obey superiors, etc., etc.;[2] and then they received them under their protection, and gave notice of it to Miantonomo, and to the whites in those parts. About this time (1643), Miantonomo had been murdered by Uncas, with the advice and assistance of the whites (ch. xxx.),

[1] Savage, in Winthrop, vol. ii., p. 121. See copy of Deeds, from Trumbull's MSS.

[2] Winthrop, vol. ii., p. 122.

so he was out of their way; his brother, Pesacus, a young man of twenty years, succeeding him.

The case of Gorton seemed to Massachusetts, a clear one.

1. Some of the whites asked protection.

2. Some of the Indians asked protection.

3. Gorton's opinions were offensive, and were believed to be dangerous.

4. "The place might be of use to us; and it was the part of wisdom not to let it slip."

GORTON OUGHT TO DIE.

Gorton's case was prejudged. He demanded of the Court liberty of speech, which being granted, he held forth, after the manner of those days, copiously, ranging hither and thither, in all directions, mainly in a religious and mystical strain. This did not help his cause; and all the Magistrates, except three (!) were of opinion, that he ought to die; but the deputies (the people) would not listen to it; what then could be done? Various means were tried to convert him to true opinions (those of the Magistrates), but he would not revoke his "hellish blasphemy.[1] So he and six of his friends were distributed into seven towns, to be kept at work, and to wear irons on one leg, and not to maintain their blasphemous errors by writing; if they did, they were to be condemned to death, and to be executed.[2] Further than this, finding the expenses of this matter considerable, amounting to some £160, which in the poverty of the Colony could not well be spared, they sent down to Gorton's settlements, and took his cattle to pay for his own defeat, for they were the Victors. This Napoleonic abuse of power now meets with condemnation, and provoked then only hatred and bitterness against the Puritans. But such things, common in all countries in that day, were rare in New England. Let it also be remembered, that men were then held to be responsible for their opinions—that is, they could believe right (as the

[1] Hubbard's History, p. 403.

[2] Winthrop, Journal. See 2 Hist. Coll., viii., 68–70. Governor Hopkins.

Church or State ordered) if they only would ; and if they would not, they were heretics and dangerous, and ought to be cut off. Such an one Gorton seemed to them ; but we can find no excuse for their extension of Jurisdiction over Gorton's territory, except in covetousness. After all this the matter did not end well, for the sympathies of the people were alive, and cruelty did not meet with favor. The hearts of women were moved towards Gorton and his friends, and their doctrines insidiously spread, and converts were made, "so, not knowing what else to do, it was at length decided to set them at liberty," and give them fourteen days to get out of the Jurisdiction.

A great deal of trouble grew out of this effort of Massachusetts to extend their power over Gorton's settlement, for the Plymouth Colony was jealous, and Gorton carried his complaints to England. Through many years this continued, till, at last, in 1658, Massachusetts gave it up, and relinquished all claim for jurisdiction.

Gorton's activity plunged him into all movements, and he was as thoroughly abused as any man in New England.[1] He was as clear and logical as to the necessity of keeping the duties of the Magistrates to civil things as Roger Williams was.[2] His religious opinions were strongly colored by his abundant individuality, so that no other person could fully comprehend or accept them. Yet he had followers who stood by him through good—rather through evil report. The last of these Dr. Styles found living at Providence in 1771—not a Quaker, or a Baptist, or anything but a Gortonist. He said, " Gorton wrote in Heaven, and beat down all outward ordinances of Baptism and the Lord's Supper with unanswerable demonstration," as Roger Williams did not. So he said, " that his eyes were a fountain of tears—that he wept day and night for the sins and blindness of the world."

[1] See Gorton's " Simplicities Defense."

[2] Rhode Island Hist. Coll., vol. ii., p. 15.

This method of water-cure availed little then, and has always failed.

Gorton seems to have been an active rather than a great man, and was a skirmisher in the van of the Armies of Liberty and Truth.

CHAPTER XXXIV.

THE CONFEDERATION.

NEW HAVEN—CONNECTICUT—PLYMOUTH AND MASSACHUSETTS—RHODE ISLAND EXCLUDED.

THE colonies were now scattered from the River Kennebeck to Long Island Sound. They were in danger from the Indians; the Dutch at Manhadoes (New York) claimed Connecticut and New Haven; while England at the same time, was distracted with civil wars. As early as 1637 some of the Connecticut people proposed a CONFEDERATION, and from time to time the plan had been revived; but it was not till 1643 that it was brought to a decision. Commissioners came from New Haven, and Connecticut, and Plymouth, who, with some of the principal men of the Bay, agreed upon a Confederation, to be called "The United Colonies of New England," consisting of New Haven, Connecticut, Plymouth, and Massachusetts Bay, Rhode Island being rigidly excluded. It provided for an appointment of two Commissioners from each Colony, whose duty it was to see to the general defense, and to attend to such matters as concerned All, but which could not be left to any one, and it continued in force with some intervals till 1686, when James II. vacated the Charters. It was a simple and sensible agreement, and grew out of an inevitable necessity, and it forcibly proves how well men can and do govern themselves, when saddles are not put on their backs by Kings, aristocracies, or pedantic and infidel statesmen.

This confederation was the child which grew into a youth after a century and a half, and now waxes toward manhood as the United States of America.[1] (See Appendix).

[1] Hazard, vol. ii. Hubbard, p. 465. Winthrop, vol. ii., p. 101. Hutchinson, vol. i., p. 124. Davis in Morton, p. 229. Bancroft, vol. i., p. 423.

CHAPTER XXXV.

THE VASSAL AND CHILDE DISTURBANCE.

THE HINGHAM ELECTION—VASSAL, CHILDE, MAVERICK, AND FOWLE PETITION—RESISTED—SONS OF BELIAL—APPEAL TO ENGLAND—SEARCHES, FINES, AND IMPRISONMENT—WINSLOW SAILS—POWER OF THE COLONIES—WINTHROP'S SPEECH.

THE Hingham folks had had some trouble about the election of their military officers, and had petitioned the General Court—referring in their petition to English law, and had been fined one hundred pounds for doing so; for the Magistrates put down all threats of Appeal to England. Out of this matter had grown ill blood, and a hostile and suspicious state of feeling.

One more assault upon the integrity of the Colony, soon came from within. William Vassal, "a gentleman of a pleasant, affable disposition," "one of the best and wealthiest men in Scituate,"[1] who came first in 1630, and was one of the Patentees and Assistants, had returned in 1635, and settled in Scituate, in Plymouth Colony. With him were joined Dr. Robert Childe, a young gentleman who had studied in Padua; Samuel Maverick, an Episcopalian, who had been admitted a Freeman before the condition of church membership was made; Thomas Fowle, a merchant, and some others. These sent a petition to the General Court [1646] and to the Plymouth Court, stating that their civil and religious rights were denied them. They claimed to live under the laws of ENGLAND, which they said were set at naught. They claimed the right of Religious Worship, which was denied them; they claimed the rights of Freemen, of holding office, which

[1] Baylie's Memoir.

were denied them, unless they entered through some of the Churches of the Colonies ; and they prayed that civil and religious liberty might forthwith be granted, or at least if it were not, that they might be exempt from taxes, and from impressment as soldiers, and so on, in a positive and aggravating style, as the Massachusetts Rulers thought. Now all this was founded in truth and reason, and could not well be gainsaid ; but the first and last necessity of the Magistrates, was to preserve the unity and strength of the Colonies against the politicians of the Church and State of England, who were only hindered from riding down these non-conforming colonists, by distance, and by nearer dangers at home. It seemed plain to the Magistrates, that all dissent and division must be put down in Massachusetts. They could not yet see, that truth, where it has a fair field, is stronger than error ; nor that by granting these men their individual rights, they would have taken arms out of their hands, and by necessity have converted them into loyal citizens to the New, rather than lingering friends of the Old World. As it was, some of the Ministers grew warm, and called the Petitioners, "Sons of Belial," "Judases," "Sons of Corah," and the like. The Court published a declaration denying their petition, and vindicating the Government ; and then Vassal and his friends claimed the right to appeal to the Commissioners for Plantations in England ; but this was not allowed. Some of the petitioners then prepared to go to England, when their papers were seized, and they were detained. Mr. Cotton preached against them (Canticles, ii., 15) showing how God's judgments were shown upon such as were going to England for mischief. In reply, they told how Mr. Winslow's horse had died under him, as he was coming to Boston, on his way to England to act against them, and so God was surely against him also. But the Court fined them all, from ten to two hundred pounds each, searched their houses and trunks, and imprisoned them, so that they should not sail in the ship, or till such time as their fines should be paid. Mr. Winslow went on his way, in spite of the warning mentioned (of God's killing his horse), and made interest with the Parliament for the Colonies. Now, if the petitioners had gone, they might have injured the Colony, and so have hindered its progress toward an Independent State. But if the Magistrates and Clergy had granted those rights which, not only the Charter, but the nature of man demanded, all cause for fear would surely have been removed. During the trouble, the Magistrates and Clergy held a conference with closed doors, after Mr. Hubbard, of Hingham, had been requested to withdraw—he being "suspect"—to consider their powers under the Charter. They concluded, that they owed allegiance to England, and a fifth part of the gold and silver found, but otherwise had full powers for self-government, which they determined to exercise, "and wait upon Providence for the preservation of their just Liberties."[1]

Winthrop, then Deputy-Governor, opposed the Petition of Childe and others for Freemen's privileges; and we may gather from this extract of his speech, about the Hingham trouble, 1645, what influenced so mild and just a man in his opposition to what now seemed a fair demand. He said in open Court, before the people, who were justly tetchy upon their individual rights: "Nor would I have you to mistake in the point of your own liberty. There is a liberty of corrupt nature, which is affected by both men and beasts to do what they list, and this liberty is inconsistent with authority—impatient of all restraint. By this liberty, *sumus omnes deteriores;* it is the grand enemy of truth and peace, and all the ordinances of God are against it. But there is a civil, a moral, a federal liberty, which is the proper end and object of authority; it is a liberty for that only which is

[1] Winthrop, vol. ii., p. 261. Hubbard, p. 499. Hutchinson, vol. i., p. 145. N. E. Jonas cast up; M. H. C., 2d series, vol. iv. Puritanism, or a Churchman Defense (*Coit*).

just and good. For this liberty you are to stand, with the hazard of your very lives, and whatsoever crosses it is not authority, but distemper thereof. This liberty is maintained in a way of subjection to authority; and the authority set over you will, in all administrations for your good, be quietly submitted to by all but such as have a disposition to shake off the yoke, and lose their true liberty, by their murmuring at the honor and power of authority." So Winthrop, one of the best of Patriots, spoke—he being in authority; and it is correct, that men have liberty to do right—never to do wrong. But what is right? and shall authority, only, decide it? Precisely this doctrine had been practiced in England, to justify the persecution of the Nonconformists, and had been held to sustain all acts of tyranny, from the foundation of society even to the present year. Concentrated into a few words, it is simply this: "Authority is for your good, and is to be quietly submitted to, because it maintains a civil, a moral, a federal liberty; whereas the liberty which you want is beastly and corrupt; and we (the Authorities) are to judge, not you."

It seems that the claims of Vassal and Childe were just; that the denying of those claims drove them to appeal to England; that it became necessary then to crush them, lest the Self-government of the Colonies should be overthrown by England; and so they were put down by force.

The first position of the Magistrates was wrong; and other grievous wrongs grew out of it.

CHAPTER XXXVI.

PERSECUTION OF THE QUAKERS.

INTOLERANCE—NEW DANGERS—MARY FISHER AND ANN AUSTIN—QUAKERS ARRIVE—ARE TRIED—IMPRISONED—WOE! WOE!—BANISHED—LAWS PASSED—DEATH—WOMEN WHIPPED—CHILDREN SOLD—EARS CUT OFF—ROBINSON AND STEVENSON HUNG—MARY DYER HUNG—LEDRA AND CHRISTOPHERSON—REPRIEVE—CHARLES II. STOPS PERSECUTION—WHAT DID THE QUAKERS BELIEVE?—GREAT SOULS KNOW—GEORGE FOX—THERE IS A GOD—PRINCIPLES—PERSECUTIONS IN ENGLAND—EXCESSES OF THE QUAKERS—WALKING ABOUT NAKED—WILLIAM PENN—THE "HOLY EXPERIMENT."

TOLERATION in religious things was not considered practicable in the seventeenth century, except in the few years when Cromwell controlled the power of England.[1] Despotism in Church or State needs a rigid censorship, for whatever can not bear examination and discussion must be sustained by force, till its hour of destruction comes. The Roman Catholic Inquisition presumed to punish people for their THOUGHTS, and it is hardly necessary to bring further proofs of the common belief and practices of that day. The magistrates in New England held that it was not only their right, but their duty to punish people for open, outspoken heresy, and that view prevailed, except with a few individuals, such as Roger Williams, Samuel Gorton, Oliver Cromwell, George Fox, and their adherents. Thousands at the present day are not aware that their own religious intolerance leads directly to the perpetration of cruelties, which shock them in the page of history; and the world owes it to a free press which appeals to a free public opinion, that such cruelties are not practiced now. Rival sects find satisfaction in the fact, that the Puritans indulged in religious cruelties, and that they too were bigots. The fact, then universal, need not be dwelt upon with pleasure.

[1] See ch. xxiv., Toleration.

NEW DANGERS.

We have seen how the minds of people and Ministers, both, had been disturbed and excited by the opinions of Roger Williams, Mrs. Hutchinson, and Samuel Gorton; and now a new danger threatened them. In July, 1656, Mary Fisher and Ann Austin came to Boston from Barbadoes ; and shortly after, nine others, men and women, arrived in the ship Speedwell from London. It was at once known, for they did not wish to conceal it, that they were "FRIENDS," vulgarly called "Quakers ;" and the Magistrates at once took them in hand, determined that no people holding (as they considered them) such damnable opinions, should come into the Colony. A great crowd collected to hear them questioned, and Boston was stirred up by a few illiterate enthusiasts. They stood up before the Court with their hats on, apparently without fear, and had no hesitation in calling Governor Endicott plain "John." That seemed to many a portentous thing, and they said among themselves : "What is the world coming to ?" "Is this one of the fearful 'vials' foretold in the Apocalypse ?" The replies which these men and women made, were direct and bold, and were considered rude and contemptuous. Numbers of Quaker books being found in their trunks, those were seized, and ordered to be burned ; while they themselves were committed to prison, for their "Rudeness and Insolence ; there being no law then under which they could be punished for being Quakers. Shortly after that the Governor was walking solemnly from church on a Lord's day, with several gentlemen, when Mary Prince called out to him, from the prison window, saying :

"Woe ! woe ! Thou vile oppressor ! Thou tyrant ! Thou who killest the children of God, as Herod did ! Thy day shall come when the Lord will smite thee, and give thy carcass to the dung-hill ! Thou shalt be devoured by worms!" and so on.

When the Ministers went to her, she reproached them as "Hirelings, Baal's priests, deceivers of the people, of the brood of Ishmael;" and such like, in the words of the Bible. Nothing seemed to intimidate or appease these Quakers, so they were banished, "Thrust out of the jurisdiction."

Laws were passed against them, of exceeding severity (1656),[1] and published by beat of drum; laying a penalty of £100 for bringing any Quaker into the Colony: forty shillings for entertaining them for an hour; Quaker men who came against these prohibitions were, upon first conviction, to lose one ear, upon the second, the other ear; and women were to be whipped. Upon the third conviction, their tongues were to be bored with a hot iron.[2] But these things seemed useless, for the Quakers, knowing their fate, swarmed into Massachusetts; and the Magistrates were fast getting more business than they could attend to. It was then determined to try greater severity, and in October, 1658, a law was passed in Massachusetts (resisted by the Deputies, urged by the Magistrates), punishing Quakers who had been banished, with DEATH.

Gorton, in 1656, wrote to the four Quakers, who arrived in Boston, expressing his sympathy, and wishing them to join him; he said: "I marvel what manner of God your adversaries trust in—who is so fearful of being infected with error; or how they think they shall escape the wiles and power of the Devil, when the arm of flesh fails them," etc.[3]

William Brend, Thomas Thurston, Christopher Holder, and John Copeland, wrote "from the common Jail in Boston, this 28 of Seventh, 1656," in reply, how "The Lord is come and is coming to Level the Mountains," "to dwell in men, so that they shall be his people henceforth and forever;" that they were unwilling to go away from Boston, but that the Magistrates had cast the Captain of tho ship into prison because he refused to give securities

[1] Hazard, vol. i.

[2] Plymouth, Connecticut, New Haven, adopted these laws; Rhode Island refused, though strongly urged.

[3] R. I. Hist. Coll., vol. ii.

to land them again in England ; the expense of which they declined paying.

Ann Burden came from London to attend to some business in New England. (1657.) She was imprisoned for some three months, and then sent back to England, at her own expense. Mary Dyer was imprisoned, but finally released, at considerable expense to her husband. Mary Clark, who came over from London to "warn the persecutors," was whipped on her naked back "twenty stripes of a whip with three cords, as thick as a man's little finger, having each some knots at the end."

Christopher Holder and John Copeland were also severely whipped and imprisoned. Lawrence and Cassandra Southwick, were imprisoned and fined for having entertained Holder and Copeland, and they and their son were afterward whipped and fined, for attending "Quaker meetings." Daniel and Provided Southwick, the children of Lawrence, were fined ten pounds for absenting themselves from the legal meetings, and not being able to pay it, and refusing to work, the Court ordered that they should be sold in Barbadoes, or Virginia. This order was signed by Edward Rawson, Secretary ; but no shipmaster would carry them. Sarah Gibbons, Dorothy Waugh, and Hored Gardner, were whipped. William Leddra, and William Brend (an old man), were imprisoned, and Brend was whipped with a rope, by the jailor. Twelve persons were fined at Salem, for not coming to church. John Rouse, John Copeland, and Christopher Holder, had their right ears cut off.

William Robinson (merchant of London), was whipped in Boston streets, and then banished, with Marmaduke Stevenson, Mary Dyer, and Nicholas Davis.[1]

The three first returned, and Governor Endicott pronounced sentence of death against them. They were marched to prison ; and on the 27th of October, in the afternoon, a guard of two hundred men, attended with

[1] Sewall's History of the Quakers, New York, 1844. W. H., p. 282.

a drummer, conducted them to the gallows. Mary Dyer walked between her friends, Stevenson and Robinson, clasping their hands. Robinson was first hanged, protesting that he died for conscience' sake; then Stevenson was hanged; and then Mary Dyer, having the rope about her neck, and her face covered with a handkerchief, lent by the Rev. Mr. Wilson, was reprieved. Her mind was made up for death, and her reprieve brought her no joy. She was taken away by her son.

The Quakers charge, that Minister Wilson was that day insulting and cruel to these poor people.

Mary Dyer was a "comely and valiant woman," and in the next Spring, she returned. What now was to be done?

The law said she must be hung, and Endicott again pronounced sentence, and she was led out to die a felon's death. Some scoffed and jeered her, but the most pitied; she died bravely, fearing nothing.

Then came Patience Scott, a girl of but eleven years of age, who said she too, was a Quaker. What could the Magistrates do? It would be ridiculous to put such a child to death; they, therefore, concluded that "Satan had employed her," and they allowed Captain Hutchinson to take her home to Providence.

Few can appreciate the sad duty which the Magistrates felt compelled to undertake, in killing these, because they were Quakers; and they felt it necessary to publish a vindication, defending themselves, and citing the practices against Jesuits in England.

But there seemed no end; for Quaker after Quaker came; they were tried, they were whipped, and the prison was full; so much did their sufferings move the hearts of the common people, who really care little for the distinctions of Theology, that a guard had to be put around the prison, to protect them from visiting and sympathizing with the prisoners.

William Ledra came back (September 1660), and

was subject to death. They offered him his life, if he would go away and promise not to return; he said,

"I came here to bear my testimony, and to tell the truth of the Lord, in the ears of this people. I refuse to go." So he was hanged in the succeeding March. (14th.)

WENLOCK CHRISTOPHERSON, or CHRISTISON, came, and was tried and condemned to die. "What have you gained," he said, "by your cruel proceedings? For the last man that was put to death here, five are come in his room, and if you have power to take my life from me, God can raise up ten of his servants, to take my place, and so you may have torment upon torment." This seemed true, and for the present he was imprisoned.

The death of Ledra, and the return of Wenlock Christison, brought confusion among the Magistrates, and some said, "Where will this end?" and declared it was time to stop.

Governor Endicott found it difficult to get a Court to agree to sentence Christison to death; but he halted not, and pronounced the sentence, and Christison was led back to his friends, in prison, with the crown of Martyrdom on his head. But a few days afterward, the jailor opened the prison doors, and Wenlock (with twenty-seven others), was set at liberty, much to his and their surprise. Peter Pearson and Judith Brown only, were stripped and whipped at the cart's tail, through the quiet streets of Boston.

The body of the people had long been averse to these cruelties, and were growing restive. Persecution, as an epidemic, had for a time, filled their hearts and blasted their sympathies and affections; but it was past, and moral health began once more to assert its power.

CHARLES II. ORDERS THE PERSECUTION TO BE STOPPED.

The friends of the Quakers in England were earnest, and they prevailed upon King Charles II. to order the persecutions to cease in New England [Sept. 1661]. Samuel Shattock, a banished Quaker, was sent from England by Charles, with a letter to Governor Endicott, commanding that no more Quakers should be hanged or imprisoned in New England, but should be sent to England for trial. This ended the persecutions ; for, on the 9th of December, 1661, the Court ordered all Quakers to be set at liberty. The order was obeyed, not so much because it came from the King, as because Excess had cured itself, and the cruel and wretched punishments were then abolished from their statute-book. Let us give our attention for a few moments to the principles and practices which made these people so obnoxious.

WHAT DID THE QUAKERS BELIEVE ? The Great Principles and Instincts, upon which human nature rests, are universal, existing in every race and clime, and are active or latent in every individual. But individuals appear from time to time, in whom these instincts shine out clear and convincing, and occasionally with marked results upon their own time and upon coming ages. Most men are hedged about and bounded by Custom and Habit ; they say "this is proper, because others do it," or, "that is right or true, because some one has said so whom we trust." This kind move in masses, unable to stand alone ; yet they gravitate toward the truth, and grow better unless ruined by an overwhelming selfishness, which vitiates their perceptions.

The Great Souled Men trust themselves, and most often stand alone ; commonly are killed or crucified. They appeal to God, and rest upon him ; they must think, speak, and live what they know to be true. They listen to, and hear the voice of God in their souls, and then they say,

"I KNOW."

When told that the Church or the King says "this or that is true," they reply "Those can not speak for me ; I must ask of God in my own consciousness." Socrates appealed to his "Dæmon," Plato to his "Domestic God," and George Fox, the founder of the Quakers, to his "Inner Light." These men restore us, as the Ages rush by, to our native manhood, and Redeem us from the follies and falsehood which gradually gather upon the usages of Life. They assert, once again, that the Essence of Manliness consists in Truth, Honor, Kindness, and Courage ; not in Titles, Wealth, Palaces, and Patronage ; and when dead, we recognize their greatness, and thank them.

GEORGE FOX.

During the struggle between Charles I. and the people of England (headed by Hampden, Eliot, Pym, and Cromwell), George Fox was a poor shoemaker's apprentice. It was a time when mind and conscience, both were excited to action, and men were everywhere dealing with the great questions of Life and Death. George Fox arose from his bench, and asked,

"What does this life mean ?" "What is Truth ?"

He left the shop, and wandered alone in the fields, to tend his master's flocks, and he asked these questions of all men. He went to the priests, and they told him to be quiet, to dance and frolic, and all would be well with him. This did not answer him. He would not seek for glory in Cromwell's army, nor for wealth ; the struggle went on in his soul, and at last, through darkness, came a voice, saying,

"There is a God."

From this time his spiritual life began, and he went among men, eager to reform, to raise and to save them. He said to poor and rich, learned and unlearned, alike, "Trust not the Scholars, trust not the Church, trust not the King, trust not the Magistrates.

The Scholar is a man,
The Bishop is a man,
The King is a man.

But you are also a MAN. God speaks to them, but he also speaks to you ; in the eye of man you may be despised, but in the eye of a just God you are the equal of any. Stand up, then, trust yourself, be your own master, and no longer a slave." He spoke bitterly against the Church and its machinery ; against hireling priests, who rolled in wealth, shearing, not feeding the flock. He spoke against Force and War, saying nothing was gained by it, for it was as often that the wrong was the strongest in Swords as the right. He spoke against persecution, for in all sects there is some truth ; and he asserted the political rights in England of the Catholics, whose theories and practices he abhorred. He spoke against symbols and ordinances, such as Baptism and Priesthood, saying that the letter killed, the spirit alone gave life. He scorned titles and aristocracy, and said Kings are but men ; and when he stood before them, before Cromwell or Charles, he kept on his hat, and said "thee" and "thou," and "yea" and "nay" to them, as he would have done to a beggar. Oaths, he said, were wrong, contrary to the Bible, which said, "swear not at all." He accepted the Bible (the Constitution of Protestants) as one form of Revelation, but to be judged by the Inner Light, and binding so far as it agreed with that. He held to the spiritual equality of the sexes, and that Women had as much right to preach as men ; he opposed all tricking and adorning of the person, and estimated lightly the advantages of learning and the Fine Arts. Such were some of the positions of George Fox. They are surprising now ; they were considered damnable then ; but his earnestness and fervor, and the democratic tendency of his teachings, commanded attention, and the common people heard him gladly. His doctrines found favor, and crowds resorted to him. But the whole power of the Church and State, of the Clergy and Magistrates, of the titled, and of the learned, of the rich and the gay, bore down upon him and his followers, for his doctrines destroyed their privileges and practices, root and branch.

His followers were called "Quakers," in derision ; they were ridiculed and persecuted, were whipped, cropped, maimed, thrown into dungeons, fined, sold to slavery, and killed ; but these things availed not.

Fox never faltered nor feared, the number of his disciples increased, and in time his doctrines were accepted by persons of wealth and standing, like Penn and Barclay. Their eyes, at last, turned to America, as a refuge for the poor and persecuted, and their missionaries came over to New England, as we have seen, to meet with persecution there—except in Rhode Island, where Roger Williams had established and maintained liberty of worship.

EXCESSES OF THE QUAKERS.

In the enthusiasm, excited by the enunciation of new truths, ill-balanced minds are sure to rush to excess, and thus to curse the cause they wish to forward; an open enemy is often better than an unwise friend. This was especially the case among the first followers of George Fox. Trusting to the "Inner light," forgetting that the instincts and inspirations of the soul are always to be examined and PROVED by experience and reason, ill-regulated persons yielded themselves blindly to any impulse or whim of the moment, and claimed, that that was an inspiration, and therefore holy. Under such excitements, they rudely interrupted religious exercises, at various places in Massachusetts; they went through the streets, crying, "Woe! woe!" and declaring curses; Thomas Newhouse went into meeting at Boston, and dashing together two glass bottles said: "Thus will the Lord break you in pieces:" and one woman went through the streets of Salem, bearing her testimony, NAKED as when she came into the world. In 1663, Lydia Wardwell, "a young and chaste woman—being given up to the leading of the Lord," went naked into the meeting at Newbury, to denounce the "wickedness of your priests and rulers." She was tied up to a post and severely whipped for it. Such things caused confusion and scandal, and in the eyes of even liberal men excused the bitter persecutions which were practiced against the whole body of Quakers, and not toward these monomaniacs only. It should be remembered that so soon as the persecutions ceased, these excesses also ceased; so certain is it, that one wrong will induce another one. The "Friends" everywhere, then became peaceable, industrious, honest citizens, remarkable for their simplicity and truth. These characteristics have remained with them, though many of their reforms have now become formulas, and they have thus lost the spirit which inspired George Fox. As a distinctive sect, they will not continue, for the reason above given; and because they undervalued Art, Literature, Learning, and Amusement; and because the world about them has, in a great degree, accepted their great truths.

But the Quakers grew in numbers, and in grace, till in 1682, William Penn at their head, they came to the banks of the Delaware to try their "HOLY EXPERIMENT." They brought no arms, they spoke their simple theories to the Indians, which were understood and well received; the Indians said,

"We will live in love with William Penn and his children," and they did.

No man claimed privileges; people were to tax themselves; to make their own laws, and to elect the officers to execute them; indeed the whole power was in the people. It was an organized democracy, except that the office of Lord-proprietor, vested in Penn, was hereditary. Virtually it was a better experiment of the power of truth and of self-government, than the world had before seen, except in Rhode Island; and it was an inevitable result of the doctrines of GEORGE FOX called the QUAKER.[1]

[1] Morton's Memorial. Hutchinson's Mass. Bay, vol. i. R. I. Hist. Coll., vol. ii. Hazard's H. Coll.

Lest any should suppose, that these persecuting laws were peculiar to New England, it will be well and satisfactory to know, that the laws of Episcopal Virginia at this time, were as follows: £100 fine for bringing a Quaker into the Colony; Quakers to lie in prison until they should give security to depart; if they returned a third time to be treated as Felons. Entertaining Quakers, subject to a fine of £100; and all Quaker books positively forbidden.—Anderson's Colonial Church, vol. ii., p. 27.

CHAPTER XXXVII.

THE KING'S JUDGES.—REGICIDES.

CHARLES I.—STRAFFORD AND LAUD—THE COMMONS—CIVIL WAR—CHARLES BEHEADED—OLIVER CROMWELL—THE REGICIDES FLY—WHALEY AND GOFFE—THEY FLY TO NEW HAVEN—HUE AND CRY—KELLOND AND KIRK—THE JUDGES' CAVE—GOVERNOR LEETE—THE JUDGES DISAPPEARED—DIXWELL—GOFFE DEFENDS HADLEY—DEATH.

CHARLES I. in England determined to rule without law, and to lay taxes without the consent of Parliament. The Earl of Strafford was his councillor in matters of State, and Archbishop Laud, in the affairs of the Church. They were determined men, and their word was "Thorough." The Commons, led by Eliot, Pym, Coke, Hampden, Cromwell, and others, were equally determined that the king in England should not be a despot. The struggle in Parliament continued in words for many years; till, in 1640, Charles marched his soldiers into Parliament, to seize the seven obnoxious members; violating the privileges of the House, and his own solemn pledge to his ministers that he would only act with their advice. Then Laud and Strafford lost their heads, and the country was plunged into armed strife. The result was, the king left London. The country was divided into the King's party and the Parliament's party, and Civil War (began in August, 1642) continued till Charles was taken prisoner. Then various attempts were made at a reconciliation, but Charles (respectable as he was for private virtues) falsified his promises; he did not hold his word as binding, and repeatedly betrayed those who trusted his public pledges. A High Court was convened, composed of some sixty members of Parliament, before which Charles was brought to trial, accused of crimes against the nation, and sentenced to death. He was beheaded in front of Whitehall, in 1649, and for a few years the government was in the stern but steady hand of Oliver Cromwell. But the people of England were used to the style of a "King, Lords, and Commons;"—they were not used to the rigid discipline of the Puritans, and remembering only the pleasant things of the past, they sighed for the flesh-pots of Egypt, as the Jews had done before. The aristocracy saw their places usurped by unknown, and, in some cases, ignoble, men; and after Cromwell's death, the nation hastened to prostrate itself at the feet of Charles's son—who became the most dissolute and corrupt king that England had ever enjoyed or suffered.

THE REGICIDES FLY FROM ENGLAND TO ALL LANDS.

When that time came (1660), the friends of Cromwell had no safety in England; but more than all, were the Regicides in danger, and many fled. Two of them, Colonel Whaley and Colonel Goffe, arrived in New England, on the 27th of July, 1660, and with Colonel Dixwell, who came afterward, are now known as the REGICIDES.

The sympathies of most of the people in New England had been with the Parliament, not with the King; for they had felt the power of Church and State, and were hopeful of better things, from the stand which had been made against it. The Regicides made no attempt at concealment on their arrival, but waited upon Governor Endicott, and were visited and well-received, by the first men in Boston. Even the children knew them, and as they walked in the streets, said to one another, "There, look, those are two of Cromwell's men!"

They were grave, serious, and brave, and knew their danger, though they were not the most obnoxious to the new King's friends; but the trying and killing of a King, was a strange thing in History, and his friends could not be expected to spare them, when they got power, as they now had. However, Whaley and Goffe lived quietly through the Autumn, and walked together in the beautiful woods, which crowned the hills (now Mount Auburn), and fringed the borders of Fresh Pond, speculating as to what might be their fate; perhaps an act of indemnity might spare them; but if not, to whom could they fly? On Lord's-days and Fast-days, they went publicly to meetings, and sat among the old men; many looked upon them with respect, many with pity, and some with dislike. Goffe kept a diary through seven years, from which, Hutchinson[1] has preserved some facts. In November, the act of indemnity reached the Colony, and then it appeared that they were NOT pardoned; some of the leading men in Boston became alarmed, and spoke among themselves, as to the harm that might come to the Colony for allowing shelter and protection, to these condemned men; and it became a question, whether the Magistrates were not bound to secure them. In February (22d), the Court of Assistants was called together by the Governor, to consider the matter; but the policy of the Magistrates had always been, to postpone and protract, and so, in the end, procure their own way; and now some said,

"It will be time enough to take extreme action, when we are required to do it." And there the matter then rested. But Whaley and Goffe were warned that they might not be safe, should a requisition from England arrive, and that their friends might not be able to protect them; so, on the 26th of February, they left Cambridge, and for the next two weeks, in broken, bitter weather, made their way South, to New Haven. They had hardly gone, when there came from England, a "Hue and cry," demanding their bodies, as Traitors, and the Court felt bound to issue a warrant, and to make some effort to secure them (March, 1660-61); but it was too late, they were beyond reach.

JOHN DAVENPORT, THE MINISTER.

It is worthy of notice, that Davenport, the Minister at New Haven, received them, and stood by them, and so did the people there; they believed that in punishing Charles, justice

[1] Vol. i., 214.

was done, and they were not ready to deliver these fugitives, to vindictive and sudden death for the part they had taken against him. But word of the King's Proclamation came through the wild country, and reached New Haven in course of a month, and many were troubled ; so Whaley and Goffe left New Haven, and showed themselves in Milford, and told who they were, and then disappeared. Toward the end of April, news came to Boston, that ten of the Regicides were executed, and that the Magistrates there, must seize and send over, Whaley and Goffe ; and then there was alarm. To save themselves from accusation, the Magistrates now gave a Commission to Kellond and Kirk, two zealous young royalists, to scour the country, and search, and seize, the fugitives ; with their guides they made their way through the untraveled country, to New Haven, where they had reason to believe they should unearth their game. Where were the Regicides? Securely sheltered and cared-for, in the house of the Minister John Davenport, at New Haven. Fast friends had brought them word, that Kellond and Kirk were hot in pursuit. They came, they searched, they brought letters to Governor Leete, at Guilford, who showed alacrity, but did not discover the Regicides ; they offered rewards, they hired Indians to catch them. The fugitives were not then in the cellar, nor in the garret, of Mr. Davenport's house? No, they had slipped away with Sperry and Burril ; and as the story goes, had once a narrow escape, being under the bridge of Mill-river, when Kirk and Kellond spurred over it.

THE JUDGES' CAVE ON WEST ROCK.

The young royalists spared no pains to take them, but the Regicides and their friends were too subtle to be caught ; and their hiding-place was the nest of rocks on the top of "West Rock ;" known to this day as "The Judges' Cave." There they stayed nigh a month, food being brought by friends. The pursuers searched the country as far as Manhadoes (New York), and then returned to Boston, threatening vengeance against Mr. Davenport. The Minister said, "I will not bewray the outcast, nor deliver the wanderer. A few men, their enemies, may declare them guilty of death ; I do not think them so. I will judge for myself, and I will not help deliver them to destruction." He knew that he might be condemned to fine, imprisonment, and even death, yet he would not yield the sacred right and duty, of judgment and action. When the Regicides heard of his danger, they came down and showed themselves in New Haven, and privately informed Governor Leete that they would yield themselves, rather than any should come to harm. Through some months they lived a dreary life in the Rocks, and then, for two years, were concealed in Thomkins's house, near Milford, their only exercises being religious. But on the arrival, in 1664, of the King's Commissioners, in Boston, they again sought their cave ; where, after a few days, some hunting Indians accidentally discovered them, and they were there no longer safe ; then they disappeared, and for some fifteen years, few persons knew where they were.

They themselves read in some English papers, that they were dead in Switzerland, which news they enjoyed ; but they did not dare leave their hiding-place, for the friends of the King were every day grasping more and more of the power in the Colonies. In 1664 [Feb. 10], Colonel Dixwell, another of the Regicides, joined them at their hiding-place, but it is not known how he escaped from England. With them he continued for some years ; and then there came to New Haven one James Davids, Esquire, who married and lived peacefully, leaving one son, whose descendants now respect his name, which was John Dixwell. A handsome monument erected by one of them, marks the place of his burial on the New Haven Green.

During the King Philip's war, the people of the town of Hadley, in Massachusetts, while at Church, were thrown into consternation by the onset and war-whoop of the Indians, and were distracted, having no leader. Suddenly, a grave, elderly man appeared among them; he put himself at their head, rallied, encouraged, and instructed them, and the Indians were repulsed. Hadley was saved, but where was their deliverer? He was not to be found. The people were surprised and alarmed, and some said that he was a supernatural visitant. It was Colonel Goffe who had led them on to defense and victory.[1]

He and Whaley had been received and concealed by Mr. Russell, the Minister of the place. Goffe had kept up a correspondence with his wife in England, through which he and Whaley received money, as they did from Richard Saltonstall and some others in the Colony. There Goffe lived till about the year 1679 (Whaley having died some years before), banished from society and from all useful occupation. Life was to them a burden, and death, when it came, a relief.

[1] Hutchinson, vol. i. Stiles's Judges. Hazard, vol. ii.

CHAPTER XXXVIII.

THE INDIANS.

THE COUNTRY DESOLATE—WINSLOW AND COBATANT—THEIR WOMEN—THEIR CHILDREN—A BELLE SQUAW—BEGGARS—GAMBLING—IN SICKNESS—THEIR SPEECHES—WAR—THEIR DRESS—THEIR RELIGION—KIETAN AND HOBBAMOCK—THE COMMANDMENTS—POWOWS—ORIGIN OF EVIL—SACRIFICES—BURIAL—BELIEFS—THEIR GOVERNMENT—SACHEMS AND SAGAMORES—DISEASES—THEIR FOOD—DREAMS—THEIR HOUSES—THEIR KINDNESS—GOOKIN'S SUMMARY—TREATMENT OF INDIANS—MASON AND SASSACUS—AGGRAVATION—NINIGRETT—LANDS—PLOTS—SLAVES—WANALAUNSET.

HISTORY says that two things, about equally potent, destroyed the Indian nations of America:

First. They were in the way of the whites.

Second. They learned to love Rum.

A blazing star had appeared, some four years before the landing of the Pilgrims, which, to credulous minds, foreboded dreadful disaster. A plague and destruction of the Indians followed, and they were swept off, so that when the Pilgrims landed, they found the country nigh desolate; and it was easy for some of the Pilgrims to believe, that God had killed off the Indians to make room for them; so many reasoned. As it was, the weakness of the Indians removed one obstacle to the permanent occupation of the country by the whites. Some short extracts from the writings of persons who were among them, will best inform us of the Indians and their habits.

THE COUNTRY DESOLATE WHEN THE PILGRIMS ARRIVED.

Edward Winslow, in a letter to a friend in England, thus speaks of the untamed children of the New England forests: "We have found the Indians very faithful in their covenant of peace with us, very loving and ready to pleasure us. We often go to them, and they come to us. Some of us have been fifty miles by land in the country with them. Yea, it hath pleased God so to possess the Indians with the fear of us, and love unto us, that not only the greatest King amongst them, called Massasoit, but also all the princes and people round about us, have either made suit unto us, or been glad of any occasion to make peace with us; so that seven of them, at once, have sent their messengers unto us, to that end. Yea, an isle of the sea, which we never saw, hath also, together with the former (?), yielded willingly to be under the protection, and subject to, our Sovereign Lord, King James; so that there is now great peace among the Indians themselves, which was not formerly, neither would have been but for us; and we, for our parts, walk as peaceably and safely in the wood, as in the highway in England. We entertain them familiarly in our Houses, and they are friendly in bestowing their venison upon us. They are a people without any religion, yet very trusty, quick of apprehension, ripe-witted, just."[1]

Winslow and Hampden, on their return from a visit to Massasoit, spent the night with Cobatant, at Mattapuyst. Winslow describes it thus: "By the way, I had much conference with him, so likewise at his house—he being a notable politician, and full of merry jests and squibs, and never better pleased than when the like are returned upon him. He demanded further, how we durst, being but two, come so far into the country? I answered, where was true love, there was no fear; and my heart was so upright towards them, that for mine own part I was fearless to come amongst them. But said he, if your love be such, and it bring forth such fruits, how cometh it to pass, that when we come to Patuxet [Plymouth], you stand upon your guard, with the mouths of your pieces presented towards us? Whereupon, I answered, it was the honorable and respective entertainment we could give them; it being an order amongst us, so to receive our best respected friends; but shaking his head, he answered, that he liked

[1] Chronicles of Pilgrims, p. 232.

not such salutations." Cobatant was no fool, and Winslow was not quite true with him. He liked all the Commandments, he said, but the seventh, thinking it might be very inconvenient to be tied to one woman; though the Indians, for savages, were remarkable for chastity. Of their Women, we read as follows:

In the "Relation of our voyage to Massachusetts," this little incident finds a place. "Having well spent the day, we returned to the Shallop, almost all the women accompanying us to trucke, who sold their coats from their backs, and tied boughs about them, but with great shamefastness (for indeed they are more modest than some of our English women are), etc." Josselyn says the same of them.[1] Their women were their drudges.[2] They hoed corn; they gathered wood, carried the luggage, etc.; yet they seem not to have been subject to cruelty, unless this was one. But they throve so surprisingly under it, that the pains of child-birth were nothing, not enough to excite a groan (?), and in two days the women were again at their work. Williams states that the children were born white, neither of which statements should be received as true. Most men had but one wife (though polygamy was not forbidden), and to her they were constant. Their affections toward children were strong, so that Williams says, he has known a father to cut and stab himself with grief and rage, at the loss of a child. Josselyn, in his New England Rarities (London, 1672) thus gives his account of what he saw among the Indians:

DESCRIPTION OF A BELLE SQUAW.

"The men are somewhat Horse Fac'd, and generally Faucious; that is, without beards; but the women, many of them, have very good Features, seldom without a *Come to me* or *Cor Amoris* in their countenance; all of them black-eyed, having even short teeth, and very white; their hair black, thick and long; broad-breasted; handsome, straight

[1] Josselyn, Voyages.

[2] Winslow's Good News. Higginson's N. E. Plantation.

bodies, and slender, considering their constant loose habit; their limbs cleanly, straight, and of a convenient stature, generally as plump as Partridges, and, saving here and there one, of a modest deportment. Their garments are a pair of sleeves of Deer or Moose-skin drest, and drawn with lines of several Colours into Asiatic works, with Buskins of the same, a short Mantle of Trading Cloath, either Blew or Red, fastened with a Knot under the Chin, and girt about the middle with a Zone, wrought with white and blue Beads into Pretty Works. Of these Beads they have Bracelets for their Neck and Arms, and Links to hang in their Ears, and a fair Table, curiously made up with Beads likewise, to wear before their Breast. Their Hair they Combe backward, and tye it up short with a Border, about two handfulls broad, wrought in Works as the others with their Beads."

Such was the appearance of a belle Squaw in 1672. BEGGARS and neglected children were not known among them. Their women seem to have been peculiar, in that two families could live in the same small house without quarreling. The principal wife of the Sachem ruled the rest; she was equal to him in birth, otherwise "their seed would become in time ignoble." They loved Excitement of all kinds, and especially that of GAMBLING, which they did with a kind of dice; and villages would often pit themselves against one another. Inveterate gamblers asked the aid of the gods, and were fond of a sort of charm—a chrystal, which they believed to be a piece of thunderbolt, and kept it by them. Williams, in his simple way, says, "I have not heard any of these prove losers." "It happened," says Winslow, "that two of their men fell out as they were in game (for they use gaming as much as anywhere, and will play away all, even their skin from their backs; yea, and for their wife's skins also, as I have seen), and, growing to great heat, killed one another, etc."[1]

[1] Winslow, Good News, p. 22.

In sickness the Indians were very attentive to one another, till their death or recovery. "If any die, night and morning they mourn for them many days in a 'most doleful manner,' so as to draw tears from their eyes, almost from ours also."

Another custom is thus indicated: "Now, it being a commendable manner of the Indians, when any (especially of note) are dangerously sick, for all that profess friendship to them, to visit them in their extremity.[1] When Massasoit was sick, the tenderness and sorrow of the Indians was very great. Hobbamock broke forth, "My loving Sachem, my loving Sachem! many have I known, but never any like thee." "He was no lyar—he was not bloody and cruel, like other Indians." [2]

WHAT WAS THEIR MENTAL CAPACITY?

Williams concluded that, "in quick apprehensions and accurate judgments, to say no more, the most high and sovereign God and Creator hath not made them inferior to Europeans." They delighted in news, and would sit around with their pipes, listening in deep silence to him who spoke. So Paul found it with the Athenians and Cæsar with the Gauls. These circles often contained a thousand, and their speakers were copious and emphatic, using action, sometimes for an hour and more at a time. When Williams spoke of the friendship of the Whites, Cobatant took a stick, and broke it in ten pieces; as he laid down each piece, he related an instance which gave him cause to fear, and to say this was not so; and Williams could not wholly answer him. Two brief speeches of Indians on record may be interesting; but it is evident that they are constrained, and are not such as they made to themselves.

Boudinot[3] describes the Speech of the Indian Chief at New York to General Knox in 1789. He seemed much dejected at looking at the City, and said,

[1] Winslow, Good News, p. 26. [2] Winslow, Good News, p. 27.

[3] Star of the West. Trenton, 1816.

"I have been looking at your beautiful City—the great Water—your fine country, and see how happy you all are. But then I could not help thinking that this fine country, and this great water, were once ours. Our ancestors lived here—they enjoyed it as their own in peace. It was the gift of the Great Spirit to themselves and their children. At last the white people came here in a great canoe.

"They asked only to let them tie it to a tree, lest the waters should carry it away; we consented. Then they said some of their people were sick, and they asked permission to land them, and put them under the shade of the trees. The ice came, and they could not go away. They then begged for a piece of land to build wigwams for the winter. We granted it to them. They then asked for some corn to keep them from starving. We kindly furnished it to them, they promising to go away when the ice was gone.

"When this happened, we told them they must go away with their big Canoe; but they pointed to their big guns round their wigwams, and said they would stay there, and we could not make them go away.

"Afterward more came.

"They brought spirituous and intoxicating liquors with them, of which the Indians became very fond. They persuaded us to sell them some land. Finally, they drove us back from time to time into the wilderness, far from the water and the fish and the oysters. They have destroyed the game—our people have wasted away, and now we live miserable and wretched, while you are enjoying our fine and beautiful country, This makes me sorry, brethren! and I can not help it."—p. 137.

Such was the speech of a man who had had intercourse with whites. These speeches were usually sententious, and full of metaphor.

This was the talk of the Stockbridge Indians (1774).

"Brother!" said Uhpaunnouwaumet, "we have heard

you speak by your letter. We thank you for it. We now make answer :

" Brothers ! you remember when you first came over the great waters. I was great, and you was little, very small. I then took you in for a friend, and kept you under my arms, so that none might injure you. Since that time we have ever been true friends. There has never been any quarrel between us.

" But now our Conditions are changed. You have become great and tall. You reach the clouds. You are seen all around the world ; I am become small, very little. I am not so high as your heel. Now you take care of me, and I look to you for protection."

He can not understand the quarrel, but will stand by the New England people ; but he says :

" Brothers ! one thing I ask of you, if you send for me to fight, that you will let me fight in my own Indian way. I am not used to fight English fashion. Therefore you must not expect me to train like your men. Only point out to me where your enemies keep—that is what I want to know." [1]

IN WAR, it was the part of a brave man to follow his arrow when it hit, and to seize and cut off quickly the head of his enemy ; and with their enemies' heads and hands they ornamented their dwellings. Though they were subject to pestilences, and to rheumatisms, and to the tooth-ache, yet under excitement they seem to have had great powers of body ; as Williams states, he has known many to travel on foot from eighty to one hundred miles of a summer's day, and without injury. "In our first war with the Indians," says Eliot, " God pleased to show us the vanity of our military skill, in managing our arms after the European method. Now we are willing to learn the skulking way of war, and what God's end is" (quaintly adds the Reverend Eliot), "in teaching us such a way of discipline, I know not."[2]

[1] Ward's History of Shrewsbury. Boston, 1847.

[2] Letter to Robert Boyle, M. H. C., vol. iii.

War was the only noble occupation for men among them, and the best fighter was the greatest man; as to this day he is among the French and other white people. Their war-dances are too well known to need description. Among them a man is not accounted a man until he doth some notable act. The men take much tobacco, "but for boys so to do, they count it odious." Their chastity is remarkable. They keep account of time by the moon, and know divers stars by name, in particular the north star, which they call "maske," or the bear. "They are weather-wise also."[1]

THEIR DRESS was simply a waist-cloth and a mantle of skin or cloth, which was commonly laid aside. Yet nakedness did not result in indelicacy, for Williams says, "I have never seen that wantonness among them as with grief I have heard of in Europe." That they were fond of dress, as all uncivilized and most civilized people are, is a matter of course, and cheap ornaments of glass or metal could buy from them their choicest furs.[2]

THE INDIANS' RELIGION.

Like all nations, they had a religion and a belief of God. Winslow saw reason to change his opinion, "that the Indians were without religion;" for he says, "therein I erred, for as they conceive of many divine powers, so of ONE, whom they call KIEHTAN,[3] to be the principal, and maker of all the rest, and to have been made by none. He, they say, created the heavens, earth, sea, and all creatures contained therein; also that he made one man and one woman, of whom they, and we, and all mankind came; but how they became so far dispersed, they know not. At first, they say, there was no sachem or king but Kiehtan, who dwelleth above in the heavens, whither all good men go when they die, to see their friends, and have their fill of all things." "Another power they worship, whom they call Hobbamock;—this, so far as we can conceive, is the devil. Him they call upon to cure their wounds and diseases."

[1] Winslow's Good News. [2] Roger Williams's Key.

[3] This was the Manitou, or "Great Spirit."

"Further, observing us to crave a blessing on our meat, before we did eat, and after to give thanks for the same, he asked us what was the meaning of that ordinary custom. Hereupon I took occasion to tell them of God's works of creation and preservation, of his laws and ordinances, especially of the ten commandments: all of which they hearkened unto with great attention, and liked well of: only the seventh commandment they objected against, thinking there were many inconveniences in it, that a man should be tied to one woman; about which we reasoned a good time. Also I told them that whatsoever good things we had, we received from God, as the author and giver thereof, and therefore craved his blessing upon that we had, and were about to eat, that it might nourish and strengthen our bodies." "This all of them concluded to be very well; and said they believed almost all the same things, and that the same power we called God, they called Kiehtan." So writes Winslow, apparently much pleased.

There is no doubt of their belief in Manitou or Manit (or Kiehtan), the Great God, and to him some seem to have referred all good, because he was pleased, and all evil, because he was angry; a solution of the "origin of evil" which has one great merit, namely, brevity. But they branched their gods into many parts, and if they had been a Church-going people, would have been split into many sects. Their powaws, like other priests, led their invocations with strange gestures, even unto fainting, and were principally useful in sickness. "They do bewitch the people," Williams says, "and not only take their money, but do most certainly, by the help of the devil, work great cures:" but he says, "commonly they die under their hands;" so they or the devil must have been poor doctors. In modern times, division of labor prevails, and between priests, doctors, and the devil, we may well hope that the latter gets no more than his share. They laid their dead by the mouth of the grave, and then sat down and wept, tears running down the faces of the stoutest captains, as well as of little children. "The principal office of the *powah* or pow-wow is to call upon the devil, and to cure diseases. Many sacrifices the Indians use, and in some cases kill children."[1] (This last statement needs confirmation.) The Narragansetts make great offerings of their goods, which the priests burn in one great holocaust. The devil was believed to strengthen and protect the chiefs, and to appear familiarly to them. "Their sachems are commonly men of the greatest stature, such as will endure most hardness, yet are more discreet, courteous, and humane in their carriages than any among them, scorning theft, lying, and the like base dealings; and stand as much upon their reputation as any man." A style of Ruler not then extant in Europe.

When the son of Canonicus died, all his favorite weapons and articles were buried with him, and then the father, in sign of his great grief, and in humble expiation to the gods, burned down his palace, and all his goods to a great value. One peculiarity these savages had which may well be noted:—"A modest religious persuasion, not to disturb English, Dutch, or any in their conscience or worship." They believed also, in the after-life, that the good would go to the South-west, and have a good time; while murderers, thieves, and liars, would wander restless.[2]

THEIR GOVERNMENT.

Their society was clannish. At the time of the settlement of the country, they were divided into some twenty tribes, extending from Maine to New York, ranged under their Chiefs or Sagamores; counting, in fighting men, from twenty up to some hundreds to each. The principal of these, were the Tarratines, about the Kennebeck; the Wampanoags, in Massachusetts; the Narragansetts, the Mohegans, and the Pequods, on Long Island Sound; and the Senecas and Mohawks, to the West and North of these.[3]

[1] Winslow's Good News, p. 55. [2] Roger Williams's Key.
[3] Hubbard's History, p. 33.

Their Government was a simple Monarchy, or rather a patriarchal state ; for the Sachem concluded no important thing—wars, laws, or subsidies—to which the people were decidedly adverse. As murders, robberies, adulteries, and such like, common " among the English," were not common with them, the duties of the Sachem, were light. So that even Indian History shows, how crimes are nearly all offenses against property, and grow out of that hunger for wealth ; every man wanting to get, or to keep, more than his share.

Higginson said, " The greatest Saggamores among us, can not make above three hundred men (fighting men), and other less Saggamores, have not above fifteen subjects, and others, near us, but two."[1]

From Morell's Poem, on New England, we take as follows:

"Their Kings give laws, rewards to those they give,
That in good order, and high service live;
The aged widow, and the orphans, all
Their Kings maintaine, and strangers, when they call.
The next in order, are their well-seen men,
In herbs, and roots, and plants, for medicine,
With which, by touch—with clamours, teares, and sweat,
With their curst magick, as themselves they beat,
They ease—but when they cannot save,
But are by death surprised, then with the grave,
The devil tells them, he could not dispence;
For God hath killed them for some great offence." [2]

Their poetry, Morell does not seem to have enjoyed ; for he says,

"And recall Odes, which us affect with griefe,
Though, to their minds, perchance they give relief."

Before the English came, there were two diseases, of

[1] Higginson's N. E. Plantation.

[2] Morell's Poem on New England. Morell was an Episcopal Clergyman, come over in 1623, with Captain Robert Gorges, who intended to be Governor-General of New England. Mass. Hist. Coll., vol. i.

which the Indians usually died: Consumption and Yellow Fever.[1] The Smallpox became, too, a terrible scourge; and they suffered greatly from Rheumatism and Toothache.

Consumption destroyed many of those Indian youths who were being educated at Harvard, and elsewhere, for the Ministry; this destroyer was "frequent among the Indians." Some of them turned back from the path of learning, and loved more the trail of the hunter; so that there seemed to be "awful providences of God," designed to prostrate the attempt at making Indian preachers of the Gospel. Upon the theory, that every disaster or discouragement, was a special act of God, this conclusion was inevitable.

But in spite of this theory, the good sense of some led them to conclude these disasters were incident to all enterprises, where experience has not taught men the road. Further than that, the struggle between the Devil and the God, was always going on, and there was no certainty, that in some way, this mischief was not Satan's work.[2]

THEIR FOOD.

From the South-west came corn and beans, out of the Great God—Cowtantowit's—field. Corn and beans were their principal food, prepared simply (from them come the names of "Samp," "Succatash," etc.); varied with the produce of the hunt and the sea. Altogether, they were good livers, when provisions were plenty, but were improvident. If any stranger came, they gave the best they had, and with a large hospitality, common among barbarous nations. Tobacco was universal, every man carrying his pipe and bag; and in its cultivation only, did the men condescend to labor; but occasionally all would join, the whole neighborhood, men, women, and children, when some one's field was to be broken up, and then they made a loving, sociable, speedy time of it; but the men would not submit to constant act-

[1] Thomas Cooper's Fabulous Traditions. Mass. Hist. Coll., vol. i.

[2] Gookin's account. Heb. xiii. 5. Matt. xxviii. 19, 20.

ive effort, and they produced no results to themselves, or to mankind.[1]

Dreams, as among the Jews, and all uncivilized nations, of whom we have histories, were supposed to proceed from God, and if bad, inspired fear, and provoked prayer.

"THE HOUSES were made with long, young saplings, bended, and both ends stuck in the ground. They were round, like unto an arbor, and covered down to the ground, with thick and well-wrought nets; and the door was not over a yard high, made of a mat, to open. The chimney was a wide hole in the top; for which they had a mat to cover it close, when they pleased. One might stand and go upright in them. In the midst of them, were four little trunches (truncheons) knocked into the ground, and small sticks laid over, on which they hung their pots and what they had to seethe. Round about the fire they lay on mats, which are their beds. The houses were double-matted; for as they were matted without, so were they within, with newer and fairer mats. In the houses, we found wooden bowls, trays, and dishes, earthen pots, hand-baskets, made of crab-shells, wrought together, also, an English pail or bucket; it wanted a bail, but it had two iron ears. There were, also, baskets of sundry sorts, bigger, and some lesser, finer, and some coarser; some were curiously wrought with black and white, in pretty works, and sundry other of their household-stuff. We found also, two or three deer's-heads, one whereof had been newly killed, for it was fresh. There was also, a company of deer's-feet, stuck up in the horns, harts'-horns and eagles'-claws, and sundry such like things there was; also, two or three baskets full of parched acorns, pieces of fish, and a piece of broiled Herring. We found, also, a little silk grass, and little tobacco-seed, with some other seeds, which we knew not. Without, were sundry bundles of flags, sud-ledge, bullrushes, and other stuffs, to make mats. There were thrust into a hollow tree, two or three pieces of veni-

[1] R. W.'s, Key.

son, but we thought it fitter for the dogs, than for us. Some of the best things, we took away with us, and left the houses standing still as they were."[1]

Cushman said : " They were wont to be the most cruel and treacherous people in all these parts, even like lions ; but to us they have been like lambs, so kind, so submissive and trusty, as a man may say ; many Christians are not so kind and sincere."[2]

They seem to have been gentlemen ; for it is told that Chickatabot, being at Boston upon a visit of amity (1631), being in English clothes, the Governor set him at his own table, where he behaved himself as soberly as an Englishman. Of course he did not get drunk, as many white folks in those days did, and more Indians.

Gookin, who was many years among them, sums up his experience somewhat to this effect :

They were idle—given to war and hunting, rather than tillage :

Kind to their children ; very hospitable ; fond of dancing and reveling ; addicted to gambling ; fond of drink and excitement ; revengeful ; proud.

Houses were of bark or mats, sometimes a hundred feet long.

Clothing was of skins.

Food was Indian Corn, fish, and flesh boiled. Their vessels of clay.

Bodies straight, rarely deformed.

Government monarchical and autocratical.

Mixed Religion. They worship for God, the sun, or the moon, or the earth ; but had two chief deities (supreme) called Woonaud or Mannitt (Good), and Mattand (Evil). Their Powaws were a kind of priests, using enchantments and spells, with which to propitiate or frighten the evil spirits. To most of the whites the Indians were, of course, hateful.[3]

[1] Pilgrim's Journal. [2] Elder Cushman's Discourse, Hazard, vol. i., p. 147.
[3] Gookin, Mass. H. C., vol. i.

It is a very common notion, that all the white men were just, merciful, humane Christians, because that was the name of them, and all the Indians, bloody, vindictive savages. It is well to set this matter right, and to vindicate God, in asserting the manhood of the men of color—the Red Men of America. The action of the governments of Plymouth, Massachusetts, Rhode Island, and Connecticut, was, in the main, just and honorable—but there were individual men by scores, who cared nothing for the Indian, nothing for Ideas, nothing for perfection. Such were they of Weston's Colony, and at Merry-mount, who sold rum, and guns, and trash of any kind, to the Indians; who cheated them in all ways; who treated them with reckless brutality, even to shooting and killing them, as they would wolves. The Indians saw and felt all this—some of them keenly; and the fierce, and more manly Pequots determined to resent it with violence. They endeavored to combine all in a plan of destruction to the whites. The justice of Williams to the Narragansetts, secured him their confidence, and a knowledge of the conspiracy, so that he was able to prevent their joining the Pequots, and also to give information to those who had banished him. A known evil is curable; so the whites fell upon the Pequots, and at last, under Major Mason, at Fort Mystic (May, 1637), nearly destroyed the tribe, and the remainder (prisoners) were dispersed among the other tribes, or sold. Sassacus, their sachem, was treacherously murdered by the Mohawks, to whom he had fled. This was the beginning of the Indian Extermination.[1] A few incidents and facts will show how and why the Indians were aggravated.

We have seen how Hunt, one of John Smith's men, seized and carried off a number and sold them as slaves, in the year 1614. When Weston's men cheated and abused the Indians, and stole their corn, the Indians were not allowed to fall upon and destroy them, as they should have done, but were themselves attacked, and some killed,

[1] See Chapter xxix.

by a party from Plymouth, headed by Standish.[1] This injustice aggravated them greatly.

Miantonomo, the chief of the Narragansetts, and one of the most capable Indians in New England, the friend and favorer of Roger Williams, was taken prisoner by Uncas; who referred the matter to the Ministers at Hartford; they decided that he ought to be put to death—not for what he had done, but because they feared him—so he was murdered in cold blood.[2] Ninigrett had a quarrel with some of the Long Island Indians; the whites sent a messenger, to tell him that he must not go to fighting. He replied that it was his own affair, and concerned himself only, and that he should take his own course; "he doth desire that the English will let him alone," he said; "I do but right my own quarrel, which the Long Islanders began with me."[3] But the Colonists sent down a troop of horse and foot, and forced him to desist; simply because they, the whites, desired quiet. The Indians saw their lands gradually going out of their control, and though the right to land, consists really in its use, not in its possession, yet they felt themselves the owners of it; and although there was a show of buying it, still shrewd Indians, like Miantonomo and Philip, felt that it was a farce, and were provoked by it.

The colonies were always on the alert as to plots of the natives. When they heard that any of them were collected, they sent off at once their Captain (Underhill), with muskets, with orders to disperse them, which was done.[4] At one time, some five or six Mohawks, well armed, having appeared in the neighborhood of Boston, and having entered a house to get food, the authorities took possession of them, seizing their arms, and cast them into prison; not for what they had done, but for what they *might* do. The Massachusetts Indians (their enemies) pressed it upon the whites, that they should at least be

[1] Chapter xiv.
[2] Chapter xxx.
[3] Hazard, vol. ii.
[4] Prince's Chron., p. 401.

given up to them. "As well let six wolves go loose as these," said they. And indeed, it seemed to many Christians, that the Lord had delivered them into their hands. The poor fellows—young men who had come far to gratify their curiosity—were in the Lion's den. But more humane counsels prevailed, and it was thought best to dismiss them, with kind words and careful cautions, lest hereafter their friends should retaliate their treatment upon the whites.[1]

In 1683, Eliot, writing to Sir Robert Boyle, states that a vessel carried away a great number of our surprised Indians, intending to sell them for slaves, but that the nations whither they went would not buy them, and finally she left them at Tangier; "there they be, so many as live." He begs of him that some means may be used to get them home, "for Christ sake."[2]

At another time, Wanalaunset, a principal Sachem, fled—the wicked English youth having carelessly and basely killed some of them (the "praying Indians"). He was persuaded to come in again; but the English having plowed and sowed his corn-land with rye, there was nothing for him to eat.

It is not necessary to repeat instances in which the strong oppressed the weak, or to explain that these things provoked bitterness, violence, murders, and finally destruction, in King Philip's war, elsewhere recounted.[3]

[1] Gookin's Hist. Act. [2] Mass. Hist. Coll., vol. iii. [3] Chap. xl.

CHAPTER XXXIX.

ELIOT AND THE INDIANS.

THE LOST JEWS—40,000—ELIOT BEGINS—A DEMOCRAT—TRANSLATIONS—FIRST CONVERT—ELIOT'S FIRST SERMON—WABAN—1649—CONTRIBUTIONS—MATERIAL BASIS—TOTESWAMP'S BOY—DIFFICULTIES—NINIGRET—UNCAS—PHILIP—QUESTIONS—MOHAWK FIGHT—ELIOT'S LETTERS—INDIAN BIBLE—OTHER MISSIONARIES—TOWNS OF PRAYING INDIANS—NATICK—SABBATH EXERCISES—HATREDS—ELIOT INSULTED—STOCKBRIDGE INDIANS—HAWLEY—DRUNKENNESS—CAPACITY FOR CIVILIZATION—INTELLECTUAL RELIGION—THE INDIANS VANISHED—WHY?—ELIOT'S FAMILY—DEATH—"WELCOME JOY."

THERE was much speculation in the early times, as to who the Indians were, and many were inclined to believe them in some way the lost Jews; so Eliot thought.

Gookin, who had much official and other experience with the Indians, evidently inclined to the hypothesis, that they were an emanation or branching of the ten tribes of Israel, which Salamanasser carried away captive.[1] Not that there are any ethnological data for it, but because men's minds seize and hold any hypothesis, rather than none. He concludes, at last, that they are "Adam's posterity, and consequently children of wrath," and "objects of Christian pity and compassion."[2]

He mentions the principal tribes in New England: 1. Pequots; 2. Narragansetts; 3. Pawkunnawkuts; 4. Massachusetts; 5. Pawtacketts.

Much ingenuity was exercised in trying to show a resemblance between the Indian and Jewish languages. But Eliot said: "I have found a greater affinity in it with the Greek tongue than with the Hebrew." There is no probability that their dialects had any connection with

[1] A. M. 3277. 2 Kings, ch. xviii., vs. 9, 12. [2] Mass. Hist. Coll., vol. i.

either ; but according to Eliot and Gookin, there was a similarity and unity in their own languages throughout New England. At the time of Eliot's beginning his labor among the Indians, their numbers in New England, loosely estimated, were between thirty and forty thousand, much divided and scattered. These are classified as a part of the Algonquin race, whose languages are similar.

We come now to the year 1646, when the labors of Eliot among the Indians, began, remarkable for their faithfulness and unproductiveness—ending only with his death. But though the Indians were not civilized or Christianized, to any encouraging extent, and though they could not be preserved in the country, those single-hearted labors were not lost upon Eliot or upon us.

JOHN ELIOT, of Nasing, in England, had a good deal of work in him, and he came to New England in the year 1631 [November 2], to do it ; he had been well educated at Cambridge, in England, and in 1632 (then twenty-eight years old), was settled to preaching at Roxbury, near Boston.

The excellent young woman to whom he was engaged, followed him to New England, and in October, 1632, they were married, and lived well together through a long and useful life.

He seems to have been inclined toward Democratic principles, for in 1634, he severely blamed the Magistrates for having made peace with the Pequots, without consulting the people ("*plebs inconsulta*") ; the same tendency came more fully into notice, in a work called the "Christian Commonwealth," published in 1660, which the Governor and Council formally censured, and called upon Eliot to retract the seditious notions, which he did.

Besides the usual labors of a minister and teacher among the Indians, he was engaged, with Weld and Richard Mather, in making the first book published in America—"The Psalms in Meter :" 1640. Of his other literary works, "The Christian Commonwealth" was published in 1660, his translation of the New Testament in 1661, and that of the Bible in 1663.

About the year 1645, he became interested in trying to serve "those ruins of mankind," the Indians, and devoted himself to the work from that time to the day of his death. He believed, beyond doubt, what David said (Ps. ii. 8), "Ask of me, and I will give thee the heathen for thine inheritance." He believed the Indian, with his dusky skin, was a man and capable of salvation. He framed first, two catechisms in the Indian tongue. His motives were, "1. The glory of God in their conversion. 2. His compassion and affection. 3. The promise of the Colonists to the King, that the Gospel should be extended." He translated the Catechisms, Primer, Singing-Psalms, The Practice of Piety, Baxter's Call, the Bible, and some other things, which were printed at the expense of the Society in London.

The first Indian converted in the new Colonies, or rather, who left some "good hopes in their hearts that his soul had gone to rest," was Hobbamock (in the Settlement of Plymouth), "who was transported with great wonderment of the power the English had with their God;"[1] because when they prayed to him for rain, it did rain; and so he concluded to join them and their God. Little seems to have been done for many years in Christianizing of Indians; for the reason that much more pressing work was at hand. And when Eliot did begin to urge it, the Indian met him with the question:

"If Christianity be so necessary, why for so many years have you done nothing in proving it to us?"

But in the year 1646, the General Court passed an order to promote the diffusion of the Gospel among the Indians, and the churches were requested to consider how it might best be done. Eliot's thought had been to do something; he had been to work to learn their language,

[1] Hubbard, p. 650.

and he now applied himself with his usual energy and determination.

On a day in October (28th, 1646), he went out into the wilderness, to seek and convert heathen Indians. He was met by a grave man (attended by five or six others), whose name was Waban; and to them he preached, in a wigwam, at Nonantum; which is near Watertown, on the south side of the Charles river.[1] He preached from the 37th chapter of Ezekiel: "Then said he unto me, Prophesy unto the wind ('Waban' is said to mean wind), prophesy, son of man, and say to the wind, Thus saith the Lord God, Come from the four winds, O Breath, and breathe upon these that they may live; so I prophesied as he commanded me, and the breath came unto them, and they lived and stood upon their feet, an exceeding great army." This discourse lasted for an hour, and one would be gratified now to know what Waban thought of it all.

HIS FIRST SERMON.

Waban was converted, and was one of the principal men in the Indian town of Natick, to which the Nonantum Indians removed (1651). Eliot could get but little assistance at the outset, and one reason no doubt was, that the Colonists were too poor. But in the year 1649, an Act of Parliament was passed, intended to promote the spread of the Christian Gospel among the Indians. Large collections also were made in England, yielding a revenue of five or six hundred pounds, which were increased by those made in New England; Boston alone contributing five hundred pounds. The first President of this Society was Judge Steel. The Society was incorporated in 1662, and Robert Boyle was named its Governor. After this time, much effort was made, with some result, among the Indians, and Eliot organized an Indian Church at Natick in 1651.

The Indians were in some cases made into Magistrates and teachers in the towns of "praying Indians;" and the

[1] Homer's History of Newtown, M. H. C.

following "State paper" is yet extant, curious among such writings for its brevity and point. It is a warrant addressed to an Indian constable :

"1. I, Hihoudi. 2. You, Peter Waterman. 3. Jeremy Wicket. 4. Quick you take him. 5. Fast you hold him. 6. Straight you bring him. 7. Before me, Hihoudi."[1]

In 1674, the number of "praying Indians," as they were called, amounted to some thirty-six hundred, collected in various settlements ; mostly in Martha's Vineyard, Nantucket, Plymouth, and Massachusetts. But few of the number were admitted to communion, the strictness of examination being too great for these ignorant and uncivilized men.

They were children, with the same elements as the rest of men ; but they had not learned to subject the carnal to the spiritual nature, or to live obedient to principle, rather than impulse : this they could learn only by living in settled communities, with some of the necessities of civilization pressing upon them. The Indian missionaries expected too much from the preaching of love to man and love to God. They, as so many others have done, forgot how many influences work together to make up the civilization of the world. Mr. Bourne, who was at work among the Indians at Plymouth, saw and noted one of these things, and he considered it as vain to try to propagate Christianity among a people who had no territory, where they might remain at peace, without fear of being ousted. Governor Hinckley[2] speaks of another monstrous evil which stood in their way, which has long stood in the way of all effort for reform and amelioration : it is a Upas-tree, and deadly. "It is the great appetite many of the young generation have for strong liquors, and the contrary evil humor of sundry of our English in furnishing them therewith, notwithstanding all the Courts' orders and means used to prohibit the same." This and another cause, the presence of a superior race, hastened

[1] Davis, in Morton. Appendix. [2] Davis, in Morton. Appendix.

the departure of the native tribes, till now, after two centuries, they vanish from sight, almost from memory.

Eliot did not have an easy time of it. The Indians bought rum of the bad whites, and not content with getting themselves drunk, they gave some to Toteswamp's little boy, about eleven years of age, and got him drunk, so that he lay out all night, and then they fought among themselves. "When Toteswamp heard this, it was a great shame and breaking of heart unto him, and he knew not what to doe." "Word was brought to me," says Eliot, "a little before I took horse to go to Natick, to keep the Sabbath with them: the tidings sunk my spirit extreamly; I did judge it to be the greatest frowne of God that ever it met withall, in the work. I could read nothing in it but displeasure; I began to doubt about our intended work. For one of the offenders was he that hath been my Interpreter, whom I have used in translating a good part of the Holy Scriptures; and in that respect I saw much of Satan's venome, and in God I saw displeasure."

The men were set in the stocks, and whipped; and the child was set in the stocks, and whipped by his father, Toteswamp, "with many tears."

"When I returned to Roxbury," says Eliot, "I related these things to our Elder, to whom I had before related the sin and my grief; who was much affected to hear it, and magnified God."

With money raised in England, tools and various useful things were sent for the Indians, to encourage them to work; schools were established and teachers paid; in one place we learn that Eliot's salary (paid by the Society) was £50; though he still continued to preach at Roxbury. He worked in all directions, he preached, he taught, he catechized, he established towns, he instituted agriculture; in addition to these he stirred the ministers of the Colony to action, and it was mainly through his efforts that others devoted themselves actively to the work.

We may well suppose, that Eliot found difficulties,

which would have discouraged a weak man. He began without means, with an imperfect knowledge of the language, with no co-operation on the part of the whites. The Indians were ignorant and undisciplined; accustomed to idleness, and a wandering life; they were vitiated with rum, and were despised or feared by the whites. Their chiefs opposed the new religion; and the sachem Ninigret resolutely and persistently declined having the white man's God and religion introduced among his people; saying: "For what reason? Let me see that your religion makes you better than us, and then we may try it." Uncas, sachem of the Mohegans, went to Hartford, and told the Commissioners his extreme dislike to having Christianity introduced among his people. Philip, chief of the Wampanoags, holding the button of one of the missionaries, said, "I care no more for your religion than for this button."

Not only were these things so, but they put to Eliot subtle questions, which each man finds it hard to answer; some of them were as follows:

"Why did not God give all men good hearts, that they might be good?" and, "Why did not God kill the devil, that made all men so bad—God having all power." "If an Indian had two wives, before he was converted, which should he put away?"

"Whether all the Indians who had died hitherto, had gone to hell, and why only a few now, at last, were put in the way of going to heaven?"[1]

"How can we reconcile the Scriptures which say, 'Save yourselves from this untoward generation,' with, 'We can do nothing of ourselves?'"

"Why did Judas sin in giving up Jesus, when it was what God had appointed?"[2]

"What is the effect of your religion? We have no contentions about property, and no man envies his neighbor."[3]

[1] Francis's Life of Eliot.
[2] Hutchinson, vol. i.
[3] Gov. Lincoln, in M. H. C., vol. v.

"Whether the good child of a bad man would be punished, because the second Commandment says, 'He visits the sins of the fathers upon the children?'"

"If I do that which is a sinne, and do not know that it is a sin, what will God say to that?"

"Why must we be like salt?"

"Why doth God say—I am the God of the *Hebrews*? Why?"[1]

Roger Williams said, that when he discoursed of the creation of the soul, of its danger and need of salvation, they assented—but when he spoke of the resurrection of the body, they cried out, "We will never believe that."[2]

His efforts were interrupted, too, by such affairs as this: In 1669, the Massachusetts Indians gathered themselves (some seven hundred men), and marched away into the Mohawk Country, to fight their enemies, and glut their revenge. Neither Eliot nor Major Gookin could dissuade them. Their principal chief, Chickatabut, led them, and they loitered on their way, and boasted; so the report of them reached the Mohawks sooner than they did. They attacked one of the Mohawk forts but did nothing, and when after a few days, their provision being spent, they turned homeward, the Mohawks waylaid them, cut them up, and killed many of their leaders; this was their last great battle.

But Eliot's labors never ceased, and although many of his converts were Backsliders, yet he kept up his courage, and worked on; he writes to his friend, Robert Boyle (November 4th, 1680), "Our praying Indians, both in the Islands and on the Main, are, considered together, numerous; thousands of souls, of whom, some true believers,

[1] The Day-breaking, if not the Sun-rising, of the Gospell with the Indians in New England. London, 1647 (Eliot). The Clear Sunshine of the Gospel, etc., By Thomas Shepard, Minister, etc., London, 1648. The Glorious Progress of the Gospel among the Indians in N. E. By Edward Winslow, London, 1649. The Light appearing more and more toward a perfect day. By Henry Whitfield, London, 1651. A late and further manifestation of the Progress, etc. By Eliot. London, 1655.

[2] Hutchinson, vol. i.

some learners, and some are still infants, and all of them beg, cry, and entreat, for Bibles."[1]

As he grew old and near his end, his urgency to complete the Bible,[2] was so great, that he writes his patron Boyle, to "change the object of your bountiful Charity from their Bodies to their Souls." "My age makes me importunate," he says, "and my heart hath much ado to hold up my head, but both daily drive me to Christ." The sturdy old apostle stood by his darling work ; yet he wished Sir Robert to draw a Curtain of Love over his failures, if he shall have been too urgent. He acknowledges the receipt of £460, toward the work, and says, "the work goeth on, I praise God." Again he acknowledged (April 22d, 1684), the receipt of £400, "which doth set a diadem of Beauty upon all your former acts of pious Charity."[3]

Again he says, "The great work that I travel about, is the printing of the whole Testament, that they may have the whole Bible. I desire to see it done before I die, and I am so deep in years, that I can not expect to live long ; besides we have but one man (viz., the Indian printer), that is able to compose the sheets, and correct the press, with understanding.[4]

From this it seems that Eliot's principal assistant and right-hand man, was an Indian.

HIS BIBLE.

His translation of the Bible, is a wonderful monument of Patience, Industry, and Faith. He labored against every difficulty, and overcame all. The first Edition consisted of the New Testament, of 1661, and the Old Testament, of 1663. The second Edition was the New Testament, of 1680, and the Old Testament, of 1685. Of the first Edition, between one and two thousand copies were printed, and of the second, two thousand copies, at a cost of £1,000.

The Language and the Race, are extinct, but Eliot and his Bible remain.

[1] Mass. Hist. Coll., vol. iii.

[2] Second Edition.

[3] This must have been from the Society.

[4] Eliot to Boyle. Roxbury, 1682–3.

To illustrate the difficulty of making the first translation, it is told, that when Eliot read to the Indians, and described the verse, "The Mother of Sisera cried through the Lattice," and they gave him their word for lattice; he afterward discovered, that it read, "The Mother of Sisera cried through the Eel-pot," that being as near his description of Lattice, as they could get.

Cotton Mather tries to exaggerate the wonder of Eliot's work, by saying, that the whole translation was written with one pen; which possibly he believed.

The title-page, and a few verses of the First Chapter of Genesis, are here given:

MAMUSSE

WUNNEETUPANATAMWE

UP-BIBLUM GOD

NANEESWE

NUKKONE TESTAMENT

KAH WONK

WUSKU TESTAMENT.

Ne Quoshkinnumuk Nashpe wuttinnemoh Christ

Noh Asoowesit

JOHN ELIOT.

CAMBRIDGE:

Printeuoopnashpe Samuel Green kah Marmaduke Johnson.

1663.

NEGONNE OOSUKKUHWHONK MOSES,

NE ASOWEETAMUK

GENESIS.

CHAP. I.

1. Weske kutchinik ayum God kesuk kah Ohke.

2. ,Kah Ohke mo matta kuhkenauunneunkquttinnoo kah monteagunninno, kah pohkenum woskeche moonoi, kah Nashauanit popomshau woikeche nippekontu.

3. Onk noowau God wequi, kah mo wequai.

4. Kah wunnaumun God wequai neen wunnegen; kah wutchadchanbeponumun God noeu wequai kah noeu pohkenum.

5. Kah wutussowetamun God wequai kesukod, kah pohkenum wutussoweetamun Nukon: kah mo wunnonkooook kah mo mohoompog negonne kesuk.

6. Kah noowau God sepakehtumooudj noeu nippekontu, kah chadchapemooudj nathauweit nippe wutch nippekontu.

7. Kah ayimup God sepakehtamoonk, kah wutchadehabeponumunnap nashaueu nippe agwu uttiyeu agwu sepakehtamoonk, kah nashaueu nippekontu attiyeu ongkouwe sepakehtamoonk, kah monkonnih.

8. Kah wuttidoweetamun God sepakehtamoonk Kesukquath, kah mo wunnonkooook, kah mo mohtompog nahohtoeu kesukok.

9. Kah noowa God moemooidjnip pe ut agwu kesuk quathkan pasukqunna, kah pahkemoidi nanabpeu, kah monkoninih.

10. Kah wuttisoweetaman God nanabpiohke, kah moeemoonippe wuttissoweetamun Kehtoh, & wunnaumun God neen wunnegen.

July 7th, 1688, Eliot writes, "I am drawing home," but, as ever, his desire is to finish his work. He wishes to dispose of 30 pounds, long ago entrusted to him by Sir Robert Boyle, and he hoped the honorable corporation "will print Mr. Shepherd's Sincere Convèrt and Sound Believer" for the Indians. Various others engaged in the work. Mr. Bourne in the Plymouth Colony followed his lead, and after him Mr. John Cotton; the Mayhew's father and son, and Mr. Peter Folger labored in Nantucket and Martha's Vineyard; Mr. Pierson and Mr. Fitch in Connecticut about Norwich; and Mr. Leveredge in and about Sandwich;[1] and Roger Williams, as has been said before, was active in Rhode Island.

THE TOWNS OF PRAYING INDIANS.

The principal town of Converted Indians was Natick, "the place of Hills." It contained one hundred and forty-two persons, with some six thousand acres of land, established 1651. Eliot gave them the same advice as to government that Jethro gave to Moses; so they assembled, and chose their rulers of hundreds, fifties, and tens, and proclaimed, "That God should rule over all." Their houses were Indian huts, built of bark, except their meeting-house, which was after the fashion of the whites. In this Eliot had a room, and a bed. Their fort was palisaded, and strong against Indian attacks; but they had more to fear from Civilization than from Barbarism. Cupidity and Rum were, from the beginning, more potent forces than the tomahawk or scalping-knife. An enumeration of the more important of these settlements of "Spoilt Indians," as some chose to think them, will suffice:

Natick—No. of Indians,	145
Pahemilt, or Punkapaog, in Stoughton,	60
Hassanamesitt, Grafton,	60
Okommakamesit, Marlborough,	50
Wamesit, Tewksbury,	75
Nashobah, Littleton,	50
Magunkaguog, Hopkinton,	55

These 7 were the oldest towns. There were also:

[1] Gookin; Hist. Coll.

Manchage, Oxford, No. of Indians, ...	60
Chabanukongkomun, Dudley, ...	45
Maanexit, Woodstock, ...	100
Quantisset, near Norwich, ...	100
Wabquisset, in Woodstock, ...	150
Puckachoog, in Wooster, ...	100
Waeuntmag, in Uxbridge, ...	50
	1100

Besides these (in the year 1674) they numbered in Martha's Vineyard, Plymouth, and Nantucket, some 2,500 more.

Eliot enumerated to Sir Boyle the following places where the Indians meet on the Sabbath since King Philip's war: in the Massachusetts only four, viz., Natick, Ponkipog, Wamesit, and Chachaubunkkakowok; which last whosoever can, may speak. In Plymouth ten places; in Martyn's (Martha's) Vineyard ten places; in Nantucket five places. The usual exercises were praying, reading the Bible, and preaching, by a white person, or one of their own teachers. Then they sang, "which sundry are able to manage very well;" and some were called up for catechism. Then "if there be any act of public discipline (as divers times there are, there being many failures among us) the offender is called forth, and exhorted to give glory to God, and confess his sin."

The Missionaries all found some material encouragement necessary, such as food or presents, to gain the ear of the Indians, and to keep them in orderly ways. They found it also a matter of imperative necessity that their Converts should have fixed homes.[1] Much interest was shown till the breaking out of King Philip's war; that brought out the hatred of Race, and thenceforth little sympathy was felt for the Indians; they were neglected and hated, and rapidly sunk into degradation and insignificance. Still some efforts for their Conversion continued as far down as the year 1754. The excitement against the Indians during Philip's war ran so high that the Mis-

[1] Clapp's Letter, 1792, M. H. C. Eliot's Letter to Sir Robert Boyle.

sionaries, Eliot and Gookin, were insulted in the streets, and were in danger of corporal harm.

STOCKBRIDGE INDIANS.

The Rev. Mr. Hawley[1] was "set apart to the work of evangelizing the Western Indians of Massachusetts, in the old South Meeting-house in Boston, in July, 1754." He went among them, and followed them alone, through the forests to the west of Albany (" Schohary") where they went to Summer, Preaching and Teaching. Deacon Woodbridge and Jonathan Edwards were at that time enlisted in the same cause; and the Dutch, then strong around Albany, had established Colonists and Lutheran Churches among them. But with most men, it was vastly more important to trade for furs, and to get their lands, than to Christianize the Indians; so it ended in removing most of them further west. Mr. Hawley went into the State of New York, and conciliating Colonel Johnson (the Magistrate of those parts, who lived near the Mohawk towns, 36 miles from Albany), he was enabled to make a good beginning with the Savages; but the results seem to have been small; for he says, " there is rarely a male professor of the Gospel, who will not falsify his word, drink to excess, and commit other immoralities." " There are two instances in the whole Six Nations, and two only, of persons who, since their conversion to Christianity, have not been intoxicated." He observed in the wilderness no singing birds, and concluded that they only haunted about habitations. On one occasion (July 1, 1753) he was in great danger, for the Indians had got Rum, and were proceeding to hold a drunk; the women and children were skulking about, secreting hatchets and guns, well knowing what must be the result. Mr. Hawley and Deacon Woodbridge, with their Interpreter, proceeded at once on their way; were pursued, but escaped, after being well frightened; and with reason, for a drunken Savage is as dangerous as a drunken white man.

[1] Rev. Gideon's Hawley's Account, M. H. C., vol. iv.

WERE THE INDIANS CAPABLE OF CIVILIZATION?

The assertion, so often made, that the Indians could not be tamed—that they were fierce, natural wild beasts, like tigers and hyenas, who could live only in riotous liberty and carnage, who died when tamed and brought to habits of order—does not seem to be true. From the very beginning, individual Indians accommodated themselves to the manners and dress of the whites; and under the direction of Eliot and others, they formed themselves into orderly assemblies. Gookin bears witness to their "reverence, attention, and modesty, in their religious exercises—the menkind sitting by themselves, and the womenkind by themselves, in a comely manner." Having no bells, they came together at beat of drum, on Lord's, fast, and lecture days; then one of their teachers, either Indian or white, led them through the usual services, in which (such as singing) they joined actively.

They seem to have had some gifts for disputation or discussion, and but little for continuous religious discourse. There can be no doubt, that they were pleased with the notice, and attention, and kindness, which these efforts at Christianizing them expressed. Their consequence was on the wane, and they were fast growing to be despised, when Eliot revived the religious zeal of the Colonists; for they were no longer feared as savages, and they had little land to give or to sell. That the hopes and expectations entertained of the Indians were not gratified, is true; but it seems more philosophical, and more satisfactory now, to explain this disappointment, upon other hypotheses, than that they were different from the whites in kind; or, in other words, not human, and therefore incapable of civilization. The hard pressure of hunger and necessity, had not forced them into the restrained, and conventional, and drudging habits of body or mind, existing among the English; and when the novelty of these new ways wore off, they were glad to escape from the monotony and work of routine life, to the free life of the forest. No man loves to hoe corn all the day ; the man who does that, and only that, continually, will go mad or become idiotic ; so the Indians thought. Again, it may be exciting or entertaining to discuss or dispute, where subtilty meets subtilty, and sharp shot is returned by sharper thrusts. But set an Indian youth to wade through the dreary morass of theological literature of that day, so that he may reconcile " Free-will and pre-ordination," or to make clear the statements of Dr. Athanasius, and he will certainly flee away to the boundless and unexplored forests. Such, in most cases, was the result of the endeavors to convert Indian boys into steady teachers. Gookin, who had many years' experience as their Magistrate and Teacher, speaks in a qualified way : he was satisfied, "according to the judgment of Charity, that diverse of them do feare God, and are true believers; will not deny that there may be some of them hypocrites, that profess religion, and yet are not sound-hearted." In that day they believed, and never doubted it, that God had given Jesus " the heathen for his inheritance," and that Jesus had called them to gather the dusky crop for him ; and that the sickle to reap this abundant Harvest, was the accepted "theology of the Church," in Massachusetts.[1]

They preached moral truths, but they addressed the intellect with subtle propositions. The Indians could and did receive the great statements of a first cause—God, and of right and wrong, and of their obligation to these ; in other words, duty to one another, and to the highest responsibilities of their nature, they recognized in common with all mankind, to some extent. But the precedence of Justification or Sanctification ; whether a Covenant of Works or a Covenant of Grace, secured Salvation ? whether the word " Person" could be applied in Trinity ? whether that part of the Trinity called the Holy Ghost, did or did not dwell in true believers ?—all these questions, which in that day distracted the religious mind,

[1] See Eliot's Life, Catechism, etc.

were as Greek to the minds of the unpedantic Indians. Theology would not move them, while Goodness would.

The people of New England were not the only people who came to believe that the essence of religion is in the intellect, rather than the soul, and that Christianity consists in the assent to some intellectual doctrines, rather than in the aspirations of the spirit.

The frightful cruelties and unpitied murders, and bitter injustice and untold sorrows, that have disgraced the name of Religion, may be explained by the fact, that the intellect, instead of the spirit of man, has been appealed to; and therefore, that assent to certain phrases or problems was required, or a man "should perish everlastingly." The Indians at once detected glaring difficulties. "How is it, then," said they, "that Mr. Wilson is ready to drive Mr. Wheelwright into the sea, and Mr. Williams is hunted from his home among Christian men, and Mrs. Hutchinson's body is shut up in prison, and her character blackened? Why is this; for do not all appeal to the Bible, and stand fast upon it?" Few in that day, except "fanatical Quakers," appealed to the Inner Light—to the voice of God in the soul of man. Some of the praying Indians were slow to accept the beliefs of Eliot and their teachers; but when they did, they followed blindly. What Mr. Eliot, or Mr. Bourne, or Mr. Gookin gave for truth, they took; and they could not be converted again. "Trouble us no further," they said to the Quakers, "with your new doctrine, for we do not approve it."[1]

But notwithstanding their capacity for religious education and for civilization, they faded away and vanished from the face of the earth. If they were capable of civilization and improvement, if they were truly men, why was this? This is the answer: Their color (as with the African) marked their race; they were in the way of the whites, who wanted their lands; quarrels grew, and the Indians were hated; bows and arrows, and gladiatorship,

[1] Gookin, in Mass. Hist. Coll., vol. i.

could not stand against combination and gunpowder; the Indian became the conquered race; his color checked his assimilation with the white man, and insured his gradual extermination; he was a marked man and race; he was beaten and cowed; he lost his own strength and manhood, and did not acquire the strength of civilization.

What little self-respect a weak and overpowered people might have had, was destroyed by Rum; and inherited vagrancy was brought to vagabondism by drunkenness.[1] Any race, White, Black, or Red, is certain to disappear, when its courage, and energy, and self-respect, are broken by defeat, or slavery, or degraded habits. History has shown this to be the law of God, and the American Indians confirm this law.

Ceasing to hope, the Indian no longer exists; we drop a tear over the extinction of a race, but would not bring it back, for it made the world no wiser—no better—and no more beautiful—and we bid it a sorrowful FAREWELL.

Eliot left a daughter, and one son; of his descendants, scattered through the country, some sympathized with him, in his hatred of tobacco, long hair, and fine clothes; and some are like him in yielding too easily to the persuasions of policy, and the frowns of power. Many of his descendants have been faithful ministers, but none did so much work as he.

Three years before his death, his wife died (1687). He stood by the coffin of her he had so long loved, and as the tears streamed down his old face, he said to the people:

"Here lies my dear, faithful, pious, prudent, prayerful wife—I shall go to her, but she shall not return to me." And he turned away, alone.

He sat waiting for death; and when Minister Walton came to see him, he said, "Brother, you are welcome, but retire to your study, and pray that I may be gone." He spent his last hours in teaching some negroes and a little blind boy; for nothing in his character was more beautiful

[1] Gov. Shute's Letter, M. H. C., vol. v.

than his ready sympathy for children. He had done his work, and was ready to go; he said in those days, "My memory, my utterance, fail me—but, I thank God, my charity holds out still."

His faithfulness, perseverance, tenderness, and courage, had earned him the title of

"The Apostle."

He was called so in his own day, and he is called so still.

But to this good man, the end here was come. As he sat in his chair on the 20th of May, 1690, full of peace and hope, Death came and led him away, as a little child going to his father; and his last words were:

"Welcome Joy."

Works Consulted—Francis's Life of Eliot—Hutchinson, Mass. Hist.—Gookin, in Mass. H. C.—Eliot, in Mass. H. C.—Morton's Memorial—Allen's Biog. Dict.—Winthrop's Journal—Mather's Mag.—Graham's Hist. of U. S.—Mass. Hist. Colls.—Roger Williams's Key—Hubbard's Hist.—Hazard H. C.—Penhallow's Indian Wars.—Gov. Shute's Letter to Jesuit Ralle, M. H. C., vol. v.—Gyles's Memoirs—Doolittle's Account.

CHAPTER XL.

KING PHILIP'S WAR.

WAMSUTTA AND METACOM—UNCAS—ALEXANDER TAKEN PRISONER—DIES—KING PHILIP—SIGNS OF TROUBLE—A PARLEY—THE INTERVIEW—NEW TREATY—JOHN SASSAMON—INDIANS HANGED—INSULTS—PHILIP A COWARD?—PHILIP INTRIGUES—PHILIP AN IDEALIST—THE INDIANS GATHER—FIRST BLOOD—36,000—CANONCHET—SWANZEY ATTACKED—WEETAMORE—BAD NEWS—THE COUNTRY RAISED—SUPERSTITIONS—DEERFIELD AND HADLEY DESTROYED—BEERS AND LATHROP ARE CUT UP—THE NARRAGANSETT FORT FIGHT—DESTRUCTION FOLLOWS—CANONCHET SHOT—INDIANS SOLD—PHILIP AGAIN—SLAUGHTERS WADSWORTH—CAPTAIN TURNER—GREAT FIGHT—MARY ROWLANDSON'S CAPTIVITY—EXASPERATION—INDIANS DISCOURAGED—RESULTS OF THE WAR—PHILIP NOT A BARBARIAN—AT HOME—HIS BOY SOLD—PHILIP FELL SHOT THROUGH THE HEART.

WAMSUTTA (ALEXANDER) AND METACOM (PHILIP).

MASSASOIT (Ousamaquin) died somewhere about 1661, near eighty years old, and his son, Wamsutta (Alexander), was King in his stead. Years before (1642) he and Metacom (Philip), then young men, had come alone into Plymouth, and renewed the friendship existing between their father and the whites, and had received the names by which we now know them. Both of these Indians seem to have been bold and talented men, and no doubt had more Indian ambition, and less admiration for the English, than their father; for Hubbard says, Alexander had neither fear of them nor respect for their religion; and Philip told Eliot, he cared nothing for it. Alexander, to sustain his position, had warred against Uncas, Chief of the Mohegans, who lay along west of Rhode Island; and Uncas intrigued with the Hartford Colonists against him; so that from Boston the Plymouth settlers heard that Alexander was plotting against them with the Narragansetts. They waited for no more proof, but at once sent Winslow with a company of armed men, to bring him to the Court. This was not neighborly; it certainly was not courteous, nor kind; for Alexander was the son of their friend; and the sachem of a tribe, and their treaties recognized him as an equal.

Winslow, on his way westward, surprised him at his hunting-lodge, with some eighty of his followers. Alexander was at peace and at ease; he looked for no danger, and reposed in his house. Winslow was a man of action and decision: he secured the weapons which were outside the lodge; he entered the house, and, with pistols to his breast, required the presence of Alexander at Plymouth. The Chief was astounded and excited; he consented to go, and though Winslow offered a horse, he declined it, as the women of his party must walk. But the exasperation of his free uncontrolled nature was too great, and his rage and indignation threw him into so violent a fever, that he could not go on, and he asked to be permitted to return home, which was granted, upon certain conditions. But he died on his way—as the learned, vain, and unjust Cotton Mather said, of "the inward fury of his own guilty and haughty mind." He was carried home on the shoulders of men, and borne to his silent grave near Mount Hope, in the evening of the day and in the prime of his life, between lines of sad, quick-minded Indians, who well believed him the victim of injustice and ingratitude; for his father had been the ally, not the subject, of England, and so was he, and the like indignity had not before been put upon any sachem.

KING PHILIP.

Few will deny to his brother Philip the possession of sagacity, and few can doubt that this insult sank deep into his heart, and lay unextinguished, like the smoldering fire of the volcano. He would have been dull, not to see that the whites were encroaching on every side, and that, throwing aside their former courtesies, they were quite ready to carry matters toward the Indians with a high hand. But whatever may have been his thoughts, he kept his own counsel, and renewed the league with the Plymouth Colonists. By his own people, he was accepted with unusual rejoicing, and no honor possible to give, was withheld from the youngest and only son of their long-beloved Ousamaquin.

It was not till the year 1671 that there was a troubled sign in the peaceful sky; then Philip did not fear to complain, openly and bitterly, of the encroachments of the whites upon his hunting-grounds. He said:

"My father gave them what they asked; they have had townships and whole Indian kingdoms for a few blankets, hoes, and flattering words; but they are not content;—the white man's throat is wide!"

And it was so; for they were greedy for good lands, and lay out far to find and possess them. The Plymouth people heard this of Philip, and they heard that Philip's men were sharpening their hatchets, and mending their guns; for if this was the note of their chief, what would be the song of his children? So they sent messengers to consult the Massachusetts government, and they sent men to confer with Philip.

Philip was out with his men, in the early spring days, when the messengers arrived. He listened to their words, he heard their inquiries; but he spoke little. He said:

"What have I done? I have not fought with Uncas as Wamsutta did, that I should answer to the white man. I have not molested any; and may not my young men prepare their weapons and follow their prey as in other days?"

He declined a parley then, but on the 10th of April (1671) he sent a messenger to the officers of the Plymouth government, inviting them to a conference. They were at Taunton, with some gentlemen from Massachusetts, who had come down to assist in preserving peace. Philip lay at Three-Mile River, about four miles away. Governor Prince urged him to come in, and guarantied his safety; so Philip and his followers advanced toward the village

THEIR INTERVIEW AT TAUNTON.

to Crossman's-mill, and sent in another messenger, desiring a meeting there. Both parties were suspicious. The Indians posted their sentinels on the hill, and were wary and watchful; the towns-people were indignant, and ready to fall on the Indians. So the Massachusetts Commissioners took the hazard, and went out to confer with Philip, who agreed to come to the meeting-house at Taunton, one half of which was to be occupied by himself and his men.

The old meeting-house had never seen such a sight. On one side stood the serious, stern, determined Puritans. The Indian warriors marched in, not with the martial tramp of armed men, but with the soft, silent tread of the subtle savage. They stood on the other side, with their long hair hanging on their shoulders, and their dark eyes lighted with the fire of latent defiance. No man was unarmed, neither Puritan nor Indian. But the time for blood had not come.

Philip alone was their orator. He said:

"Why should there be war between the white man and the Indian? Was not my father the friend of the English? Was not my brother at peace with them? and am not I? Is God angry, that there should be blood on our hatchets, and that the hearths of the English should be red? Let there be justice and peace between us, and let Metacom and his warriors sharpen their hatchets only against the fierce Narragansetts, who hate the English!" So he spake, and the Puritans listened, while the Indians gave their peculiar, almost silent assent.

The Commissioners and Governor Prince replied. They cited cases of aggression on his part, and convinced themselves, if not him, that he had been practicing and plotting mischief against them. It is clear that Philip was a politician, and whatever were his plans, his time for action was not yet come. He seemed to yield the point, and the English drew up a paper for him to sign, admitting that "through my indiscretion and the naughtiness of my heart," "I have violated and broken my covenant," etc., and promising to give up his English arms. If his purpose was to gain time, it made no more difference what he signed, than if he had been a French Emperor or a chivalrous Diplomat. He signed, and gained time. The meeting was over, but the Indians kept their arms, for the present. Fear and suspicion were not lulled, nor was ill-will allayed. But in the course of the summer (August), the Plymouth government summoned Philip to appear there; he went to Boston instead, and strengthened that government in his favor; so that though letters from Plymouth came the same day, declaring in favor of war forthwith, the Massachusetts government so strongly opposed it, that both parties consented to a new conference at Plymouth; which resulted in Philip's agreeing to pay one hundred pounds "in such things as he had," and five wolf's-heads yearly, "if I can get them." None of which he did. Yet peace continued without suspicion for the coming three years.

One of the principal clauses, of the Treaty between Philip and the Plymouth Colony, was, that the whites should not buy, nor the Indians sell, their lands, except by mutual consent of Philip and the Governor. But nothing could hinder the whites from buying, or cajoling away the farms of the Indians. Philip saw that they violated the Treaty, and that his possessions and power were thus slipping out of his hand. He remonstrated; he wrote, "If any English or Engians speak about aney land, he pray you to give them no answer at all." That this matter was serious, is evident, for Eliot and Gookin, in a petition, to the Massachusetts Government, in 1684, about certain fraudulent purchases, said, "Was not a principal cause of the late war, about encroachments on Philip's land, at Mount Hope?"

Now, at this time (about 1674), John Sassamon, who had been somewhat educated at Cambridge, and had been employed as a teacher, among the Indians, was Philip's

Secretary and confidential friend. Hubbard and Mather, speak of him, as a "Cunning Indian," who left Christianity, and went back to Sin with Philip, "like a heathen;" he seems to have been an Indian, "badly spoilt," for he deserted Philip, and betrayed his secrets to the English, and went to preaching and praying again, under Eliot, at Natick. Such a fellow, no decent Indian could respect; yet he left the whites, and again came among them, and went about in the territory of his Chief, whom he had so basely served; for awhile he did this, and then disappeared. The whites sought for him, for they knew the hatred he must have provoked, and they at last found him, a dead Indian, at the bottom of Assawomset Pond (in Middleboro'), his hat and gun lying on the ice. Now had he drowned himself, tired of this miserable mongrel life? The Plymouth people thought not, and, on the testimony of another Indian, "found by a strange providence," who said he saw from the top of a hill, the murder done, they seized three Pokanoket Indians, one of them, a man of distinction, and forthwith hanged them.

Philip brooded over these things. He thought of the many and repeated kindnesses done the whites by his Father, he remembered his gifts (for in fact they were such), of lands, and his steady refusal to join in their extermination (in Weston's time), when they were weak; he thought of the indignity and death of his brother at their hands; he saw that they were grasping, that his corn-lands and hunting-grounds, were rapidly growing less; that the Rum introduced by the whites, was poisoning his warriors; and that his men were seized, and now, at last, without consultation with him, were put to death. This was insult. As he walked among his fighting men, they begged for war. They said, "that will be better than this; better to die bravely than perish like dogs," and they cursed the English. But Philip continued silent and moody; he did not restrain their anger, yet he did not declare war; he visited the graves of his fathers, and thought of the past, when they were Chiefs in the land ; he stood by the mound, yet ungrassed, where the body of Wamsutta lay, and remembered that he had perished, not in war, and by the hand of a brave enemy, but that insult had blasted him in his prime, and that women, not men, had sung his song of death. Philip's Indian heart was moved with pity, indignation, and revenge, and he swore before his God, that he, or the whites, should perish.

There were those among the Sachem's own tribe, who said "Philip is a coward, Philip dares not meet the English." Philip knew this, but he spoke nothing to them ; his squaws watched him fearfully, and his Indian boy played no longer with his hatchet. But he was not idle ; that subtle brain was on fire, and his feet knew no rest, nor his eyes sleep. Alone he threaded the forests, and found the places of his rivals, once his enemies ; they were such no longer, if they had Indian hearts and Indian sympathies, and would listen to his story. All through 1674–75, until the breaking out of the war, Philip was busy. The powerful Narragansetts, on the West, gave him their hands ; the Nipmucks along the Connecticut, listened, and promised aid ; and there is reason to believe, that Philip's lithe and dusky figure was seen further West. Many Indians had felt the same iron that had entered his soul ; and only waited an opportunity for revenge, which came too soon. But the Mohegans, and the Pequots, turned a deaf ear to the Sachem's seductive song (perhaps they remembered the bloody destruction at Mystic fort, ch. xxix.); and the "Praying Indians," then numbering between one and two thousand, stood by the whites.[1]

Philip spent his strength ; he spared no arts, he lived only for one purpose, and that was to unite the Indians of New England (thus far split into clans), into one body ; strong enough to maintain themselves against the whites. He was now become an Idealist—no longer a dirty sensual Indian, bent upon gaining wampum (money), and Rum,

[1] Gookin's Account in Mass. Hist. Coll., vol. i.

and scalps—and his idea raised him, as ideas always do, from the crowd of mercenaries into the rank of Heroes. A SPIRIT now possessed him, and inspired every fiber of his brain, and every muscle of his body.

There was a slight tremble in the earth, and a hush in the sky, which portended danger; but the whites had been, for more than a century, at peace with the Indians, and felt themselves to be their masters; and it was not likely now, when the whites had grown in numbers, and in power, that a Chief of six hundred warriors, would venture to begin the struggle. Still the minds of men were agitated and anxious, and in every quarter preparations were made for war, which might come, none knew when.

THE INDIANS GATHER.

In the spring of 1675, Philip's men gathered from all quarters to Mount Hope; they came in day by day in parties, every man bearing his arms, ready for action. None of them feared war, and, as their numbers swelled, their bitterness and fury increased. They knew not policy, nor how to reserve their anger, as Philip did; and this feverish condition could not be allayed. The Execution of the three Indians for the murder of Sassamon was not forgotten for a moment, and that served to fire the mine. It was on the 24th of June, 1675,[1] that, in a discussion at Swansea, the Indians expressed themselves so as to exasperate the whites, one of whom discharged his musket, and wounded an Indian. This was the first blood shed, and it began the King PHILIP'S WAR. Philip wept when he heard of it, for he was not ready, and he knew that when he struck the blow, it must be with destruction. It was too late for tears; blood had been shed, and it maddened the Savages beyond the control of the Sachem.

At this time, according to loose estimates, there may have been some 36,000 Indians, and 60,000[2] whites in

[1] Thatcher's Indian Biography.

[2] Holmes's Annals say 120,000. Turnbull's Hist. Church's Indian War. Hildreth's Hist., vol. i.

New England ; 10,000 of the former fit for war, and 15,000 of the latter capable of bearing arms. But the Indians had no duties, no restraints, and no property—nothing to hinder them from war. Still, at the outset, the Narragansetts, numbering 2,000 warriors, did not actually second Philip's resistance. But Canonchet, their Sachem, might well remember the death of his father Miantonomo (see ch. xxx.), and Philip might safely hope that some wanton, blundering violence would drive him to exasperation. The whites now began to gather their forces, from the various towns to Taunton, under the command of Major Bradford and Captain Cudworth, assisted by that indefatigable partisan, Captain Church ; and it was not long before a party of Militia from Boston, led by Captain Savage, with Hutchinson, Prentice, and Moesly (the old Buccaneer) joined them (28th June), and rendezvoused at Miles's house near Mount Hope, Bristol, the country of Philip and his Wampanoags. General Josias Winslow, of Plymouth, was at the head of the whole of the forces. Major Appleton, of Boston, commanded the Massachusetts men ; Major Treat the Connecticut men ; and their united troops numbered between 1,500 and 2,000 men.[1] No efforts at conciliation seem to have been made by either party ; for the whites felt their superiority [were they not " the Lord's chosen people ?"] ; and Philip knew the desperate nature of the struggle between united and well-armed whites, and divided uncontrolled savages ; yet when the emergency came he met it, and never faltered or plead from that day forth.

The Indians at first plundered and killed cattle ; but soon two men belonging to a small garrison were shot, which was followed up by an attack upon a part of Swanzey [Swansea], in which eight whites were killed, and their heads left exposed on poles, a ghastly sight to the coming troops. The Indians dispersed in parties over the Neck, and shot the whites from their ambushes ; none

[1] Moore's Governors.

could tell where the Indians might not be. It was clearly Philip's policy, and it was Indian warfare never to face the enemy. But the whites soon gathered information and confidence, and not finding Philip, marched away into the Narragansett's country,[1] (15th July), and exacted pledges from them, which could as easily be broken as given. One provision of this treaty was, that Philip's head should be paid for with twenty good trucking-coats, and every common Indian's head the Narragansetts brought in should command one coat. Captain Church, the bush-fighter, was busy, and with such squads of men as he could get, he kept on the track of Philip, who he discovered had left Mount Hope without a fight, and gone to Pocasset [Tiverton], probably to join the squaw Sachem—Weetamore—and her Indians.

She stood by Philip from the first to the last ; and he had strong men with him, in his own Chiefs Anawon, Tiasq, and Akkompoin.[2] Pumham, too, had been supplied with arms by Massachusetts, to act against Gorton. He now joined Philip, and turned them against Massachusetts and the whites. Philip felt confident of the Connecticut River Indians—the Nipmucks—and had hopes of other powerful tribes.

THE GREAT SWAMP FIGHT, JULY 16.

The white troops from Massachusetts, Plymouth and Connecticut, after a march of 18 miles, [July 16], came to the great swamp, where the Indians were, and immediately entered it. The first of them were shot down, but those behind pressed on ; the ground was soft and the cover tangled, and every man fought on his own judgment, and shot at every bush where he thought an Indian might be concealed. They penetrated to the Indian houses in the center of the swamp, but found them deserted ; and night coming on, they surrounded the swamp, and determined to watch the prey, so nicely caught. The game being thus trapped, the Massachusetts and Connecticut troops

[1] Hutchinson, vol. i.

[2] Church's History, p. 210.

both turned their steps homeward, and left the Plymouth men to finish the work.[1] But the game was not yet taken, and on the first of August, Philip and his followers ferried themselves over the great Taunton River on Rafts, and in great triumph marched away to the Nipmucks, around Springfield [5th Aug.], who had already attacked Mendon [37 miles S.W. from Boston], and killed some whites.

One easy victory could be easily won ; but a warlike and desperate spirit seemed now to be roused in the Indians, which refused to stay beaten ; and they had a leader in Philip as determined and full of resource as the country was wide, and the irritation deep. News did not then travel fast, but all too soon it came through the frightened villages to Boston, that Mendon was taken ; that Captain Hutchinson, who had been sent from Boston to make a league with the River Indians, was killed [Aug. 2], with a large part of his twenty horsemen ; that Brookfield had been beset, and all the houses but one, where the people had gathered, burned ; and that the Indians had pushed up to that a cart loaded with combustibles by means of a long spliced pole, and were only prevented from consummating the destruction, by the arrival of Major Willard with a party of troopers from Lancaster. They heard, too, that the Hadley Indians had joined Philip ; and the timid trembled, while the strong men roused themselves, and girded themselves for a struggle, which had not been foreseen nor provided for. The Hartford men were raised, and organized under Major Treat, and in every town and scattered village, young men and old scoured up their firelocks, and enrolled themselves to guard their homes, and the lives of their frightened women and children.

Their vague dread was increased by the wildest fancies of superstition, which converted the simplest things in na-

[1] Trumbull's Connecticut, vol. i. Hutchinson says the Massachusetts troops were stationed around the swamp, vol. i., p. 293.

ture into dire omens. The thin cloud seemed an Indian's bow; the shadow of the earth in an eclipse, a white man's scalp over the sun; the sighing of the wind, the whistle of bullets; other sounds seemed the gallop of invisible horsemen; and the clergy, by no means cowards, were ready to seize the moment to rouse the people to a sense of their sins, and gather them into the Church. Even the General Court of Massachusetts, after consulting with the Elders, pronounced the war a special judgment of God upon them, for such sins as wearing long hair, profane swearing, leaving meeting before the blessing was asked, Sabbath-breaking, and so on—not including harshness and injustice in dealing with the Indians.

DEERFIELD IS BURNED. HADLEY IS ATTACKED.

But the judgment was come, and disaster followed fast. Deerfield was attacked and burned [September 1, 1675], and on the same day—and that Fast-day, while the inhabitants of Hadley were in meeting, imploring the protection of God—they were startled by the whoops and shouts of savages. In fearful confusion, not knowing where to fly, a white-haired stranger put himself at their head; his clear voice rallied them around him, and leaving the women and children in the house, they rushed against the undisciplined savages, drove them back and dispersed them. This vigor and valor still lingered in the person of General Goffe, an old compatriot of Cromwell's, who, as one of the Regicides, had been hunted from place to place, and now appeared for a moment, and then disappeared forever.[1]

The destruction of Northfield followed; and a few days after [September 11], Captain Beers, who was going to its relief, was slain with twenty of his men. On the 18th September, Captain Lathrop, with a party of nigh a hundred men, convoying a large quantity of grain from Deerfield to Hadley, was cut off almost to the last man. On the 5th of October, Springfield was attacked and fired, but

[1] Stiles's Judges.

was saved by the sudden arrival of Major Treat. Then Hatfield was attacked [October 19]. Not only were these things done there, but the fury was kept alive in and about Mount Hope by Pumham and Weetamore. The Narragansetts, in Rhode Island, too, were growing restive. The spark spread toward the East, and the Indians along the Merrimack began to attack the towns.

Winter now drew on [1675–6], and many of Philip's Indians were believed to have returned from the North, and to be harbored among the Narragansetts. It was uncertain where he was; but as he was alive, and as there were signs of hostility among the Narragansetts, it was decided to crush them before the spring should come, or a new league be formed. So a thousand men were raised (five hundred and twenty-seven, led by Major Samuel Appleton, from Massachusetts; one hundred and fifty-eight, led by Major Bradford, from Plymouth; and three hundred and fifteen, led by Major Robert Treat, from Connecticut), and placed under the charge of Governor Winslow, of Plymouth, who led them into the Narragansett country. Whatever had been the hesitation of Canonchet and his Narragansetts, the news of this expedition told them, that the whites looked upon them as enemies. Winslow and his troops marched through the snow, to the great Swamp-fort of the Indians, in what is now South Kingston. They reached it at day-break, and pushed on to the entrance of the Fort. It was the "Lord's day," and the 19th day of December. Parties of Indian scouts waylaid them, and were waylaid by parties of the whites, led by Church and other bush-fighters; while Davenport, Gardiner, Gallop, and Marshall (all of whom were killed) assaulted and rushed into the fort. The destruction was frightful: nigh two hundred whites were wounded, eighty killed; and of the Indians some three hundred or more (Hubbard reports, from an Indian, seven hundred), men, women, and children, perished, and "as many more captivated." The forts and wigwams were fired, and in their flames, many old men, women, and children perished. Great stores of corn were consumed, so that starvation now stared in the face the once powerful, now broken, tribe. They were houseless, homeless, and hungry, and all through the winter, lived by devastation, or died in despair. The whites had broken the strength of the tribe, but had turned loose on their own villages bands of desperate men ; and what was the result ? Lancaster was burned, and forty of the inhabitants killed [February 10th, 1676] ; Medfield was partly burned, and Weymouth was attacked ; Groton and Warwick were destroyed [17th March], and Providence was partly burned [28th March], in spite of the moral influence of Roger Williams to protect it. Captain Denison, of Connecticut, with his brave volunteers, swept the Narragansett country; but the Indians doubled upon their track, and appeared in unexpected places. All over the Plymouth country, the destruction went on; town after town was attacked and burned ; and fear and horror everywhere ruled, till even Plymouth Town itself, on the 11th of May, was attacked, and sixteen houses were burned.

CANONCHET IS TAKEN AND SHOT.

In the spring, Canonchet, the Sachem of the Narragansetts, came down from the Nipmuck country, to get seed corn from his own land, and was surprised by Captain Denison, while telling his exploits to some of his tribe. He fled, was seized by a swift Pequot, and made no resistance, but refused to answer him or a young white, who next came up. "You too much child," he said ; "let your Captain come." When told "he was to die," he said : "I like it well ; I shall die before my heart is soft, or I say any thing unworthy of Canonchet." He was shot at Stonington, and died as he had lived, simply and bravely, refusing to make peace.

Captain Denison, of Connecticut, and Church, of Plymouth, carried on their partisan warfare through the summer [1676], hunting up, dispersing and destroying parties of Indians, and sending the prisoners (whom they took, or who surrendered themselves) to Plymouth, whence they were mostly transported, and sold as slaves, in spite of what Mr. Earl, Captain Els, or Church "could say or argue, plead or beg;" and Church avows his belief, that in a great degree, it hindered the pacification of the Indians. The price they brought, was low, for Major Bradford, in a letter, says: "That day [December 16], we sold Captain Davenport forty-seven Indians, young and old, for £80 money."[1]

Philip led the Indians in their attack upon Lancaster (Feb. 10), and in their furious attack upon Sudbury (18th April), where "they swallowed up the gallant Captain Wadsworth and all his men." Then the Indians appear to have gathered to the Falls of the Connecticut,[2] where they were busy in taking fish, for all their corn was cut off. Captain Turner, of Boston, learned where the Indians were, and that they felt strong, and were fearless and careless. He concerted a plan of attack with Captains Holyoke of Springfield, Lyman of Northampton, and Kellogg and Dickinson of Hadley. They hastily gathered one hundred and sixty volunteers, and being well mounted, led by Benjamin Wait and Experience Hinsdale, they started, and passed through Deerfield at midnight, crossed the river at Cheapside, and rode on through the meadows and woods, till they came to the west bank of Fall River. Here they dismounted, tied their horses, and left them in charge of a guard. The Indians were encamped above the Falls, half a mile from where Turner and his men dismounted. He then gave the orders:

"Every man to see to his priming—to make his way in silence—to keep together—and not to fire until the word was given."

Then they stole along the bank of the river, and it was just day-break when they came in sight of the Indian camp. It was the 18th of May. Turner and his friends,

[1] Hutchinson, vol. i., p. 301.

[2] Montague Falls, or Great Falls, or Turner's, or Miller's Falls.

sheltering themselves behind the trees, listened but could hear no sound; the Indians lay about, sleeping in their camp, many not even sheltered with tents of boughs. It was evident that they had had a grand feast the night before; and indeed some of the settlers' beef had helped them. Turner then told his men to creep up, and when he fired, to mark their men and pour in a volley. No Indian stirred—they dreamed of plenty of fish, and plenty of plunder.

The sharp crack of Turner's musket broke their dreams in the stillness of the morning, and then a rattling volley carried death and amazement among the sleeping Indians. Many were killed—many were wounded, and howled with pain—the rest rushed wildly to the river, shouting—

"Mohawks! Mohawks!" and in a panic of fear, threw themselves into their canoes, and pushed out into the river; they waited not, even for their paddles; the swift current caught the drifting canoes and swept them over the falls—dashing them in pieces. Turner, Holyoke, and their men, kept up this murderous attack, and slew the bewildered and unarmed savages. Five fell by the hand of Holyoke alone. More than a hundred were killed in the camp, and nigh two hundred were lost in the falls—a few escaped to tell the dreadful tale.

Turner then burned the huts and retired; he found his guard defending their horses from another party of Indians; one party had come upon them from above, and another from below, and Turner's work seemed yet but half done. He and his men retired fighting. Holyoke defended the rear, and was nigh being taken prisoner by a daring Indian, whom he shot. Their retreat was hastened by the report of one of their captains, that King Philip was in pursuit with a thousand Indians. They reached Green River and crossed it; and there a bullet, with "Death" written on it, struck Captain Turner; he fell from his horse, and soon died. Captain Holyoke kept up his retreat fighting, through Green River meadows, till he at last reached Hatfield, with a loss of thirty-eight men.[1]

Among the prisoners taken in this war, was Mary Rowlandson ; her narrative of her captivity and sufferings was once among the famous books of New England. Some extracts from it are as follows :[2]

"On the 10th of February, 1675," she begins, "came the Indians, with great numbers, upon Lancaster : their first coming was about sun-rising ; hearing the noise of some guns, we looked out ; several houses were burning, and the smoke ascending to heaven."

A few short extracts will serve to show the condition of both Indians and captives.

"It is not my tongue or pen can express the sorrows of my heart, and bitterness of my spirit, that I had at this departure ; but God was with me in a wonderful manner, carrying me along, and bearing up my spirit, that it did not quite fail. One of the Indians carried my poor wounded babe upon a horse ; it went moaning all along, *I shall die! I shall die!* I went on foot after it, with sorrow that can not be exprest. At length I took it off the horse, and carried it in my arms till my strength failed, and I fell down with it."

"These nine days I sat upon my knees, with my babe in my lap till my flesh was raw again. My child being even ready to depart this sorrowful world, they bid me carry it to another wigwam (I suppose because they would not be troubled with such spectacles), whither I went with a heavy heart ; and down I sat with the picture of death in my lap. About two hours in the night, my sweet babe like a lamb departed this life, it being about six years and five months old."

They keep removing from place to place thenceforward.

[1] Memoir of Williams in "Williams's Redeemed Captive." Ed. 1853.

[2] A Narrative of the Captivity, Sufferings, and Removes of Mrs. Mary Rowlandson, who was taken Prisoner by the Indians, etc. Written by her own hand. Boston, 1805.

"The water was up to our knees and the stream very swift, and so cold that I thought it would have cut me in sunder. I was so weak and feeble that I reeled as I went along.

"My master had three squaws—living sometimes with one, and sometimes with another. Onux, the old squaw at whose wigwam I was, and with whom my master had been then three weeks: another was Wettimore, with whom I had lived. A severe and proud dame she was, bestowing every day in dressing herself, near as much time as any gentry of the land; powdering her hair, and painting her face, going with her necklaces, with jewels in her ears, and bracelets upon her hands. When she had dressed herself, her work was to make girdles of wampum and beads. The third squaw was a younger one."

Mrs. Rowlandson passed several months among them, when she was allowed to go home, for some small ransom. "So I took my leave of them, and in going along, my heart melted into tears, more than all the while I was with them; and I was almost swallowed up with the thoughts that ever I should go home again."

She found her husband at Boston, and her two children were afterward ransomed and returned to her—but one she had held in her arms, never came back more.

Up to the spring of 1676 (excepting the terrible destruction of the Narragansetts), the successes of Philip and the Indians had been surprising; and it is not to be wondered at, that the superstitious fears of the whites led many to believe that God had consented to their destruction. But there were men among them who were not fatalists, and who had determined to die hard, and their courage and determination rose with the emergency. The exasperation of the whites toward the Indians was now extreme; so great that even their color aroused the whites to cruelty, and various towns of the peaceable "praying Indians" were driven into Boston, and confined for safety on the islands in the harbor, subject to wretched shelter and bad food. It seemed hardly worth while to observe even honor with the Indians in arms : parties who made terms, and were sent in by Church, were treated as spoil, not as friends, and were sent, part to the gallows, and part to slavery. So it was with a large party who came together to treat for peace at Dover (N. H.) ; they were seized by Major Waldron and sent to Boston.[1] Some men of Marblehead had been killed, and shortly after it, two Indians were brought in prisoners on a Sunday; WOMEN then coming out of meeting fell upon them and murdered them.[2] One concludes it were pleasanter to have been an Indian dead than a woman living.

It is easy enough to condemn these things, and they deserve it, but due allowance ought to be made to the desperate nature which the war had assumed. The whites believed the Indians could not be trusted, and that heathen who refused to be converted, might with safety be exterminated, as the Amalekites had been. The hatred of Philip at this time was vindictive, and could he have been taken, he would have had no mercy, and we might now be forced to blush for our ancestors. "Hell-hounds," "catiffs," "dogs," were applied by Mather and others to Philip and the Indians.

Philip withdrew from men, and wandered on the banks of the beautiful Connecticut : he looked at the past, in which he had made desperate efforts, had borne untold fatigues, and had escaped death and capture through a thousand dangers ; he had spared no arts to unite the Indians and to destroy the overbearing whites ;—but he had not succeeded ; and the Nipmucks were now charging their miseries upon him. The Indians could never persevere in a continuous war, and now grew weary of it. Their stores of corn, never large, were consumed or destroyed, and in the past year they had raised none ; they could not fish or hunt with safety, for parties of whites were falling upon them, and they were also in danger from

[1] Hildreth, vol. i., p. 490.

[2] Letters of J. Mather to C. Mather. Hutchinson, vol. i., p. 307.

prowling bands of unfriendly Indians. Philip saw his danger, and that destruction must come, and he longed once more to return to his old haunts, once more to look upon the sea, and to die, if die he must, by the graves of his fathers.

His determination was taken, and he returned to the band, yet formidable, who held by so determined a leader. He spoke to them; he silenced their remonstrances; he recapitulated the past, and praised their courage; he said: "You wish for peace. I consent. We have done what we could, and the white man is too strong for us; but as for me and my Wampanoags, we will return to the Land of our Fathers, and there we will live or die; but we will not be the slaves of the whites."

RESULTS OF THE WAR.

And what had been the results of this war, inevitable as it seemed, and so lightly undertaken? It had destroyed the Wampanoags, the Narragansetts, and the Nipmucks. It had killed off more than two thousand of the savages, who were in the way of the advancing civilization; who would otherwise have passed away quietly, under that law which removes the weak without violence, to make room for the strong. But how had it been done? With what peril—with what suffering—with what cost—with what destruction? 'Tis true, Pumham was dead, and Canonchet, and King Philip was nearly spent; but Turner was also killed, and Lathrop, and Beers, and Johnson, and Siely, and Wadsworth, beside six hundred more, the prime strong men of the Colonies; and war had done what war always does, unsettled many, and debauched many, and injured all. Fear had made young women old, and mourning was in every heart and house in New England. The destruction of property in these infant States was fearful. Some thirteen towns were destroyed, and hard-earned property to the amount of half a million of dollars.[1]

[1] Twelve white captains had been killed. Gallop Siely and Marshall (of Connecticut); Hutchinson, Beers, Lathrop, Davenport, Gardner, Johnson,

Yet let us remember that the Puritans fought it through alone, and stood by their principle of self-dependence; they made no whine to England, and asked no help, and received none from her. They may justly be charged with cruelty and hard-heartedness toward the irresponsible natives; but their apparent necessities will excuse them in a large degree; yet more is to be laid to their belief, that the vindictive barbarities practiced upon the Hivites and the Philistines were worthy of imitation. Nor is it necessary for the present generation—who have stood by and aided in a barbarous war against Osceola and the Seminoles, in Florida, who have been quite willing to take possession of the Indians' lands, everywhere—to be righteous over much, in condemning the Puritans.

PHILIP WAS NOT A BARBARIAN.

It can not be charged that Philip was cruel or brutal; he did not murder in cold blood. There is not a report of his having maltreated a captive, and Mary Rowlandson, in the account of her "doleful captivity," shows that he was even at that time, capable of humor. He spared James Brown, of Swansea, when the Indians cried out that he should be killed; for his father had "charged him to show kindness to Mr. Brown;" and he gave strict orders, that his friends, the Leonards (Blacksmiths at Raynham) should be spared, as they were through the war.

And now (about July), Philip turned his face homeward, with his Chief, Anawon, and the remnant of his tribe. The Squaw-Sachem, Weetamore, with her Indians, still lurked in the swamps and fastnesses of the Plymouth country, and kept up a feeble struggle; neither flattery nor fear had detached her from Philip; and when he appeared once more in his old places, and among his old

Wadsworth, and Turner, of Massachusetts; and Prince, of Plymouth. Also about six hundred men. Twelve hundred houses were burnt, eight hundred head of cattle killed, and some three thousand Indians. The loss to the Colonists was computed at £150,000 sterling. Backus's History, vol. i., p. 433.

followers, their spirits revived; but Philip knew that surrender would end in Slavery, and War must end in Destruction. He chose DEATH! and when one of his Indians stood up at the Council, and urged peace, Philip sunk his hatchet in his skull.

Word came down to Plymouth, on a Sabbath morning, in the last of July, that a great number of Indians were gathered toward Taunton, or Bridgewater. Governor Winslow sent for Captain Church, to come out of meeting, and to get together what company he could, and march away at once, to watch, or fight, the Indians. Church found, that some of the Bridgewater men had shot Akkompoin, the old Uncle of Philip, as he was crossing a river on a tree. The next morning, Church being out on a scout, with a friend-Indian, discovered an Indian sitting silently on the opposite bank of the river; he raised his gun to shoot, when his Indian laid his hand upon his arm, saying, that it might be a friend. It was Philip—who at the moment, discovered them, and bounded down the bank; Church's lead could not touch him. Church and his party crossed the river, and dashed among the Indians, and took some prisoners, among whom, was Philip's wife and son, a boy of about nine years. He was the last of his race, except Philip, and was sent prisoner, to Plymouth, and was finally shipped to Bermuda, and sold as a slave, against the advice of Cotton, and some Ministers, who said—"death."

The struggle was now between Philip and Church, both skilled in Indian War; but Philip had to contend with treachery, also; his prestige was gone, he was a defeated man, and there were Indians, base as any white men, who worship only success; they tnrned from the setting sun, and carried news of every movement of Philip's, to the whites; who had gathered their forces at Taunton, Captain Talcott, with the Connecticut troops, among them. Yet, in spite of these odds, he kept up the war through July.

PHILIP FELL, SHOT THROUGH THE HEART.

It was on the 11th of August, that an Indian was seen on Sandy Point, "over against Tripp's," who hallooed and made signs to be ferried over the river. He reported himself from Mount Hope, and had fled from Philip, who had slain his brother, for proposing peace; and he proposed to pilot Church, to where he might find, and capture the Chief. Church was away at once, for his blood was up, and Philip would be a prize. Before day he stationed his men in parties around the swamp, and directed one party to rush in, shouting, so as to drive the Indians toward his ambush. This was done, Philip came dashing out, and then fell, shot through the heart by the Indian who had guided the whites. He fell near the foot of Mount Hope, his old seat, and by the hand of one of his own tribe (August 12, 1676). His body was dragged through the mire, treated with indignity, and was quartered, and hanged on the trees; while his head was sent to Plymouth, and his hand to Boston. They were afterward shown about as a sight, whereby Elderman (the Indian who shot him), "got many a penny." Few doubted whither the soul of Philip went; for Doctor Mather, in 1790, after the fury of the war had subsided, could write, "It is not long since that the hand which now writes, took off the jaw from the exposed skull of that blasphemous leviathan." But for the body, the Earthly Tabernacle, this was the end of Metacom, King Philip, Sachem of the once powerful Wampanoags.[1]

[1] The works consulted and referred to for the account of Philip's war, are, Church's Indian Wars; S. G. Drake's Notes; Thatcher's Indian Biography; Gookin; Mass. Hist. Coll., vol. i.; Trumbull's Connecticut; Hubbard's Indian Wars; Hutchinson, vol. i.; Records of United Colonies, Hazard, vol. ii.; Hist. Coll. of Mass. H. S.; Hildreth's U. S., vol. i.; Bancroft's U. S., vol. ii.; Anne Rowlandson's Captivity; Knowles's Life of Roger Williams; Penhallow's Wars of New England; Prince's Annals; Holmes's Annals.

CHAPTER XLI.

RECALL OF THE CHARTERS.

VIRGINIA CHARTER CANCELED—MASON AND GORGES IN ENGLAND—CHARTER OF MASSACHUSETTS ORDERED HOME—NOT SENT—£600 VOTED FOR FORTIFICATIONS—THE GREAT SHIP DESTROYED—QUO WARRANTO—NAVIGATION ACT—THE COLONIES KEEP THEIR CHARTERS.

THROUGH the years 1630 to 1640, there had been a constant effort on the part of the enemies of the Puritans, to procure a recall of their Charters. As early as 1623, James I. had determined to cancel the Charter of Virginia, and agents were sent there to look after the affairs of the Colony, which were rather tumultuous. Their General Assembly urged the rights of the popular legislatures, and of imposing their own taxes; for in the air of freedom—freedom grew fast. But in 1624, the Courts in England decided against them, and their patents were canceled; so Virginia became a royal province, subject to the laws and the Church of England; but, being neglected afterward, she gradually took her own shape.

Sir Fernando Gorges and Captain Mason laid claim to a large part of Massachusetts, and they made use of Morton, Ratcliffe, and Gardiner, who had been sent out of the Colony in a rather high-handed manner, and owed the Puritans no love. Gorges wrote to Gardiner and Morton [1631], developing his designs, which letters the Magistrates took possession of, and so were forewarned. Humphrey, Saltonstall, Downing, and Cradock, had much trouble in counteracting Gorges in England; but they were persistent, and they had the Earl of Warwick on their side; however, in 1633, the Privy Council ordered that the Charter should be returned, that it might be regulated, but it was not returned. In July, 1634, Mr. Cradock was ordered by the authorities in England to return the Charter, and wrote to the Governor and Council in Massachusetts to send it to him. They decided to answer his letter, but not to return any answer to this demand. Afterward they decided that it could only be done by order of a General Court. At the Court held in May, 1634, laws were made against tobacco, immodest fashions, extravagant apparel, etc., but the principal thing done was, that money (£600) was voted for fortifications; for word had come that a Grand Commission was granted to the two Archbishops, and others—lords and gentlemen—to regulate all plantations, and to call in Patents, and remove Ministers and Governors, and to inflict punishment, even death. The Colonists were advised that this was intended especially for them, and that force would be used to compel them to receive a new Governor, and to accept the discipline of the Church of England. They, therefore, hastened their fortifications, and took measures "to discover their own minds." [1]

But things did not go well in England—"The Lord frustrated their design." In June [1635] their great ship, built to bring over the Great Governor of all the Colonies, fell in sunder in the midst as soon as she was launched, and Captain Mason, the chief mover against them in England, soon after died, "the Lord in mercy taking him away," and so the business then fell asleep.

A "Quo Warranto" was brought against the Charter in 1635, and judgment was given against them, but the Colonists stood firm; and the Ministers being consulted, said, "We ought to defend our lawful possessions if we are able—if not, to avoid and protract." Whenever Commissions were sent out, the Magistrates simply did nothing; they refused even to examine witnesses upon a Commission from the Court of Chancery [1636]; and they declined in 1641 to put themselves under the pro-

[1] Winthrop's Journal. Say's Letter. Hubbard, p. 180.

tection of the Long Parliament, lest "it might prove prejudicial to us." It is clear, that at that early day, the leading minds had determined to govern themselves.

Again, in 1639, order came that the Charter should be returned. The Lords Commissioners averred, that they did not propose to take away the Liberties of the Colony, "but only to regulate, etc., etc." The Court refused to listen to them, decided that they did not wish to be regulated, and had courage to abide threats; so they went on, as though they had never any knowledge of such an order, and they forbade the messenger to write, that he had delivered to them the letters.[1]

In 1641 England claimed the monopoly of the Commerce of the Colony, which the Navigation act of Charles II. afterward enforced, and then began a dispute, which never ended till the war of Independence in 1776.

The Freeman's Oath [1634] secured fidelity to the Massachusetts rather than to England; and, in 1643, seeing that King Charles I. had violated the privileges of Parliament, and had made war, they "decided for the present" not to include the declaration of allegiance to him, even in the Governor's Oath.[2]

If these things were not rebellion and independence in that early day, they looked quite like it. When Charles I. and the Parliament came to open quarrel, and Charles fled from London, the New England Magistrates declined to take part in it, although their sympathies were with the Parliament. But the Colonists were not the more ready, to put their necks into the yoke prepared for them by the Long Parliament. It may well be suspected how some in the Colony, whose sympathies were with the mother country, and the disaffected, and the men with free democratic ideas, looked jealously upon this centralizing tendency in the Magistrates and Clergy; which, however, by securing unity, strengthened the Colony, though it tended inevitably to despotism. From despotism they

[1] Winthrop's Journal. [2] Winthrop's Journal.

were then saved, because the material power of the Colony was in the Militia of the towns, and not in a Pretorian Guard or Standing Army, ready to work the will of any rulers. They were also guarantied against despotism, because there was conscience, and honor, and a fear of God in the hearts of the Ruling Class, who have been a prey to selfishness and ambition everywhere beside.

Massachusetts resisted the attempts to revoke her Charter for half a century, but then the evil day came, as we shall see.

CHAPTER XLII.

THE KING'S COMMISSIONERS.

THE RESTORATION—MAVERICK—THE KING'S LETTER—THE MAGISTRATES' ORDERS—THE FOUR COMMISSIONERS ARRIVE—GO TO WORK—DEAD LOCK—MANHADOES SURRENDERS—PLYMOUTH VISITED—RHODE ISLAND AND CONNECTICUT—MASSACHUSETTS REFUSES—MAINE VISITED—THE COMMISSIONERS RETIRE.

THROUGH the Civil War in England, between Charles I. and the Parliament, Massachusetts prudently recognized the authority of Parliament, and afterward of Cromwell; at the Restoration of Charles II. (1660) she tardily proclaimed him king (August, 1661); and the people waited for assurances that the Restoration was certain. Their sympathies, however, were with Cromwell and the Independents, not with the Court and Church party. This the king and his managers knew; though, with his lazy good-nature, he cared little about it, so long as he could enjoy his wits and his women. But there were courtiers who hated the name and person of a Sectary or Reformer; whose bitter hands they had found so heavy in the Commonwealth-days; there were, also, disaffected men in the Colonies, who had been harshly treated by the authorities there, mainly because they were Church of England men —of these Samuel Maverick was one. He went to England, and used his influence to have Commissioners sent over, to put things to rights, and to protect the liberties and privileges of British subjects in the Colonies, even if they did not belong to the Churches there.

The king sent a letter, in 1662, commanding that the Oath of Allegiance to him should be taken, and that people should have liberty to use the PRAYER-BOOK, and to worship as they chose; and that all persons of honest lives, orthodox opinions (not Quakers), and of good estates, should be voters. This was a signal-gun, and gave rise to anxiety. But they were not easily moved, and no concession was at once made by the magistrates, except to administer justice in the king's name. Through some thirty years, the question of Religious Toler..tion was under discussion, and it was not established till after the Revolution in England, of 1688.

As the king required it, the Magistrates sent over Bradstreet and Minister Norton, as agents to England, to explain and report about matters; the result of which was not satisfactory, either to the Colony or to the king. Then in 1664, rumors came from England, that ships of war were coming over, and that great men were coming over, and that all portended danger to the young State, yet in the milk of its growth. In this year also, there was a large comet in the heavens, which was looked upon by most of the people as a bad omen. Although Heaven might be against them, the Magistrates met the threatened danger vigorously. They ordered the Captain of the Castle in the harbor, to keep a sharp watch, and to give speedy notice of any signs of ships; they appointed a committee to go on board at once, and to receive the gentlemen courteously, and to see that but few sailors or soldiers were allowed to come ashore at a time ("for," they said, "it behooves us to be careful of the morals of the town!"); they appointed a day of fasting and prayer, and they ordered the Patent to be copied, and to be deposited for safe and secret keeping, with four members of the Court. In their Petition to the King, they said: "Let our government live, our patent live, our magistrates live, our laws and liberties live, our religious enjoyments live—so shall we all have further cause to say from our hearts, Let the king live forever." These things toned up the public mind to the proper key.

In March of this year, Charles had given his brother, the Duke of York, extensive grants, in which were included Long Island and Manhadoes (New York), then occupied by the Dutch. War ensued between Holland and England in March, 1665.

At last, on Saturday, July 23d, 1664, the Royal Commissioners arrived in Boston Harbor, in English ships, the sound of whose guns trembled along the Massachusetts shores. The threatened evil was upon them ; but no evil is so great when it comes, as an anxious imagination pictures it ; and so it resulted now. The Commissioners were—Colonel Richard Nichols, George Cartwright—Esquire, Sir Robert Carr, and Samuel Maverick—Esquire.

The Commissioners, of course, went to their work at once and vigorously. The Magistrates met them with great courtesy, coolness, and caution. The Commissioners said : We suggest this, and that ; we see that so, and so, and so, needs reform ; and that such and such things should be made to conform to the laws of England. The Magistrates said : We have been used to doing thus, and not otherwise ; and the people wish things as they are now; and finally we stand by our Charter. They practiced a masterly inactivity; and they pretended that they doubted the genuineness of the king's letter, which the Commissioners had brought over.

What could the Commissioners do with men who would not move ? Things were at a dead lock, and they concluded to leave matters there till their return from Manhadoes, which place it was their business to take from the Dutch, and bring under English rule, by negotiation or by force. Massachusetts voted to raise two hundred men for their assistance, and sent Thomas Clark and John Pyncheon to act as Commissioners of the Colony.

The Dutch surrendered without fighting (August, 1664), so that no troops were needed.[1] On the return of the Commissioners from the reduction of Manhadoes, they endeavored to enforce their authority in Massachusetts, but without success ; then they went to Plymouth, and thence

[1] Valentine's History of New York.

to Rhode Island. These last treated them with more consideration, and consented to their demands, for they had some favors to ask of England. They were also well received by Governor Winthrop of Connecticut, and the Assembly there complied with their demands. They came again to Boston (May, 1665), where they had many conferences with the Magistrates, not always amicable. The Magistrates reasoned in this way :

" We will stand by our Charter, and retain our privileges and liberties. If we yield them, then they are of course lost ; and it will be no worse if they should be taken away by force, which may never be used."

So they did not yield ; and their courage is only to be spoken well of ; for the effect certainly was to inspire the whole community with moral power.

It is worth while to notice, with what tenacity the authorities in Massachusetts stood by their customs and rights. They received the Commissioners politely, and that was all ; and they were sustained by the people. Rumors flew about from mouth to mouth, how the Commissioners had come over to raise £5,000 for the King ; how twelve pence was to be collected upon every acre of improved land ; and how all liberties and privileges were in danger. The Commissioners were obliged to take steps to disabuse the people of these fears, and even to try to prove to the authorities of Massachusetts, that they really were duly authorized by the King ; but the Magistrates declined to act upon their authority, and refused to hear the voice of the charmer, charm he never so wisely. They obstinately said : " We prefer to stand by our Charter." They declined to act in concert with the Commissioners, or to appear before them to answer complaints, or to call the people together at their instance ; and when the Commissioners proposed to settle a claim for damages, the Magistrates brought the same case before themselves, and so took it out of their hands. There was an evident conflict of jurisdiction, and the people's government, not the king's, prevailed.

Finding it not easy to accomplish their plans in Massachusetts, the Commissioners went to Maine and New Hampshire; and decided there in favor of the claims of Mason and Gorges;[1] but the people in New Hampshire did not favor that decision. In Maine, they overthrew the jurisdiction of Massachusetts; but it was resumed [in 1668] after they had left. Colonel Nichols remained in New York as Governor. The other Commissioners soon left, and Cartwright (bursting with wrath), who took home the minutes and papers, was captured by the Dutch. His papers were lost, so he could do little harm. Besides this, the King and Court had their hands full at home with the Dutch war, and with various intrigues and ambitions.

So, for this time, the Colonies, though shaken, maintained their liberties and their integrity. They were not yet rich enough, to make their taxation and plunder an object worthy of much trouble or time, and so they were left to go their own way.[2]

[1] See chap. xxvi.

[2] Morton, Hutchinson, Hildreth, Hazard. M. H. Coll. Lucas's Charters Valentine's History of New York.

CHAPTER XLIII.

ANDROS—THE REBELLION.

HOW TO GOVERN COLONIES—CHARTER ANNULLED—EDWARD RANDOLPH—JAMES II.—EDMUND ANDROS, GOVERNOR—HIGH-HANDED MEASURES—TITLES TO LAND DESTROYED—THE CHARTER OAK—THE REVOLUTION—THE REBELLION IN NEW ENGLAND—THE MOB ACTED—THE FORT STORMED, AND ANDROS MADE PRISONER—THE PROVISIONAL GOVERNMENT—THE OTHER COLONIES—THE NEW CHARTER OF MASSACHUSETTS.

WHILE Colonies are poor, they are neglected by the parent State; when they are able to pay taxes, then she is quite ready to "govern them;" she is willing to appoint various dependants to important offices, and to allow the colonies to pay liberal salaries; she likes also to tax them to the amount of the surplus production, which is transferred to the managers in the Mother Country. Surprising as this is, it is what many call "Government," and is common everywhere. England has been no exception to this; and her practice in New England was of this character, till in the year 1776, the back of the people was so galled, that it threw its rider, with violence.

We have seen how, at various times, attempts were made to destroy the Massachusetts Charter. At the restoration of Charles, in 1660, the enemies of the Puritans roused themselves. All who scented the breath of Liberty in those western gales—all who had been disappointed of fond hopes in those infant States—all who had felt in New England too, the iron hand of ecclesiastical tyranny, who chafed in the religious manacles which there, as everywhere else, were imposed upon the minority—all united against them; and in 1664, Commissioners were sent over with extraordinary powers, as has been said. The Colony withstood them to their ability; but at last, in 1676, a

"Quo warranto" was issued, and judgment was obtained in England, against the Massachusetts Charter.

In 1683, the quo warranto was brought over, by Edward Randolph, who had been appointed Collector of the Port of Boston in 1681, but had not been allowed to act. He was the "messenger of death" to the hopes of the Colony. The Deputies refused to appear in England, and plead, and judgment was entered up against them at last, in 1685, and the Charter was abrogated. Charles died, and the bitter and bigoted James II. came to the throne in 1684. The Colonists then had rumors that Colonel Kirke, the fiercest hater of the non-conformists in England, was coming over, as Governor; which filled them with dread. The Colony now seemed to be at the mercy of the Churchmen, or worse than that, of the Papists, for such was James. Mr. Rawson, Secretary of the Colony, about this time wrote, "Our condition is awful."

EDMUND ANDROS, GOVERNOR.

Mr. Joseph Dudley was appointed Governor, and acted for a short time, but was succeeded by Sir Edmund Andros, who arrived (December 19, 1686), with a commission from James II., to take upon himself the absolute government of all New England. Andros was supposed to be a bigoted Papist, and he certainly carried matters with a high hand; the poisoned chalice of Religious despotism, which these Pilgrims had commended to the lips of Roger Williams, the Browns, Mrs. Hutchinson, Gorton, Clarke, and the Quakers, was now offered to their own lips, and the draught was bitter.

First, THE PRESS WAS MUZZLED; then marriage was no longer free. The Minister Moody (1684), was imprisoned six months in New Hampshire, for refusing to administer the Communion to Cranfield, and others, according to the manner and form set forth in the book of Common Prayer.[1] The Congregational Ministers were as mere laymen, and danger menaced public worship and the meeting-houses.

[1] Adams's Annals of Portsmouth.

But this last extremity was saved them, by the necessity which James was under, of securing the triumph of *his* Church, in Protestant England; the first step toward which, was the proclamation of Religious toleration. This, of course, secured the Colonists, and the Pilgrims were saved that fearful misery, of being driven out from their own cherished altars. Andros carried things with as high a hand in Massachusetts, as his master did in England; absolute subjection, they both insisted on. Besides the denial of political and religious rights, the practice of arbitrary taxation was asserted by Andros, and all titles to lands, were questioned; in the brutal phrase of the time, it was declared, that "the calf died in the cow's belly;" that is, having no rights as a State, they had none as individuals; so fees, fines, and expenditures, impoverished the people, and enriched the officials. All seemed lost in Massachusetts.

THE CHARTER OAK.

Andros went down to Hartford, in Connecticut, with his suite; and with sixty troops, took possession of the Government there, and demanded the Charter. Through the day (October 31, 1687), the authorities remonstrated, and postponed. When they met Andros again in the evening, the people collected, much excited. There seemed no relief. Their palladium, their Charter, was demanded, and before them stood Andros, with soldiers and drawn swords, to compel his demand. There was then no hope, and the roll of Parchment—the Charter, with the Great Royal Seal upon it—was brought forth, and laid upon the table, in the midst of the excited people. Suddenly, without warning, all lights were extinguished! There was darkness and silence; followed by wonder, movement, and confusion. What meant this very unparliamentary conduct, or was it a gust of wind which had startled all? Lights were soon obtained, and then—

"Where is the Charter?" was the question that went round the assembly.

"What means this?" cried Andros, in anger.

But no man knew where the Charter had disappeared to; neither threats nor persuasions brought it to light. What could Andros do? Clearly nothing, for the Authorities had done all that could be asked; they had produced the Charter in the presence of Andros; and now it had disappeared from his presence. He had come upon a fool's errand, and some sharp Yankee (Captain Wadsworth), had outwitted him. Where was the Charter? Safely hidden in the heart of the Great Oak, at Hartford, on the grounds of Samuel Wyllys. There it remained beyond the reach of tyranny.

The Oak stands to this day, and is known as the "Charter Oak." The Indians had always prayed that the tree might be spared; they have our thanks.[1]

Andros wrote on the last page of their Records, FINIS, and disappeared—but that was not the end of Connecticut.

It was a dark time for Liberty, in New England, and a dark day for Liberty, in Old England; for there James II.

[1] "The famous old Charter Oak, so noted in song and history, fell with a tremendous crash, during the great storm, at quarter before 1 o'clock, on the morning of August 21st, 1856. This famous monarch of the forest, whose history is so intimately intwined in that of Connecticut, was supposed to be upward of a thousand years of age.

"Before Governor Wyllys came to America, he sent his steward forward, to prepare a place for his residence. As he was cutting away the trees upon the hill-side, of the beautiful 'Wyllys place,' a deputation of Indians came to him, and requested that he would spare that old hollow Oak. They declared that it had 'been the guide of their ancestors for centuries.'

"On the 31stof October, 1687, Sir Edmund Andros, attended by members of his Council, and a body-guard of sixty soldiers, entered Hartford, to take by force, the Charter granted to the Colony, by Charles II., in 1662. By stratagem, however, the Charter was removed from the Assembly-room, and concealed by Captain Jeremiah Wadsworth, a patriot of those times, in the hollow of Wyllys' Oak, afterward known as The Charter Oak.

"In 1689, King James abdicated, and on the 9th of May, of that year, Governor Treat, and his associate officers, resumed the government of Connecticut, under the Charter, which had been preserved in the *Old Hollow Oak*."
—*Guild.*

and his unscrupulous Ministers, were corruptly, grossly, and illegally trampling down the rights of manhood. Andros was doing it in New England, and he found in Dudley, Stoughton, Clark, and others, sons of New England, ready feet. In 1688, Randolph writes, "We are as arbitrary as the great Turk;" which seems to have been true. The hearts of the best men in both countries, sunk within them, and they cried in their discouragement, "Oh, Lord, how long!"

Thus matters stood, when, during the Spring of 1688–9, faint rumors of the landing of William Prince of Orange, in England, came from Virginia. Could this be true? It brought Andros up to Boston (April), where he gave orders to have the soldiers ready, against surprise.

THE REBELLION IN NEW ENGLAND.

"Liberty is the most ardent wish of a brave and noble people;" and is too often betrayed by confidence in cultivated, and designing, and timid men. Liberty was the wish of the people of New England, and for the want of brave men then, and since then, they suffered.

When, on the 4th of April, John Winslow brought from Virginia, the rumor of the English Revolution, and the landing of the Prince of Orange, it went through their blood like the electric current, and thrilled from the city along the byways into every home. Men got on their horses, and rode onward, to the next house, to carry the tidings, that the Popish King was down, and William was up, and that there was hope; through town and country the question was eagerly asked, "Shall we get our Old Charter? Shall we regain our Rights?"

"What is there for us to do?" cried the people.

Andros put out a proclamation, that all persons should be in readiness to resist the forces of the Prince of Orange, should they come. But the old Magistrates and leaders silently prayed for his success; the people, less cautious, and more determined, said one to another, "Let us do something. Why not act?" and this went from mouth to mouth, till their hatred of Andros, and the remembrance of his dastardly oppressions, blazed into a consuming fire.

"On the 18th of April, 1689," wrote an onlooker,[1] "I knew not any thing of what was intended, until it was begun, yet being at the north end of the town, where I saw boys running along the streets, with clubs in their hands, encouraging one another to fight, I began to mistrust what was intended, and hasting towards the Town-Dock, I soon saw men running for their arms; but before I got to the Red Lion, I was told that Captain George and the Master of the frigate were seized, and secured in Mr. Colman's house at the North End; and when I came to the Town-Dock, I understood that Bullivant, and some others, were laid hold of, and then immediately the drums began to beat, and the people hastened and ran, some with and some for arms," etc.

So it was begun, no one knew by whom; but men remembered yet their old liberties, and were ready to risk something to regain them; they remembered, too, their present tyrants, and longed to punish them. But in all this, men of property took no part—they are always timid. It was the "mob" who acted.

Governor Andros was at the fort, with some soldiers, and sent for the clergymen to come to him, who declined.

The people and train-bands rallied together at the Town-house, where the old Governor Bradstreet, and some other principal men met to consult as to what should be done. The king's frigate, in the harbor, ran up her flags, and the lieutenant swore he would die before she should be taken, and he opened her ports and ran out her guns; but the captain (prisoner in Boston) sent him word not to fire a shot, for the people would tear him in pieces if he did. In the afternoon the soldiers and people marched to the fort, took possession of a battery, turned its guns upon the fort and demanded its surrender. They

[1] Hutchinson, vol. i., p. 374.

did not wait for its surrender, but stormed in through the port-holes, and Captain John Nelson, a Boston merchant, cried out to Andros, "I demand your surrender." Andros was surprised at the anger of an outraged people, and knew not what to do, but at last gave up the fort, and was lodged prisoner in Mr. Usher's house.

The next day he was forced to give up the castle in the harbor; and the guns of the battery from the shore, were brought to bear upon the frigate. But the captain prayed that she might not be forced to surrender, because all the officers and crew would thus lose their wages; so she was dismantled for present security. All through the day people came pouring in from the country, well armed and hot with rage against Andros and his confederates; and the cooler men trembled, lest some unnecessary violence might be done; so Captain Fisher, of Dedham, led Andros by the collar of the coat, back to the fort for safety.

THE PROVISIONAL GOVERNMENT.

On the 20th, Bradstreet, and other leading men, met, and formed a kind of Provisional Council. They carefully abstained from resuming their old Charter, partly from fear and partly from doubt, and called upon the towns to send up deputies. When these met, on May 22d, 1689, forty, out of fifty-four were for "resuming," but a majority of the Council opposed it, and time was spent in disputes; but at last the old Governor and Magistrates accepted the control of affairs, though they would not consent to resume the Charter. Thus the moment for action passed, and the Colony lost that chance for re-establishing its old rights.

Rhode Island and Connecticut resumed their Charters, which had never been legally vacated. Mr. Treat was OBLIGED to take again the office of Governor in Connecticut, when the amazing reports of the Revolution, and seizure of the Governor in Massachusetts, reached them. They issued loyal addresses to William and Mary, in which they said: "Great was that day, when the Lord who sitteth upon the floods, did divide his and your adversaries like the waters of Jordan, and did begin to magnify you like Joshua, by the deliverance of the English dominions from Popery and slavery."

Andros escaped, but was apprehended at Rhode Island, and sent back to Boston, and in February, 1689, with Dudley and some others, he was sent away to England.

THE NEW CHARTER OF MASSACHUSETTS.

Mr. Increase Mather, the Agent of the Massachusetts Bay Colony, with the aid of friends in England, endeavored to gain the restoration of the old Charter from King William, but was unsuccessful; a new one was granted (1691) which contained many of the old privileges; but the king would not grant them the power of appointing their own Governor; that power was reserved; and appeals from the Colony Courts to England, were allowed. The Governor and the King both had a veto upon all colonial legislation. By it all religions, except the Roman Catholic, were declared free, and Plymouth was annexed to Massachusetts.

Thus two important elements of a free government were lost to Massachusetts; and powers which had been exercised over fifty years were, for nigh a hundred years, taken away. In Connecticut and Rhode Island they continued to elect their own rulers and to exercise all the powers of government.

The new Charter was brought over by Sir William Phipps, the new Governor appointed by the king, who arrived on the 14th of May, 1692.

Thus ended the Rule of the Theocracy in Massachusetts; and from this time forward, the ministers and church members possessed no more power than the rest of the people.

The first period of Colonial History may now be said to have passed, and before entering upon the next century, we may pause for a few moments, and turn our attention to some matters of Church and State, which we have not been able to dwell upon in the order of events.

CHAPTER XLIV.

PURITAN LAWS.

BLUE LAWS—PETERS—COTTON'S DRAFT—WARD'S DRAFT—BODY OF LIBERTIES—CAPITAL LAWS—VIRGINIA LAWS—LUDLOW'S CODE—THE NEW HAVEN CODE—CODDINGTON'S LAWS—FREEMEN—CHURCH MEMBERS—DIVISION OF PROPERTY—SWEARING—DRUNKENNESS—LIQUOR LAW—TOBACCO—PUNISHMENTS—UNCLEANNESS—SUMPTUARY LAWS—LAWYERS.

It is not necessary to go into an elaborate explanation of the origin and working of the Laws of New England. Their great value was, that they were mainly the growth of the time, and being made by the people, were as good as they then knew how to make. Those who are disposed to seek for erroneous legislation, will find it in New England, and they will find it wherever they look. Errors of legislation are not, therefore, to be traced to the religious views of a nation alone, but also to its want of intelligence and virtue, and to physical causes.

"The Blue Laws," so often referred to, do not exist; most of the scandalous stories and libels now quoted, were coined by Peters, a Royalist Minister, who was expelled from New England, and wrote a history to revenge his wounded feelings.[1] Among his laws were such as these: "No woman shall kiss her child on the Sabbath or Fasting day." "No man shall read Common Prayer, keep Christmas or Saints'-days, make mince pies, dance, play cards, or play on any instrument of music, except the drum, trumpet, or Jew's harp." He also stated that the waters of the Connecticut river were so compressed in the narrow passage at Bellowsfalls, that they became

[1] Peters's History of Connecticut. London, 1791. New Haven Edition, 1829.

solid, and that iron would float on the surface. His scientific and historical statements are equally true.

The Laws of a Country are one of the most significant evidences of its intelligence and civilization, and therefore demand attention. At first the Magistrates controlled the Legislation, but the people, by their Representatives, steadily gained upon them ; for, as the Rev. Mr. Fobes, in his description of Raynham,[1] says, "The inhabitants of this town, especially those who attend public worship here, have been distinguished for their zealous attachment to Republican Government, to learning, to military discipline, and Church Music." This description may apply to most of the people of New England, if we except their proclivity to music. There is not a doubt, that they looked in the Jewish laws for the model of many of their laws, and much of their polity ; and that many of their mistakes arose from an attempt to adapt the customs of a foreign climate and people to the wants of New England. Slowly they have learned better.

Punishments at first were arbitrary, being left to the discretion of the Magistrates ; sure of their own integrity, and confident of their own wisdom, they were averse to a written "Body of Liberties," and quoted Scripture against it. But the people of Massachusetts, being leavened with a spirit of Liberty, and moved by a wholesome fear, as early as 1635, requested the Governor and Magistrates to have a body of laws prepared, which all might know, and which might therefore govern each man's action. No very definite steps were taken in the business till 1636 ; then Rev. Mr. Cotton, being requested to assist the Magistrates, drew up and presented "A copy of Moses his judicials." These are printed under the title of "Abstract of Laws of New England, published in London, 1641."[2]

But they were not adopted by Massachusetts, and were never the laws of New England.

[1] M. H. Coll., vol. xiii. [2] M. H. Coll., vol. v.

THE BODY OF LIBERTIES.

With greater variety of interests, and a more complex society, came more difficult questions, and a greater need of referring them to some settled principles, which should be a test when differences arose. The people began to ask for this in the year 1635, and, against the wishes of the Magistrates, insisted upon it, till it was done. Efforts were made to arrive at a Constitution. One was prepared by Minister Cotton, and the one drawn up by Nathaniel Ward, Minister of Ipswich, was accepted in 1641. It contained ninety-eight laws or statements, which were called "Fundamentals." These challenge comparison with any constitution of the day, and in most respects are up to the standard of the present time. They rest in some cases upon the laws of Moses, but in most upon the Rights of Man. They recited the Rights of the Individual as they were then understood, and, in the main, well understood. They provided for Legal proceedings, and admitted the employment of Pleaders, who were not to be paid. Among other things, they provided that no man should be "beaten above 40 stripes," and that no Gentleman should be whipped, unless the case was very flagrant. Trial by Jury was of course established (29). Men were not permitted to whip their wives (80), which was allowed by the laws of England. Servants flying from cruel treatment were protected by law (85). Foreigners and strangers were to be free and welcome, provided they professed "the true Religion" (89). The indenture of Servants for seven years was provided for. Slavery and a Slave-trade, based upon the Jewish practices, were recognized and protected (91). Church censure could not degrade any civil officer (60). Townships were to make their own laws (66). Primogeniture was forbidden (81). Private meetings of all sorts of Christians were allowed (95), etc., etc. (See Appendix.)

Their capital offenses were twelve in number, and were all strongly sustained by Scripture texts.

These were punished with death:
Idolatry;
Witchcraft;
Blasphemy;
Murder, willful, guileful, or in passion (3);
Buggery;
Sodomy;
Adultery;
Man-stealing;
False witness, to take away life;
And Treason.

THE BODY OF LIBERTIES was adopted in 1641, and copies were sent to the towns, to be tested by their experience for three years. F. C. Gray, LL.D., some years ago discovered a manuscript copy of these, which is printed in the Massachusetts Historical Collections.[1] Mr. Gray says truly:

"The Body of Liberties exhibits, throughout, the hand of the practiced lawyer, familiar with the principles and the securities of English Liberty; and although it retains some strong traces of the times, it is, in the main, far in advance of them, and in several respects, in advance of the English Common Law at the present day. It shows that our ancestors, instead of deducing all their laws from the Books of Moses, established at the outset a code of fundamental principles, which, taken as a whole, for wisdom, equity, adaptation to the wants of their community, and a liberality of sentiment, superior to the age in which it was written, may fearlessly challenge a comparison with any similar production from Magna Charta itself, to the latest Bill of Rights that has been put forth in England or America."

With regard to their capital offenses, it is well to know, that the heads of the law-makers were harder than the hearts of the people, and that very few convictions took place under them. Lest it should be inferred, that these

[1] 3d Series, vol. viii.

New England laws were beyond measure severe, it will be well to read the following, which preceded them but a few years.

In Virginia, by their laws, Death was the punishment of a great variety of offenses, as appears from the copy published 1611. These laws were to be read by the Clergymen every Sunday :

1. Speaking impiously against the Holy Trinity.
2. Traitorous words against His Majesty.
3. Derision of God's Holy Word.
4. Sabbath-breaking ; death upon third offense.
5. Murder.
6. Sodomy and Adultery.
7. Sacrilege.
8. Stealing.
9. False witness.
10. Calumniating the Council or Magistrates.
11. Unlawful trading with Indians.
12. Conspiracy against the Government, or concealment of it.
13. Robbing gardens or stealing corn.
14. Deserting with vessels to another country.
15. Running away to the Indians.
16. Robbing Indians.
17. Officers defrauding the Colony.

So far was death.

Refusing to receive the instructions of the Minister, was punished with whipping.

These laws were approved in Virginia, "by Sir Thomas West, Lord Lawain, Lord Governour, and Captain General," the 1st of June, 1610.[1]

THE CODE OF MASSACHUSETTS.

Though well satisfied with the "Fundamentals," or Body of Liberties, the people desired to have the laws passed, written out and published ; and though Magistrates opposed it, and urged that it was an innovation, and dangerous, it was

[1] Peter Force's Tracts, vol. iii.

finally done [1649]. No copy of this code exists,[1] so far as is known; but some of its provisions we know.

THE CONNECTICUT CODE was compiled by Roger Ludlow, who had one of the best legal minds at that time in New England. This was in 1649.

In Ludlow's Code, the capital offenses were twelve in number. In many respects it is the same as the Massachusetts Body of Liberties. Among other things, it provided that:

Children were to be taught to read the "Inglish toungue," and also some "shorte orthodox catechisme;" they were also to be brought up in "some honest, lawful calling, labour, or employment."

All persons were to attend the stated exercise of worship on Sundays, and fast-days, under penalty of 5*s.*

Armed Guards were stationed at meetings. The Court ordered, that twice in every year, one of the Ruling Elders, accompanied by Thomas Stanton, should go among the Indians, "to convey the lighte and knowledge of God and his worde to the Indians and natives amongst us."

That the people should provide for the pay of the Ministers, by voluntary contribution; but if any refused to pay, they were to be taxed, and the tax to be collected as was customary with other debts.

A person swearing, was fined 10*s.*, or the stocks.

Tobacco was not to be used by any under twenty, except by recommendation of a physician; and every public use of it by any person, was fined 6*d.*

THE NEW HAVEN CODE, compiled by Governor Eaton,[2] has the same general character as the Laws of the other New England Colonies, and bears, as they do, the marks of the Mosaic dispensation. Some sixteen crimes were punishable with death; and there is no evidence that

[1] Hildreth, vol. i., p. 369.

[2] In "New Havens Settling in New England, and some Lawes for Government, Published for the use of that Colony." London. Printed by M. S., for Livewell Chapman, at the Crowne, Pope's Head Alley, 1656. MS. Copy in State Library, at Hartford.

Trial by Jury was resorted to. The testimony of two witnesses was sufficient ; yet I nowhere find, that the punishment of death was applied for the large number of offenses for which it was provided, such as Adultery, Blasphemy, etc.

Education was provided for, as in Connecticut, as were the salaries of Ministers. Absence from meeting was subject to 5*s*. fine. Widows' dowers were to be one third of the Real Estate. Heresy was punishable with Banishment ; and intention of Marriage was to be openly published three times.

In 1651 Coddington assisted in preparing the Laws of Rhode Island.

CHURCH MEMBERS FREEMEN.

In Massachusetts, Freemen were required to be members of the Church, and of course large numbers were left out. Jugde Story thinks four sixths of the people were thus disfranchised.[1] Lechford, in his " Plain Dealing," says, " here is required such confession and profession, that three parts of the people of the country remain out of Church."

This continued in force till Charles II. sent instructions to the contrary in 1662 ; and it was not entirely given up till the new Charter of 1691.

In Connecticut, by Ludlow's Code, the Church qualification was not a condition of citizenship.

Chalmers states that " A freeman must be orthodox, above twenty years old ; worth £200. [2]

Those who paid ten shillings taxes to a single rate, appear to have been held persons of competent estate, entitled to vote.[3]

In 1650 a vote was passed in town meeting at Haverhill, that the Freeholders should attend the town meetings, and stay them out, on penalty of paying half a bushel of Corn.

We find, that before the Civil War in England, the

[1] Coit's Puritans. [2] Chalmers's Annals, M. H. C., vol. iv.

[3] 1665, Com. Letter, M. H. C.

people of Massachusetts took an oath of fidelity to the Commonwealth, not to the King.[1] In Connecticut also, the Freemen took the Oath to support the Commonwealth.

By King William's Charter of 1691, Liberty of Conscience was allowed, except to Papists ; and freeholders, who had forty shillings sterling a year, or £40 of personal estate, were counted freemen.

All Oaths were taken standing, holding up the right hand. Kissing the book was considered idolatrous.

Property was divided, one third to the widow, and the balance among all the children (male and female) ; the eldest for a time had a double portion. This practice was confirmed by the English Courts in 1729.[2]

The Court ordered [1632] that "no person shall take tobacco publicly, and that every one shall pay a penny sterling for every time of taking tobacco in any place."[3]

Tobacco seems to have been a very troublesome thing ; for,

"Att another Session of the Generall Cou^r^te of Elecçons held at Boston y^e^ $7^{8}_{mo.}$, 1646,

"Itt is ordered, y^t^ if any yson shall take any tobacco w^th^in the Roome where the Courte is sitting, he shall forfeite for evey pipe so taken, 6d., and if they shall offend against in contemni'ng this wholesome order, he shall be called to y^e^ bar for his delinquency, or pay double his fyne voted."[4]

This was a good law, and was also contained in the Connecticut Code.

Some brief extracts will best show peculiarities, and can not fail to interest:

In the first Court in Massachusetts Bay, August, 1630, it was ordered that the Ministers have £30 and £20, their salaries paid at the public charge, and that

[1] See Freeman's Oath, M. H. C., 2d Series, vol. iv. N. England's Jonas cast up.
[2] Hildreth, vol. ii., p. 348.
[3] Prince's Chronology.
[4] Colony Records.

"Carpenters, Joiners, Bricklayers, Sawyers and Thatchers, take no more than 2 shillings a day," This legislation was afterward revoked to be again resorted to, and again revoked. Severe laws were made against Cursing and Swearing. Laws against Drunkenness were also severe.

March, 1631–2, Ales and Revels were forbidden by law, and the same were denounced in the Churches. This vexed Laud, as the Pilgrims were led to think, and threats were made; but the Colonists were not to be turned or dismayed. Good order they were determined to have, if in their wisdom they could get it.

In 1639 the Court abolished the "Vain Custom" of drinking healths—inasmuch as

It was a thing of no good use.

It induced drunkenness and quarreling.

It wasted wine and beer.

It was troublesome to many, forcing them to drink more than they wished.

LIQUOR LAW.

At the Court held in Boston, July 2, 1633, it was ordered that "no man shall sell wine or strong water without the leave of the Governor or Deputy, and that no man shall sell or give any strong water to any Indian." The same law was passed in Connecticut. (See Code of 1649.)

PUNISHMENTS.

Every town was required to provide itself with a "Whipping-post" and a pair of "Stocks;" and also with a drum, which at first was used to call people to meeting. The maker of the Shrewsbury Stocks was the first who sat in them, and his own fine went to pay his own bill. The Meeting-house, Stocks, and Whipping-post stood together in the center of the settlements.[1]

September 4th, 1632, the Court ordered a man to be severely whipped for cursing, swearing, justifying the same, and glorying in it; and another to be whipped and branded in the Cheek, for selling arms to an Indian.

[1] Ward's Shrewsbury.

Ratcliffe, a servant of Mr. Cradock, "for foul, scandalous invectives against our churches and government," was whipped, cropped, and banished the Colony, and was afterward active against it in England.

A young man in 1631 was whipped for soliciting a squaw to incontinency, she and her Indian standing by to see it done.

Henry Linne also was whipped and banished for writing slanderous letters to England.

Mrs. Oliver, of Salem, "for ability of speech far before Mrs. Hutchinson," was whipped for reproaching the Magistrate.[1] She stood without tying, and bore her punishment bravely, glorying in her suffering. She had also a cleft stick put on her tongue for half an hour.

In 1663 Elizabeth Webster was sentenced at Newbury for taking a false oath, "to stand at the Meeting-house dore, next lecture day, from the ringing of the bell until the Minister be ready to begin prayer, with a paper on her head, written in capitall letters, FOR TAKING A FALSE OATH," or to pay a fine of five pounds. "She made choice to stand at the doore."

Ann Walker [in 1638] was cast out of the Church for intemperate drinking, and was tied, with shoulders naked, to the Whipping-post; but being with child she was not whipped.

Josselyn, in his second voyage,[2] speaks of some of their laws in this way; but he is not to be relied on. "For being drunk, they either whip or impose a fine of five shillings—so for swearing and cursing.

"For kissing a woman in the street, though in the way of civil salute, whipping or a fine.

"For single fornication, whipping or a fine.

"Scolds they gag and set them at their doors, for all comers and goers to gaze at.

"Stealing is punished with restoring four-fold, if able; if not, they are sold for some years, as are poor debtors."

[1] Winthrop's Journal. [2] 1663, Mass. Hist. Coll.

He says also :

" There are none that beg in the country."

At New Haven (1643) the daughter of one of the Magistrates (Malbon) was publicly whipped, her father joining in the sentence.[1] In 1644, two ministers' sons, students at Cambridge, robbed a house, and were publicly whipped. In the same year, a drunken man, sitting in the stocks, was liberated by one of La Tour's Frenchmen, who was seized by the constable, and after a struggle, made to sit in the stocks himself.

It was thought that whipping should not exceed forty stripes—that being the *Scriptural* number.

One Plain (of Guilford, near New Haven) was executed for sodomy (1646).

One Fairfield was sentenced to be whipped ; and if he went out from Boston Neck, to have his nostrils slit, etc. This was for forcing a child eight years old.

" As the people increased, so sin abounded," said one. So it became necessary in one case to punish sensual intercourse with a cow, with death, and it was done.

Again, a man and woman, for adulterous practices, were carried to the gallows, with ropes round their necks, and made to sit upon the ladder for an hour.

At New Haven, a man was suspected of having had connection with a sow, and when charged, confessed it. He was put to death (1641).

An English woman admitting some unlawful freedoms from an Indian man, was, for twelve months, obliged to wear " an Indian cut in red cloth" upon her left arm.

Hugh Bewett was banished (1640), upon pain of death if he returned to the Bay, for maintaining that he was free from original sin, and from actual sin for half a year before.

In the records of York (1651), it is ordered, " That Mrs. Batcheller, wife of Rev. Stephen Batcheller, Esq., for her adultery, shall receive forty stripes, save one, at the

[1] Winthrop.

first town-meeting held at Kittey, six weeks after her delivery, and be branded with the letter A."[1]

"One Britton," not being able to pay a fine for speaking reproachfully of a book defending the Church, was openly whipped.[2]

In 1662, the town-meeting at Portsmouth "ordered that a cage be made, or some other means be invented, to punish such as sleep on the Lord's day," etc.

In 1671, the Select-men agree with John Pinckey to build a cage twelve feet square, with stocks in it, and a pillory on the top, a convenient space from the west end of the meeting-house.

Deputy-governor Dudley was had up (1632) for selling a man seven and a half bushels of corn, to receive ten for it after harvest. Winthrop and others thought it usurious.

All this was in character with the time, and though much of it was barbarous, brutal, and tyrannical, it was common in the most civilized countries, such as England and France. Yet some people say there is no Progress!

UNCLEANNESS.

Even in the earliest days of the Massachusetts Colonies, they were sore troubled with incontinence, both among married and single people, and every means was resorted to, to stay the evil. Persons were whipped, imprisoned, fined, set on the gallows, and compelled to wear a badge telling their dishonor. Drunkards were often marked with a red letter D; but they were past shame. Sodomy was not uncommon. Desponding persons, with weak digestion, who find it hard to believe that society does improve, will be interested in the following event, which happened in Plymouth in 1642, and which is impossible of to-day. A young man, some seventeen years of age, was discovered having intercourse with a beast. "Horrible it is to mention, but ye truth of ye history requires it," it was discovered that

[1] Lewis's History of Lynn. [2] Winthrop's Journal (1638).

he was guilty of intercourse with "a mare, a cow, two goats, five sheep, two calves, and a turkey."[1] He was brought for trial before a jury, and the Ministers were consulted, and he was condemned to die. He was executed in September, 1642; and before his eyes were brought all the animals; first the mare, and then the rest were killed, and cast into a "great and large pitte," and then he was put to death.

These fearful abuses and crimes, according to Winthrop, and others, seem to have disappeared in fact, when they were banished from the Statute-book.

The following sentence will show what was meant by whipping at the cart's tail:

"John Browne & Peter Peirson, having binn indicted at the last Court of Assistants, for Quakers, & there standing mute, Refusing to give any Answer, being bound ouer to this Court to Ans[r] theire Contempt, & here standing mute also, The Court Judgeth it meete to Order that they shall by the Constable of Boston, be forthwith taken out of the prison & stript from the Girdle upwards by the executione[r] & tyed to the Carts Tayle & whipt thro' the Towne wth twenty stripes, & then Carried to Roxbury and delivered to the Constable there, who is also to tye them or cause them in like manner to be tjed to a Carts tayle & againe whip them thro' the Towne wth tenn stripes, & then Carried to Dedham & deliuered to the Constable there who is Againe in like manner to Cause them to be tjed to the Carts Tayle & whipt with tenn stripes thro' the Towne, & from thenc they are immediately to depart this Jurisdiction at theire perrill."[2]

SUMPTUARY LAWS.

Ornaments of Gold, Silver, Silk, and Thread, also slashed and embroidered garments, silver girdles, belts, etc., were forbidden;[3] wearing of laces, etc., was prohibited. (1636.) Sleeves were to reach to the wrist, and not to be more than half an ell wide;

[1] Bradford.

[2] Mass. Records, vol. vi., p. 380. 1661.

[3] Mass. Records. 1634.

immoderate great breeches, knots of ribbon, double ruffs, etc., were discouraged ; churches were advised to deal with all offenders against simplicity in dress.[1]

"Although severall declaratjons and orders have binn made by this Courte against Excesse in Apparel, both of men and women, which haue not taken that Effect as were to be desired ; but, on the contrary, wee cannot but to our griefe take notice, that intollerable excesse and bravery hath crept in upon us, and especially among people of mean condition, to the dishonor of God, the scandall of our profession, the consumption of Estates, and altogether unsuitable to our povertie ; and although we acknowledge it to be a matter of much difficultie, in regard of the blindness of men's minds, and the stubborness of their wills, to sett down Exact rules to confine all sorts of persons, yet wee cannot but account it our duty to commend unto all sorts of persons, the sober and moderate use of those blessings which beyond Expectation the Lord hath been pleased to afford unto us in this wilderness, & also to declare our utter detestation and dislike that men or women of mean condition, should take upon them the garb of Gentlemen, by wearing gold or silver lace, or buttons, or points at their knees, or to walk in great boots, or women of the same rank to wear silks, or tiffany hoods, or scarfs, which though allowable to persons of greater Estates or more liberal Education, yet we cannot but judge it intollerable in persons of such like condition. It is, therefore, ordered by the Court and the Authorities thereof, that no person within the Jurisdicçon, or any of their relations depending upon them, whose visible Estates, real and personal, shall not Exceed the true and Indifferent value of Two hundred pounds, shall weare any gold or silver lace, or any bone lace above two shillings per yard, or silk hoods or scarfs, upon the penalty of ten shillings for Every such offence."

"It is further ordered by the Authoritje aforesajd, that

[1] Vol. i., pp. 261, 262. 1639.

the select men of every town * * are hereby enabled and required from time to time to have regard and take notice of apparel * * * and whosoever they shall judge to Exceed their ranks and abilities in Costumes or Fashion of their apparell in any respect, Especially in the wearing of Ribbons or great Boots (leather being so scarce a commodity in this countrye), lace pointes, silk hoods or scarfs, the Selectmen aforesajd shall have power to assesse such persons so offending * * * in the Country rates at Two hundred poynds Estates * * * provided this law shall not Extend to the restraint of any magistrate or public office of this jurisdiction their wives and children, who are left to their discretion in wearing of apparell, or any settled millitary officer or soldier in the tjme of military service, or any other whose education and Imployments have been above the ordinary degree, or whose Estates have been considerable though now decayed."[1]

The proviso at the conclusion of the order just recited shows the *animus* that dictated it, and comment is unnecessary. The number of laws on this subject was great; we will give one or two more : "Whereas there is manifest pride openly appearing amongst us, in that Long Haire like woman's Haire, is worn by some men, either their own or other's Haire, and their Cutting, Curling, and Immodest laying out there Haire, which practice doth prevail and increase, especially amongst the younger sort. This Court does declare against this ill Custom as offensive to them and diverse sober Christians amongst us, and therefore do hereby exhort and advise all persons, to use moderation in this respect : and further do empower all grand jurys to present to the County Courts, such persons whether male or female, whom they shall judge to exceed in the premises. And the County Courts are hereby authorized to proceed against such delinquents either by admonition, fine, or correction, according to their good discretion."[2]

[1] Vol. iv., pp. 57, 58. 1651.

[2] Vol. v., 58, 1675.

"Notwithstanding the wholesome law already made by this Court, for restrayning excess in Apparel yet through Corruption in many, and neglect of due execution of those laws, the evil of pride in apparel, both for Costlines in the poorer sort, and vayne, new, strange fashions both in poore and riche, wth naked breasts and arms, or, as it were perceived with the addition of superstitious Ribbons, both in Haire and apparell, for redress whereof, It is ordered by this Court that the County Courts, from time to time doe give strict charge to present all such persons as they shall judge to exceed in that kind, and if the Grand Jury shall neglect theire duty herein, the County Court shall impose a fine upon them at their discretion."

LAWYERS were unpopular, and for the first half century seem hardly to have existed as a distinct profession. In 1701, an oath of office was required of them, upon being admitted to practice. In 1768, there were but twenty-five barristers in Massachusetts.[1]

In 1646, a fine was laid in Massachusetts, of twenty shillings an hour, for any speech more than one hour long, made by any attorney or person before a Court.

Various other legal provisions will be found in the next chapter, on Church Matters.

[1] The Judicial History of Massachusetts. By Emory Washburn. Boston, 1840.

CHAPTER XLV.

CHURCH MATTERS.

NOT SEPARATISTS—THE CHURCH COVENANT—FIRST CHURCHES BUILT—TAXATION—VOLUNTARY SYSTEM—CONGREGATIONALISM—THE MINISTERS—THEIR PAY—THE CAMBRIDGE PLATFORM—THE SABBATH—SATURDAY NIGHT—MARRIAGE—NAMES—THE HALF-WAY COVENANT—HERESY—WHIPPING OF BAPTISTS—SATAN—SPECIAL PROVIDENCES—METEORS—EPISCOPACY—THE MEETING-HOUSES—FASTING—SINGING—DEATH—FUNERALS—EPITAPHS.

THE Massachusetts Bay Colonists were afraid of the suspicion of being Separatists, "Brownists." They were not conscious of their own position, and how completely they had cut themselves loose from the Church of England. It would have prejudiced the authorities in England, and many of their own friends too, against them, had they avowed themselves Independents; as in reality they were, though they had not taken the last step. There was something of the philosophy, which "would run with the hare, yet hold with the hounds," lurking among them.

To guard against the charge of being Separatists, Winthrop and his friends, before sailing for Massachusetts, issued (April 7, 1630) from the Arbella at Falmouth, an Address to the people of England, desiring their prayers and blessings; cautioning them against rumors, and desiring them "to take notice of the principal and body of our Company, as those who esteem it our honor to call the Church of England, from whence we rise, our dear mother."[1]

But this feeling was soon changed by the projects of Laud and the Churchmen for establishing a hierarchy in

[1] Hubbard's Hist., p. 127. Young's Chronicles.

New England (1635). These plans were never forgotten, and a bill for the purpose was prepared, but was stopped by the death of Queen Anne, in 1714; to be again revived before the Revolution (1768).[1]

THE CHURCH COVENANT.

One of the early proceedings of the Massachusetts Colony, was the confirmation of it as a Religious Government; a Covenant was drawn up which ran thus:

"In the name of our Lord Jesus Christ, and in obedience to his holy will and divine ordinance—We, whose names are here underwritten, being by his most wise and good providence brought together into this part of America, in the Bay of Massachusetts, and desirous to unite into one Congregation or Church, under the Lord Jesus Christ, our head, in such sort as becometh all those whom he hath redeemed and sanctified to himself, do hereby solemnly and religiously, as in his most holy presence, promise and bind ourselves to walk in all our ways, according to the rule of the Gospel, and in all sincere conformity to his holy ordinances, and in mutual love and respect to each other, as near as God shall give us grace."

This was signed by Governor Winthrop, Deputy-Governor Dudley, Mr. Johnson, and the Rev. Mr. Wilson, in the name of the whole community, at Charlestown, on the 30th July, 1631.

The First Church, or Meeting-house, in Boston, was begun in 1632,[2] on Cornhill. In 1639, a new one was built, which in 1711 was destroyed by fire; in 1712, the "Old Brick" was raised, and in it was the first organ admitted into a Congregational church in the town. In this church was a good bell and a town clock.[3]

The first Episcopal church was a wooden building in Tremont-street, called King's Chapel (1688); before that time the society had met at the house of their minister,

[1] Backus, vol. ii., p. 28. De Berdt's Letter, Mass. State Papers.

[2] Winthrop's Journal.

[3] See List of Ministers, in M. H. C., vol. iii. Description of Boston.

John Ratcliffe. The corner-stone of the New Hewn Stone Chapel, was laid by Governor Shirley, in 1749. In 1785 it adopted a Unitarian Liturgy which it still continues.

The first Baptist church was built in 1679, and rebuilt in 1771.

In 1710, the Quakers, or Friends, erected a meeting-house. Few of the sect remain now in Boston.

The Congregations were called together, and each man put down what he was willing to pay toward the support of the Church, the rest was raised by tax. Those who paid were entitled to vote in settling the minister, though they might not be "Professors."[1]

Mr. Cotton, in a Sermon preached in 1639,[2] showed how the Churches were in a declining condition, "when the Magistrates are forced to maintain the Ministers;" and how this should be done, not by revenues or tithes, but by the voluntary contribution of the Members.

So "the Lord," says Winthrop, "directed him to make it clear by the Scripture, that the Minister's maintenance, and the charges of the Church should be paid out of a fund raised by weekly contributions."

The County Courts of Massachusetts were empowered in 1654 to assess a rate for the support of the Ministers, when the voluntary contribution was not enough; but the Churches in Boston were always supported by voluntary contributions (weekly), and many of the Clergy were doubtful of the lawfulness of receiving support in any other way.[3]

In 1692, a law was made in Massachusetts, that every town should support an orthodox Minister. The voters of the town had the power of appointment, not the Church members only. In 1693, this was modified so as to allow the Church members to select the Minister, and present him to those voters who were to pay taxes to support him for confirmation.[4]

[1] Knowles, p. 317. Trumbull's Connecticut, ch. xiii.

[2] Winthrop's Journal. [3] Hutchinson, vol. i., p. 427. Backus.

In case the Professors and congregation did not agree, a Court of Ministers was to decide it [1695].

Cotton Mather advocated the plan, practiced in some towns, of involving the Minister's salary in the general town tax. There was no law exempting Baptists and other sects from paying taxes to support the orthodox ministers, till 1728.[1]

In 1692, the members of the Church of England, in Boston, had never been taxed for the support of the Congregational Ministers.[2]

In 1727, was passed the Five-mile Act, which provided, that taxes paid by members of the Church of England, residing within five miles of an Episcopal Church, should be applied to the support of that Church. At that time, there were but three Episcopal Churches in the Province, besides those of Boston. Before 1734, Anabaptists, and Quakers also, were exempted from taxation for the benefit of the Congregational Churches.[3] It seems however, at that time, in the Colony of New York, Presbyterians, both people and Clergymen, were taxed to support the Episcopal Church.

CONGREGATIONALISM.

The Democratic tendency of the Puritans, showed itself first in the Church organization, as has been said before ;[4] and the first planters, with Endicott, agreed that the authority for ordination rested not in the Ministers, but in the congregations, and each of these was competent to call and ordain its own Ministers, and to make its own rules.[5] But when this came to be exercised, it was found rather *too* Democratic for the Magistrates and Ministers ;[6] and the General Court then ordered, that no Church should call a Minister, without the approbation of some of the Magistrates, as well as of some neighboring churches. In 1653, the authorities forbade the North Church of Boston, to choose

[1] Backus. [2] Mass. Hist. Coll. Rev. Andrew Eliot's Account.
[3] Mass. Hist. Coll. [4] See chap. xvi. The Plymouth Church.
[5] Mass. Hist. Coll., vol. ix. [6] See Salem Church and Roger Williams.

Mr. Powel, "a man of sense and character" for their teacher, because he had not had a learned education.

Cotton Mather, writing in the year 1718, says: "The only declared basis for union among them (the Congregational Churches) is that solid, vital, substantial piety, wherein all good men of different forms are united; and Calvinists with Lutherans, Presbyterians with Episcopalians, Pedobaptists with Anabaptists, *beholding one another to fear God*, and work righteousness, do with delight sit down together at the same table of the Lord." [1]

It is well to know that the laws against Anabaptists and Quakers were not then repealed, and that Cotton Mather is one of the most unreliable of historians.

At an assembly of Ministers and others, held at Newtown, 1635, the question was brought up by Mr. Shepard, as to the number which make up a Church? It was agreed that three (3) was too small a number, but that *seven* persons might do; still, as there was no rule laid down in Scripture, it might fairly be considered a matter non-essential.

Some took these positions:

"In Adam's and Noah's time, there was not above seven or eight. Will you deny them the being of a *Church?*" [2]

"A visible Church, in the New Testament, consists of no more in number than may meet in one *place*, in one *congregation*." [3]

THE MINISTERS.

There is not a doubt that the Ministers of New England were the steady encouragers of education, the friends of goodness, and the advocates of piety. They made mistakes, had quarrels, were too urgent for class-legislation, jealous of their influence, and among them were base men; yet with all their

[1] Cotton Mather's Letter to Lord Barrington, 1718. Mass. Hist. Coll., vol. i.

[2] A Defense of Sundry Positions, etc.; by Samuel Eaton, Teacher, and Timothy Taylor, Pastor, etc. London, 1645. [3] 1 Cor. xi., 20, and xiv., 23.

faults, they may well ask comparison with the clergy of any sect anywhere. They were men, with common weaknesses, follies, and vices, and are to be judged like other men; their occupation was their only difference. But any community will be the better, safer, and richer, which can secure a *good* pulpit (and a good press); that of New England was equal, at least, to the intelligence and virtue of the time. The clergy ought to lead in the right way, and should belong to the advancing, moving party.

Some of the New England ministers were bigots and ascetics, but not all. That some were kindly and warm-hearted men, who loved the world and the things of the world, properly, is probable. Some indeed were jocose, and Mather Byles (born 1706) is known to this day as a wit, rather than a clergyman. An old picture exists in Massachusetts (date lost), painted on a panel, divided in the center: one half shows a pleasing landscape—such as could probably be seen from the windows—and the other half presents a meeting of ministers, in wigs and gowns, met for conference. They are well supplied with pipes and tankards, and sit in easy positions, as though bent upon having a pleasant time.

The practice of reordaining ministers who had been episcopally ordained, was common, if not universal, and was consistent with the doctrine, that their authority was derived from the people, rather than the Church.

We find that in the preaching of early days, they were freer than now to speak upon the worldly interests of the day.

The laity, too, were at liberty, and were expected, to speak in Church, as they are not now.

We meet with such notices as this from time to time: "The Governor went on foot to Agawam, and because the people there wanted a minister, spent the Sabbath, and exercised by way of prophecy [preaching], and returned home on the 10th."[1]

[1] Winthrop's Journal, 1634.

The pay of ministers was not large, but was at least equal to the ordinary incomes of men then. The salaries, mentioned in a list of twenty-six towns of New England, published in 1648, were from £20 to £90; which list includes such men as Mr. Cotton in Boston, and Hugh Peters at Salem.[1]

In the year 1713, it appears that there were forty-three Ministers in Connecticut, or about one to every four hundred people.

The Colony Records of Connecticut inform us, that in the year 1676 the Court recommended Ministers to see to it as to the observance of family worship, and in case persons obstinately refused, that the Grand Jury should present them for trial.[2]

The Ministers of New England also took an active and leading part in matters of State, and, as has been said elsewhere, often erred in their attempts to make the necessities of the people of New England, bend to the practices and laws of Moses. The Churches followed the example of the people of Massachusetts, who provided themselves with a Civil Constitution;[3] and after several meetings, agreed upon a Church Constitution, called the Cambridge Platform.

The first steps for holding this Synod were taken in 1646; the Massachusetts Churches having invited the Churches of the other Colonies to unite with them in the work. It was not till 1648 that it was finally agreed upon. Rather than draw up a new Confession of Faith, they adopted that of the Westminster Assembly of Divines (of 1643), and then proceeded to agree upon their Platform. Afterward, in 1680, the "Savoy Confession" was adopted, which does not greatly differ from the Westminster.

[1] Good News from New England. Mass. Hist. Coll., 4th Series.

[2] Trumbull's Records of Connecticut. See vol. ii., "The Ministers."

[3] See Body of Liberties, ch. xliv., vol. i.

Hubbard, who knew many of the Ministers present, speaks of them in this way:

"They were men of great renown in the nation (England) from whence the Laudian persecution exiled them. Their learning, their holiness, their gravity struck all men that knew them, with admiration. They were Timothies in their houses, Chrysostoms in their pulpits, and Augustines in their disputations." We may bear it in mind that Mr. Hubbard was one of them, and make due allowance for his brotherly affection. Among them were such men as Wilson and Cotton of Boston, Norton of Ipswich, Eliot of Roxbury, Shepard of Cambridge, Mather of Dorchester, Allen of Dedham, Rogers of Rowley, and Partridge of Duxbury.

The composing of the Platform has been attributed to the Reverend Richard Mather of Dorchester. It met with almost universal acceptance in New England, and was the rule of the Churches in government and discipline, till the Saybrook Platform was adopted in Connecticut in 1708.[1] It was recognized as such by the General Court of Massachusetts, and has not been formally superseded, though in the course of events it has ceased to have any binding force.

When the business of making the platform was ended, the Synod closed, "with the singing the Song of Moses and the Lamb, recorded in the fifteenth chapter of the Revelations"—Thus, says Scotto, "the ravening Wolves of Heresy, and the Wild Boars of Tyranny, being chained up from Devouring the Lord's poor Flock, and from Rooting up his Heritage."[2]

THE SABBATH. They early dropped the Heathen name for Sunday, and called it Sabbath, or Lord's day. In "Lechford's Plain Dealing,"[3] is an inter-

[1] See vol. ii., ch. vii.

[2] A Narrative of the planting of the Massachusetts Colony, by Joshua Scotto. London, 1694.

[3] Published in London, 1641. Mass. Hist. Soc. Coll., 3d series, vol. iii.

esting account of how they spent Sunday in Boston in those "good old colony times."

"Every Sabbath, or Lord's day, they came together at Boston by ringing of a Bell, about nine of the Clock or before. Their pastor begins with solemn prayer, continuing about a quarter of an hour. The teacher then readeth and expoundeth a Chapter; then a psalm is sung, whichever one of the ruling elders dictates. After that the pastor preacheth a sermon, and sometimes extempore exhorts. Then the teacher concludes with prayer and a blessing. Once a month is a Sacrament of the Lord's Supper, whereof notice is usually given a fortnight before, and then all others departing, except the Church [which is a great deal less in number than those that go away], they receive the Sacrament, the Minister and ruling Elders setting at the table, the rest in their seats, or upon forms. About two in the afternoon they repair to the meeting-house again, when the services are much the same as in the morning. After that ensues Baptism, one of the parents being of the Church, no sureties are required, which ended, follows the contribution, one of the deacons saying, 'Brethren of the Congregation, now there is time left for contribution, wherefore, as God has prospered you, so freely offer.' The Magistrates and chief gentlemen first, and then the Elders, and all the Congregation of them, and most of them that are not of the Church, all single persons, widows, and women in absence of their husbands, came up, one after another one way, and bring their offerings to the deacon at his seat, and put it into a box of wood for the purpose, if it be money or papers; if it be any other chattel, they set or lay it down before the deacons, and so pass another way to their seats again, which money and goods the deacons dispose toward the maintenance of the Minister and the poor of the Church, and the Church's occasions, without making account ordinarily." Again—prophesying is, "When a Brother Exerciseth in his own congregation, taking a text of Scripture, and handling the same according to his ability; notwithstanding, it is generally held in the Bay by some of the most grave and learned men among them, that none should undertake to prophesy in public, unless he intend the work of the ministry." But Lay preaching for a long time was permitted; for "Gifted men, viz. [so reputed by competent judges, though] not called to the ministry, nor intended for it, may preach."[1]

Thus, in this simple and natural way, did they carry on their worship, and their Teaching, and their Lord's-days, in the early time of the Puritan Church.

In 1668 it was ordered by the Court in Connecticut that all unnecessary traveling or playing during public worship, or staying away unnecessarily, should be punished with a fine of five shillings.

The Law of Connecticut, laying a fine of 10 shillings for neglect of public worship, was repealed in 1770.[2]

There was high authority for this Sabbath Legislation; for, by the 35th of Elizabeth's reign, staying away from Church was punished with severe penalties.[3]

To avoid all sympathy with Heathenism, they dropped the old names for days and months, and used numbers; beginning with Sunday, which was the "first" day, and March, which was the "first" month.[4]

A singular order exists in the Records of Hampton [1661]—A fine of five shillings was imposed upon any person who shot off a gun, or led a horse into the Meeting-house.[5]

The keeping of Saturday night, a custom peculiar to New England, dates back to the early days of the Colony. It seems to have originated in a wish to prepare thoroughly for Sunday; and we find in one of the Company's letters to Endicott, at the very founding of the Colony, a direction to cease labor early on Saturday afternoon. The

[1] Acts ii., 19, and viii. 14.
[2] Backus, vol. ii. p. 42.
[3] Kingsley's Historical Discourse. New Haven, 1838.
[4] Lechford, Plain Dealing, M. H. C., 3d series.
[5] Coffin's Newbury.

Reverend Mr. Cotton, gave to this the weight of his character, talents, and reputation; and they found it practicable to quote Scripture to sustain it—for the Bible said, "the Evening and the Morning were the first day." Nothing then was more easy, than to believe that Sunday began with the sunset of Saturday. When that hour came, the cattle were housed, tools were laid up, and doors and gates were carefully closed; the chickens went to roost, and the singing of birds was no longer heard; a universal hush settled upon New England, as the shadows of evening came over the landscape. Then, after six days of labor, old men and women, young men and children, sat down to rest; and the stillness of the hour penetrated their hearts. It is not to be supposed, that the thoughts of all were turned inward, only to religious things, and that in silence they bewailed the corruption of their hearts; but it was the hour for self-communion, and the steady voice of the old man, repeating the earnest words of the prophets, or trembling in prayers toward Heaven, recalled wandering thoughts. The Sabbath was at hand, and when at nine o'clock, the Curfew tolled through the forest, every one went quietly to bed, and slumbered till the Sabbath morning broke; disturbed, if at all, only by dreams of the sweet voice of love, premonition of the coming Sabbath night; or of rushing rains destructive to the new-cut hay; or of the shrill savage whoops, and the cries of frightened women. But the morning's sun dispelled fearful fancies, and strengthened shadowy hopes.

MARRIAGE was looked upon, by the Puritans, as a Civil Contract, and not as a Sacrament at all; and the ceremony, at first, was performed only by the Magistrates, or by some Civil person, duly appointed. But in 1692, the General Assembly of Massachusetts, passed a resolve, that Ministers might marry, as well as Justices of the Peace, "which hath Encouraged me (said the Rev. Bailey), to do it at the Importunity of friends."[1]

[1] Rev. Bailey's Memo. See Francis's Watertown. Appendix, p. 141.

Bradford says they followed "ye laudable Custom of ye Low-Countries in which they had lived—and nowhere in the Gospel was it layed on the Ministers."

The Connecticut Code said, "For as much as many persons intangle themselves by rashe and inconsiderate contracts," etc., persons should not entertain a motion in way of Marriage, without knowledge of their parents or guardians. And, also, that all contracts should be PUBLISHED in some public meeting in their town, at least eight days before the time of marriage."

This custom has prevailed there, till within a few years; and was called "Publishing the Banns."

There was a great fondness for Scripture NAMES, and for such as expressed a virtue or good habit. The names of Brewster's children were, "Fear," "Love," and "Wrestling;" the two first were women. And the names of Joy, Mercy, Thankful, Prudence, Patience, Hope, Charity, etc., were common. It is even said that some men were baptized "Hateful," which needs confirmation.

"THE HALF-WAY COVENANT," grew out of the discussion, in 1656, about Infant baptism. Some persons said, if there were any use of Baptism, it seemed cruel to deprive children of its benefits, because their parents were not members of the Church, as had been the custom. The pressure of public opinion was such, that the Ministers felt obliged to act; so in 1662, at Boston, they contrived a way, called the "Half-way Covenant." It provided, that all persons of sober life and correct sentiments, without being examined as to a *change of heart*, might profess religion, or become members of the Church, and have their children baptized, though they did not come to the Lord's table.[1]

Great confusion and discussion resulted, and the Country was in a ferment; but public opinion sustained the "Half-way Covenant."

Such questions as this were thus answered:

[1] Knowles's R. W., p. 315.

Quest. 1. Who are the subjects of Baptisme?[1]

Ans. 1. They that according to Scripture are members of the Visible Church, are the subjects of Baptisme.

2. The members of the Visible Church, according to Scripture, are Confederate visible Believers in particular Churches, and their infant seed, *i. e.*, children in minority, whose next parents, one or both, are in Covenant.

3. The Infant-seed of confederate visible Believers, are members of the same Church with their parents, and when grown up are personally under the Watch Discipline and Government of that Church.

4. These Adult persons are not, therefore, to be admitted to full Communion, meerly because they are and continue members, without such further qualifications as the Word of God requireth thereunto.

5. Church members who were admitted in minority, understanding the Doctrine of Faith, and publickly professing their assent thereto; not scandalous in life, and solemnly owning the Covenant before the Church, wherein they give up themselves and their children to the Lord, and subject themselves to the Government of Christ in the Church, their Children are to be Baptised.

6. Such Church Members, who, either by death or some other extraordinary Providence, have been inevitably hindered from publick acting as aforesaid, yet have given the Church cause in judgment of Charity, to look at them as so qualified, and such as had they been called thereunto, would have so acted, their children are to be Baptised.

7. The Members of Orthodox Churches being sound in the Faith and not scandalous in life, and presenting due testimony thereof; these occasionally coming from one Church to another, may have their children baptised in the Church whither they come, by virtue of a communion of Churches; but if they remove their habitation they

[1] From the Answer of the Elders and other Messengers of the Churches assembled at Boston, in the year 1662, to the Questions propounded to them by Order of the Honoured General Court. Cambridge, 1662.

ought orderly to Covenant and subject themselves to the Government of Christ in the Church where they settle their abode, and so their children to be Baptised. It being the Churches duty to receive such into Communion, so far as they are regularly fit for the same.

By the Code of Massachusetts, the following persons were deemed worthy of banishment: Whoever "shall go about to subvert and destroy the Christian faith and religion, by broaching and maintaining any damnable heresies; as, denying the immortality of the soul, or the resurrection of the body," "or denying that Christ gave himself a ransom for our sins, or shall deny the morality of the fourth commandment, or oppose the baptizing of infants, or shall purposely depart the congregation at the administration of that ordinance, or shall deny the ordinance of the Magistracy, or their lawfull authority to make war, or to punish the breaches of the first table," etc.[1]

It was decreed that whoever should carry himself contemptuously against the "Word of God," or the Ministers, should, on the second offense, be obliged to stand two hours openly, upon a block, four foot high, on a lecture day, with a paper fixed on his breast written in capital letters, "AN OPEN AND OBSTINATE CONTEMNER OF GOD'S HOLY ORDINANCES."

WHIPPING THE BAPTISTS.

Clarke, Crandall, and Holmes, Baptists, and leading men at Newport, went to visit a brother at Salem, and gave a public exhortation at his house; they were arrested and taken to hear the proper preacher in the afternoon. They were afterward carried to Boston, imprisoned, fined, and Holmes was whipped, "The man striking with all his strength (yea, spitting in his hand three times), as many affirmed."[2]

Sir Richard Saltonstall wrote from England to Mr. Cotton and Mr. Wilson, after these doings against Dr. Clarke, Mr. Holmes, and Mr. Crandall: "It doth not a

[1] Hazard, vol. i.

[2] See Ill News from New England, by John Clarke. London, 1652.

little grieve my spirit, to hear what sad things are reported daily of your tyranny and persecution in New England, as that you fine, whip, imprison men for their conscience," etc. Cotton, who was a mild man, replied very sharply: "If our ways (rigid ways, as you call them) have laid us low in the hearts of God's people, yea, and of the saints (as you style them), we do not believe it is any part of their saintship. Nevertheless I tell you the truth, we have tolerated in our churches some Anabaptists, some Antinomians, and some Seekers, and do so still this day; we are far from arrogating infallibility of judgment to ourselves, or affecting uniformity. Uniformity, God never required; infallibility, He never granted us."[1]

When Turner, Gold, Drinker, Osborne, and their friends (in 1665), were prosecuted for holding meetings, and for being Anabaptists, and were imprisoned and banished, the effect was the reverse of what was intended, for sympathy and publicity made more converts.

These things were unfortunately turned against the Puritans in England, when remonstrance was made against the persecution there of the Independents. The bishops replied: "Why, you persecute in New England those who differ with you."

THE DEVIL. SATAN.

Satan was always a large power in the Old Colonies; at any and all seasons, he seems to have been busy. "He stirred up a spirit of jealousy at Charleston, between Mr. James and his people; he was very busy with Mr. Williams," etc. "At Providence also, the devil was not idle" (1638), for the rights of conscience having been there asserted, people went to churches and meetings as often as they would; and the women would not be restrained by their husbands.

"Another pest the old Serpent had against us, by sowing jealousies and differences between us and our friends at Connecticut." It is so much easier to lay the fault to

[1] Knowles's Life of R. W., p. 245.

the devil than to ourselves, that to this day some persons find it difficult to get along without him.

"The devil would never cease to disturb our peace," for "One Mrs. Oliver, for appearance and speech far before Mrs. Hutchinson," claimed the sacrament of the Lord's Supper, and stood up in meeting to plead for her right. This was contrary to all custom, and she was had before the Court to answer for her audacity, and was put in prison, till her husband's bond liberated her. But she still held to her opinions—imprisonment did not give her any new light—which devilish opinions were:

"1. That the Church is the heads of the people," etc.

"2. That all who dwell in the same town and will profess their faith in Jesus Christ, ought to be received to the Sacraments:

"3. That Excommunication is no other, but when Christians withdraw private communion from all that hath offended."[1]

In December, 1638, "Satan persuaded Dorothy Tabbye to break the neck of her child, that she might free it from future misery." The Puritans hanged her! though they judged her crazed.

Special Providences seem to have been universally believed in, in that day; but they were considered as such, only under peculiar circumstances. When any misfortunes happened to those who opposed the Magistrates or the Church, they were counted as certain Judgments of God against them. But such misfortunes happening to themselves, were usually counted as Griefs or "Tryalls"—and did not stop them from going on as they wanted to.

"We can not but all take notice," wrote Mr. Shirley, "how the Lord hath been pleased to cross our proceedings, and caused many disasters."

The following were remarkable judgments of God:

In 1633, John Edy, a religious man, went distracted.

In 1635, August 15, was a terrible storm of wind and

[1] Winthrop's Journal, 1638.

rain, the like of which never was known; it worked great destruction to all, godly and ungodly.

In 1633, Mr. Peirse's ship was lost on the coast of Virginia, which caused great injury to the Colonists; whereby some concluded that "many are the afflictions of the righteous, and that in outward things all things come like to all."[1]

A man, lighting his pipe in a boat, set fire to a barrel of gunpowder, and blew himself and the whole up; he had scoffed at their ways, so he was destroyed, and it was looked upon as a remarkable judgment of God.

Two men were after oysters, and the boat drifting away, they were drowned. This, too, was a judgment, because one of them before that, being desired not to do something for fear of Hell, said "he would do it if Hell were ten times hotter."

Two men, going for wood to Noddles Island, were lost; they were much lamented, were counted very religious, so that apparently they could not have been destroyed by God's anger. Morton repeatedly attributes various physical evils to spiritual sins. A fiery meteor appeared in 1664, which he thought was an exhalation or natural appearance, but was sent by God "to awake the secure world." Newton and Halley had not then shown that Comets are some of the natural appearances, and governed by laws. Morton gives an account of the dreadful evils which had followed or attended upon Comets, which is entertaining and instructive, showing, as it does, how untrustworthy the unscientific and uncultivated mind must be, even in its capacity for observation.

Meteors.—A wonderful meteor appeared on the night of December 11th 1719, which surprised and alarmed the people. What was singular about it beyond its red light, was its appearing and disappearing three times in the same night. It was described as "somewhat dreadful." "The dreadfulness, as well as the strangeness

[1] Hubbard's History, p. 202. (This smacks of Neology.)

of this appearance, made one think of Mr. Watts's description of the day of judgment, in English sapphick.

> "'When the fierce northwind with his airy forces
> Rears up the Baltic to a foaming fury, etc.'"

But remember how open to credulity the world then was, and then note the bravery of the writer, who adds, "as to prognostications from it, I utterly abhor and detest them all, and look upon these to be but the effect of ignorance and fancy."[1]

Dr. Increase Mather said in his discourse, that, "when blazing stars have been seen, great mutations and miseries have come upon mortals," and many believed him.

God manifested his displeasure this year against New England, Morton says, by striking three men dead in Marshfield by a "Blow of Thunder," as well as cattle; so that the historian in his perplexity rather quaintly said, "how doth the Lord go on gradually, first by striking cattle, and then one person at a time, and this year seven, besides some cattle also."

When the ship "Mary Rose" was blown up with her own powder, Winthrop thought the judgment of God was in it, because they "were scoffers at us and the ordinances of religion here."

Winthrop also mentions as a singular fact, that in his son's room was a book containing the Greek Testament, psalms, and "Common Prayer;" the mice ate *every* leaf of the *Common Prayer*, but touched not the other parts of the book.

He also mentions, that in a great storm of 1638, which blew down some strong new houses, God "miraculously preserved old weak cottages." The inference is, that he blew down the others. He mentions how Magistrate Humphrey and three Ministers, returning to England [1642], were caught in a great storm; how they had spoken against the Churches and Colony, and how they

[1] Mass. Hist. Coll., vol. ii.

now confessed their sin in so doing ; and then that "it pleased the Lord to turn the wind, so as they were carried safe to the Isle of Wight by St. Helens."

Episcopacy always hung over them, full of threatenings. That they feared the Hierarchy of the English Church, and dreaded its interference, is plain on every page of New England History ; and this will sufficiently explain their stubborn opposition to insignificant things, such as organs, ceremonies, keeping Christmas and saints' days, and especially to praying with a book.

In the answer to the King's letter [1662] Governor Endicott of Mass., says, concerning Liberty, to use the Common Prayer Book, "none as yet among us appear to have desired it ;" he carefully abstaining from saying, that its use will or will not be admitted ; various other things were carefully touched upon, but were not answered satisfactorily to the King.

Andros took possession of the old South Meeting-house in Boston, and the Episcopalians at last succeeded in establishing a Church of Worship in Boston [1686]. Kings' Chapel was built in 1688.[1]

The Churches or Meeting-houses were cold, desolate-looking places ; and quite down to our own day the warming them has been considered a questionable matter, whether indeed it was not a concession to the carnal man, and so sinful ? We little know what our religious ancestors suffered. Judge Sewall in his Diary writes :

January 24, Sunday [1686], "So cold, that the Sacramental bread is frozen pretty hard, and rattles sadly into the plates."

The people were seated in the Meeting-house yearly by a Committee, and there were no pews. Every person was expected to sit in his own seat ; and, in 1669, John Walcott and Peter Toppan were fined £27 4s. for being disorderly, and "Sitting on a seat belonging to others."

The children sat by themselves, and a man was ap-

[1] For accounts of Ministers and Episcopacy, see vol. ii.

pointed to keep them in order, which was no easy matter to do. He carried a staff of office, with a knob at one end and a feather brush at the other. With the knob, he knocked the heads of the men who slept, and with the feathers, he tickled the faces of the women.

One day, the officer got himself into serious difficulty, for rapping the head of a man who seemed nodding with sleep, while in truth he was only signifying his assent to the preacher. It behooved him thereafter to classify the nods. In 1643, Roger Scott, of Lynn, struck the man who waked him up, and was afterward severely whipped, to cure him of his sleeping habit.

The women and the men sat separately, as they do still in most of the Methodist Churches. In 1677, it appears that the Selectmen of Salem, gave a few young women permission to build a "pew," in the women's gallery. For some reason, this excited the anger of some young men, so that they broke the window of the meeting-house "in pessis," and demolished the pew, and were fined ten pounds a piece for it.

FASTING was a resource in every kind of trial and adversity; and when things seemed at the worst, solemn appeal was made to the Lord. This was tried when the weather was unfavorable for crops; when it was too wet or too dry; when the caterpillars were bad; also when danger threatened the Charter; when the Bishops were plotting Episcopacy; when the Indians were restless; when the Churches and ministers quarreled; when Sectaries broke in—"that God would prevent ye spread of errors in this place, especially the errors of the Quakers." And there was, beside these small and private Fasts, a great Annual Fast, in which, by appointment, the whole people joined. I come upon this curious incident, illustrative of one peculiarity. For some public sin, a venerable lady and her daughter decided to hold a day of fasting on their own account. The record states, that they began after breakfast, of a crisp September day, and went on well till past the dinner hour; when the elder lady sought her daughter and said to her: "Mary, I feel faint and weak, and I begin to doubt whether we shall do the Indians much good, after all; I think we had better have something to eat;" to which the young woman assented.

There was an abiding faith that prayer and fasting would move the purposes of God; yet this belief seems not to have paralyzed human effort. They themselves put the shoulder to, and whipped the horse, as the Greeks, before them, were wont to do.

SINGING was at first done by the congregation—some one person leading them. The tunes were few; such as York, Hackney, Saint Mary's, Windsor, and Martyrs.[1] But about 1714, Rev. John Tuffts published a singing-book, containing twenty-eight tunes. It created great interest and some dismay. One writer in the New England Chronicle [1723] said: "Truly I have a great jealousy, that if we once begin to sing by rule, the next thing will be to pray by rule and preach by rule, and then *comes popery*." And though it did not result in popery, it brought to pass singing-men and singing-women in New England; and a singing-gallery, in which they stood on Sundays, to "praise the Lord." A singing-school followed, where in the cold winter nights, hard-handed young farmers sat by the side of tender-eyed girls, and holding the book between them, they chaunted "Mere" and "Wells," till their soft young hearts were attuned to harmony. Hand-in-hand, they walked homeward, and felt that that was bliss. The Puritans resisted church-organs, even to the present day; but now a few sound their pipes in Congregational Churches.

The prejudice against organs extended to other instruments of music; and this seems strange, too, when they read in the Old Testament how David's minstrels played on the "cornet, flute, harp, sackbut, psaltrey, dulcimer, and all kinds of music." How Moses provided

[1] Coffin's Newbury

horns for the Temple, and David himself played upon a Harp. The pitch-pipe seems to have been the first petard, after the singing-book had lulled the garrison; this was a sort of wooden whistle, made no doubt by the chorister, with which a faint approximation to a key-note could be had. A small squeak from this warned the audience to be ready, and then the chorister stood up in his place, and led his band through the Psalm, all the while beating time with his arm, and singing—now bass, now treble, now falsetto, in the face of the Lord and his people. Next to the Minister, the Chorister was, on Sundays, the greatest man—by far before the Deacon or the Tything-man. During the singing, little boys were still, and the Tything-man could close his eyes in peace, and rest from his impossible labor—the keeping boys quiet for three hours on hard benches, who could not keep quiet. The Flute, and Bass-viol [Violincello], and Fiddle, and Clarionet, gradually crept in after the Pitch-pipe; and at this day, the Sunday bands of the New England meeting-houses are sometimes startling.

DEATH was always a serious matter in New England, for two reasons:

First: the people had many plans—work to do—and much to live for.

Second: they feared Hell and the terrors of the Lord.

When they heard the bell slowly tolling, they listened and counted, and said: "There 's another soul departed; whose turn comes next?"

The bodies of the dead were sacred, and were cared for; to protect them from all possible outrage, the custom was to bury them around the church in the center of the town; where even to the present day they lie, in some of the villages of New England. When the solemn sound of the bell, tolling slowly, struck the hour for interment, the minister came to the house of the dead; the whole people suspended their labors, and, decently clad, came also to show respect for the departed, or to mingle their tears with the living. Every word of the prayer, or exhortation, went to the hearts of the people, and the air of the town was heavy and sad.

Funerals were not performed on the Sabbath. It was customary to give wigs and gloves to the Ministers and pall-bearers ; and a supper was provided for the company. The funeral expenses of the Rev. Thomas Cobbett, Minister of Lynn and of Ipswich, who died in 1680, were as follows :

"1 Barrel Wine, ...	£6	8	0
2 " Cider, ...	0	11	0
82 lbs. Sugar, ...	2	1	0
½ Cord of Wood, ...	0	4	0
4 Doz. Prs. of Gloves, for Men and Women, . .	5	4	0
And some Spice and Ginger for the Cider."			

Those of Robert Ward, a cooper of Charlestown, who died 1736—and whose estate was worth but £241 17s. 3d. —were :

"Funeral Expenses in part, 17 prs. Gloves, . .	£5	10	6
Wine, ...	0	18	0
1 pint Stomach Water, ...	0	1	8
Paid the Porters, ...	1	10	0
Use of the Pall, ...	0	10	0
Tolling the Bell, ...	0	3	0
Mourning Scarfs for 3 Heirs, ...	30	0	0
	£38	13	2

These expenses were so great that in the time of the Revolution they were forbidden, as was the use of mourning garments ; which greatly relieved the poor.[1]

The brown slabs which mark the graves of that early day, bore on them the most frightful engravings of the departed, intended to represent them as cherubs risen to everlasting bliss. If their feelings were faithfully represented by the funereal artists, their torments must have been past description, and one could but shudder at their future state. These gravestones perpetuated the honors

[1] Ward's Shrewsbury.

and titles, which the buried had borne in his day on earth; and we find engraved, those of, Esquire, Deacon, Captain, Ensign, Sargent, and Corporal. Some lines, broken up into poetry, were often engraved; and the making of epitaphs was quite an art. One of the best I have seen is upon the tombstone of the Rev. Samuel Russell, of Branford (1731); as follows:

"From vulgar dust distinguish'd lies,
The active herald of the skies,
Whose voice salvation did attend,
Could comfort to the seeker send,
And make the stubborn-hearted bend;
With honor watch his urn around
And ne'er forget the silver sound,
Till trumpets bid the final day,
And laboring angels rouse his clay.
By Heaven dismissed, you 'll shine his crown,
And bow his head with glory down," etc.

"In slumber bound fast by his side,
The tender part, his pious bride,
Reclines her head.
So round the oak, the ivy twines,
With faithful bands in spiral lines,
Though both are dead."

On the Rev. Samuel Newel's tomb, at Bristol (1789), we find:

"Death! Great Proprietor of all! 'tis thine
To tread out Empires, and to quench ye Stars."

But whether Mr. Newel is complimented as an empire, or a star, the sorrowing reader is left to decide.

Rev. Mr. Bailey's (of Watertown) epitaph of his wife, was as follows:

"Pious Lydia made and given by God, as a most meet help to John Bailey, Minister of the Gospel:

Good Betimes—Best at Last.
Lived by Faith—Died in Grace,
Went off Singing—Left us Weeping;

"Walked with God till translated, in the 39th year of her age, April 16, 1691.

"Read her epitaph in Prov. 1, 10, 11, 12, 28, 29, 30, 31."

Added to Governor Eaton's monument, was this :

"T' attend you, sir, under these framed stones,
Are come your honored Son and daughter Jones,
On each hand to repose their weary bones."

Of Deacon Joseph Kingsbury (Farmington), it was engraved :

"Here lies a man, no one prized Religion more,
The same our fathers brought from Europe's shore,
A strict supporter of the good old ways
Of Puritans, in their most early days."

On the tomb of "The truly honorable and pious Roger Newton, Esq., an officer," etc. (1771), was the following :

"His mind returned to God, intombed here lies
The part the *Hero* left beneath the skies.
Newton as steel, inflexible from right,
In Faith, in Law, in Equity, in Fight."

Upon the tomb of a young girl (1792), was :

"Molly, tho' pleasant in her day,
Was suddenly seized and sent away.
How soon she's ripe, how soon she 's rotten,
Laid in the grave, and soon forgott'n."

Upon another in Middletown (1736), we find :

"EPITAPH.

"So fair, so young, so innocent so sweet—
So ripe a judgment and so rare a wit,
Require at least an age in one to meet;
In her they met, but long they could not stay,
'T was gold too fine to mix without allay."

Another one (1764) :

"A loving wife and tender mother,
Left this base world to enjoy the other."

Mr. Daniel Noyes's epitaph ran thus :

"As you are, so was I,
God did call and I did dy.
Now children all, whose name is Noyes,
Make Jesus Christ
Your only choice."

At Windsor this epitaph exists :

> "Here lyeth Ephraim Hvit sometimes
> Teacher to ye Chvrch of Windsor, who dyed
> September 4th, 1644.
> "Who when hee lived wee drew ovr vitall breath,
> Who when hee dyed his dying was ovr death,
> Who was ye stay of state, ye chvrches staff,
> Alas, the times forbid an epitaph."

The judicious reader will observe that the last line was kept till the last.

The inscription to Captaine Richard Lord (1662), has a brusque, crisp sound :

> "Bright starre of ovr chivallrie lyes here
> To the state covnsillovr fvll deare
> And to ye trvth a friend of sweete content
> To Hartford Towne a silver ornament
> Who can deny to poore he was reliefe
> And in composing paroxyies he was chiefe
> To Marchantes as a patterne he might stand
> Adventuring dangers new by sea and land."

The knowledge of the virtue of "composing paroxyies" the Historian is deficient in, he can therefore only commend it to the attention of the virtuous reader.

To so great a pass had this writing of epitaphs come, that a rather dull fellow, named Calef, took it up, and no dead person escaped him. Some neighbor complained of this seriously, in print: and said that even the "neat cattle" had taken up the practice, and a "calf" in their neighborhood was carrying it to an alarming extent. It is possible that the fear of an epitaph will go far to explain the dread of death in New England, and if so, should be added to the two reasons already laid down. It is plain that elegiac poetry had not in those early days reached the dignity of a fine art in New England.

CHAPTER XLVI.

COLLEGES, SCHOOLS, AND BOOKS.

NEW LAW—HARVARD COLLEGE—MASTER DUNSTER—COLLEGE RULES—DEGREES—FREE SCHOOLS—PENALTIES—"THE PECULIAR INSTITUTION"—SCHOOLMASTERS—YALE COLLEGE—RECTOR CUTLER—BISHOP BERKLEY—ORTHODOX TESTS—RANK—"SCHOLAR"—PUNISHMENTS—FAGS—THE COMMONS—THE BUTLER—DRUNKENNESS—DARTMOUTH COLLEGE—BROWN UNIVERSITY—PRINTING AND BOOKS—"THE BAY PSALM BOOK"—CENSORSHIP—TITLES OF BOOKS—"THE HEART OF NEW ENGLAND RENT"—THE PRIMER—POETRY—"THE SIMPLE COBBLER OF AGAWAM"—"THE DAY OF DOOM"—ANNE BRADSTREET—"PIETAS ET GRATULATIO"—NEWSPAPERS.

THE Encouragement of Education from the beginning of the New England Colonies was second only to that of Religion. It is so still, and the last year [1855] was signalized in Connecticut by the passage of a law, requiring applicants for citizenship to be able to read the laws they are to obey. No false oath can make a voter of him who can not read.

HARVARD COLLEGE.

In 1636 the General Court of Massachusetts gave four hundred dollars toward a public school at Newtown, to which grant was afterward added the income of Charlestown Ferry. Mr. Harvard, one of the liberal and noble men of the Colony, died in 1638, leaving for it £800 ; and, in 1639, by order of the Court, the name was changed to Harvard College ; and Newtown was thenceforth called Cambridge.

Master Dunster was the first President (1640), a "learned, conscionable, and industrious man."[1] There were twelve overseers appointed, six from among the Magistrates, who were "to see that every one be diligent and proficient in his proper place." The rules clearly

[1] New England's first fruits. M. H. C., vol. i.

provide for a religious training, without which, in those days, there could be no proper public education.

1. Every scholar was to understand Tully or some Latin classic before entering, and something of Greek.

2. Every student was to be plainly instructed, that the main end of his life is to know God and Jesus Christ, which is life Eternal.

3. Every student was to exercise himself in reading the Bible.

4. They were not to profane the Word or the ordinances, or the Worship, or the Name of God.

5. They were to be studious, modest, and punctual.

6. They were to shun the society of dissolute men.

7. They were to attend prayers and lectures carefully. Their studies were Logic, Physics, Ethics, Politics, Arithmetic, Geometry, Astronomy; Greek, Latin, and Hebrew Languages; Divinity, Rhetoric, and Declamations.

"Every scholar, that on proof is found able to render the originals of the Old and New Testament into the Latine Tongue, and to resolve them Logically, withall being of Godly life and conversation, and at any public act hath the approbation of the overseers and masters of the Colledge, is fit to be dignified with his first degree."

Whoever presented and defended a system of Logic, Philosophy, Arithmetic, Geometry, and Astronomy, and had the above other qualifications and endorsements, was worthy of the second degree.

"If any scholar shall be found to transgress any of the Laws of God or the School, after twice admonition, he shall be liable, if not adultus, to correction; if adultus, his name shall be given up to the Overseers of the Colledge, that he may be admonished at the public monthly act."

The Commissioners in 1644 recommended the Ministers to stir up their people, to contribute toward the maintenance of "Poor Schollars at the Colledge at Cambridge," if only a peck of corn from each family.

So in 1645, by agreement, each family in the Colonies gave one peck of Corn, or one shilling in cash, to Cambridge College.

A collection was made in 1672 for rebuilding Harvard College, amounting to £1895 2s. 9d.; and a £100 was given by Sir Thomas Temple, "as true a gentleman as ever sat foot in America."[1]

The Treasurer's report for the year 1855 stated that the pecuniary affairs of the College were in a prosperous condition, its property well invested, and that its expenses during the past year had not exceeded the income.

FREE SCHOOLS.

The Boston Records of 1635 show that Philemon Purmont was appointed schoolmaster there; but in 1645 a number of Free Schools were organized at Roxbury and Boston, and other towns followed their example; to be supported by a voluntary contribution or by tax. These were legalized in 1649.

In 1665 the Secretary of Massachusetts, in a note to the Commissioners—Nichols and others—said, beside Harvard College, "there is by law enjoined a school to be kept and maintained, in every town, and for such towns as have one hundred families, they are required to have a Grammar School." Dr. Belknap, in answer to Judge Tucker (1795), wrote,[2] "It is a very easy thing for the children of the poorest families here to acquire a common education, not only at public, but even at private schools." In some cases the school-mistress, in the intervals of reading, set the children to putting wires into wool-cards, thus paying her own expenses, and teaching them both reading and card making.

The practice of Connecticut and Plymouth was mainly the same as Massachusetts; and thus "Free Schools" have grown to be the security and pride of New England, and, with some slight exceptions, of all these United States. The Connecticut Code of 1650 specified, that

[1] Hutchinson, vol. i.

[2] M. H. C., vol. iv.

every township of fifty householders, should provide a teacher for the children, and that towns of one hundred householders should provide for a grammar school, to fit persons for the University. It also directed the select men of every town to see to it, that no "families should suffer so much barbarism," as not to have their children and apprentices taught to read and write, as well as to know some orthodox catechism.

Connecticut ordained [1677], that every town which neglected to keep a school, "above three months in the yeare," should forfeit five pounds for every defect.

And that every County town which neglected to keep a Latin school should forfeit ten pounds.[1]

And it was ordered, that they should be maintained by way of Rate (tax), unless the town otherwise provided. Until 1768, they were supported partly by voluntary contributions, and partly by taxes.[2]

One instance will show the way they took to introduce and support common schools. The Magistrates [in 1644] of Salem, ordered notice to be given on Lecture day, that all should hand in the names of their children, who were fit for school, "and what they will give for one whole year;" also that the children of poor bodies should be paid for by rate on the town.

In 1647, the penalty exacted from towns not providing schools, was five pounds, which was increased, till in 1718, it was 30 to 40 pounds.[3]

In 1745, schools in Norwich were supported by County rate—40*s*. on £1,000—and by payments from parents beside.

Women teachers were paid half the wages of men.[4]

In 1691, the town of Dedham was indicted for not keeping a grammar-school.[5]

The Grand Jury said. "We present the Selectmen of

[1] Colonial Records.
[2] Felt's Salem, vol. i., p. 428.
[3] Holland's West. Mass.
[4] Calkins's Norwich.
[5] Worthington's History of Dedham. Boston, 1827.

the town of Kittery, for not taking care that their children and youth be taught the Catechism, and Education, according to law.[1]

Various towns early made public appropriations of moneys to sustain schools [1656]. Massachusetts represented to the Commissioners, that Plymouth was wanting in a due acknowledgment of, and encouragement to, the Ministers of the Gospel. So the General Court of Plymouth passed a law [1657] requiring towns to tax themselves for the support of Churches and schools.[2] The salary of Schoolmaster, 1693 to 1700, is mentioned at thirty-three pounds a year; in 1765 at fifty-three pounds.

About the year 1705, there was a regulation at Plymouth, that children sent to school, not subscribers to the school fund, living within one mile of the school, were to pay four pence the week for being taught Latin, writing, and ciphering; those who lived beyond one mile, half that—the poor only excepted, who were to come free. A school fund was formed, after the year 1705, from the sale of lands.

THE PECULIAR INSTITUTION OF NEW ENGLAND.

The little brown, one story school-house, was a "peculiar institution" of New England, for a century; and was then transformed, by paint, into a red one. Travelers on horseback, would notice these institutions standing in the villages, and at the forks of roads in the most out-of-the-way places; but when the hour of nine o'clock came, from every wood-road and lane, little children, with their books and dinners, were seen flowing to the school-house like rills to a lake; and when the windows were opened, there came forth at times, a confused sound of voices, like the murmur of many waters; this was the result of a habit which then prevailed of studying the lessons aloud, which has now given way to a quieter method. The simple branches, Reading, Writing, and Arithmetic, were taught to all, and it was not respectable to be ignorant of these; but other

[1] Mass. Hist. Coll., vol. i.

[2] Hildreth, vol. i., p. 394.

studies were also pursued; and now the High Schools (common too), furnish an education sufficient for the highest position of life.

When four o'clock came, the lessons were over, and boys and girls poured out of the modest doorway, shouting and dashing about, free as their own mountain-streams.

The Synod of 1679, discourses in this way of Education as one of the remedies for the evils which afflict the State; and they fortify their position by Scripture citations, and examples new to most readers of this day.

They say, "The interest of Religion and good Literature have been wont to rise and fall together. We read in the Scripture of Masters and Scholars, and of Schools and Colledges.[1] Was not Samuel (the great Reformer), President of the Colledge at Najoth,[2] and is thought to be one of the first founders of Colledges. Did not Elijah and Elisha restore the Schools erected in the land of Israel?"

In 1640, Rev. Robert Lenthel, was called to keep a public School, in Rhode Island, and one hundred acres of land were given to him, besides four acres in Newport, to encourage him; and one hundred acres more were set apart for the use of the School.[3]

Rhode Island adopted the New England School-system more slowly, but adopted it. So did New Hampshire, Maine, and Vermont. In all these States, Free-Schools are universal; lying at the base of honest labor, and Free thought and Speech.

In the early days, the Schools were kept by men; for few women then could write, though most could read. The Legal papers executed in the first century, by well-to-do women, were mostly signed with a +.

THE SCHOOLMASTERS OF NEW ENGLAND.

The Schoolmasters became a breed in New England; they were apt to be long, loose-jointed, young men, with high, nervous organizations; not strong enough for the rough work of the

[1] 1 Chron. xxv., 8. Mal. ii., 12. Acts xix., 9, and xxii., 3.
[2] 1 Samuel, xix., 18, 19. [3] Peterson's Rhode Island, p. 30.

farm, or the chase, or the sea ; too shy for the pulpit ; too awkward to bask in the smiles of beauty, and too unworldly to drive sharp bargains, and grow rich by trade. But they were clear-headed and faithful teachers, and in the School-room, their shyness vanished, and there they reigned supreme. Next to the Minister, the Schoolmaster was entitled to respect, for in New England too, they wondered,

"How one small head could carry all he knew."

It was the custom for him to be "boarded 'round," in the families of his pupils ; and every week he took his pocket-handkerchief full of "Luggage," to new quarters ; where he slept in new beds, fed on new Dough-nuts, gossipped with the Elders, talked of the wonders of Geography with the children, and sang Psalms, and perturbed the hearts of New England's fair daughters.

Many of them lived and died Schoolmasters.

Private schools were established from the first, and have always continued.

YALE COLLEGE AT NEW HAVEN.

In the year 1698, the Rev. Mr. Pierpont, of New Haven, Andrew of Millford, and Russel, of Branford, were active in organizing a College in Connecticut, for the Education of young men for the Ministry, and various departments of civil life. It resulted in starting with Ten Trustees, in the year 1700. Each gentleman gave some books, and as he laid them on the table, said, "I give these books for the founding of a College in this Colony." The College was incorporated in 1701, and, at first, it was agreed that it should be established at Saybrook ; but as the Rector, Rev. Abraham Pierson, lived at Killingworth (now Clinton), it was begun there.

The name of "Yale" College, came to be applied in anticipation of gifts (£800), which were made by Elihu Yale (1716), a rich London merchant, who was born in the Colony. In the year 1717, its location, after violent opposition at Saybrook, was fixed at New Haven, where a building had already been begun; and in 1718, a Grand Commencement was held, at which all the Clergy, the Governor, and other dignitaries assembled, to take part in an inspiriting inauguration. The College was in favor, and donations, at various times, have been made by private individuals, while the State had made grants amounting to $71,582, up to the year 1816.[1] The College has steadily increased in popularity, and is extending the basis of Instruction to matters of Practical life. In 1722, the whole Colony was moved by the revolt of Rector Cutler (with Daniel Brown, the Tutor), against Independency, and his conversion to Episcopacy. It was found impossible to convince him of his Error, though Governor Saltonstall himself, held a dispute with him, and was thought by the majority to have the best of it. So the Rector was quietly excused from further service, and took his place among the Clergy of the Church of England.

BISHOP BERKLEY.

One of the benefactors of Yale College was George Berkley, Bishop of Cloyne, in Ireland, who came to America in 1729, with the vague but benevolent purpose of converting the Indians to Christianity, by founding a College for their education in one of the Bermuda Islands. He waited at Newport, Rhode Island, for the action of the English Ministry, and for some two years seems really to have believed that they would keep their promises made to him. While there, he purchased a fine farm, on which he lived, devoted to literary pursuits. There he wrote out his "Minute Philosopher," published in 1732.

His character was charming, and his influence, during the short time he remained, was good and civilizing upon all those who came within his reach. Finding his expectations hopeless, he returned to England in 1731. He gave his farm to Yale College (he was an Episcopalian himself), to support and encourage scholars, and he made it a present also of a thousand volumes.

[1] Annals of Yale College, by Baldwin.

He was industrious, scholarly, enthusiastic, generous, subtle, and visionary, but altogether lovely.

A new charter for the College was granted in 1745, and in 1792 an amendment was made, which introduced some members of the State government into the Board of Fellows. This was a wise provision.

The distraction of Religious things which grew up after the "Great Revival" [1740 to 1750] induced the founding of a Professorship of Divinity, and a College Church in 1755; and Napthali Daggett was the first Professor who filled that chair. Rector Cutler's defection, in 1722, had given great cause for fear, and it was decided that the orthodoxy of the Professors should be tested. In 1753, this was carried into operation by a resolution, which provided that they and the Fellows (the Board), should give their assent to the Westminster Catechism and the Confession of Faith, which was afterward modified into an assent to the "Saybrook Platform." Those who think there is no progress, and especially none in College Boards, will be glad to know that this test was abrogated in 1823.[1]

Some notices of the manners and customs which prevailed in Yale College (much the same in Harvard) will be interesting.

As late as 1768, students were entered in the catalogues, according to the rank of their fathers. Descendants of Noblemen and Knights had the first place; then of Governors, then of the Councillors; then of Ministers; and so on; and it was a punishment to degrade a boy below his father's rank; all which was upset by the breeze of Republicanism which the Revolution raised.

To pass through the four years of College life safely, and to get a "Degree," was to take high rank at once; and ever after, however great the Dunce, he was known and called "Scholar," for he was College-bred, and knew Latin.

In both Yale and Harvard, bodily punishments (boxing

[1] President Woolsey's Discourse, 1850.

and whipping) prevailed, as they do yet in some English schools. But with us, these barbarisms have given way, before a decent regard to public opinion; and a young man who needs to be whipped, soon discovers that he is not fit for the University Hall, and so disappears.

The most rigorous marks of respect were then required from the Students toward the Officers of the College. They were always to stand in their presence; to remain uncovered and silent; and in the College yard were to go bare-headed if any Officer was present.

But the treatment of Freshmen was both gross and brutal; they were the slaves, the Fags, of the Seniors, The Seniors could order up a Freshman, or the whole class, for reprimand "as to manners," or instruction in College rules. The Freshman was always to remain uncovered in their presence, and to stand; not to go through a gate or door, if a Senior was coming within three rods of it; he could not play with them unless he was invited; he was to run of errands for them, and was responsible for any damage done to articles intrusted to him to carry. And these rules applied, not only at the College, but anywhere within the City limits of New Haven.[1]

It was long the custom for the students to board in common, which conduced neither to good manners nor morals. A public Hall was provided, where they did their eating. The following rations, ordered by the Trustees in 1742, will show their fare: "For breakfast, the Steward shall provide one loaf of bread for four, which (the dough) shall weigh one pound. For dinner for four, one loaf of bread, as aforesaid, two and a half pounds of beef, veal, or mutton, or one and three quarter pounds of salt pork about twice a week in the summer time, one quart of beer, two pennyworth of sauce (vegetables). For supper for four, two quarts of milk and one loaf of bread, when milk can be conveniently had; and when it can not, then apple pie, which shall be made of one and three quarter

[1] Freshman Laws of 1764.

pounds dough, one quarter pound hog's fat, two ounces sugar, and half a peck apples."

President Woolsey states, that during the Revolutionary war, the Steward was quite unable to procure food, and the students were obliged to disperse into various towns.

For a long time, there existed an officer called the Butler, who had the monopoly of sales to the students, of cider, metheglin, strong beer (to the amount of not more than twelve barrels per annum), loaf-sugar, pipes, tobacco, books, stationery, and fresh fruits, which the students were not at liberty to buy elsewhere; still they did do it, and drunkenness and riot were not uncommon, even down to very recent times. As early as 1737, the trustees endeavored to prevent the excessive use of wines and liquors on commencement days; but the evil grew so alarmingly —the seniors in 1760 having brought in such quantities of rum and produced so much mischief—that the commencement exercises were suspended, and their degrees were not given, till after a public confession of the class.

DARTMOUTH COLLEGE grew out of a project of John Sergeant (a missionary among the Indians at Stockbridge, who died 1749) for a school to educate and drill the Indian children. It was revived by Dr. Eleazer Wheelock of Lebanon in Connecticut; who found these children tractable, and was encouraged to push the plan forward. Efforts were made to collect money in Scotland and England, with success, and a board of trustees there was appointed, of which the Earl of Dartmouth was head. A remarkable Indian preacher, Sampson Occum, visited England, and excited great attention.

The Governor of New Hampshire invited Dr. Wheelock to remove to that State, and in view of valuable grants of land (some 44,000 acres), and a charter for a university (1769), Dr. Wheelock removed his family and school, consisting of eighteen whites and six Indians, into that wilderness in the year 1770. It now stands secure and prosperous in the beautiful town of Hanover.[1]

BROWN UNIVERSITY, of Rhode Island, originated with James Manning, a Baptist minister, who came from New Jersey to Newport in 1763. In 1764 a charter was obtained, and the first commencement was held (1769) at Warren, where the president, Mr. Manning, resided. In 1770 it was removed to Providence, where it is now presided over by Rev. Dr. Wayland. Its name was given in honor of Nicholas Brown, whose donations began in 1804, and continued to the time of his death, 1841. His heart was large and his generosity was ample. At "Brown," the university system prevails; the students select their own studies, and are not all put through the same courses. Three degrees are given, according to the studies which have been pursued.

PRINTING AND BOOKS.

March 1, 1638, "a printing house was begun at Cambridge, by one Daye, at the charge of Mr. Glover, who died on sea hitherward. The first thing which was printed was the Freeman's Oath; the next was an Almanack made for New England by Mr. William Pierce, mariner; the next was the Psalms newly turned into meter."[2]

"In 1640 this American book was published in Cambridge (it being the first published in what are now the United States), which was soon after reprinted in England, where it passed through no less than eighteen editions, the last being issued in 1754; thus maintaining a hold on English popularity for one hundred and fourteen years!"

This was the "Bay Psalm Book." It passed through twenty-one editions in Scotland, where it was extensively known, the last bearing date in 1759; and as it was re-

[1] Belknap, vol. ii., p. 271. "A Plain and Faithful Narrative of the Original Design, Rise, Progress, etc., of the Indian Charity School at Lebanon, Connecticut. By Eleazer Wheelock, A.M. Boston: 1763." Continuation of the Same. Boston: 1771.

[2] Winthrop's Journal.

printed without the compiler enjoying pecuniary benefit from its sale, we have irrefutable proof that England pirated the first American book, being in reality the original aggressor in this line. The first American work enjoyed a more lasting reputation, and had a wider circulation, than any volume since of American origin, having passed in all through seventy editions—a very remarkable number for the age in which it flourished.

These Psalms were put into verse by the Revds. Mr. Weld and John Eliot of the Roxbury Church, they being acquainted with the original Hebrew.[1]

The title, and a few of the verses, are here given:

"The whole Booke of Psalmes, faithfully translated into English Metre: Whereunto is prefixed a Discourse declaring not only the Lawfulness, but also the Necessity of the heavenly Ordinances of singing Scripture Psalmes in the Churches of God." Imprinted, 1640.

"If, therefore [concludes the Introduction], the verses are not always so smooth and elegant as some may desire or expect; let them consider that God's Altar needs not our pollishing (Ex. xx), for wee have respected rather a plaine translation, than to smooth our verses with any paraphrase, and soe have attended conscience rather than elegance, fidelity rather than poetry, in translating the hebrew words into english language, and David's poetry into English Meetre; that soe wee may sing in Sion the Lord's songs of prayse according to his oune will; untill hee take us from hence and wipe away all our teaers, and bid us enter into our master's ioye to sing eternall Halleluias."

PSALM I.

O Blessed man, that in th' advice
of wicked doth not walk:
nor stand in sinners way nor sit
in chayre of scornfull folk—

---

1 Thomas's History of Printing. Worcester: 1810. Vol. i., p. 232.

But in the law of Iehovah
  is his longing delight:
and in his law doth meditate
  by day and eke by night.

And he shall be like to a tree
  planted by water-rivers:
that in his season yields his fruit,
  and his leafe never withers.—&c.

Verse 10 in Psalme li. may be properly quoted as one of the "unpollish'd" ones:

"Create in mee cleane heart at last,
  God: a right spirit in mee make,
Nor from thy presence quite me cast,
  thy holy Spright nor from me take."

Sternhold's and Hopkins' edition of 1648 renders the same verse as follows:

"Make new my heart within my breast,
  and frame it to thy holy will:
Thy constant Spirit in me let rest,
  which may these raging enemies kill."

PSALM CXXVIII.

A SONG OF DEGREES.

1. Blessed is every one
  that doth Iehovah feare:
that walks his wayes along.

2. For thou shall eate with cheere
  thy hand's labour:
blest shalt thou bee,
it well with thee
  shall be therefore.

3. Thy wife, like fruitful vine,
  shall be by thine house side:
the children that be thine
  like olive plants abide
    about thy board.

4. Behold, thus blest
that man doth rest
that feares the Lord.

5. Iehovah shall thee blesse
from Sin, and shall see
Ierusalem's goodnesse
All thy life's days that bee.

6. And shall view well
thy children then
with their children,
peace on Isr'ell.

It is not easy to explain the popularity of such verses. A simple incident, however, may help us to a comprehension of it, if we can apply it. It is but a few years ago that a member of a small congregation of "Come-outers," describing the perplexity to which they were subject, said: They had tried a good many ministers but none suited. "The truth is," he continued, "we are an ignorant congregation, and we want an ignorant preacher; those we have had, shot too high"—that charge can not with safety be made of the verses of the "Bay Psalm Book."

Eliot's Indian Bible was completed, and printed in New England, in 1664; while the first English edition of the Bible, in America, appeared in 1752.

"Wherever American enterprise penetrates, the printing-press is found. We have shown that printing was exercised in America in 1639. The first typography executed in Rochester, Kent—the seat of an English bishopric—bears date, 1648, or nine years after the art was introduced into the forests of Massachusetts; and the earliest printing done in the great manufacturing city of Manchester, was in the year 1732, or nearly one hundred years subsequent to the establishment of a press in America. The art was first practiced in Glasgow and Cambridge in the same year; at Exeter, thirty years later than in the United States, and not in the great commercial city of Liverpool until after the year 1750 (one hundred and eleven years later than in the United States), where the population was not far short of 25,000, nor was a newspaper printed there before May, 1756—New York, Philadelphia, and Boston, were immensely in advance of her then (as they are now), with fewer inhabitants."[1]

In 1662, the General Court appointed two persons Licensers of the Press, without whose consent no books were allowed to be published; and in 1667, it directed "a book that imitates Christ, written by Thomas Kempis, a popish minister," to be revised by the Licensers, and the printing of it not to proceed further then.

LITERATURE for the first century was mainly devoted to religious writings, and to controversial theology. The titles of books will sometimes show the state of society. These are two of that day:

NEW ENGLAND'S SALAMANDER

DISCOVERED,

BY AN IRRELIGIOUS AND SCORNEFULL PHAMPLET CALLED NEW ENGLAND'S JONAS CAST UP AT LONDON, &c., &c., OWNED BY MAJOR JOHN CHILDE, BUT NOT PROBABLE TO BE WRITTEN BY HIM,

or,

A Satisfactory Answer to many Aspersions cast upon New England therein;

Wherin our Government there is showed to be legall and not Arbitrary, being as near the Law of England as our Conditions will permit,

Together

With a Brief Reply to what is written in Answer to certain Passages in a late Book called Hypocrosie Unmasked.

BY EDW. WINSLOW.

London, 1647.

[1] Trubner's Bibliographical Guide to American Literature. London.

THE HEART OF NEW ENGLAND

RENT AT THE

BLASPHEMIES

OF THE PRESENT

GENERATION,

or,

A Brief TRACTATE concerning the Doctrine of the Quakers, Demonstrating the destructive nature thereof, to Religion, the Churches, and the State, with Considerations of the Remedy against it. Occasional Satisfaction to Objections and Confirmation of the contrary Truth.

By JOHN NORTON,

TEACHER OF THE CHRIST CHURCH AT BOSTON,

Who was appointed thereunto by the Order of the General Court.

CAMBRIDGE IN NEW ENGLAND.

1651.

A glance into "The Heart of New England rent," shows something of the state of religious feeling and opinion in New England, two centuries ago. The purpose of the Rev. Mr. Norton is to expose the absurdities of the Quakers and the viciousness of their doctrines, and of course he proceeds to do that in the best way he can.

"What is Truth?" is not germain to his argument. He states "that Apollo (that is, Satan) caused the pythoness to quake, as he has at various times others in a strange manner as he now does the Indian Powows;" therefore, it is clear to him, that it is the devil who is quaking the Quakers. They replied that Isaiah (ch. xx., 2) went about three years *naked*, and that Ezekiel smote and stamped (ch. vi., 11), and that Daniel (ch. x., 7) had a great quaking, when moved with the Spirit; therefore, it may be worth while to believe that the Spirit of God still moves men. But Norton said their cases were "divine circumstances to Edification, Extraordinary," but the Quakers were surely moved with the devil. There was no other way for him to get along with the case. The Tract then proceeds to argue the Trinity at large—"personal God"—the necessity for the Scripture after Moses's time, though not before, and that the "inner light," "which lighteth every man," will not do. He then shows that the presence of the Quakers is a sign that God is about to inflict vengeance upon such as do not receive "the Truth in the Love of it;" says much about false prophets (the Quakers, of course, being such, in his opinion), goes on to prove the "destructiveness of their doctrines unto Religion, the Churches, and Christian states," and the great necessity for the Magistrates putting a stop to the teaching of Heresy and Blasphemies, at whatever cost, "with weapons and punishment," etc. All of which was objected to by Roger Williams, and some others, at that day, and is now repudiated by all, except the Holy Roman and some few other Religious sects.

THE NEW ENGLAND PRIMER is one of the oldest and most curious books published in New England. There is an advertisement of a second impression, as early as 1691. This small book contained matter for small children, beginning with the Alphabet, and ending with a very strange poetic dialogue, between "Christ, A Youth, and the Devil." A few fearful illustrations illuminate the text; among them, the burning of Mr. John Rogers; whose wife, with "nine *small* children and one at the breast," followed him to the stake, "with which sorrowful sight he was not in the least daunted."[1] It contains the Assembly's Shorter Catechism, and Mr. Cotton's Milk for Babes, in both of which the children of New England were sorely exercised, both on Saturdays and Sundays. The Assembly's Catechism is so important a document, and was for so long a period the guide to a religious education, that it deserves to be preserved in History.

[1] Many, with such a family, would have gone gladly.

The people were too much occupied with the hard struggle of life, and in resolving religious doubts, to pay much attention to Literature or Art.

Neither Poetry nor the Fine Arts flourished during the early days of New England. With the exception of the "Bay Psalm Book," we find but little poetry of any kind, and but little of that worthy of notice. Many of the Ministers tried their hand at it, and left verses, some of which, survived their sermons; but nearly all of both are forgotten now.

One curious book in verse, was—

"The Simple Cobbler of Aggawam, in America, willing to help mend his native country, lamentably tattered, both in the upper leather and sole, with all the honest stitches he can take. And as willing never to be paid for his work by old English wonted pay.

"It is his trade to patch all the year long gratis,
Therefore, I pray, Gentlemen, keep your purses.

"By Theodore de la Guard. *In rebus arduis ac tenui spe, fortissima quoque consilia tutissima sunt.—Cic.*

In English,

"When bootes and shoes are torne up to the lefts,
Coblers must thrust their awls up to the hefts;
This is no time to feare *Appelles gramm:*
Ne Sutor quidem ultra crepidam.

"London: Printed by J. D. & R. J., for Stephen Bowtell, at the signe of the Bible, in Pope's Head Alley. 1647."

Such is the title of one of the quaintest and most curious books that appeared in New England. It was written by Nathaniel Ward, Minister of Ipswich. It is a satire, and is aimed at what the old Minister considered follies, and mostly at those rife in England; full of barbarisms and affected words; it is not now worth much attention, though many things are well hit. The following little poem in it is good, addressed to King Charles :

Their lives cannot be good,
  Their faith cannot be sure,
Where truth cannot be quiet,
  Nor ordinances pure.

No King can King it right,
  Nor rightly sway his rod,
Who truly loves not Christ,
  And truly fears not God.

He cannot rule a land
  As lands should ruled been,
That lets himself be ruled
  By a ruling Roman queen.

No Earthly man can be
  True subjects to this state,
Who makes the Pope his Christ,
  And heretique his mate.

Then peace will go to war,
  And silence make a noise,
When upper things will not
  With nether equipoise.

The Upper world shall rule
  While stars will run their race;
The nether world obey,
  While people keep their place.

As Michael Angelo's "Last Judgment" arrests the attention of the curious in Italy, so Michael Wigglesworth, A. M.'s "Day of Doom," or A poetical description of the great and last Judgment, demands our attention in New England. He opens with a description of the world before Christ's coming to Judgment :

1.

"Still was the night, Serene and Bright,
  when all men sleeping lay;
Calm was the season, and carnal reason
  thought so 't would last for ay.
Soul take thine ease, let sorrow cease,
  much good thou hast in store :
This was their Song, their Cups among,
  the Evening before.

2.

"Wallowing in all kind of Sin,
  vile wretches lay secure," &c.

They are much surprised with the coming of Christ, which is described ; and then comes the Trump :

17.

"Before his Throne a Trump is blown, 1 Thes. iv. 16.
proclaiming the day of Doom:
Forthwith he cries, *Ye dead arise,*
and unto judgment come.
No sooner said, but 't is obeyed, John v. 28, 29.
sepulchers opened are:
Dead bodies all rise at his call,
and 's mighty power declare."

Then they all gather to the throne.

22.

"At Christ's right hand the Sheep do stand,
his holy Martyrs, who"—&c., &c.

27.

"At Christ's left hand the Goats do stand
all whining hypocrites, &c.
Who Sheep resembled, but they dissembled," &c.

The various wicked are then described quite in detail. Jesus then calls the Elect, and speaks to them:

40.

"These men be those my father chose
before the world's foundation,
And to me gave, that I should save Job xvii. 6.
from Death and condemnation." Eph. i. 4.

They are received into joy; and the wicked are brought forward, who plead all sorts of excuses; and the hypocrites say:

82.

"We did believe, and oft receive
the precious promises: Acts viii. 13. Isa. lviii. Heb. vi. 45.
We took good care to get a share
in endless happiness.

"We pray'd and wept, we Fast-days kept,
lewd ways we did eschew;
We joyful were thy word to hear,
we form'd our lives anew.

83.

"We thought our Sin had pardon'd been,
that our Estate was good,
Our debts all paid, our peace well made,
our Souls washed with thy Blood, &c.

84.

"The Judge incensed at their pretenced
self-vaunting Piety,"

proceeds to expose them, and refuses to listen to their prayers and excuses.

92.

"Then were brought nigh a Company
of Civil, honest Men,
That lov'd true dealing, and hated stealing,
ne'er wrong'd their Bretheren;"
&c.

But they were rejected with the rest.

107.

"A wondrous crowd then 'gan aloud
thus for themselves to say,
We did intend, Lord, to amend,
and to reform our way.
Our true intent was to repent, Prov. xxvii., 1. Jam. iv. 13
and make our peace with Thee;
But sudden Death, stopping our breath,
left us no Libertie."

Then others came;

"They argued, We were misled,
as is well known to Thee,
By their Example, who had more ample
abilities than we."
&c.

130.

"Others Argue, and not a few,
is not God gracious?
His Equity and Clemency
are they not marvellous?

Thus we believe: are we deceived?
cannot his mercy great,
(As hath been told to us of old)
asswage his anger's heat?"

To all,

147.

"Christ readily make this Reply,
I damn you, not because
You are rejected, or not elected,
but you have broke my laws;" Luke xiii. 27.
&c.

148.

"Whom God will save, such he will have Acts iii. 19, & xvi. 31.
the means of life to use;
Whom he'll pass by, shall chuse to dy 1 Sam. ii. 25.
and ways of life refuse."

The Heathen plead:

157.

"Thy written Word (say they), good Lord,
we never did enjoy;
We nor refus'd, nor it abus'd;
Oh! do not us destroy!"

To whom Christ replies:

164.

"You sinful Crew have not been true Rom. i. 20.
Unto the Light of Nature,
Nor done the good you understood,
Nor owned your Creator."

"Reprobate Infants plead for themselves," who had been born but to die. These were condemned because Adam, their federal head, had sinned; but,

181.

"A crime it is, therefore in bliss
you may not hope to dwell;
But unto you I shall allow
the easiest room in Hell."

The Judge pronounceth the sentence of condemnation :

201.

"Ye sinful wights and cursed sprights,
  that work iniquity,
Depart together from me forever,
  to endless Misery;
Your portion take in yonder Lake,
  where Fire and Brimstone flameth;
Suffer the smart, which your desert
  as its due wages claimeth."

The wicked are then cast in with the Devils.

209.

"With Iron bands they tied their hands
  and cursed feet together,
And cast them all, both great and small,
  into that Lake forever,
Where day and night, without respite,
  they wail, and cry, and howl, Matt. xxii. 13, & xxv. 46.
For torturing pain which they sustain,
  in body and in soul."

The versification of the Reverend poet is careful and satisfactory, and his theology is as unmitigated in verse as in prose.

The following title-page introduces us to Anne Bradstreet :

"Several Poems, compiled with great variety of Wit and Learning, full of delight ; wherein especially is contained a Compleat Discourse and Description of the Four Elements, Constitutions, Ages of Man, and Seasons of the Year, together with an Exact Epitome of the Three First Monarchies, viz., the Assyrian, Persian, and Grecian ; and the beginning of the Roman Commonwealth to the end of their last King, with divers other Pleasant and Serious Poems : By a Gentlewoman of New England." Printed at Boston, 1640 ; at London, 1650, under the title of "The Tenth Muse lately sprung up in America."

This "Gentlewoman of America" was Anne Bradstreet,

daughter of old Governor Dudley, and wife of one who was afterward the Governor of the Colony. Her poems are full of delicate touches, and indicate a fine poetic nature, and are remarkable as the productions of a woman at a time when most women did not know how to write their own names :—

EXTRACT FROM CONTEMPLATIONS.

Under the cooling shadow of a stately elm,
  Close sat I by a river's goodly side,
Where gliding streams the rocks did overwhelm;
  A lovely place with pleasures dignified.
I, once that loved the shady woods so well,
Now thought the rivers did the trees excel,
And if the sun would ever shine, there would I dwell.

While on the stealing stream I fixed mine eye,
  Which to the longed-for ocean kept its course,
I marked nor crooks nor rocks that there did lie,
  Could hinder aught, but still augment its force.
"O happy flood," quoth I, "that hold'st thy race,
Till thou arrive at thy beloved place,
Nor is it rocks or shoals that can obstruct thy pace.

"Nor is't enough that thou alone mayst slide,
  But hundred brooks in thy clear waves do meet:
So hand in hand along with these they glide
  To Thetis' house, where all embrace and greet.
Thou emblem true of what I count the best—
O could I leave my rivulet to rest!
So may we press to that vast mansion ever blest.

"Ye fish that in this liquid region 'bide,
  That for each season have your habitation,
Now salt, now fresh, when you think best to glide
  To unknown coasts to give a visitation,
In lakes and ponds you leave your numerous fry:
So Nature taught, and yet you know not why—
You wat'ry-folk, that know not your felicity!"

Look how the wantons frisk to taste the air,
  Then to the colder bottom straight they dive,
But soon to Neptune's glassy hall repair,
  To see what trade the great ones there do drive,

Who forage o'er the spacious sea-green field,
And take their trembling prey before it yield,
Whose armor is their scales, their spreading fins their shield.

While musing thus, with contemplation fed,
And thousand fancies buzzing in my brain,
The sweet-tongued Philomel perched o'er my head,
  And chaunted forth a most melodious strain,
Which wrapt me so with wonder and delight,
I judged my hearing better than my sight,
And wished me wings with her a while to take my flight.

"O, merry bird," said I, "that fears no snares;
  That neither toils nor hoards up in thy barn;
Feels no sad thoughts, nor cruciating cares
  To gain more food, or shun what might thee harm:
Thy clothes ne'er wear, thy meat is everywhere;
Thy bed a bough, thy drink the water clear,
Reminds not what is past, nor what's to come dost fear.

"The dawning morn with songs thou dost prevent; [1]
  Sets hundred notes unto thy feathered crew;
So each one tunes his pretty instrument,
  And warbling out, the old begins anew,
And thus they pass their youth in summer season,
Then follow thee into a better region,
Where winter's never felt by that sweet airy legion."

After a few verses of reflection, she closes—

So he that saileth in this world of pleasure,
  Feeding on sweets that never bit of the sour,
That's full of friends, of honor, and of treasure—
  Fond fool! he takes this earth e'en for heaven's bower.
But sad affliction comes, and makes him see
Here's neither honor, wealth, nor safety:
Only above is found all with security. [2]

"Pietas et Gratulatio Collegii Cantabrigiensis, Apud Novanglos. Bostoni, Massachusettensium, Typis J. Green & J. Russell, M.DCCLXI." was a book of poetical addresses to George III. upon his accession. It was printed and bound in a superb style—in a style which Boston at this day can hardly rival. It abounds in the fulsome

[1] Anticipate.
[2] Griswold's Female Poets of America.

flatteries common to such works, which have too long disgraced literature and literary men; and is now almost forgotten, for the King and his flatterers were shortly after this hated and despised.

NEWSPAPERS. In 1704, the first newspaper was begun in Boston. This was its style:

N. E. Numb. 1.

The Boston News-Letter.

PUBLISHED BY AUTHORITY.

From MONDAY, April 17, to MONDAY, April 24, 1704.

It is printed on half a sheet of pot-paper, with a small-pica type, folio.

The first page is filled with an extract from "The London Flying Post," respecting the Pretender's sending Popish Missionaries into Scotland; then comes the Queen's (Anne's) Speech to Parliament; then a few Boston items, and four from New York, Philadelphia, and New London. This, with *one* advertisement, formed the whole of its contents. The advertisement is as follows:

"This News-Letter is to be continued Weekly; and all Persons who have any Houses, Lands, Tenements, Farmes, Ships, Vessels, Goods, Wares, or Merchandizes, &c., to be Sold or Lett; or Servants Runaway; or Goods Stoll or Lost, may have the same Inserted at a Reasonable Rate; from Twelve Pence to Five Shillings, and not to exceed. Who may agree with *Nicholas Boone*, for the same, at his Shop, next door to Major Davis's Apothecary, in Boston, near the Old Meeting-House.

"All persons in Town or Country, may have said News-Letter, Weekly, upon reasonable tearms, agreeing with John Campbell, Post Master, for the same."

It was printed by B. Green.[1]

In 1719, the second newspaper, in New England, was started by J. Franklin ; it was called the Boston Gazette.

The New England Courant, was started in 1721, by James and Benjamin Franklin. It satirized Religious Knaves ; was censured by the Ministers, and suspended by the Assembly, in 1723.

The Rhode Island Gazette was begun in 1731.

In 1748, the number of papers in Boston, had increased to five.[2]

The Connecticut Gazette, was first published in 1755.

The New Hampshire Gazette, was started in 1756.

In 1771, Dr. Franklin states, that twenty-five newspapers were printed in America ; but at the opening of the Revolution, there appears to have been thirteen newspapers printed in New England, as follows :

In Massachusetts,	7
In New Hampshire,	1
In Rhode Island,	2
In Connecticut,	3
Total,	13

In all the Colonies, Thirty-four.[3]

[1] Thomas's History of Printing, vol. ii., p. 191.

[2] Ibid.

[3] Ibid.

CHAPTER XLVII.

MANNERS AND CUSTOMS OF THE PEOPLE.

ARISTOCRACY—GENTLEMEN AND FREEHOLDERS—MAGISTRATES FOR LIFE—TITLES—THEIR HOUSES—CLOTHES—OCCUPATIONS—FARMING—MAIZE—OTHER CROPS—WHEAT AND BERBERRIES — POTATOES — DRINKS—TEA—MONEY— SHIP-BUILDING—HUNTING—FISHING—WHALES — EXPORTS — FREE-TRADE — TRAVELING—CARRIAGES—WINTERS—THE POOR—CHARACTERISTICS—MEADOW LANDS—THE HUSKING—LOVE—"TO SALT"—SPINNINGS—SLEIGH-RIDES — THE SABBATH-DAY—THE SAINTS — COURTING—CHASTITY—RELIGIOUS MELANCHOLY—A DUEL—THRIFT AND PIETY—"THE GOOD OLD TIMES."

THOSE who came first to New England, were not of the kind described thus by Captain John Smith—"who would live at home idly (or think himself of any worth to live), only to eate, drink, and sleep, and soe die? Or by consuming that carelessly, his friends got worthily; or for being descended nobly fine, with the vaine vaunt of great kindred, in penurie; or to maintain a silly shew of Bravery, toyle out thy heart's soule and time basely by shifts, tricks, cards, and dice?"[1] No, they were men who came to work, and were able to do it. The occupations of new countries are mainly the same—Farming, Hunting, and Fishing; and such they were in New England.

"If he have nothing but his hands he may set up his trade," wrote Captain Smith. These things he may get, "Herring, Cod, and Ling, the Triplicity; Salt upon Salt; Beavers, Otters, Martens, and furres of price. Mines of Gold and Silver, Woods of all sorts, Eagles, Gripes, Hawkes, &c., Whales, Grampus, Haddock, &c.; Moose, Deere, Beares, Beavers, &c.; all in their season; for you cannot gather cherries at Christmas, in Kent."

ARISTOCRACY.

The feeling of class, held on among the Puritans for a long time. The well-bred and well born were entitled to be called Gentlemen, and

[1] Smith's Description of New England, p. 31.

these had the prefix of Mr.; the common folk being called Goodman and Goody. So much was the title of Mr. valued, that Josias Plaistow, in 1631, for stealing corn from the Indians, was fined five pounds, and forbidden to be called Mr. Thenceforth he was plain Josias.

In 1636, Lords Say, Brook, and other "persons of quality," proposed to emigrate to New England, upon certain conditions; which were briefly—

"That there should be two distinct ranks of men" in the Colonies, one Gentlemen, and the other Freeholders.

That the Gentlemen should make one house in the Legislature, and the Freemen the other; that none should be admitted to the first rank, except by vote of both houses; that they should sit separately; and that the Governor should always be chosen from the first rank. To all of which the reply was, that to these things the Colonists in Massachusetts agreed, and that in most things their practices were conformed. But Church-membership was the condition of citizenship, rather than property or blood, as Lords Say and Brook proposed.

Mr. Cotton, in his letter to them (1636), said:

"As for monarchy and aristocracy they are clearly approved and directed in Scripture, yet so as referreth the sovereignty to himself and setteth up Theocracy in both."[1]

But although clearly approved in Scripture, as Mr. Cotton said, the people were on the alert, and refused stubbornly to elect a Governor for life; and in 1639 rescinded an order, which confirmed some of the magistrates for life.

"What is this but Aristocracy?" they said; "Why should we put riders on our backs?" and so they entirely refused to do it. The community steadily grew more democratic, insisting that every man should have political rights, and should exercise them as his own judgment and conscience (not as any man or class) should dictate.

[1] Hutchinson, Append.

"Honorable," was applied to Governors after 1685.

TITLES.

"Esquire," was applied to a few persons in the early days; and in the country towns is now used to designate persons connected with legal matters—to lawyers and judges.

"Gent." or "Gentleman" was applied to some few, who were of good birth in England.

"Mr." was the common title of well-born and well-bred persons.

"Yeoman," was the common designation of well-to-do men.

"Goodman," and "Goody," "Gammer," and "Gaffer," were applied to the working classes, who had no pretensions to education or superiority.

"Major," "Corporal," and all military titles were much valued, and were engraved on the tombstones.

"Rev." and "Deacon," were also prized.

THEIR HOUSES.

Winthrop, Dudley, and some of good estate, in the Colonies of Massachusetts Bay, New Haven, and Connecticut, very early built fine houses; but at first the people mostly built with logs; then there soon grew up all over New England, comfortable double houses with a long, sloping roof behind, which covered a kitchen and closets. It is one of the striking peculiarities of New England that the people there would not then live shabbily or in dirt, and that they will not now.

The houses at first were of one story, but soon were built of two stories, the upper one projecting about a foot. Great timbers were used, and showed on the inside in the rooms. Some of these houses are still in good preservation. They commonly faced the south, so that the sun might shine square, and then they could tell when noon-time came. The windows were small, with diamond-shaped glass. A great stone chimney reared itself in the middle of the house; in which, wood four and six feet long was used, and thirty to sixty cords a-year was a fair allowance. In those great chimneys the bacon was hung, and in the corners the children sat; and, looking up, saw the stars shine in the day-time. Along the joists were hung strings of dried apples and ripe pumpkins; and on the hooks hung a "king's arm" and a spontoon. Many a copy of "King Charles's Twelve Good rules" were preserved on the walls, though they had transgressed the second.

THE TWELVE GOOD RULES.

Profane no divine ordinance.
Touch no State matters.
Urge no Healths.
Pick no Quarrels.
Encourage no Vice.
Repeat no Grievances.
Reveal no Secrets.
Maintain no ill Opinions.
Make no Comparisons.
Keep no bad Company.
Make no long Meals.
Lay no Wagers.

Dress, always a matter of prime necessity in a cold country, was so in New England—and in such a country the question early came up, "How was it to be had?" "You are like to want clothes hereafter," etc.; to which it was answered, "First, Linen fustians; Dimities, we are making already; secondly, sheep are coming on for woolen cloth; thirdly, in meantime we may be supplied by way of trade with other parts; fourth, Cordevant, deere, seale, and moose skins (which are beasts as big as oxen, and whose skins are buff) are there to be had plentifully, which will help this way esspecially for servants' clothing."

THEIR CLOTHING.

In New England's First-fruits,"[1] the following, among other blessings, are enumerated: "In

[1] London, 1643, Mass. H. Coll. Vol. i.

prospering hempe and flaxe do well, that its frequently sowen, spun, and woven into Linen-Cloth ; (and in a short time may serve for cordage) ; and so with Cotton Wool (which we may have at very reasonable rates from the islands) ; and our linen yarn we can make dimittics and fustians for our Summer Clothing, and having a matter of 1,000 sheep which prosper well, to begin withall, in a Competent time, we hope, to have woollen cloth there made. And great and small cattel, being now very frequently killed for food, their skins will afford us leather for Boots and shoes and other uses ; so that God is leading us by the hand into a way of Clothing."

But sad to say, some soon ran into Expenditures, which were in excess ; and as early as 1631, the Court sent for the Elders, and Charged them to urge it upon the consciences of the people, that they should avoid this Costliness of Apparel and following of new Fashions : which they indeed promised to do. It was a rash thing, for "divers of the Elders' wives were partners in the general disorder," and the Court did not enough consider what was to befall the Elders, who took this thing in hand. Winthrop quietly ends this matter by saying that little was done about it.[1]

Broad Skirted Coats were worn, with great pockets. Small clothes were the full dress, for boys as well as men. Shoe-buckles and a ring were highly prized. The men often wore red cloaks ; and scarlet broad-cloth cloaks of domestic manufacture were used by women subsequently to the Revolution. Trains or trails were in use from the Earliest days. And hooped skirts of the amplest dimensions appeared in the 18th century.

Ultimately, several laws were passed against excessive expenditure and Extravagant Fashions, which are mentioned in another place.[2]

Governor Eaton's Estate at New Haven was £1440 15 7, some portions of which were as follows :

[1] Journal, Oct. 1638.

[2] See ch. XLV. Puritan Laws.

Wearing Apparel, . . .	£50	0	0
Item in Plate, ...	107	11	0
Item in a piece of Gold, 20*s.* and Silver, 25*s.* 5*d.* .	2	5	0
Item in two signet rings of gold, . .	2	12	0

The value of money may be judged by this : John Winthrop bought one of the best houses and Lots in New Haven for £100.[1]

Most of the men wore Short hair and Long beards.

Drunkenness soon prevailed to an alarmiug extent, and various laws were made to restrain it. Tobacco was chewed and smoked in excess ; and various efforts were made to restrain this. In 1669 the Massachusetts Court ordered that any persons found smoking tobacco on the Lord's-day, going to, or coming from Church, should be fined twelve pence. And it is asserted that they even smoked in meeting.

THEIR OCCUPATIONS.

Farming, Fishing, and Hunting, as before stated, were the three principal occupations for the men. The women were busied with household matters. Idleness was not popular, and it was the duty of the magistrate to see to it. The Grand Juries, among other presentments, made these :

"We present Charles Potrom for living an idle, lazy life." "We present Adam Goodwine, for denying the morality of the fourth commandment."

Their staple crop was maize, or Indian corn, which they found rudely cultivated by the Indians, and which they soon came to like ; but English grains and other crops were at once introduced. Squanto showed them how to cultivate it, and how to manure it with fish, as is done now. At first their ground was prepared, and their crops put in with hoes ; till they could get cattle and plows. CATTLE were brought to Plymouth in 1624, and nigh 100 head were brought over in 1629 for the Massachusetts Bay Company. Many losses were had, and the

[1] Bacon's Disc. Appen.

prices of Cows in 1636 were from £25 to £30 each; yet a quart of milk could then be bought for a penny. Of course, Cattle were not then used for eating.

In the year 1630, food was at great prices. Wheat-meal cost fourteen shillings; Peas, eleven shillings. In 1632, Corn was sold at 4*s.* 6*d.* a bushel, These are enumerated as food (1631): "fat hogs, kids, venison, poultry, geese, partridges, &c." Again it is mentioned, that two or three boys brought in a bushel of eels, and sixty great lobsters. In one of Winthrop's Letters to his son, the following articles in use are mentioned: "Meal, Peas, Oatmeal, Malt, Beef, Prunes, and Aquavitæ."

Farmers had their troubles then, as they have now; Frosts sometimes killed their unripened crops, and drought shortened them greatly. In the year 1633 (May), great numbers of "a sort of flies, like for bigness to humble-bees," came out of the ground, eating up every green thing, and making "such a constant yelling noise" as to deafen the hearers. These were what we now call locusts.

Pumpkins, Squashes, Melons, and Beans, which they found in the country, they soon came to love; and from the Indians they learned the ways of raising and cooking them.

In 1674 the Luxury of Molasses became common.

About the year 1664, Wheat began to blast, which greatly perplexed the farmers. Every theory as to the cause and cure seemed to fail; and, at last, for want of a better cause, it was laid to the Berberry bushes, which, brought from Europe, were beginning to grow along every fence and hedge-row. Unsparing war was made upon the beautiful shrub for nigh two centuries, and the belief in their malignity yet prevails.

Mills were not common, and families were provided with a large mortar, in which Indian Corn could be pounded for use.

Potatoes were introduced by Emigrants from Ireland, and were raised by Mr. Nathaniel Walker of Andover.

Their popularity grew very slowly; and, as late as 1750, a crop of five bushels would glut the market.[1]

Breakfast, Dinner, and Supper, were hearty meals, and went with the Sun: at Sun-rise—Mid-day—and Sun-down; and when Nine o'clock came, the Meeting-house bell rung the Curfew, and then most people went to bed.

The DRINK of the people was Water, which is good throughout New England — Beer, which every family brewed from its own Barley Malt, as was the custom then in England—Milk, which their Cows and Goats yielded—Cider, which after a few years was ground out of their apples.

Tea, "the Cup which cheers, but not inebriates" the female heart, and imperceptibly brings the nerves to the finest condition of excruciating sensibility, appears to have crept in from England about 1720,[2] though it was used here and there in New England in the beginning of the century.

In the Old Country it was used only by the rich, and was much longed-for by the poor. For a time the sufferings of those in the Colonies who attempted to use it were fearful. They only knew that it was fashionable, and of course desirable; but how to use it few knew, and many experiments were tried; among others, the leaves were boiled, and eaten with butter, like "Greens." Its use, however, was soon learned, and, before the Revolution, smuggled Tea was in almost every house. When the Excise laws were enforced, we shall see that, dear as it had became to the tired nerves, and delicious as the stimulant was felt to be, women then equaled men in their devotion to the cause, and formed voluntary associations, pledging themselves against the use of any which had paid duty to England. Its production and importation have now come to be immense; while Beer and Cider have nearly gone out of use in New England. "A Tea

[1] Coffin's Newbury. [2] Holmes.

Equipage" of Silver was highly prized ; and it was common in those early days for women to carry their own china cup, saucer, and spoon to visiting parties, and the "Chaney" of that day was prettier than that of to-day.

The high prices of Food depended somewhat upon the scarcity of money, as well as upon the scarcity of food. In 1626, when Mr. Allerton went to England upon business for the Plymouth Company, he was obliged to borrow there £200, for which he paid 30 per cent. interest.[1] In "New England's First Fruits" we find it said,

"But you have no money there ?"

Ans.—"It is true we have not much, though some there is, but we have those staple commodities named, that will fetch money from other parts. Ships, fish, iron, pipe staves, corne, bever, oyle, etc., will keep us with money and other things also." "We can trade among ourselves by way of Exchange, one commodity for another, and soe doe usually." Yet the greed for gold was so great even then (1624), that Bradford says, "it makes men rave and cry out," and Roger Williams said much the same thing. The first money coined in New England was struck in the year 1652 ; this was the Pine-tree shilling, a few of which are extant.

SHIP-BUILDING was begun early, Governor Winthrop's Bark, called the "Blessing of the Bay," being launched July 4, 1631. In 1648 there were trading to Virginia seven ships from New England, beside some twelve from England, and twelve from Holland.[2]

HUNTING.

The Hunters at once grew into a class in New England. They were a breed by themselves, a kind of cross between the Puritan and Indian, with all the "grit" of the one, and lawless love of liberty of the other. They were at first the friends of the savages, lived with them in their cabins, and with them learned the ways and haunts of the beasts of the

[1] Bradford's Letter Book, M. H. C., vol. iii.

[2] Bancroft, vol. i., p. 210, M. H. C., vol. i., p. 118.

Forest. Bear, Deer, Beaver, Wolves, and Foxes abounded, and the hunters tracked, trapped, and shot; the carcases furnished them with food, and the pelts brought them money, or its equivalent in powder, lead, brandy, and clothes. The towns, also, paid a bounty for wolf's scalps, which were nailed up on the Meeting-house. Besides the wild beasts, the streams and ponds then abounded with ducks, geese, and fish, and it was not easy to starve those hardy fellows. Hunters' blood is impatient of routine and drudgery, and flows quick at the mention of the chase or adventure. This class of men is not the kind that builds houses, and hoards wealth, and gathers in cities, and divides labor, and fosters science, and loves Art and Literature. The hunter is competent for all his wants; he builds his own house; he raises his own food; he makes his own clothes, nets, and tools; he does his own thinking; knows nothing of books, but every thing of trees, brooks, mountains, and woodcraft; and every foot-track fires his imagination, and tells a story, which keeps his eyes from sleep. It is easy to see that the boundless free forest, developed all the hunter instincts in this class of men, and that they ranged wide, regardless of Public Opinion, of Schools, and of "Church Privileges."

Out of this class came Captains Stone and Oldham, who were killed by the Indians—Captain Underhill, who kissed his neighbor's wife, and "got his religion over a pipe of tobacco"—Thomas Morton, of Merry-mount, and afterward the Bush-Rangers, such as Stark, and Putnam, and Allen, and Baker.

The Indians merely possessed the Continent; the Hunters were the pioneers of civilization, who cleared the way for new and increasing nations. The nations came, to put all things to USE, for the support of man, and his ultimate complete and perfect development. The Hunters, at first fraternized with the Indians; but when the interests of Whites and Indians clashed, they turned all their skill to the destruction of Indians, which before had been devoted to Bear and Deer; and their superior energy overcame the Red-man. From out this Hunter class came some of the most wary and indefatigable bush-fighters, men inured to danger, so that when war came in the next century, bearing down upon them in the white-winged navy of England, they were not afraid to meet it.

FISHING.

The Banks which stretch along the New England coast, beyond Newfoundland, abounded with Cod, Halibut, and Mackerel; and in catching and curing these, the first enterprises were engaged. The Fishermen were brothers to the Hunters; one ranged over the land, the other over the seas. Rude huts were clustered along the coast, sheds were made, and racks raised, where the harvests of fish could be dressed and cured for the European markets. Smacks and fishing-boats were built in every bay, and when the fishing season came, swarmed out bold and reckless, to catch their finny prey. The Hunters have disappeared from New England, but the Fishermen still inhabit along the coast, from New Bedford to Cape Race. They are an open-handed, open-hearted, free, manly set, half farmer, half fisherman, amphibious, often reckless, but almost always honest. They weaken neither New England nor this Nation.

In 1793, in March, a codfish was sold in Newbury, weighing ninety-eight pounds, five and a half feet in length, and girth at the thickest part, three feet four inches.[1]

WHALES were often found on the coasts, and were attacked and killed by people in boats. The Whale Fishery originated at Nantucket in 1690, in boats from the shore. It increased steadily, and the vessels extended their adventures to the coasts of Guinea, Brazil, and the West Indies, while their returns varied from five thousand to thirty thousand barrels annually.[2]

Captains David Smith and Gamaliel Collings, of Truro, were the first who adventured to the Falkland Islands in pursuit of them: this was in 1774.

[1] Coffin's Newbury. [2] Mass. Hist. Coll., vol. iii.

EXPORTS FROM NEW ENGLAND.

The first exports were mainly furs and fish, which grew steadily in importance till the time of the Revolution. "The best sort of fish is sent to Spain, Portugal, and the Straits; the nett proceeds of which are remitted to England. Oil, Bone, Masts for the Royal navy, timber of all kinds (which is now sent home in rafts), ships of every kind, pot-ash, furs, etc., etc.; many of which England was obliged to other nations for (before New England was known), are the immediate exports to Great Britain. In return for all, they receive the manufactures of England, and thereby give bread to thousands of British Subjects. Thus all their labor centers in England, except their daily food."[1]

In 1648, Winthrop writes to his son that the iron works go on well, and that they are making seven tons a week, mostly out of brown earth which lies under the bog mine, and that "their bar iron is as good as Spanish."

Free Trade seemed little understood in those days. In 1639, Robert Keaine, merchant, was fined £200 for taking too large profits on his goods—"sixpence in the shilling, and in some small things, above two for one." He was thought to hold false principles, such as:

That if a man lost in one commodity, he might make it up in another:

That a man might buy as cheap as he can, and sell as dear as he can, etc.

And Mr. Cotton preached a sermon upon the matter, which apparently did nothing to clear things up.

"One Taylor, of Linne," on his passage over, sold the milk of his cow at twopence the quart, and after hearing a sermon upon extortion, went distracted.

Wages of mechanics were fixed by the Court in 1630 at two shillings a day; but again left free, by order of Court, March 22, 1631. When, in 1640, it was found that workmen would move to where their wages were

[1] A Brief Review, &c. London, 1774.

better, the legal limitation was removed, and towns fixed their own rates, if they pleased.

In 1649, the municipal regulations of Springfield, in Massachusetts, provided that the wages of laborers in winter months should not be beyond sixteen pence, and in summer twenty pence a day; and tailors were to receive but twelve pence. It was also a fineable offense to stay away from town meetings, or to refuse to receive office.

When John Dunton went out to visit the Indians, "he carried Madame Brick," the flower of Boston, "behind him on his horse;" who, "in this case, proved but a beautiful sort of luggage to me." The usual way of going from place to place, was on foot or on horseback.

Very few wheeled carriages existed till near the time of the Revolution; where now they are manufactured by the thousand, and sent abroad over the world.

DRINKING.

Rum and tobacco seem to have held their usual place in this Colony too; a boat-load of stores was blown up in 1632 by a man who was lighting his pipe, and "some in the boat were so drunk" that they did not wake. In 1630, Governor Winthrop, in view of the "inconveniences" resulting in England from drinking of healths, restrained it at his own table, and wished others to do the same, and it grew into disfavor. In 1639 a law was made against the practice. But spite of all laws drunkenness increased fearfully.

The Connecticut laws provided that no man should be allowed above half a pint of wine at a time, or should tipple over half an hour, or after nine of the clock at night.

Thomas Morton's song at the raising of the May-pole ran thus:

"THE SONGE.

"Drink, and be merry, merry, boyes,
Let all your delight be in the Hymen's joyes,
So to Hymen now the day is come,
About the merry May-pole take a roome.

Make green garlans, bring bottles out,
And fill sweet nectar freely about;
Uncover thy head, and fear no harm,
For here is good liquor to keepe it warme.
Then drink and be merry," etc.

They soon sent this roystering blade out of the Colony.

DISEASES.

Besides consumption, which prevailed from the beginning, the small-pox raged at times, and when Cotton Mather introduced inoculation, and Doctor Boylston had the courage to inoculate his family, the startled public cried out, "That they should wait their Maker's will concerning it, and not force a disease upon themselves which perhaps they might otherwise escape."[1] Vaccination has taken the place of inoculation, and the small-pox is almost banished.

BOSTON IN 1673.

In Chalmers's Political Annals is a "curious paper," and in it such facts as these about Massachusetts in 1673:

"There be—five hundred persons worth each £3,000—about fifteen hundred families in Boston. No beggars (!) Not three persons put to death for theft (annually). There are no musicians by trade. A dancing-school was set up, but put down." Which things indicate a primitive, simple state of society, growing naturally toward strength and vigor.

Some of the WINTERS seem to have been exceedingly severe, such as are now quite unknown.

In the Winter of 1741, Francis Lewis drove his horse on the ice, all the way from New York to Barnstable.[2] In the year 1717, the year of the great snow, it fell to the depth of from ten to twenty feet. Deers were killed by wolves; and Winthrop says, "we lost at the island 1,100 sheep, horses, and cows." Twenty-eight days after the storm, two sheep were taken out alive, having fed on the wool of the others.

In 1729, was a great snow storm, which was strangely varied with much thunder and lightning.

[1] Description of Boston, M. H. C., vol. iii. [2] Boston Post-Boy.

POVERTY is no crime, but it has never been considered an evidence of merit in New England. Every person was expected to support himself, by industry and economy; and nearly all did it. But the people recognized their obligation to protect paupers from outright suffering—no more; and each town took such action as it saw fit, to provide for its own poor. A house was commonly provided by the town, and an overseer; or some person in the town was paid a sum for taking care of the poor, he making what use he could of their labor.

It was the practice at Lynn, to warn every new-comer, out of the town, formally. Not because it was wished or expected that they would go, but to secure the town against the support of other towns-poor, in case they should become paupers. But sometimes it must have created surprise; and one old gentleman, upon being warned off from Lynn, consoled his wife, by saying,

"It is not so very desirable a place, after all!"

CHARACTERISTICS.

Thrift, Chastity, and Sabbath-keeping, were the three cardinal virtues of New England, in those "good old Colony times." That the people who came to New England, were bent on improving their worldly condition, as well as enjoying their religious worship, no one need doubt; they would not have lain out so far, on the banks of the Connecticut, the Piscataqua, and the Kennebeck, had they not wanted good Meadow-land. They did want it, and they were right in wanting it; and the desire for it is essential to a healthy individual and natural growth. The individual or the nation which devotes its energies to the pursuit of gold alone, or to the engrossing hazards and demands of Trade, will surely come to naught. Let the forced and unnatural lives of the money-dealing Jews, witness this; and let the fate of Tyre and Venice, warn us at this day, not to forget the true basis of Civilization. Cut off from the associations of land and farms, men lose sight of the Real sources of wealth, and forget the bountiful mother, who bears all and nourishes all. Men engaged in trade, pride themselves, if by any art or combination, they succeed in gathering thousands to their coffers, rather than in doing fair work for fair wages; while the Farmer, if honest and true, rejoices, when by skill and industry, he persuades the rugged earth to yield her fruits in abundance, for his own sustenance, and that of his toiling fellow-men. He knows the times, and the seasons, the sunshine and the shower, and does not forget the relations of man to nature; so also does the Fisherman—and the Miner, though less perfectly. They learn that Nature, with her wealth of growth and variety of beauty is not naught; that the Forests and the Mountains, the Oceans and the Tempests, and the Plains and the Valleys, are something, and that Gold is not all of Life. Therefore, let every man, as soon as he can, own a little land, and let him cultivate it well; as they did in the early days of New England.

The Meadow-lands, which lie along the New England rivers, tempted the settlers away from Boston and Plymouth, where the ground is not fertile, but sterile; and there through a century, they cultivated their corn, with the hoe in one hand, and the musket in the other. Now and then the war-whoop startled them, and a life was lost; but was not even this better than hopeless poverty, and spiritual starvation, in England?

So at least the Puritans thought. There was manhood enough then, to risk something to gain all, and to secure a better future. They did risk and they did gain what they wished.

The yellow Indian-corn shot up on their small but fertile plains, the grass waved in their eyes, and their cattle lowed on a thousand hills. Spring loosed the ice-bound earth, and all men went to their labors as to a work of love, for they saw their reward before them. Young and old worked in the fields; women and children converted the grassy pastures into golden butter; and wove the fleecy wool into warm clothing for winter. The summer sun shone fiercely, but it was to bless them with ripened harvests ; and when the autumn came, and yellow crops were heaped in their barns, every man had his reward ; and he knew that the greater share would not be taken for taxes, as in England, to support the army, and the court, and the church of the aristocracy of England.

This was no small good, and the student of New England history, can not but note how jealous the people were, even of Winthrop, fearing lest in some way an upper-class might fix itself on their necks.

THE HUSKING.

When the corn was gathered, the heaviest work was done, and anxious fear was past. Then in every neighborhood, the good custom was, for the young men and the blooming girls to gather in troops, and under the roof-tree, on the broad barn-floors, to strip the husks from the ripened ears.

"Many hands make light work," was their proverb ; and their hearts were as light as their work ; both were in harmony with the glorious autumn world. In the clear, crisp, November days, this went on from house to house. Does the reader of to-day suppose that it was done with long faces, sad eyes, and straitened and distressed consciences ? That they began with prayer, and, sitting stiff and straight on the barn-floors, they then enlivened the monotony of their work, with texts of Scripture, and mutual exhortations to godliness ? That these determined Puritans were indeed no longer human ?

Such was not the case—by no means. Jokes, broad and rich, went round the company ; and the dusky light in the old barn-roof, was purified with peals of laughter, and flashes of wit ; there the hay could not grow musty, but was sweet, and carried its sweetness through the rich udders, till at last it came home again, and clustered around the hearts of those boys and girls to keep their sympathies and memories young.

At this distance along the way of time, it will do no harm to mention a fact, which some seem to have forgotten, in thinking or writing of the Puritans—it is this:

Most of these young people were in love with one another! Startling as this may seem, to those who considered the Puritans as made of oak and iron, strung together with sinews drawn from Calvin's Institutes, it is nevertheless true; and researches into the past prove to me, that Cupid shot his shafts right and left in New England, and that they quivered in hearts as soft and as true, as if they had beat in "Merry Old England." Here and there, one more awkward, or more ugly,[1] or more shy than the rest, stood alone; but every bird finds its mate, and there every one found his fellow. Every one—for land was plenty, and marriage easy.

When the work was done, and the supper-table, spread by clean and industrious hands, loaded with loaves of bread and cake, with seed-cakes and dough-nuts, with pies and with tarts—sustained with pitchers of milk, and flagons of beer—when this table needed their presence, then they went to do justice to it; and many a sweet thing was whispered behind a dough-nut, and many a "sentiment" lurked in a pie. Good, "round, romping games" closed up the Husking and the evening, and then the sweethearts wended their way homeward, in the soft light of the autumn moon. To tell the whispered words, and explain the singular sounds made in the shadows of those old Puritan "stoops," is not the province of the Historian; he must dwell upon Politics and War, and leave such things to the imaginations of the young, and the memories of the old.

Nor can the Historian dwell long upon the holiday, which in the summer or autumn weather, those Puritan farmer families loved to enjoy, in a trip to the shores of the sea. They went to it as the buffaloes went to the licks—to salt; and the sea yielded of its fruits; oysters and clams, fish and lobsters, were pleasant to the palates

[1] New-English for "homely."

of Puritans. And the wonders of the broad and great deep, were borne in upon the souls of the little children, who spent the day well among the rude rocks, and along the sandy beaches.

The reader would hardly excuse the Historian who should devote his pages to a full description of those "Spinnings," where every woman, bearing her "wheel," went forth to a neighbor's, and sitting together, in a single afternoon spun out knots upon knots of thread, to be woven into linen, and whitened into sheets, for the outfit of the coming bride. Nor will his assertion be fully believed, that without the stimulating cups of fragrant tea, the noise of tongues silenced the hum of revolving wheels the live-long day.

Time would fail, too, to describe at large the sleigh-rides which jingled all over New England, in those winter days and nights. Rude sledges made of saplings, answered every purpose ; and wrapped in blankets, and bedded in straw, sweethearts and wives enjoyed the exhilaration of New England winter weather, and aired their charms.

These things are touched upon, not because they are worthy the attention of that singular myth, called "The Dignity of History," whom all respect, but because they serve to show, that the straitened New England Puritans were fellow-creatures, with large and ready sympathies.

The New England "Thanksgiving" has been mentioned ;[1] and a few words may here be given to their weekly holy-day—to Sunday, THE SABBATH DAY.

On the afternoon of Saturday, work—week-day labor—was ended. The struggle and anxiety for the supply of daily bread, were suspended, and both body and mind subsided from the six days' activity, and found rest and strength in change. The coming day was holy time, sacred to the Lord, and was to be devoted to his service in

[1] Vol. i., ch. xvi.

customary religious exercises. Prayers, in most houses, began the day, and no more work was done than barely to prepare food for themselves and their cattle. Few steps were taken, and there was little talking, and that in a subdued voice. Personal cleanliness, and a decent garb, were universal in New England on Sunday; and all people, when the sound of drum or stroke of bell called them to the meeting-house, went out of their homes, serious, quiet, and clean.

They went twice on Sunday to meeting, and they listened reverently to prayers an hour long, and to the hymns of the Bay Psalm-book, and to sermons of two hours in duration; because they earnestly wished to praise the Lord, and to save their souls. If any fell asleep, as some did, it was because tired nature's demands could not be resisted. They laid aside their hay and their harvest, their cares and their bargains, and attended to the intellectual and spiritual exercises of the day.

The Puritans believed, as the Jews did, that they were a peculiar people, dear to God; and they loved to see, in the History of the Jews, experiences like their own, and to comfort themselves in the successes of that nation. However each individual might have bewailed his own unworthiness, he held that he was eminently capable of salvation; and that the Puritans were the Saints, and that the Saints should rule the earth; and they based their State upon that idea. Whatever Formality, or Narrowness, or Phariseeism, or Persecution, grew out of it, there is no question that this idea elevated the whole body in their own estimation, inspired them with strong individuality and self-respect, and impelled them so to conduct themselves, as to be worthy of their position and their God.

This is the key to the New England character, and has produced in New England both bad and good results; but few in this day will doubt which preponderates.

These Sabbath sermons sharpened the intellect, and led

to infinite talk and discussion; tedious and strange as many of them now seem, they kept alive the better part of man, and saved them then from degenerating into the groveling Materialism, which even yet sinks the masses of Europe below the influences of improvement and true civilization.

With the sunset of Sunday the Sabbath ended, and stillness and silence were past. The subdued and tired children burst forth and ran like colts; the boys to the pasture-lot to bring home the cows, and the girls to the kitchen to prepare the cheerful supper. The old spent the evening in discussing the sermons, or their neighbors; and the youth welcomed it, for it was the time when "courting" was indulged in, and then every swain, with rose in buttonhole, sought his sweetheart.

With this exalted, even exaggerated value of the individual entertained in New England, it was not possible that men or women entertaining it should yield themselves to corrupt or debasing practices. CHASTITY was, therefore, a cardinal virtue, and the abuse of it, a crying sin, to be punished by law, and by the severe reproof of all good citizens. Among the better people, this virtue was of the first water, though its absence was too common among the poor and reckless, there as elsewhere.

Winthrop gives some instances of melancholy and distraction, growing out of an excessive anxiety about the future state of the soul and the fear of hell, which in some cases produced disastrous results; such as the following:

In 1642 a cooper's wife of Hingham, having been long in a "sad melancholie distemper," carried her little child, three years old, to the creek, and threw it into the mud and water. The child scrambled out, and taking up its clothes, came to its mother, who was sitting by. She again threw it in, as far as she could, but "it pleased God," that a young man coming by, saved it. The reason she gave was, that she herself had sinned against the Holy Ghost, and she wished to save her child from misery.

An excess of spiritual consciousness is sure to produce disease and mischief, visible in the present as well as in the past.

In contrast to this, it is mentioned that there was a public duel of WIT (1756) between Jonathan Gowen of Lynn, and Joseph Emerson of Reading. It was held out of doors, and was attended by crowds. Dr. Perkins says Gowen's wit "was beyond all human imagination;" and Emerson was completely foiled. They were a pair of those wags which may be found in almost any village of New England.

A singularly large number of the people of New England seem to have inherited from their ancestors a sort of arrested development of the nasal organs. So many of their speakers, public as well as private, indulge in an unmelodious intonation, that one is led, for want of a better reason, to conclude that the nose in New England does not reach perfection. Surely no preacher who should hear himself preach "through his nose," would consider it a superior method. But why this peculiarity should have come in with Puritanism, no one now can tell.

Another peculiar trait of New England character, which seems to date far back, has grown out of the caution of the people. They say, "I *guess*," rather than "I know." Those who have been in England know well the dogmatic character and conversation of the people: their descendants in New England may be no less positive in their opinions, but they have come to a habit of guessing at the truth, which is almost infallible. Guessing matches once prevailed, when he who guessed nearest to the weight of a good fat hog, won the prize.

A proclivity to trade seems to have been developed among this people to a singular degree; and sharp bargains are now often described as Yankee practice. Many curious stories exist about the "swopping" and trading habits of New England, which it is not necessary to repeat here. One such is told of a "remarkably conscientious" man, who rarely missed his bargain ; but he said "that if any body cheated him, his conscience would not let him rest till he had made it right, and cheated somebody else 'abeout' the same amount." Widely as the Jews are scattered, their absence from New England has been satisfactorily accounted for, in that, highly gifted as they are in bargains and trade, their superiors exist there, and they must surely come to want.

The Thrift and Piety of the New England Character may be illustrated by a simple incident, which happened within this century.

It was near the neck of Cape Cod, that a woman, dressed in profound mourning, got into the stage-coach. She said nothing, and seemed absorbed in grief. After a time, one of the passengers, a woman with active sympathies and a keen spirit of investigation, said to the mourner :

"Appear to be in affliction, ma'am ?"

"Yes," was the brief reply.

"Recent affliction ?"

"Yes."

"Loss of relatives ?"

"Yes."

"Perhaps your father 's dead ?"

"Yes."

"Your husband, too, may-be ?"

"Yes."

"And your only son ?"

"Yes."

"Were they lost at sea ?"

"No."

"Where did they die ?"

"At the South."

"Were they all three hopefully pious ?"

"Yes."

"Well, have you got their chests home ?"

"Yes."

"Now, then, if they were hopefully *pious*, and you have got their chests *home*, you have-a-great-deal-to-be-thank-ful-for!"

There was not a smile in the coach, for all respected the mourner's tears.

"THE GOOD OLD TIMES" OF NEW ENGLAND.

We have now passed over three quarters of a Century of the good old times of New England. We have seen the hunted Puritans established through much suffering, along the Atlantic shore; their churches formed, their laws established, their circle completed. Heresy has been grappled with, and Roger Williams, Mrs. Hutchinson, and Samuel Gorton are banished; the Quakers hanged, and driven away; the English Hierarchy have not been able to establish their rule in New England; but Massachusetts has lost her old independence, and for another three quarters of a century is to be wrestling with the domineering Ministry of England, and to grow strong in the struggle. Those ancient copper-colored tribes have disappeared; Miantonomo and Canonicus, and Iyanough and Philip are dead, lying in unknown, unhonored graves.

But through all this jar and friction, the people of New England have steadily improved in knowledge, and wealth, and strength, and virtue. Their homes are the best in the world, and education and decency exist as they exist nowhere else in the known world. Yet justly as her past has been praised, who would wish now to go backward to that time? It is a glorious fact of the human mind, that it forgets the evils and discomforts of the past, and remembers its enjoyments and good things: it is because the Good is of God, is perennial, and is positive; while Evil is only the absence of Good, and cannot poison the Memory of a healthy mind. Feeling acutely present struggles and meannesses, minds of a certain sentimental cast are apt to sigh for the good old times. History everywhere shows, that there were no such times; and even in full view of our own mercenary and time-serving politicians, and Christians, and cotton-spinners, no one, "sitting clothed, and in his right mind," will mourn for the past of Old, or of New England. He will be resolute in the Present time, and hope and work for the better Future.

No—we look at the present of New England, and do not regret the past, however full of promise it may have been. Good morals, and good manners, and good living, have steadily grown with her growth, and are now common there and strong. Gross crimes against nature are no longer known ; drunkenness, with poverty and its army of evils and vices, have almost disappeared. Comfort is universal, and the homes of the workmen are musical with the voices of civilized children, in harmony with the strings of the piano or guitar. The commonest houses are painted, and carpeted floors welcome the soft tread of their owners ; the rose-bush and honey-suckle bloom in the door-yard, where once was the pig-pen or wood-pile ; the time of labor is reduced to ten hours a day, and wages of men are good ; the rights of women are more and more respected ; every one can read and write, and Literature and Art are beginning to assert their powers, as superiors to greed and gold ; few exaggerated fortunes curse New England, and they are soon dissipated by just laws of inheritance, which now refuse a bounty to the luck of being first born ; a liberal state of feeling toward sects (except, perhaps, the Catholic) prevails ; the bitterness of religious rivalry is passed, and everywhere more genial and hearty and kindly feelings are overcoming the reserved and stiff manners presented to strangers. Surely no one should regret that his home in New England is in the present day, rather than in the past ; and no sound-hearted, strong-minded man will forget the good lessons of the past, and that he too must, as her fathers did, jealously and persistently watch the encroachments of Despotism, and defend his rights, at whatever cost, against the centralizing tendencies of Place-hunters, and the National Executive.

The present is better than the past, as the future must be better than the present.

In the coming volume we shall therefore see the further struggles of this people toward Liberty and Independence.

END OF VOL. I.

BOOKS CONSULTED OR QUOTED.

Allen's History of Vermont.
American Archives.
A Defense of the Ministers' Refusal of Subscription to the Book of Common Prayer, etc. Imp. 1607.
Allen's Biographical Dictionary.
Ashton's Memoir—Mass. Hist. Coll.
Annals of Providence.
Adams's Annals of Portsmouth.
Anderson's History of Colonial Church.
A Review of the Military Operations in North America, 1758.
Allen's Narrative of his Capture, 1779.
Adams's Diary.
A Narrative of the Excursion and Ravages of the King's Troops on the 19th of April. Published by Authority, 1775.
Alden's American Epitaphs.

Beamish's Discovery of North America by the Northmen.
Bradford's History of Plymouth Plantation —M. H. Coll., 1856.
Bancroft's History of United States.
Baylie's Memoir.
Bradford's Letters—M. H. Coll.
Burnaby's Travels, 1760.
Belknap's American Biography.
Belknap's History of New Hampshire.
Bowen's Documents of the Constitution.
Boudinot's Star of the West.
Baldwin's Annals of Yale College.
Bay Psalm Book.
Boston "News Letter," 1704.
Bacon's Historical Discourses.
Boston "Post Boy."
Barstow's History of New Hampshire.
Brattle's Candid Account of the Salem Witchcraft—M. H. Coll.
Barry's History of Harvard.
Barber's Historical Collections.
Bushnell's Speech for Connecticut, 1837.
Beverly's Virginia.
Boston Evening Post, 1755.
Botta's History of the War of Independence.
Bishop's New England Judged.
Backus's History of New England.
Bradford's History of Boston.

Crantz's History of Greenland, 1767.
Corbett—An Account of the Principles and Practices of several Nonconformists, etc., 1682.
Cotton's Account—M. H. Coll.
Cushman's Reasons.
Cheever's Journal of Pilgrims.
Cradock's Letter—M. H. Coll.
Chalmers's Political Annals.
Coit's Puritanism, or a Churchman's Defense.
Clapp's Letter—M. H. Coll.
Church's Indian Wars.
Coffin's History of Newbury.
Clarke's "Ill News from New England," 1652.
Calkins's History of Norwich.
Calef's Wonders of the Invisible World.
Campbell's Historical Account of New York.
Carver's Travels.
Chauncey's Thoughts on the State of Religion in New England.
Connecticut Journal, 1775.
Cooper's Election Sermon, 1756.
Copley's History of Slavery.
Clarkson's Essay: London, 1786.
Chandler's Appeal, 1758.
Curwen's Journal.
Colonial Records.
Colton's Way of the Churches, 1645.
Callender's Discourse on Rhode Island, etc.
Cushing's History of Newburyport.
Chalmers's History of Revolt of American Colonies.

Dudley's Letter to the Countess of Lincoln.
Dwight's Travels.
Doolittle's Narrative.
Drake's History of Boston.
Dunton's Journal—M. H. Coll.
Drake's Notes.
Dwight's Discourse on Slavery, 1794.
Dearborn's Bunker Hill Battle.

Eliot's Passages in History of Liberty.
Eliot's Biographical Dictionary.
Elton's Life of Roger Williams.
Endicott's Life of Endicott.
Eliot—"The Day-breaking if not the Sunrising of the Gospel, etc.," 1647.
Eliot—"A Late and Further Manifestation, etc." 1655.
Eliot's Indian Bible.
Eaton—"A Defense of Sundry Positions, etc.," 1645.
Eccentric Biography: Worcester, 1804.
Edwards's Works. Ed. 1808.
Elliott's Toussaint l'Ouverture.
Emerson's English Traits.
Everett's Life of John Stark.

Francis's Life of Eliot.
Force's Tracts.
Francis's History of Watertown.
Felt's History of Salem.

Franklin's Autobiography.
Felt's Massachusetts Currency.
Frothingham's Siege of Boston, 1849.
Farmer and Moore's Historical Collections.

Gorton's Works, 1646.
Gorge's America, 1659.
Grote's History of Greece.
Gordon's History of New Jersey.
Grahame's History of United States.
Gervinus's Introduction.
Gray's Essay.
Gammel's Life of Williams.
Gorton's "Simplicities Defense."
Gookins's Account—M. H. Coll.
Gyles's Memoirs.
Griswold's Female Poets of America.
Godwin's Lives of the Necromancers, 1834.
Godwin and Granville's Sadducismus Triumphans, 1726.
Greene's Life of General Greene.

Hubbard's History of New England.
Havens's Int. to Mass. Records.
Hunter's Letter in M. H. Coll.
Hall's New England Discourse, 1847.
Hazard's Collection.
Hutchinson's Collection.
Hutchinson's History of Mass. Bay.
Hildreth's History of United States.
Hinman's Early Settlers of Connecticut.
Hubbard's Indian Wars.
Higginson—New England Plantation.
Homer's History of Cambridge.
Holmes's Annals.
Holland's History of Western Massachusetts.
Hutchinson's Essay Concerning Witchcraft, 1718.
Hobby's Inquiry into the Itineracy of Mr. George Whitefield, etc., 1785.
Hollister's History of Connecticut.
Higginson's New England's Plantation.
Humphrey's Life of Putnam.

Johnson's Wonder-working Providence.
Josselyn—Voyages.
Journals of Congress.
Johnson's History of New England.

Keyser's Religion of the Northmen.
Knowles's Life of Roger Williams.
Kingsley's Historical Discourse, 1838.

Lucas's Charters.
Lechford's Plain Dealing, 1641.
Lewis's History of Lynn.
Lossing's Field Book of the Revolution.
Lord Bishops none of the Lord's Bishops, 1640.

Mather's Apology for the Liberties of the Churches, 1738.
Mauditt's Brief Review, 1774.
Morton's Memorial of New England.
Massachusetts Historical Collection.
Mourt's Relation, 1622.
Moore's Governors.
Mather's Magnalia.
Macsparren's America Dissected, 1752.
Mason's History of Pequot War, 1736.
Morell's Poem on New England—M. H. Coll.
Mather's Letter to Lord Barrington, 1718.
Mather's Memorable Providences, 1689.
Mather's Wonders of the Invisible World.
McGregor's Progress of America.
Minot's History of Massachusetts.
Mayhew's Discourse upon Non-Resistance, 1750.
Macpherson's Annals.
Massachusettensis, 1776.

Neal's History of New England.
"New Haven's Settling in New England etc.," 1656.
"New England's Jonas Cast Up."
New England Courant, 1721.
New England Magazine.
Norton—Heart of New England Rent.

Old Men's Tears for their own Declension, 1691.
Oldmixon's British Empire in America.

Pontopoddian's History of Norway, 1758.
Prince's Chronology.
Purchas's Pilgrims.
Plymouth Records.
Plymouth Book of Laws, 1671.
Penhallow's Indian Wars.
Peters's History of Connecticut.
Peterson's History of Rhode Island.
Philip's Life of Whitefield.
Pitkin's Statistics.
Palfrey's Life of Palfrey.
Philogathos—A Poem Commemorative of Goffe, Whaley and Dixwell, 1793.
Price's Boscawen.

Quincy's History of Harvard College.

Rafn's Antiquitates Americanæ.
Rafn's Mémoir sur la Découverté de l'Amerique au dixieme Siècle, 1843.
Robertson's America.
Rhode Island Historical Collections.
Rhode Island Colony Records.
Rowlandson's Narrative of Her Captivity, etc.
Records of the United Colonies.
Rogers's North America, 1765.
Ramsay's American Revolution.
Randolph's Memoirs of Jefferson, 1829.

Stowell's History of Puritans.
Staples's History of Rhode Island.
Sewall's History of the Quakers.
Stiles's Judges.
Shepard—The Clear Sunshine of the Gospel, 1648.
Shute's Gov. Letter—M. H. Coll.
Scotto—A Narrative of the Planting of the Massachusetts Colony, 1694.
Smith's Description of New England.
Smith's History of New York.
Shirley's Letter to the Duke of Newcastle, 1746.
Stillman's Election Sermon, 1770.
Sargent's History.
Slade's Vermont State Papers.
Sumner's White Slavery.
Sparks's Franklin.
Sabine's American Loyalists, 1847.
Sparks's American Biography.

Swett's Bunker Hill Battle, 1827.
Secret Journals of Congress.
Sparks's Washington.
Snow's History of Boston.
Stoddard's Appeal to the Learned, 1709.

The Stone-throwing Devil, 1698.
Tegner's Frithiof's Saga, 1825.
Thacher's History of Plymouth.
Thornton's Landing at Cape Ann, 1854.
Trumbull's History of Connecticut.
Thatcher's Indian Biography.
Thomas's History of Printing.
Traits of the Tea Party.
The Testimony of the President, etc., of Harvard College against the Rev. George Whitefield, 1744.
The Tyrannical Libertyman, 1795.
Tudor's Life of Otis.
Trumbull's Reminiscences, 1841.

Updyke's History of the Narragansett Church.
Upham's Second Century Discourse.

Valentine's History of New York.

Warburton's Divine Legation.
Wheaton's History of the Northmen, 1831.
Winslow's Relation.
Winslow's Good News, 1624.
Winslow's "Glorious Progress of the Gospel, etc.," 1649.
Winslow's "New England's Salamander," 1647.
Wilson.
Winthrop's Journal.
White's Brief Relation—Chron. of Pil.
Wood's New England Prospect.
Ward's Simple Cobbler of Agawam.
Williams's "Bloody Tenent."
Williams's Letter to Mason—M. H. Coll.
Williams's Fox digged out of his Burrow.
Williams's Key.
Walsh's Appeal.
Williamson's History of Maine.
Weld's Rise, Reign, and Ruin of the Antinomians, 1644.
Ward's History of Shrewsbury.
Whitfield—"The Light Appearing More and More, etc.," 1651.
Williams's Redeemed Captive.
Washburn's Judicial History of Massachusetts.
Worthington's History of Dedham.
Woolsey's Discourse, 1850.
Wheelock's Plain and Faithful Narrative of the Indian School at Lebanon, 1763.
Wigglesworth's "Day of Doom."
Wright's Sorcery and Magic, 1851.
Williams's History of Vermont.
Whitefield's Journals.
Whitefield's Letter to the President of Harvard College, 1745.
Whittier's Old Portraits.
Webster's Discourse on Slavery.
Weld's Churches of New England, 1692.

Young's Chronicles of Pilgrims.
Young's Chronicles of Massachusetts Bay.

www.ingramcontent.com/pod-product-compliance
Lightning Source LLC
LaVergne TN
LVHW020924110826
845150LV00004B/765